PICTORIAL
PRICE GUIDE
TO
AMERICAN ANTIQUES
and Objects Made for the American Market

1994-1995 EDITION

PICTORIAL PRICE GUIDE TO AMERICAN ANTIQUES

and Objects Made for the American Market

MORE THAN 5000 ILLUSTRATED AND PRICED OBJECTS

By

Dorothy Hammond

VIKING
STUDIO
BOOKS

Published by the Penguin Group
Penguin Books USA Inc., 375 Hudson Street,
New York, New York, 10014, U.S.A.

Penguin Books Ltd, 27 Wrights Lane,
London W8 5TZ, England

Penguin Books Australia Ltd, Ringwood,
Victoria, Australia

Penguin Books Canada Ltd, 2801 John Street.
Markham, Ontario, Canada L3R 1B4

Penguin Books (N.Z.) Ltd, 182-90 Wairau Road,
Auckland 10, New Zealand

Penguin Books Ltd., Registered Offices:
Harmondsworth, Middlesex, England

First published by Viking Studio Books, an imprint of Penguin Books USA, Inc.

First Printing, January 1994
10 9 8 7 6 5 4 3 2 1

ISBN: 0-525-48620-8

CONTENTS

INTRODUCTION

The *1994-1995 Pictorial Price Guide to American Antiques and Objects Made for the American Market* includes all new entries, prices and photographs. The format is designed to provide the collector and antiques dealer with an accurate market value of items sold at auction galleries from November 1992 through October 1993.

Entries are keyed to the auction house where an item was actually sold. A state abbreviation has been included for the readers' convenience, because prices vary in different parts of the country. Also, the year and the month the item sold has been indicated. This method of pricing sets this publication apart from all other price guides on the market. When the book becomes dated, it will serve as an excellent reference guide for future generations.

Although most auction houses give detailed catalog descriptions of items sold, others do not; therefore, every effort has been made to include as much information as possible. When comparing similar pieces, the reader must take into consideration that fluctuations in the market during the year, as well as the quality of an object, the region in which it sold, as well as demand determine the auction price.

What is the state of the antiques market? This is the question on everyone's mind these days because every field of collecting has been greatly effected by today's economic picture. Overall, there are many hopeful signs this fall that the beginning of the recovery is actually here. Customers are back at antiques shows and auctions—and they are buying. Good items are selling well, whereas the great stuff sells better, and reasonable auction catalog estimates have been boosting sales. The biggest problem for potential buyers these days is finding quality merchandise. Wherever items of quality—and fresh to the market come up at auctions—they seem to bring strong prices. And the fact that there hasn't been any great bargains at auctions this year, is certainly encouraging.

As always, period furniture continues to demonstrate its strength in the market with many pieces exceeding expectations—and furniture manufactured during the 30s well into the 50s is making the transition from tacky to trendy. Other fields showing signs of interest include advertising, radios—espespecially color plastic models from the 30s, baseball memorabilia, fine textiles, American art pottery, vintage photographics, American Indian items and decorative garden statuary, chairs and benches. And finally, according to the Commerce Department, trade figures indicate art and antiques to be one of the few categories where the United States has a favorable balance of trade.

Every effort has been made to record prices accurately and describe each item in the space allotted to our format. The writer cannot be responsible for any clerical or typographical errors that may occur.

— Dorothy Hammond

ACKNOWLEDGMENTS

I am very grateful to the following auction galleries that have provided pictorial material in order to make this edition a reality: Alderfer Auction Company, Hatfield, PA; Richard A. Bourne Co., Inc., Hyannis, MA; Conestoga Auction Co., Inc., Manheim, PA; Early Auction Co., Milford, Ohio; Garth's Auctions, Inc., Delaware, OH; Glass Works Auctions, East Greenville, PA; Leslie Hindman Auctioneers, Chicago, IL; James D. Julia, Inc., Fairfield, ME; Gary Kirsner Auctions, Coral Springs, FL; David Rago, Lambertville, NJ; Majolica Auctions by Michael G. Strawser, Wolcottville, IN; Northeast Auctions, Hampton, NH; Skinner, Inc., Bolton & Boston, MA; and C.G. Sloan & Co., North Bethesda, MD.

I am especially indebted to Elizabeth Yadon, project coordinator, for organizing the many entries, and others for their contributions to the outcome of this project.

ABBREVIATIONS USED IN THIS BOOK AND THEIR MEANINGS

Am.	American
c.	century
ca.	circa
©	copyright
D	deep, diameter
dec	decorated
dk.	dark
H	high
ht.	height
L	length, long
litho	lithograph
lt.	light
MOP	mother-of-pearl
NE	New England
opal	opalescent
orig.	original
pat.	pattern
sq.	square
T	tall
W	wide, width
w/	with
WMG	white milk glass

The common and accepted abbreviations are used for states.

Prices in this guide are hammer prices. Whenever an asterisk follows a price, it denotes buyer's premium was added. The buyer's premium is a surcharge on the hammer or final bid price at auction. During the 1970s, a major New York auction house introduced the premium at 10 percent, and were followed by auction houses large and small all across the country. Currently, some are charging 15 percent, graduating to 10 percent, depending on price paid.

GAN 621-623
A-OH Nov. 1992   *Garth's Auctions, Inc.*
G.O.P. SIGN, masonite, grey, red and black paint, both sides painted, tail replaced, 66" L $110.00
HOSE CADDY, black man, wood and metal, original polychrome, "Sprinkling Sambo, The Firestone Tire & Rubber Co.," 33½" H $165.00
TOURIST CAMP SIGN, plywood, original polychrome, wear, edge damage, 35½" H $181.50

A-ME May 1993   *James D. Julia, Inc.*
SIGN, Frank Fehr Brewing Co., paper, soiled, chips, 21½" x 29½" $600.00*
SIGN, Westinghouse Threshing Machines, paper, soiled, creased, tears, 26½" x 21" $600.00*

A-ME May 1993   *James D. Julia, Inc.*
TRANSFER SIGN, Penn Esther Kitchen Range, between glass, 7½" x 8½" $175.00*
DISPLAY SIGN, Carborundum File, tin, chips, rust, dents, 14" x 19½" . . . $220.00*

A-ME May 1993   *James D. Julia, Inc.*
CALENDAR, Ringler & Co. Brewers, paper, 1899, crease, stain, 16" x 24" . . $2500.00*

A-ME May 1993   *James D. Julia, Inc.*
SIGN, De Laval, tin, scratches, frame repair, 29½" x 40½" $3250.00*

A-ME May 1993   *James D. Julia, Inc.*
POSTER, Sweet, Orr & Co., scuffing, scratches, loss, 20" x 24" $1600.00*
POSTER, Runkel Cocoa, printer's proof, creasing, in-painting, 18" x 24" . . $700.00*

A-ME May 1993   *James D. Julia, Inc.*
SIGNS
ADMIRATION CIGAR, reverse glass, acid etched, silver, gold leaf, lithographed insert, 18" x 24" $2000.00*
YALE BREWING CO., reverse glass, etched, silver, gold leaf, 32" x 24" $3000.00*
THE DIAMOND WINE CO., paper, 1896 soiled, 19" x 27" $1500.00*

A-ME May 1993   *James D. Julia, Inc.*
SIGN, Ivory Soap, cardboard, creased, chips, in-painting, 17" x 24½" $450.00*

A-ME May 1993   *James D. Julia, Inc.*
SIGN, Green River Whiskey, tin, soiled, rust, 33" x 23½" . . . . $225.00"*

A-ME May 1993   *James D. Julia, Inc.*
SIGN, Dupont Gun Powder, paper, 1869, professionally deacidified and cleaned, 27½" x 22" $19000.00*

A-ME May 1993　　　*James D. Julia, Inc.*
PAPER POSTERS
Row 1, Left to Right
WWI POSTERS, 6 pcs., (2 illus.), creasing, general soiling $500.00*
HOWARD DUSTLESS-DUSTER, 18½" x 27½" $400.00*
B.F. GOODRICH CO., ca. 1901, wrinkled, stained, 18" x 29" $175.00*
Row 2, Left to Right
FIRESTONE RIMS, crease, in-painted, 20½" x 40" $850.00*
ALTMAN & TAYLOR FARM MACHINERY, breaks, losses, 36" x 14" . . $350.00*
SEED POSTERS, 2 pcs., (1 illus.), cracks, creases, 21" x 30" $200.00*

A-ME May 1993　　　*James D. Julia, Inc.*
SIGNS
Row 1, Left to Right
BROTHERHOOD TOBACCO, cardboard, creases, soiled, 17½" x 26" $125.00*
RUHSTALLER'S BEER, cardboard, damage, crease, 17¾" x 15" $250.00*
LIPTON'S COCOA, tin, ca. 1915, rust, scratches, 9" x 13¼" $400.00*
PERFECTION DYES, cardboard, crazing, soiled, 9½" x 13½" $50.00*
Row 2, Left to Right
SODA FOUNTAIN SIGNS, 2 pcs., Coca-Cola, Hires, tin, chips, holes $300.00*
GREAT WESTERN CHAMPAGNE, tin, wear, 13" x 19" $300.00*
RUHSTALLER'S GILT EDGE BEER, cardboard, 13½" x 18½" $500.00*
MULSIFIED COCOANUT OIL SHAMPOO, cardboard, stains, 22" x 34" $120.00*
Row 3, Left to Right
JUSTIN GATES, cardboard, soiled, chips, 18½" x 21" $200.00*
BODEGAS FRANCO-ESPANOLAS, embossed tin, dents, chips, 13" x 18½" $50.00*
PERMIT CIGAR, cardboard, chips, scratches, faded, 21½" x 28" . . . $200.00*
ARTIE CIGAR, tin, chips, 6¼" x 9½" $400.00*

A-ME May. 1993   *James D. Julia, Inc.*
SIGN, Roosevelt Cigar, embossed tin, bright colors, 13½″ x 19½″ $13000.00*
WINDOW, Budweiser Faust, stained glass, stress cracks to glass, 32″ x 47″ ... $4000.00*
SIGN, Splendid Plug Tobacco, paper, 4 insert cards, creases, 26″ x 40″ $1100.00*

A-MA Jun. 1993   *Skinner, Inc.*
WATCHMAKER'S SIGN, carved and painted, New England, 19th c., 29″ H, 21″ D $1540.00

A-ME Mar. 1993   *James D, Julia, Inc.*
STEREOSCOPE, Mascher's, w/daguer-reotype $370.00*

A-ME May 1993   *James D. Julia, Inc.*
TIN SIGNS
Row 1, Left to Right
COCA-COLA, "Betty," self framed, dents, chips, restored, 31″ x 41″ $1000.00*
DE LAVAL CREAM SEPARATORS, wear, in-painted, faded, 25″ D $650.00*
PURITY KISS, chips, rust, faded, 8″ D $700.00*
Row 2, Left to Right
OLEOMARGARINE, dents, chips, 13″ x 9″ $2700.00*
LE ROY CIGAR, dents, chips, 11″ x 15″ $400.00*
RAINIER BEER, rolled corners, chips, crazing, 14½″ sq. $250.00*
Row 3, Left to Right
GILBERT RAE'S AERATED WATERS, embossed, 20″ x 28″ $600.00*
ARTIE CIGARS, chips, soiled, 14″ x 10″ $375.00*
MOXIE, embossed, red, yellow, scratches, discolored, 27″ x 19″ $325.00*

A-ME May 1993   *James D. Julia, Inc.*
PAPER POSTER, Duke's Mixture, 1899, wrinkled, soiled, 20" x 30½" $200.00*

A-ME May 1993   *James D. Julia, Inc.*
PAPER POSTER, Hartford Tires, stains, 27½" x 21½" $350.00*

A-ME May 1993   *James D. Julia, Inc.*
PAPER POSTER, Hygienic Water Cure Sanitorium, stained, 36" x 24" .. $100.00*

A-ME May 1993   *James D. Julia, Inc.*
DISPLAY CABINETS

Row 1, Left to Right
DIAMOND DYES, tin front, in-painting, 22½" x 30" x 11" $1350.00*
DIAMOND DYES, chips, 22½" x 30" x 12" $950.00*
DIAMOND DYES, tin front, soiled, 22½" x 30" x 10" $1050.00*

Row 2, Left to Right
PEERLESS DYES, paper front, stained, split, 19" x 32" x 11" $600.00*
PRATT'S VETERINARY REMEDIES, tin front, in-painting, 17" x 33" x 7½"... $1400.00*
DIAMOND DYES, tin front, in-painting, 22½" x 30" x 10" $1000.00*

Row 3, Left to Right
DIAMOND DYES, tin front, restored, 15" x 24½" x 8¾" $650.00*
DIAMOND DYES, tin front, dents, rust, soiled, 22½" x 30" x 10" $600.00*
DIAMOND DYES, tin front, soiled, chips, 15½" x 19" x 9" $750.00*

A-ME May 1993   *James D. Julia, Inc.*
PAPER POSTER, Gund's Brewing Co., wrinkles, stains, 28" x 14" $300.00*

A-ME May. 1993   *James D. Julia, Inc.*
PAPER POSTER, "Girl Flying Over New York," 20½" x 16" $150.00*

A-ME May 1993   *James D. Julia, Inc.*
PAPER POSTER, Goodyear Tires, tears, soiled, 31" x 38" $450.00*

A-ME May. 1993   *James D. Julia, Inc.*
Row 1, Left to Right
DISPLAY CASE, Dr. Daniels Remedies, tin, chips, scratches, 13½" x 20" x 5" $3000.00*
DYE CABINET, Diamond Dyes, tin front, chips, 24" x 30½" x 10" $2300.00*
DYE CABINET, Diamond Dyes, 20½" x 27½" x 9½" $950.00*
Row 2, Left to Right
DYE CABINET, Diamond Dyes, tin front, dent, chips, 23½" x 31" x 11" .. $1100.00*
CABINET, Dr. Daniel's Veterinary Medicines, embossed tin front, spots, scratches, dents, 21½" x 28½" x 7½" $1550.00*
DYE CABINET, Diamond Dyes, embossed tin front, 22½" x 30" x 10" $1100.00*

A-ME May 1993   *James D. Julia, Inc.*
PAPER POSTERS
HAMILTON BROWN SHOES, ca. 1904, tears, soiled, 20½" x 30" $100.00*
UNCLE TOM'S CABIN, printer's proof, 1883, 31" x 25" $100.00*
YELLOW CAR, in-painting, tears, losses, 21" x 28" $275.00*

A-ME May 1993   *James D. Julia, Inc.*
SIGN, Walter Baker & Co., tin, chips, strong color, 13½" x 19½" $500.00*
SIGN, Rice's Flower Seeds, paper, 13¾" x 29" $1450.00*

A-ME May 1993   *James D. Julia, Inc.*
SIGN, Moxie, embossed tin, dents, wear, 27" x 19¼" $210.00*

A-ME May 1993   *James D. Julia, Inc.*
DYE CABINET, Diamond Dyes, tin front, restored, 16" x 20" x 8" $450.00*
DYE CABINET, Diamond Dyes, embossed tin front, dents, chips, scratches, 22½" x 30" x 11" $550.00*

A-ME May 1993   *James D. Julia, Inc.*
PAPER POSTER, Yellow Car, tears, 21" x
28" $450.00*

A-ME May 1993   *James D. Julia, Inc.*
PAPER POSTER, Elgin Watches, in-
painted creases, trimmed, 16" x 24" . . NS

A-ME May 1993   *James D. Julia, Inc.*
PAPER POSTER, Pierce Arrow Cycles,
creases, tears, loss, 36" x 52" . . . $700.00*

A-ME May 1993   *James D. Julia, Inc.*
SIGNS

Row 1, Left to Right
PEPSI-COLA, flange sign, enameled tin, wear, scratches, 14½" x 10" $250.00*
DERBY BOOT POLISH, paper, ca 1859, trimmed, 7¾" x 9¾" $300.00*
WILSON SEWING MACHINE, paper litho on canvas, wear, 19" x 24" $350.00*
Row 2, Left to Right
WALTER A. WOOD, paper, creased, 14" x 23" $375.00*
MERCHANT'S GARGLING OIL, paper, wrinkles, stain, 21½" x 14" $650.00*
P.S. DUVAL LITHOGRAPHER, paper, trimmed, crease, 4½" x 7" $350.00*
Row 3, Left to Right
GRAPE NUTS, embossed tin, chips, dents, in-painted, faded, 20" x 30½" $850.00*
W.H. BAKER COCOA, paper, hole, soiled, 14" x 24" $275.00*
M. HOMMEL WINE, paper, spots, scuffed, 27" x 21" $550.00*

A-ME May 1993   *James D. Julia, Inc.*
SIGN, Tip Top Tobacco, cardboard, stains,
36" x 23½" $1450.00*

A-ME May 1993   *James D. Julia, Inc.*
SIGN, Bull Durham, paper, 35" x
23½" $600.00*

A-MA Mar. 1993   *Skinner, Inc.*
"CHRISTIE'S" BISCUIT CASE, ash, 54"
H, 47" W, 12½" D $1210.00

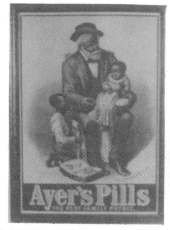

A-ME May 1993   *James D. Julia, Inc.*
SIGNS
AYER'S PILLS, paper, folds, stains, 28½" x 41" $9500.00*
COLUMBUS BUGGY, paper, creases, 40" x 26" $3000.00*

A-ME May 1993   *James D. Julia, Inc.*
SIGN, Coca-Cola, porcelain, 1930's fountain service, red, green, yellow, chips, 23" x 25½" $1700.00*

A-ME May 1993   *James D. Julia, Inc.*
BROADSIDE, Beadle's Library, creasing, breaks, soiling, 23" x 33" $1500.00*
SIGN, Bull Durham, paper, stains, 21½" x 27½" $1500.00*
SIGN, Dixon's Pencils, paper, in-painting, replacement, 13" x 29" $300.00*

A-ME May 1993   *James D. Julia, Inc.*
ARROW SIGN, Coca-Cola, painted wood, ca. 1930, soiled, scratches, loss, 23¼" x 28" $300.00*

A-ME May 1993   *James D. Julia, Inc.*
SIGN, Coca-Cola, porcelain, 2-sided, rust, chips, 26" x 25¼" $600.00*

A-ME May 1993   *James D. Julia, Inc.*
PAPER SIGNS
DR. JAYNE'S EXPECTORANT, wrinkles, tears, soiled, 13½" x 29" $500.00*
DIXON'S STOVE POLISH, creases, soiled, 13" x 28½" $400.00*
BUNTE BROS. CANDIES, trimmed, spotts, 15½" x 21" $650.00*

A-ME May 1993   *James D. Julia, Inc.*
SIGN, Coca-Cola, porcelain, 2-sided 1940's sign w/fountain and glass on both sides, rust, chips, 26" x 25¼" $600.00*

A-ME May 1993   *James D. Julia, Inc.*

Row 1, Left to Right

TRAY, Anheuser-Busch Brewing Co., tin, chips, 18½" x 15½" $2100.00*

TRAY, Leisy Brewing Co., tin, scratches, 16½" x 13½" $3650.00*

Row 2, Left to Right

TAKA-KOLA, 2 pcs., tin, tip tray, rust, chips, 4¼" D; sign, scratches, 9" x 13" $350.00*

TRAY, Anheuser-Busch Brewing Company, tin, rust, fading, scratches, chips, hole, 18½" x 15½" $450.00*

Row 3, Left to Right

CHARGER, Hoster's Beer, tin, fading, scratches, wear, 24" D $375.00*

TRAY, E. Robinson's Sons Beer, tin, chips, 13½" D $145.00*

A-ME May 1993   *James D. Julia, Inc.*

SIGN, Derby Tobacco, embossed cardboard, spots, 17½" x 22½" $4500.00*

A-ME May 1993   *James D. Julia, Inc.*

SYRUP DISPENSER, Ward's Orange Crush, tarnish, chips, 9" x 12" x 8" $575.00*

SYRUP DISPENSER, Ward's Lemon Crush, replacement, chips, 10" x 9" x 7" .. $450.00*

SYRUP DISPENSER, Ward's Lime Crush, replacement, wear, 9" x 9" x 7" $800.00*

A-ME May 1993   *James D. Julia, Inc.*

SIGN, Cooks Water, embossed cardboard, 11½" x 23½" $2750.00*

ABC PLATES — Alphabet plates were made especially for children as teaching aids. They date from the late 1700s and were made of various material including porcelain, pottery, glass, pewter, tin and ironstone.

AMPHORA ART POTTERY was made at the Amphora Porcelain Works in the Teplitz Tum area of Bohemia during the late 19th and early 20th centuries. Numerous potteries were located there.

BATTERSEA ENAMELS — The name "Battersea" is a general term for those metal objects decorated with enamels, such as pill, patch, and snuff boxes, doorknobs, and such. The process of fusing enamel onto metal—usually copper—began about 1750 in the Battersea District of London. Today the name has become a generic term for similar objects—mistakenly called "Battersea."

BELLEEK porcelain was first made at Fermanagh, Ireland, in 1857. Today this ware is still being made in buildings within walking distance of the original clay pits according to the skills and traditions of the original artisans. Irish Belleek is famous for its thinness and delicacy. Similar type wares were also produced in other European countries as well as the United States.

BENNINGTON POTTERY — The first pottery works in Bennington, Vermont, was established by Captain John Norton in 1793; and, for 101 years, it was owned and operated by succeeding generations of Nortons. Today the term "Bennington" is synonymous with the finest in American ceramics because the town was the home of several pottery operations during the last century—each producing under different labels. Today items produced at Bennington are now conveniently, if inaccurately, dubbed "Bennington." One of the popular types of pottery produced there is known as "Rockingham." The term denotes the rich, solid brown glazed pottery from which many household items were made. The ware was first produced by the Marquis of Rockingham in Swinton, England—hence the name.

BISQUE — The term applies to pieces of porcelain or pottery which have been fired but left in an unglazed state.

BLOOR DERBY — "Derby" porcelain dates from about 1755 when William Duesbury began the production of porcelain at Derby. In 1769 he purchased the famous Chelsea Works and operated both factories. During the Chelsea-Derby period, some of the finest examples of English porcelains were made. Because of their fine quality, in 1773 King George III gave Duesbury the patent to mark his porcelain wares "Crown Derby." Duesbury died in 1796. In 1810 the factory was purchased by Robert Bloor, a senior clerk. Bloor revived the Imari styles which had been so popular. After his death in 1845, former workmen continued to produce fine porcelains using the traditional Derby patterns. The firm was reorganized in 1876 and in 1878 a new factory was built. In 1890 Queen Victoria appointed the company "Manufacturers to Her Majesty" with the right to be known as Royal Crown Derby.

BUFFALO POTTERY — The Buffalo Pottery of Buffalo, New York, was organized in 1901. The firm was an adjunct of the Larkin Soap Company, which was established to produce china and pottery premiums for that company. Of the many different types produced, the Buffalo Pottery is most famous for its "Deldare" line which was developed in 1905.

CANARY LUSTER earthenware dates to the early 1800s, and was produced by potters in the Staffordshire District of England. The body of this ware is a golden yellow and decorated with transfer printing, usually in black.

CANTON porcelain is a blue-and-white decorated ware produced near Canton, China, from the late 1700s through the last century. Its hand-decorated Chinese scenes have historical as well as mythological significance.

CAPO-di-MONTE, originally a softpaste porcelain, is Italian in origin. The first ware was made during the 1700s near Naples. Although numerous marks were used, the most familiar to us is the crown over the letter N. Mythological subjects, executed in either high or low relief and tinted in bright colors on a light ground, were a favorite decoration. The earlier wares had a peculiar grayish color as compared to the whiter bodies of later examples.

CARLSBAD porcelain was made by several factories in the area from the 1800s and exported to the United States. When Carlsbad became a part of Czechoslovakia after World War I, wares were frequently marked "Karlsbad." Items marked "Victoria" were made for Lazarus & Rosenfeldt, Importers.

CASTLEFORD earthenware was produced in England from the late 1700s until around 1820. Its molded decoration is similar to Prattware.

CHINESE EXPORT PORCELAIN was made in quantity in China during the 1700s and early 1800s. The term identifies a variety of porcelain wares made for export to Europe and the United States. Since many thought the product to be of joint Chinese and English manufacture, it has also been known as "Oriental" or "Chinese Lowestoft."

As much as this ware was made to order for the American and European market, it was frequently adorned with seals of states or the coat of arms of individuals, in addition to eagles, sailing scenes, flowers, religious and mythological scenes.

CLEWS POTTERY — (see also, Historical Staffordshire) was made by George Clews & Co., of Brownhill Pottery, Tunstall, England, from 1806–1861.

CLIFTON POTTERY was founded by William Long in Clifton New Jersey, in 1905.

COALPORT porcelain has been made by the Coalport Porcelain Works in England since 1795. The ware is still being produced at Stroke-on-Trent.

COPELAND-SPODE — The firm was founded by Josiah Spoke in 1770 in Staffordshire, England. From 1847, W.T. Copeland & Sons, Ltd., succeeded Spode, using the designation "Late Spode" to its wares. The firm is still in operation.

COPPER LUSTER — See Lusterwares.

CROWN DUCAL — English porcelain made by the A.G. Richardson & Co., Ltd. since 1916.

CUP PLATES were used where cups were handleless and saucers were deep. During the early 1800s, it was very fashionable to drink from a saucer. Thus, a variety of fancy small plates was produced for the cup to rest in. The lacy Sandwich examples are very collectible.

DAVENPORT pottery and porcelain were made at the Davenport Factory in Longport, Staffordshire, England, by Joan Davenport from 1793 until 1887 when the pottery closed. Most of the wares produced there—porcelains, creamwares, ironstone, earthenwares and other products—were marked.

DEDHAM (Chelsea Art Works) —The firm was founded in 1872 at Chelsea, Massachusetts, by James Robertson & Sons, and closed in 1889. In 1891 the pottery was reopened under the name of The Chelsea Pottery, U.S. The first and most popular blue underglaze decoration for the desirable "Cracqule Ware" was the rabbit motif—designed by Joseph L. Smith. In 1893 construction was started on the new pottery in Dedham, Massachusetts, and production began in 1895. The name of the pottery was then changed to "Dedham Pottery," to eliminate the confusion with the English Chelsea Ware. The famed crackleware finish became synonymous with the name. Because of its popularity, more than 50 patterns of tableware were made.

DELFT — Holland is famous for its fine examples of tin-glazed pottery dating from the 16th century. Although blue and white is the most popular color, other colors were also made. The majority of the ware found today is from the late Victorian period and when the name Holland appears with the Delft factory mark, this indicates that the item was made after 1891.

DORCHESTER POTTERY was established by George Henderson in Dorchester, a part of Boston, Massachusetts, in 1895. Production included stonewares, industrial wares, and, later, some decorated tablewares. The pottery is still in production.

DOULTON — The pottery was established in Lambeth in 1815 by John Doulton and John Watts. When Watts retired in 1845, the firm became known as Doulton & Company. In 1901 King Edward VII conferred a double honor on the company by presentation of the Royal Warrant, authorizing their chairman to use the word "Royal" in describing products. A variety of wares has been made over the years for the Amer-ican market. The firm is still in production.

FLOWING BLUE ironstone is a highly glazed dinnerware made at Staffordshire by a variety of potters. It became popular about 1825. Items were printed with patterns (Oriental) and the color flowed from the design over the white body so that the finished product appeared smeared. Although purple and brown colors were also made, the deep cobalt blue shades were the most popular. Later wares were less blurred, having more white ground.

GAUDY DUTCH is the most spectacular of the gaudy wares. It was made for the Pennsylvania Dutch market from about 1785 until the 1820s. This softpaste tableware is lightweight and frail in appearance. Its rich cobalt blue decoration was applied to the biscuit, glazed and fired—then other colors were applied over the first glaze—and the object was fired again. No luster is included in its decoration.

GAUDY IRONSTONE was made in Staffordshire from the early 1850s until around 1865. This ware is heavier than gaudy Welsh or gaudy Dutch, as its texture is a mixture of pottery and porcelain clay.

GAUDY WELSH, produced in England from about 1830, resembles gaudy Dutch in decorations, but the workmanship is not as fine and its texture is more comparable to that of spatterware. Luster is usually included with the decoration.

HISTORICAL STAFFORDSHIRE — The term refers to a particular blue-on-white, transfer-printed earthenware produced in quantity during the early 1800s by many potters in the Staffordshire District. The central decoration was usually an American city scene or landscape, frequently showing some mode of transportation in the foreground. Other designs included portraits and patriotic emblems. Each potter had a characteristic border which is helpful to identify a particular ware, as many pieces are unmarked. Later transfer-printed wares were made in sepia, pink, green and black but the early cobalt blue examples are the most desirable.

IRONSTONE is a heavy, durable, utilitarian ware made from the slag of iron furnaces, ground and mixed with clay. Charles Mason of Lane Delft, Staffordshire, patented the formula in 1823. Much of the early ware was decorated in imitation of Imari, in addition to transfer-printed blue ware, flowing blues and browns. During the mid-19th centruy, the plain white enlivened only by embossed designs became fashionable. Literally hundreds of patterns were made for export.

JACKFIELD POTTERY is English in origin. It was first produced during the 17th century; however, most items available today date from the last century. It is a red-bodied pottery, often decorated with scrolls and flowers, in relief, then covered with a black glaze.

JUGTOWN POTTERY — This North Carolina pottery has been made since the 18th century. In 1915 Jacques Busbee organized what was to become the Jugtown Pottery in 1921. Production was discontinued in 1958.

KING'S ROSE is a decorated creamware produced in the Staffordshire district of England during the 1820-1840 period. The rose decorations are usually in red, green, yellow and pink. This ware is often referred to as "Queen's Rose."

LEED'S POTTERY was established by Charles Green in 1758 at Leed, Yorkshire, England. Early wares are unmarked. From 1775 the impressed mark "Leeds Pottery" was used. After 1880 the name "Hartly, Green & Co." was added, and the impressed or incised letters "LP" were also used to identify the ware.

LIMOGES — The name identifies fine porcelain wares produced by many factories at Limoges, France, since the mid-1800s. A variety of different marks identify wares made there including Haviland china.

LIVERPOOL POTTERY — The term applies to wares produced by many potters located in Liverpool, England, from the early 1700s, for American trade. Their print-decorated pitchers—referred to as "jugs" in England—have been especially popular. These featured patriotic emblems, prominent men, ships, etc., and can be easily identified as nearly all are melon-shaped with a very pointed lip, strap handle and graceful curved body.

LUSTERWARE — John Hancock of Hanley, England, invented this type of decoration on earthenwares during the early 1800s. The copper, bronze, ruby, gold, purple, yellow, pink and mottled pink luster finishes were made from gold painted on the glazed objects, then fired. The latter type is often referred to as "Sunderland Luster." Its pinkish tones vary in color and pattern. The silver lusters were made from platinum.

McCOY POTTERY — The J.W. McCoy Pottery was established in 1899. Production of art pottery began after 1926 when the name was changed to Brush McCoy.

METTLACH, Germany, located in the Zoar Basin, was the location of the famous Villeroy & Boch factories from 1836 until 1921 when the factory was destroyed by fire. Steins (dating from about 1842) and other stonewares with bas relief decorations were their specialty.

MOCHAWARE — This banded creamware was first produced in England during the late 1700s. The early ware was lightweight and thin, having colorful bands of bright colors decorating a body that is cream colored to very light brown. After 1840 the ware became heavier in body and the color was often quite light—almost white. Mochaware can easily be identified by its colorful banded decorations—on and between the bands—including feathery ferns, lacy trees, seaweeds, squiggly designs and lowly earthworms.

NILOAK POTTERY with its prominent swirled, marbelized designs, is a 20th century pottery first produced at Benton, Arkansas, in 1911 by the Niloak Pottery Company. Production ceased in 1946.

NIPPON porcelain has been produced in quantity for the American market since the late 19th century. After 1891, when it became obligatory to include the country of origin on all imports, the Japanese trademark "Nippon" was used. Numerous other marks appear on this ware identifying the manufacturer, artist or importer. The hand-painted Nippon examples are extremely popular today and prices are on the rise.

OHR POTTERY was produced by George E. Ohr in Biloxi, Mississippi, around 1883. Today Ohr is recognized as one of the leading potters in the American Art Pottery movement. Early work was often signed with an impressed stamp in block letters—G.E. OHR, BILOXI. Later pieces were often marked G.E. Ohr in flowing script. Ohr closed the pottery in 1906, storing more than 6,000 pieces as a legacy to his family, remaining storage until 1972.

PISGAH FOREST POTTERY — The pottery was founded near Mt. Pisgah in North Carolina in 1914 by Walter B. Stephen. The pottery remains in operation.

REDWARE is one of the most popular forms of country pottery. It has a soft, porous body and its color varies from reddish-brown tones to deep wine to light orange. It was produced in mostly utilitarian forms by potters in small factories, or by potters working on their farms, to fill their everyday needs. Glazes were used to intensify the color. The most desirable examples are the slip-decorated pieces, or the rare and expensive "sgraffito" examples which have scratched or incised line decoration. This type of decoration was for ornamentation, since examples were rarely used for ordinary utilitarian purposes, but were given as gifts. Hence, these highly prized pieces rarely show wear, indicating that they were treasured as ornaments only. Slip decoration was made by tracing the design on the redware shape with a clay having a creamy consistency in contrasting colors. When dried, the design was slightly raised above the surface. Because these pieces were made for practical usage, the potter then pressed or beat the slip decoration into the surface of the object.

RED WING POTTERY, of Red Wing, Minnesota, was founded in 1878. The firm began in the 1920s and closed in 1967.

ROCKINGHAM — See Bennington Pottery.

ROOKWOOD POTTERY — The Rookwood Pottery began production at Cincinnati, Ohio, in 1880 under the direction of Maria Longworth Nichols Storer, and operated until 1960. The name was derived from the family estate, "Rookwood," because of the "rook" or "crows" which inhabited the wooded areas. All pieces of this art pottery are marked, usually bearing the famous flame.

RORSTRAND FAIENCE — The firm was founded in 1726 near Stockholm, Sweden. Items dating from the early 1900s and having an "art noveau" influence are very expensive and much in demand these days.

ROSE MEDALLION ware dates from the 18th century. It was decorated and exported from Canton, China, in quantity. The name generally applied to those pieces having medallions with figures of people alternating with panels of flowers, birds and butterflies. When all the medallions were filled with flowers, the ware was differentiated as Rose Canton.

ROSE TAPESTRY — See Royal Bayreuth.

ROSEVILLE POTTERY — The Roseville Pottery was organized in 1890 in Roseville, Ohio. The firm produced utilitarian stoneware in the plant formerly owned by the Owens Pottery of Roseville, also producers of stoneware, and the Linden Avenue Plant at Zanesville, Ohio, originally built by the Clark Stoneware Company. In 1900 an art line of pottery was created to compete with Owens and Weller lines. The new ware was named "Rozane," and it was produced at the Zanesville location. Following its success, other prestige lines were created. The Azurine line was introduced about 1902.

ROYAL BAYREUTH manufactory began in Tettau in 1794 at the first porcelain factory in Bavaria. Wares made there were on the same par with Meissen. Fire destroyed the original factory during the 1800s. Much of the wares available today were made at the new factory which began production in 1897. These include Rose Tapestry, Sunbonnet Baby novelties and the Devil and Card items. The Royal Bayreuth blue mark has the 1794 founding date incorporated with the mark.

ROYAL BONN — The tradename identifies a variety of porcelain items made during the 19th century by the Bonn China Manufactory, established in 1755 by Elmer August. Most of the ware found today is from the Victorian period.

ROYAL CROWN DERBY — The company was established in 1875 in Derby, England, and has no connection with the earlier Derby factories which operated in the late 18th and early 19th centuries. Derby porcelain produced from 1878 to 1890 carry the standard crown printed mark. From 1891 forward, the mark carries the "Royal Crown Derby" wording, and during the present century, "Made in England" and "English Bone China" were added to the mark. Today the ocmpany is a part of Royal Doulton Tableware, Ltd.

ROYAL DOULTON wares have been made from 1901, when King Edward VII conferred a double honor on the Doulton Pottery by the presentation of the Royal Warrant, authorizing their chairman to use the word "Royal" in describing products. A variety of wares has been produced for the American market. The firm is still in production.

ROYAL DUX was produced in Bohemia during the late 1800s. Large quantities of this decorative porcelain ware were exported to the United States. Royal Dux figurines are especially popular.

ROYAL RUDOLSTADT — This hard paste ware was first made in Rudolstadt, Thuringen, East Germany, by Ernt Bohne in 1854. A second factory was opened in 1882 by L. Straus & Sons, Ltd. The ware was never labeled "Royal Rudolstadt" originally, but the word "Royal" was added later as part of an import mark. This porcelain was imported by Lewis Straus and Sons of New York.

ROYAL WORCESTER — The Worcester factory was established in 1751 in England. This is a tastefully decorated porcelain noted for its creamy white lusterless surface. Serious collectors prefer items from the Dr. Wall (the activator of the concern) period of production which extended from the time the factory was established to 1785.

ROYCROFT POTTERY was made by the Roycrofter community of East Aurora, New York, during the late 19th and early 20th centuries. The firm was founded by Elbert Hubbard. Products produced included pottery, furniture, metalware, jewelry and leatherwork.

R.S. PRUSSIA porcelain was produced during the mid-1800s by Erdman Schlegelmilch in Suhl. His brother, Reinhold, founded a factory in 1869 in Tillowitz in lower Silesia. Both made fine qualtiy porcelain, using both satin and high gloss finishes with comparable decoration. Additionally, both brothers used the same R.S. mark in the same colors, the initials being in memory of their father, Rudolph Schlegelmilch. It has not been determined when production at the two factories ceased.

SAMPSON WARE dates from the early 19th century. The firm was founded in Paris and reproduced a variety of collectible wares including Chelsea, Meissen and Oriental Lowestoft, with marks which distinguish their wares as reproductions. The firm is still in production.

SATSUMA is a Japanese pottery having a distinctive creamy crackled glaze decorated with bright enamels and often with Japanese figures. The majority of the ware available today includes the mass-produced wares dating from the 1850s. Their quality does not compare to the fine early examples.

SPATTERWARE is a softpaste tableware, laboriously decorated with hand-drawn flowers, birds, buildings, trees, etc., with "spatter" decoration chiefly as a background. It was produced in considerable quantity from the early 1800s to around 1850.

To achieve this type of decoration, small bits of sponge were cut into different shapes—leaves, hearts, rosettes, vines, geometrical patterns, etc.—and mounted on the end of a short stick for convenience in dipping into the pigment.

SPONGEWARE, as it is known, is a decorative white earthenware. Color—usually blue, blue/green, brown/tan/blue, or blue/brown—was applied to the white clay base. Because the color was often applied with a colorsoaked sponge, the term "spongeware" became common for this ware. A variety of utilitarian items were produced—pitchers, cookie jars, bean pots, water coolers, etc. Marked examples are rare.

STAFFORDSHIRE is a district in England where a variety of pottery and porcelain wares has been produced by many factories in the area.

STICKSPATTER — The term identifies a type of decoration that combines hand-painting and transfer-painted decoration. "Spattering" was done with either a sponge or brush containing a moderate supply of pigment. Stickspatter was developed from the traditional Staffordshire spatterware, as the earlier ware was time consuming and expensive to produce. Although most of this ware was made in England from the 1850s to the late 1800s, it was also produced in Holland, France and elsewhere.

TEA LEAF is a lightweight stone china decorated with copper or gold "tea leaf" sprigs. It was first made by Anthony Shaw of Longport, England, during the 1850s. By the late 1800s, other potters in Staffordshire were producing the popular ware for export to the United States. As a result, there is a noticeable diversity in decoration.

TECO POTTERY is an art pottery line made by the Terra Cotta Tile works of Terra Cotta, Illinois. The firm was organized in 1881 by William D. Gates. The Teco line was first made in 1885 but not sold commercially until 1902 and was discontinued during the 1920s.

VAN BRIGGLE POTTERY was established at Colorado Springs, Colorado, in 1900 by Artus Van Briggle and his wife, Anna. Most of the ware was marked. The first mark included two joined "A's," representing their first two initials. The firm is still in operation.

WEDGWOOD POTTERY was established by Josiah Wedgwood in 1759 in England. A tremendous variety of fine wares has been produced through the years including basalt, lusterwares, creamware, jasperware, bisque, agate, Queen's Ware and others. The system of marks used by the firm clearly indicates when each piece was made.

Since 1940 the new Wedgwood factory has been located at Barleston.

WELLER POTTERY — Samuel A. Weller established the Weller pottery in 1872 in Fultonham, Ohio. In 1888 the pottery was moved to Piece Street in Putnam, Ohio—now a part of Zanesville, Ohio. The production of art pottery began in 1893 and by late 1897 several prestige lines were being produced including Samantha, Touranda and Dicken's Ware. Other later types included Weller's Louwelsa, Eosian, Aurora, Turada and the rare Sicardo which is the most sought after and most expensive today. The firm closed in 1948.

A-PA May 1993   *Conestoga Auction Co.*
WELLER
HUDSON VASE, blue, block mark $190.00*
VASE, signed D.E. painted mark, 10" T $190.00*
HUDSON VASE, pink, rose on blue, signed McLaughlin, 9½" T $275.00*
HUDSON VASE, pink, yellow on blue, block mark, 9½" T $110.00*

A-PA May 1993   *Conestoga Auction Co.*
ROSEVILLE
Row 1, Left to Right
WHITE ROSE VASE, pink, green, 12" T $180.00*
WINCRAFT VASE, green to brown $65.00*
CLEMATIS VASE, green, 8" T .. $60.00*
Row 2, Left to Right
ZEPHYR LILLY ASHTRAY, green $45.00*
DOGWOOD II BASKET, 8" T .. $80.00*
JONQUIL VASE, 8½" T $120.00*
DOGWOOD I VASE, 6¼" T ... $85.00*
BANEDA VASE, green, 6" T ... $200.00*

A-PA May 1993   *Conestoga Auction Co.*
VASE, marked Etna Weller, green matt glaze, 12½" T $725.00*
HUDSON VASE, pastels on teal, signed Pillsbury, 11¾" T $950.00*
KNIFEWOOD VASE, squirrels on branches, no mark, 11" T $130.00*
WARWICK VASE, no mark, 9½" T $35.00*

A-PA May 1993   *Conestoga Auction Co.*
ORCHID VASE, multi-color on cobalt, dated 1942, 12" T $440.00*
SPRING FLOWER CHARGER, pastels on blue, 1928-1949, 12" D $500.00*
ANEMONE LAMP, red, blue, white, on green to blue, pottery 8" T, lamp 24" T $400.00*

A-PA May 1993   *Conestoga Auction Co.*
WELLER, MARKED
FLEMISH VASE, blue, 6¾" T .. $160.00*
BLUEWARE VASE, 12" T $170.00*
HUDSON VASE, pink, green on blue, signed McLaughlin, 10" T $250.00*
HUDSON VASE, yellow, pink, green, blue on blue, 7" T $150.00*

A-PA May 1993   *Conestoga Auction Co.*
ROSEVILLE
Row 1, Left to Right
NUDE VASE, red $300.00*
FUTURA VASE, blue, green, glaze curdling $475.00*
WISTERIA VASE, blue, 8½" T $325.00*
FUTURA VASE, blue, green, repair, 8" T $250.00*
Row 2, Left to Right
MONTICELLO BASKET, blue, 6" T $270.00*
FUTURA VASE, pink, green, glaze curdling $200.00*
FUTURA VASE, green, repair .. $350.00*
FUTURA VASE, blue-green ... $100.00*

A-ME Nov. 1992   *James D. Julia, Inc.*
Row 1, Left to Right
VASE, Haviland, raised dec., 10" T .... NS
VASE, Louwelsa Weller, brown, green on brown, 10" T .... NS
Row 2, Left to Right
VASES, pr, Royal Bayreuth Blue Mark, "Lake Megantic," 7" T $192.50*
TRAY, signed Doyal Daulton, shades of green, white, pale blue, 11½" L $104.50*
INDIAN MAIDEN, signed Van Briggle, pale green, blue, artist "CB," 8½" T..... $450.00*
VASE, Chelsea, ceramic art pottery, mottled green-brown, 7¼" T $220.00*
Row 3, Left to Right
BOWL, Saturday Evening Girl's Art Pottery, blue-gray, signed "S.E.G. TM," .... NS

A-OH July 1993   *Garth's Auctions, Inc.*

LUSTERWARE
Row 1, Left to Right
CREAMERS, 3 pcs., copper w/enameled raised dec., 3⅜" to 3⅝" T $74.25
CHILD'S MUG, canary, black transfer, silver luster, wear, flakes, 2⅝" T ... $25.30
CREAMERS, 3 pcs., copper, 2 w/white, 2½" to 3" T $5.50
TUMBLER, SHAKER, copper, pink, white, 3" T, 4¾" T $38.50
Row 2, Left to Right
PITCHER, pearlwear w/pink luster, wear, small chips, 4¾" T............ $165.00
GOBLET, CREAMER, copper luster w/ polychrome enamel, repairs, 4⅛" T, 4⅜" T $44.00
MUG, CREAMER, copper luster w/ polychrome, 3½" T, 4¾" T $99.00
CREAMER, pearlware, black transfer w/pink luster trim, wear, stains, 4¾" T $52.25
Row 3, Left to Right
PITCHER, copper luster w/polychrome enamel, purple luster, 8⅞" T $220.00
PITCHER, copper luster w/red transfer, polychrome enamel, old repair, flakes, 7¾" T $60.50
PITCHER, copper luster w/polychrome enamel, 7½" T $126.50
POT, copper luster w/pink luster dec., hairline, 6½" T $71.50

A-PA May 1993   *Conestoga Auction Co.*

MOORCROFT, ALL MARKED
VASE, multicolor on white to cobalt, ca. 1945, 7" T $385.00*
VASE, pink, cobalt, yellow on blue-green, 1953–1978, 12" T $450.00*
LAMP, red, white, purple, 1929–1949, pottery 12" T, lamp 24" T $550.00*
MAC INTYRE JUG, pewter lid, dk. green, mint green, ca. 1910, 7" T $300.00*

A-MA Nov. 1992   *James D. Julia, Inc.*

ROOKWOOD POTTERY
Row 1, Left to Right
PERFUME JUG, Limoges style glaze, "Miss Hanna," by Albert R. Valentine in 1883, mkd, 3¾" T $100.00
VASE, wax matte glaze, yellow, dated 1929, mkd., 5½" T $250.00
PITCHER, Limoges style glaze, by Martin Rettig in 1885, mkd., 5½" T $350.00
MUG, wax matte glaze, dated 1907, mkd., 7¼" T $300.00
VASE, wax matte glaze, lt. blue, dated 1924, mkd., 8¼" T $350.00
Row 2, Left to Right
VASE, high glaze, by E. T. Hurley in 1943, mkd., 8½" T $1200.00
VASE, standard glaze, dated 1887, mkd., crack, chip, 8¼" T $300.00
VASE, vellum glaze, by Carrie Steinle in 1907, mkd., 9¼" T $650.00

A-MA Dec. 1992   *Skinner, Inc.*

STAFFORDSHIRE TOBY PITCHER, 10" H.......................... $300.00*
MAJOLICA PITCHER, dated 1859, 9½" H.......................... $425.00*

A-IL Apr. 1993   *Leslie Hindman Auction*

MASON'S SOUP TUREEN, ironstone, 19th c., 15" L $1400.00*

A-OH July 1993   *Garth's Auctions, Inc.*
Row 1, Left to Right
CHILD'S TEA SET, 21 pcs., moss rose, teapot, creamer, sugar, 6 cups & saucers, 6 plates $275.00
HEN ON NEST, bisque, polychrome, 3⅞" T........................... $104.50
CHILD'S TEA SET, 6 pcs., incomplete, brown floral ironstone, 3 plates, 2 saucers, 1 cup, chip.................. $3850.00
Row 2, Left to Right
CHILD'S TEAPOT, blue transfer Staffordshire, wear, flakes, 3⅞" T $82.50
CHILD'S TEA SET, PCS., 36 assorted pcs., mostly plates, some lids $71.50
Row 3, Left to Right
CHILD'S TEA SET, 13 pcs., "Staffordshire England," ironstone, red "Water Hen" transfer, 6 plates, 3 cups, 1 saucer, creamer, waste bowl, sugar, teapot, chips $275.00
FOOT W/SHOE, milk glass, worn enamel, 3" L........................... $5.50

A-PA May 1993   *Conestoga Auction Co.*

MOORCROFT, ALL MARKED
Row 1, Left to Right
VASE, cobalt, yellow on blue-green, ca. 1950, 3½" T $85.00*
VASE, pink, purple on cobalt, ca. 1960, 6" T........................... $110.00*
VASE, pewter top, red on cobalt, 1949–1986, 6½" T $130.00*
VASE, pink, blue on dk. green, 1949–1986, 5" T........................ $120.00*
BASE, yellow, lt. green, blue on green, 1949–1986, 3½" T $90.00*
Row 2, Left to Right
VASE, yellow, red on cobalt, 1953–1978, 3" T........................... $100.00*
VASE, red on copper, 1953–1978, 5" T........................... $210.00*
BOWL, pink, purple on blue to green ground, 1949–1986, 2" H, 6" D .. $100.00*
VASE, red on cobalt, 1949–1986, 3½" T........................... $120.00*

A-MA Nov. 1991   *Skinner, Inc.*
VASE, Satsuma, Meiji period, signed "Seizan," 3⅜" T $660.00
JAR, Satsuma, Meiji period, signed "Kizan," 3⅜" T $1320.00
BOWL, Satsuma, Yabu Meizan, teak stand, 1¾" D $1430.00

A-PA May. 1993   *Glass Works Auctions*
ANNE POTTERY PIG BOTTLE, (front and back shown), incised, brown glaze, Lake Shore Saloon, chip, 8" L .. $2400.00*

A-PA May 1993   *Conestoga Auction Co.*
STANGL, MARKED
Row 1, Left to Right
COCKATOO, 6" T $55.00*
PARROT, 5½" T $70.00*
YELLOW WARBLER, 6" T $95.00*
CHICADEE, 5" T $95.00*
BLUEJAY, (unmarked), 5½" T, ... $25.00*
Row 2, Left to Right
BLUEJAY, CLIFF SWALLOW .. $85.00*
YELLOW WARBLER, 4" T $75.00*
KINGFISHER, HUMMINGBIRD
.... $110.00*

A-OH July 1993   *Garth's Auctions, Inc.*
Row 1, Left to Right
PLATE, Rose Canton, 8½" D $148.50
TEA POT, Rose Medallion, 4¾" T $71.50
PLATE, Rose Canton, 7¾" D $148.50
CUP & SAUCER, Thousand Butterfly, demi-tasse $27.50
PLATE, Thousand Butterfly, crow's foot, 7¼" D $93.50
CREAMER, Rose Canton, 4" T $93.50
PLATE, Rose Medallion, hairline, 8½" D $154.00
Row 2, Left to Right
SOUP PLATES, pr., (1 illus.), Rose Canton, 9¾" D $407.00
COVERED DISH, Rose Medallion, 8" L $550.00
HEXAGONAL DISH, Rose Canton, 11" D $302.50
TAZZA, Rose Medallion, 3¼" H, 6¾" D $110.00
FLOWER POT, Rose Medallion, 4¾" T $220.00
PLATE, Rose Canton, flakes, 9¾" D $104.50

A-PA May 1993   *Conestoga Auction Co.*
MOORCROFT, MARKED
Row 1, Left to Right
CLEMATIS VASE, multi-color on green to blue, 1949–1986, 5" T $170.00*
PLUM VASE, multi-color on cobalt, 1949–1986, 5" T $165.00*
FRUIT VASE, multi-color on cobalt, ca. 1945, 5" T $160.00*
Row 2, Left to Right
CLEMATIS CANDLESTICKS, pr., (unmarked), 3" T $180.00*
ANEMONE DISH, pink on cobalt, 1949–1986, 8½" L $110.00*

A-MA Jan. 1993 *Skinner, Inc.*
**CANTON FRUIT BASKET W/UNDER-
TRAY,** 19th c., 8½" .... NS
ARMORIAL FITZHUGH PLATE, reticulated, 19th c., 10¼" $467.50
**CANTON FRUIT BASKET W/UNDER-
TRAY,** 19th c., 9¾"........... $880.00

A-MD May 1993 *C.G. Sloan & Co., Inc.*
BLUE AND WHITE CHINESE EXPORT PORCELAIN
Row 1, Left to Right
NANKING SOUP PLATE, Qianlong, ca. 1790, 9½" D $90.00*
FITZHUGH COVERED TUREEN, Jiaqing, ca. 1800, 14" L .... NS
PLATTER, Qianlong, ca. 1770, deer and peony dec., 12¼" L $900.00*
Row 2, Left to Right
UNDERTRAY OR BASKET STAND, 9½" L $550.00*
SQUARE SALT, Kangxi, ca. 1710, 3" sq. .... NS
CUPS AND SAUCERS, pr., Kangxi, ca. 1710 .... $550.00*
BRUSH POT, transitional, ca. 1650, 7" T $775.00*
DEEP PLATTER, Quianlong, ca. 1795, 12" L............................ $500.00*
LEAF SHAPED SAUCEBOAT, Quianlong, ca. 1780, 8" L $450.00*
BOWL, Jiaqing, ca. 1800, 6" D $170.00*
FITZHUGH BOWL, Jiaqing, ca. 1800, chip, 7½" D $225.00*

A-PA May 1993 *Conestoga Auction Co.*
MOORCROFT, MARKED
POMEGRANATE VASE, cobalt, ca. 1945, 4" T....................... $180.00*
ORCHID VASE, multi-color on cobalt, 1949–1986, 4" T $285.00*
ANEMONE VASE, multi-color on cobalt, 1949–1986, 4¾" T............ $165.00*
HIBISCUS VASE, yellow, red on green to blue, 1949–1986. 4" T $80.00*

A-MD May 1993 *C.G. Sloan & Co., Inc.*
JAPANESE SATSUMA EARTHENWARE
Left to Right
SCALLOPED PLATE, Meiji period, interior w/bird and flower dec., base w/dragon dec., 8½" D $115.00*
KORO, Showa period, figural dec., 3" T................................... $150.00*
VASES, pr., Showa period, panels w/alternating figural, fan, floral dec., 6½" T .. $300.00*
VASE, Meiji period, Samurai dec., 7½" T $100.00*
KORO, Showa period, applied bows, pierced silver cover, 5" T $475.00*
QUATREFOIL VASE, Showa period, floral dec., 5" T $325.00*
CONICAL VASE, Showa period, Floral and brocade dec., 6" T $375.00*
KOGO (COVERED BOX), Meiji period, figural and brocade dec., 3¼" D .... NS

A-MA Jan. 1993 *Skinner, Inc.*
CREAMWARE PITCHER, Liverpool transfer-painted, 19th c., ship "Amelia" flying American flag, green, yellow, red, blue, black enamel, inscribed "Amelia, of New York, William S. Brooks, Commander of New-York," reverse with Washington, inscribed "First President of the United States of America, 10" H $4950.00
CREAMWARE PITCHER, Liverpool transfer-painted, ca. 1800, Independence (McCauley 172), reverse with Washington and Justice, Liberty, Victory, American eagle under spout, 8" H $1650.00

A-OH May 1993　　　*Garth's Auctions, Inc.*

Row 1, Left to Right

HANDLESS CUP/SAUCER, red spatterware, black deer, stains, flakes, crow's foot $357.50
TOBY, Staffordshire, pearlware, polychrome enamel, chips, 3¾" H . . . $165.00
HANDLESS CUP/SAUCER, gaudy, pearlware, wear, flakes $275.00

Row 2, Left to Right

TOBY PITCHER, Staffordshire, creamware, brown, black, yellow, tan, chips, 10" H $440.00
TOBY PITCHER, Staffordshire, 8½" H $440.00
TOBY PITCHER, Staffordshire, yelloware, white, black, tan, brown, blue glaze, old repair, 10¼" H $386.00

A-PA May 1993　　　*Conestoga Auction Co.*
VAN BRIGGLE

Row 1, Left to Right

PINECONE BOWL, turquoise, dated 1920, 5" H, 8" D $360.00*
VASE, turquoise, ca 1950, 4" T . . $85.00*
FIGURINE, turquoise, 7½" T . . . $130.00*

Row 2, Left to Right

VASE, persian rose, ca. 1930, 5" T $150.00*
VASE, turquoise, dragonfly dec., ca. 1920, 6½" T $325.00*
VASE, turquoise, floral dec., ca. 1930, 7½" T $75.00*
LORELIE VASE, turquoise, ca. 1960, 12" T $200.00*
VASE, turquoise, floral dec., 10" T $180.00*

A-MA Jan. 1992　　　*Skinner, Inc.*
ROSE MEDALLION VASES, pr., 19th c., 12" T $605.00
ROSE MANDARIN VASE, 19th c., 16" T $550.00
ROSE MANDARIN PUNCH BOWL, 19th c., 15½" D $1870.00
ROSE MANDARIN, 2 pcs., covered dish, oval dish, 19th c., 11¼", 8" L $220.00
ROSE CANTON PLATES, 19th c., 9¾" D $550.00

A-MA Jan. 1993　　　*Skinner, Inc.*
CANTON TEAPOT, 19th c., 5½" H $550.00
CANTON TEAPOT, 19th c., 6" H $275.00
CANTON TEAPOT, 19th c., 6" H $522.50
NANKING CIDER JUGS, pair, gilt, 19th c. 10" $825.00
NANKING TEAPOT, 19th c., 17½" $220.00
NANKING BOTTLE & RICE BOWL, (bowl not illus.), 19th c., 10½" T $357.50
CANTON GRAVY BOAT, 19th c., 7¼" . . . . NS
CANTON PITCHER, 19th c., 7½" $935.00
CANTON TEAPOT, 19th c., 6¼" H $412.50
NANKING TEAPOT, 19th c., 7" H $302.50

A-MA Jan. 1993　　　*Skinner, Inc.*
PORCELAIN CHARGER, Chinese export, 19th c., 13" $880.00

A-MA Mar. 1993　　　*Skinner, Inc.*
LIMOGES ENAMEL PLAQUES, pr., late 19th c., imperfections, 7½" D $990.00

A-MA Jan. 1993   *Skinner, Inc.*
FITZHUGH OVAL PLATTER, pierced inset liner, gilt, 19th c., 17¾" $1100.00
FITZHUGH OVAL PLATTER, 19th c., 17" $660.00
NANKING PLATTER, 19th c., 15¾" $880.00
NANKING OVAL PLATTER, 19th c., 15¾" $247.50

A-OH July 1993   *Garth's Auctions, Inc.*
Row 1, Left to Right
COVERED VEGETABLE, Canton, blue, white, 8" L $291.50
PLATTER, Canton, blue, white, 12½" L $385.00
TRAY, Nanking, blue, white, 7¼" L $220.00
COFFEE POT, cloisonne, 3½" T .. $49.50
COVERED VEGETABLE, Canton, blue, white, 10¼" L $330.00
Row 2, Left to Right
JARS, (each end of row), pr., blue, white, foo dog finials, 8¾" T $407.00
JAR, Canton, blue, white, 3" T ... $170.50
PLATE, cloisonne, 9⅝" D $104.50
DISH, Canton, blue, white, hairline, 6⅛" D $5.50
DISH, Canton, blue, white, chips, 9¼" D $302.50
STIRRUPS, pr., cloisonne $93.50

A-PA May 1993   *Conestoga Auction Co.*
ROSEVILLE
WATER LILLY VASE, brown, 4" L $40.00*
PINECONE JARDINIERE, brown, 5¼" T $1100.00*
MOSS BOWL, pink $75.00*

A-NH Aug. 1993   *Northeast Auctions*
Row 1, Left to Right
SAUCE TUREEN, Canton $550.00*
BOWL, Canton $475.00*
TEA CADDY, Canton $1800.00*
Row 2, Left to Right
SAUCE BOAT, Canton $100.00*
SOUP TUREEN, Canton $1600.00*
POTS DE CREME, set of 8, (1 illus.), Canton $900.00*
Row 3, Left to Right
PITCHER, Canton $500.00*
SOUP TAUREEN, Canton ... $1600.00*
TRAY, Canton $450.00*
TRENCHER SALT, Canton $525.00*

A-MA Jan. 1993   *Skinner, Inc.*
CANTON SERVING DISH, 19th c. 11¼" $302.50
CANTON WELL AND TREE PLATTER, 19th c., 12¾" $605.00
CANTON PLATTER, 19th c., 17¼" $330.00
NANKING PLATTER, 19th c., 14½" L $192.50
NANKING TRAY, 19th c., 9¾" sq. $495

A-MA Jan. 1993   *Skinner, Inc.*
CANTON SAUCE TUREEN W/UNDER-TRAY, 19th c., 6½" $550.00
CANTON SAUCE TUREEN W/UNDER-TRAY, 19th c., 10¼" $770.00
CANTON SAUCE TUREEN W/UNDER-TRAY, 19th c., 6½" $522.50
NANKING COVERED TUREEN, 19th c., 13½" $1210.00
NANKING COVERED TUREEN, 19th c., 12" $385.00

A-NH Aug. 1993   *Northeast Auctions*
Row 1, Left to Right
PUNCH BOWL, export, polychrome $1500.00*
TEAPOT, Chinese export $450.00*
BOWL, Chinese export, cherry picker des. $450.00*
Row 2, Left to Right
TEAPOTS, 3 pcs., Chinese export, Armorial crests $2100.00*
Row 3, Left to Right
HOT-WATER DISH, blue Fitzhugh $1500.00*
SAUCE TUREENS, 2 pcs., (1 illus.), Nanking $600.00*
CHARGER, Fitzhugh, blue, white $700.00*

A-OH March. 1993 *Garth's Auctions, Inc.*

Row 1, Left to Right

PITCHER, pink luster resist, vintage w/blue striping, chips, 4½" H $220.00
PITCHER, silver luster, black transfer, ivory ground, wear, hairline, 5⅜" H $104.50
BOWL, silver luster resist, vintage, wear, hairlines, 9¼" D, 4¼" H $165.00
MUG, silver luster resist, floral, stains, hairlines, flakes, 3⅜" H $11.00
PITCHER, silver luster, vintage w/grain, wear, hairlines, 5¼" H $49.50

Row 2, Left to Right

PITCHER, silver luster resist, vintage w/farmer's arms, wear, 5½" H $137.50
PITCHER, silver luster resist, canary, foliage, worn, 5⅜" H $302.50
TRAY, canary band, white center and rim, wear, 8¼" L...................... $192.50
PITCHER, silver luster resist, bird w/flowers, wear, 5½" H $137.50
PITCHER, canary w/silver luster trim, black English transfer, repair, 5½" H...... $93.50

Row 3, Left to Right

PITCHER, silver luster resist, bird w/flowers, stains, hairlines, chip, 6⅝" H $60.50
PITCHER, silver luster resist, floral, stains, wear, 5⅜" H $93.50
PITCHER, canary w/black striping, black transfer, "King Henry IV Part I," "The Merry Wives of Windsor," chips, hairlines, 6¼" H $110.00
PITCHER, silver luster resist, vintage, wear, stains, 5" H $71.50
PITCHER, silver luster resist, floral, wear, flakes, 6¼" H $165.00

A-MA Mar. 1993 *Skinner, Inc.*

CANTON TUREEN, chips, 12" L..................................... $770.00
CHINESE EXPORT PORCELAIN PLATES, 12 pcs., blue/white, bird and chrysanthemum dec., imperfections, 9" D $440.00
CANTON TAZZA, chip, 14¾" L $990.00
NANKING OVAL PLATTER, chips, 16" L................................. $412.50
NANKING SOUP PLATES, 13 pcs., chips, 9¾" D $990.00
CANTON ITEMS, 4 pcs., (octagonal tile illus. only) $495.00
CANTON COVERED SERVING DISH (illus.)**, UNDERTRAY, CREAMER,** ... $440.00
CANTON CANDLESTICKS, pr., imperfections, 11" H $2310.00

A-OH Jan. 1993 *Garth's Auctions, Inc.*

Row 1, Left to Right

STAFFORDSHIRE HANDLESS CUPS AND SAUCERS, pr., (each end of row), gaudy, blue, green, red $55.00
SALT, yellowware, white, brown, hairlines, 3" D $225.50
CREAMER, pearlware, blue, white, stains, 3¼" H $385.00
CHAMBER POT, yellowware, white, brown, blue, 1¾" H $192.50

Row 2, Left to Right

CUP PLATE, King's Rose, chips, 4⅜" D $55.00
CREAMER, pearlware, blue trim, wear, hairline, 2⅝" H $33.00
CUP, King's Rose, 3⅝" D $71.50
CUP PLATE, gaudy Staffordshire, impressed "Rogers," 4⅛" D $49.50
SUGAR BOWL, pearlware, blue, white Leeds dec., wrong lid, 3⅝" H $66.00
HANDLESS CUP AND SAUCER, pearlware, enameled floral dec., hairlines, chips $66.00

Row 3, Left to Right

TODDY PLATE, King's Rose, 5¼" D $93.50
CREAMER, pearlware, yellow, green, brown, blue, repair, stains, 3⅞" H.......................... $330.00
MEDALLION, yellowware, bust of Washington, 6¼" H................ $253.00
SUGAR BOWL, blue spatterware, purple, red, green, black, chips, repairs, 4¼" H.......................... $143.00
HANDLESS CUP AND SAUCER, red, green, brown, professional repairs $467.50

A-MA Oct. 1992 *Skinner, Inc.*

REDWARE PLATES, 2 pcs. (1st and 4th in illus.), slip decorated, losses, 9", 12" $412.50
REDWARE DISH, slip decorated, notched rim, chips, 11½" $1045.00
REDWARE PLATE, slip decorated, notched rim, chips, 11½" $880.00
REDWARE PLATES, 2 pcs. (one illus.), one slip decorated, imperfections, 10½", 8" $412.50

A-OH Feb. 1993 *Garth's Auctions, Inc.*

Row 1, Left to Right

STONEWARE STEIN, bear, brown, blue, grey glaze, hairline, 7⅜" H $38.50
DOULTON TUMBLER, 2-tone, tavern/hunt scenes, London mark, 4⅝" H .. $110.00
DOULTON TUMBLER, 2-tone, tavern/hunt sceans, impressed " Daulton & Co. Lambeth," 4¼" H $27.50
STONEWARE STEIN, pewter lid, grey, blue, 5" H $49.50
DELFT BOWL, polychrome design, flakes, hole in table ring, 8⅜" D, 4" H .. $550.00
DELFT PITCHER, blue, white, hairlines, flakes, 6¾" H $137.50

Row 2, Left to Right

STONEWARE EWER, tan glaze, pewter lid, lip restored, 11½" H $137.50
STONEWARE STEIN, grey salt glaze, pewter lid, porcelain insert, enameled deer, damage, 9⅜" H $82.50
POTTERY PITCHER, 2-tone glaze, tavern/hunt scenes, flake, 7⅜" H $27.50
DELFT STEIN, pewter fittings, polychrome landscape, "1807," hairlines, damage, repair, 10¼" H $275.00
STONEWARE EWER, grey w/blue, incised design, loss, chip, 11" H........ $159.50

A-OH May 1993 *Garth's Auctions, Inc.*

ENGLISH STAFFORDSHIRE W/BLUE TRANSFER

Row 1, Left to Right

PLATE, "Barrington Hall," impressed "Stevenson," wear, flake, 8⅞" D .. $192.50
PLATE, "Hawthorne, Edinburghshire," impressed "Adams," wear, flakes, scratches, 8¾" D $115.50
PLATTER, "The Letter of Introduction, from Wilkie's Designs," impressed "Clews," wear, flakes, 12⅜" L $577.50
PLATE, "Italian Scenery, Fisherman's Island . . .," impressed "E. Wood & Sons," wear, scratches, 8⅜" D $82.50
PLATE, rural homes, impressed "E. Wood & Sons," 9⅛" D $115.50

Row 2, Left to Right

PLATES, 3 pcs., (1 illus.), floral border, farm, 9⅞" D $297.00
PLATTER, "The Advertisment for a Wife," impressed "Clews," chips, repair, 16½" L $220.00
PLATE, "Llanarth Court, Monmouthshire, R. Hall's picturesque scenery," 10" D $192.50

A-MA Jan. 1993 *Skinner, Inc.*

NANKING COVERED SERVING DISH, 19th c., 12¼" $605.00
NANKING SHAPED BOWL, 19th c., 10" $880.00
CANTON COVERED SERVING DISH, 19th c., 11¼" $467.50
CANTON SCALLOPED BOWL, 19th c., 10¼" $770.00
CANTON SCALLOPED BOWL, 19th c., 7¼" $550.00
CANTON COVERED SERVING DISH, 19th c., 8¼" $275.00
CANTON SHAPED BOWL, 19th c., 9¾" $880.00
CANTON COVERED SERVING DISH, 19th c., 9⅜" $412.50

A-MA Nov. 1992 *James D. Julia, Inc.*

WEDGEWOOD

Row 1, Left to Right

PITCHER, black basalt w/floral dec., 7¾" T $150.00*
BLACK BASALT WARE, 7 pcs., 2 teapots, cup/saucer, ink well (illus.), etc., some damage $450.00*
BLACK BASALT WARE, 3 pcs., teapot (top center), 2 creamers (ends of bottom row), unsigned........ $300.00*
VASE, basalt, floral dec., 5½" T $100.00*
BOWL, basalt 11½" D $150.00*

A-OH Nov. 1992   *Garth's Auctions, Inc.*
Row 1, Left to Right
SHAVING MUG, pottery, buff clay, mottled brown glaze, flakes, repairs, 3½" H .. $49.50
DESK ORGANIZER, red clay, worn black, chips, 4⅝" H $27.50
REDWARE MILK BOWL, wear, 8" D $143.00
REDWARE JARS, 2 pcs., shiny glaze, chips, 4¼" H, 5½" H $55.00
Row 2, Left to Right
REDWARE PITCHER, mottled dk. brown metallic glaze, 6⅛" H $55.00
BIRD WATER FOUNTAIN, stoneware, white glaze, 5½" H $137.50
REDWARE PLATE, coggeled edge, chips, hairlines, 6¼" D $137.50
REDWARE JAR, black, brown, amber glaze, 5½" H $60.50
REDWARE JAR, shiny dk. amber glaze, repair, 5¾" H $49.50
Row 3, Left to Right
REDWARE PIE PLATE, yellow slip, coggeled rim, flakes, 9½" D.............. $220.00
REDWARE BOWL, brown, white, green slip, wear, chips, 10" D, 2" H $1430.00
REDWARE PIE PLATE, white, green, brown plaid slip, wear, 8" D $577.50
REDWARE PIE PLATE, yellow slip design, coggeled rim, 10¼" D $385.00

A-OH Nov. 1992   *Garth's Auctions, Inc.*
Row 1, Left to Right
CHALK ROOSTER, Original yellow, red and green paint, wear, 5⅝" H .. $687.50
CHALK RABBIT, nodder, Original yellow, red and black paint, minor wear, 6¼" L $1100.00
CHALK PIG, nodder, worn original black and red paint, stains and chips, 7½" L $770.00
CHALK BIRD, worn original green, red, yellow, black paint, 5⅛" H $330.00
Row 2, Left to Right
CHALK CAT WITH GOAT'S BODY, nodder, original red, yellow and black paint, repair, 8" L $165.00
CHALK CAT, original deep yellow, red, black paint, repair, 9½" H $990.00
CHALK BANK, basket of fruit, warn and flaked original black, yellow and red paint, 6½" H $357.50

A-MA Oct. 1992   *Skinner, Inc.*
PITCHER, Flint enamel, base marked "E," 19th c. 12½" H $825.00
BENNINGTON PITKIN & COVER, Rockingham glaze, Lyman Fenton & Co., marked, chips, 6¼" H $990.00
BENNINGTON TOBY BOTTLE, Rockingham glaze, Lyman Fenton & Co., 19th c., marked, damage, 10¾" H... $715.00
TULIP VASE, Flint enamel, 19th c., chips, 9" H $385.00
BOOK FLASK, Flint enamel, 19th c., impressed "Ladies Suffering," imperfections, 5¼" H $412.50
BENNINGTON LION, Rockingham glaze, 19th c., damage, 7½" H $1750.00
HAND VASE, Flint enamel, 19th c., 6½" H................... $275.00
BENNINGTON POTTERY, 4 pcs., boot flask (illus.), 2 Rockingham glazed door knobs, flint enamel door knob, repairs $110.00

A-MA Mar. 1993   *Skinner, Inc.*
BLUE FITSHUGH CHINA
FISH PLATTER, inset liner, chips, 18" L................................. $880.00
EGG CUP, LEAF DISH, UNDERTRAY, chips........................... $385.00
PLATTER, rim chips, 21" L $825.00
PLATTER, flake under rim, 18" L $467.50
COVERED SERVING DISHES, 2 pcs., imperfections, 8¼" L, 9¾" L $522.50
SALAD BOWL, hairline, 9¾" D $990.00

A-MA Nov. 1992   *James D. Julia, Inc.*

OLD IVORY CHINA

Row 1, Left to Right

SUGAR & CREAMER, (1 illus.), mkd. "Ohme & Silesia" $300.00
OYSTER BOWL, mkd. "Ohme & Silesia," crack $55.00
HAIR RECEIVER, Germany $100.00
SAUCE DISHES, 6 pcs., (1 illus.), (not Old Ivory), lavender w/orange $40.00

Row 2, Left to Right

MAYONNAISE & TRAY, mkd. "Silesia" $120.00
CUPS & SAUCERS, 10 sets, (1 illus.), mkd. "Silesia" $250.00
6 PIECES, (1 illus.), 2 berry dishes, 1 chocolate saucer, 1 bread & butter, 1 mustard pot, all mkd. "selisia," supper plate mkd. "Ohme & Silesia" $300.00
TOOTHPICK, mkd. "Silesia" $200.00

Row 3, Left to Right

SALAD PLATES, 3 pcs., (1 illus.), mkd. "Ohme & Silesia" $45.00
5 PIECES, (1 illus.), 2 cake plates mkd. "Silesia," 2 pepper shakers, berry dish ... $110.00
WASTE BOWL, mkd. "Ohme & Silesia" $225.00

Row 4, Left to Right

MAYONNAISE & TRAY, Germany $75.00

OLD IVORY PATTERN CHINA

Row 1, Left to Right

CAKE PLATES, 3 pcs., (1 illus.), #15, 10" "Silesia & Ohme," 11" "Silesia," 11" "Clarion" w/wear $100.00
CELERY, "Silesia & Ohme," 11½" L $50.00
9 PIECES, (1 illus.), "Silesia & Ohme," or "Silesia," wear $100.00

Row 2, Left to Right

14 PIECES, (1 illus.), 8 sauce dishes mkd. "Silesia," 5 luncheon plates mkd. "Ohme," 1 chocolate cup w/crack $100.00
18 PIECES, (2 illus.), 14 odd saucers, dresser tray, open vegetable all mkd. "Ohme & Selesia," salt & Pepper mkd. "Silesia" $100.00
PLATES, 5 pcs., (1 illus.), mkd. "Silesia & Ohme," 8½" D $100.00
3 PIECES, (1 illus.), celery mkd. "Ohme & Silesia," celery mkd. "Clarion," relish mkd. "Germany & Clarion" $100.00

Row 3, Left to Right

BERRY SET, 7 pcs. mkd. "Silesia" $110.00
SQUATTY CRACKER JAR, mkd. "Ohme & Silesia" $300.00
10 PIECES, (1 illus.), 3 cake plates, 1 berry bowl, 6 salad plates, all mkd. "Silesia & Ohme" or "Silesia" $150.00

Row 4, Left to Right

CHOCOLATE SET, pot, 5 cups and saucers, mkd. "Silesia & Ohme" $400.00
CHOP PLATTER, mkd "Silesia & Clarion" $120.00
8 PIECES, (1 illus.), 4 cake plates mkd. "Silesia & Ohme," 4 chocolate cups mkd. "Silesia" $250.00

A-MA Nov. 1992   *James D. Julia, Inc.*
OLD IVORY CHINA
Row 1, Left to Right
3 PIECES, (1 illus.), sugar bowl, berry bowl, cup & saucer $125.00
22 PIECES, (1 illus.), 3 chocolate cups mkd. "Clarion," 3 saucers mkd. "Silesia," 6 cups & saucers mkd. "Silesia," 4 footed cups $150.00
5 PIECES, (1 illus.), sugar bowl mkd. "Germany & Ohme," cup & saucer, 2 sugar bowl covers, butter dish cover $60.00

Row 2, Left to Right
8 PIECES, (1 illus.), berry bowl mkd. "Silesia & Ohme," 6 salad plates mkd. "Silesia," bouillon cup & saucer mkd. "Silesia" $100.00
BUTTER PATS, 6 pcs., 3" D $450.00
FOOTED CUPS & SAUCERS, 13 sets, (1 illus.), mkd. "Silesia" $200.00

Row 3, Left to Right
4 PIECES, (1 illus.), suger shaker mkd. "Silesia," 3 underplates for soups mkd. "Silesia & Ohme" $350.00
11 PIECES, (1 illus.), nappie mkd. "Ohme & Silesia," relish dish mkd. "Germany & Ohme," 2 tea cups & saucers, 2 saucers, 2 coffee cups, dinner plate, bread & butter plate, salad plate, lot damage . . . $100.00
4 PIECES, (1 illus.), celery dish, roll tray mkd. "Silesia & Ohme," bread & butter plate, tea cup and saucer, all mkd. "Silesia & Ohme," lot damage $100.00

Row 4, Left to Right
17 PIECES, (1 illus.), chocolate pot mkd. "Silesia & Ohme," 3 chocolate saucers, bouillon cup cover, 12 cereal bowls mkd. "Germany & Silesia" $350.00
CAKE SET, 7 pcs., unnumbered $200.00

A-OH Jul. 1993   *Garth's Auctions, Inc.*
HANDLESS CUP & SAUCER, blue spatterware, mismatched, chips $38.50
SAUCES, 2 pcs., (1 illus.), blue spatterware w/red, green, black rose, 4" D $38.50
HANDLESS CUP & SAUCER, gaudy ironstone, blue, red, green $203.50
HANDLESS CUP & SAUCER, red spatterware, mismatched, hairlines $38.50
Row 2, Left to Right
SAUCE, red spatterware w/red, blue, green, black peafowl, 5" D $170.50
SAUCE TUREEN, blue, white pearlware, chips on lid, 6½" L $192.50
HANDLESS CUP & SAUCER, creamware, black transfer "Washington His Country's Father" on saucer, Washington and Lafayette on cup, flakes, hairlines $302.50
SUGAR BOWL, pearlware, Leeds gaudy floral in blue, white, repair, 4½" T $110.00
TEA CADDY, creamware, black transfer of couple, no lid, wear, damage, 4⅛" T . . . $71.50
Row 3, Left to Right
TEAPOT, porcelain, New Hall floral dec., red, green, crack, 6" T $60.50
PITCHER, creamware, black transfer, Washington, Lafayette, flakes, 5¼" T $544.50
HANDLESS CUP & SAUCER, purple spatterware, flakes, hairlines, stains $104.50
TEAPOT, pearlware, enamel, silver luster trim, stains, chips, hairlines, 6¾" T $154.00

A-MA Aug. 1993   *Skinner, Inc.*
ROYAL CROWN DERBY DINNER SERVICE, Imari pat., 20th c., vegetable bowl, sauce tureen w/stand, ginger jar, oval bowl and platter, square dish, 2 round platters, 6 dinner plates, 9 soup plates, 16 salad plates, 7 butter plates, 7 coffee cups/saucers, 6 tea cups/saucers, figure of fox $3520.00

A-TX 1993 *Majolica Auctions*
ETRUSCAN SHELL AND SEAWEED
SPOONER, repair $165.00*
PITCHER, repair, 6" T $154.00*
COFFEE POT $522.50
CREAMER $247.50
SPITTOON $1100.00*
CUP AND SAUCER $209.00*
FOOTED BOWL, repair $220.00*
PLATE, 9¼" D $440.00*
COMPOTE, repair $1100.00*

A-TX 1993 *Majolica Auctions*
WEDGWOOD GAME DISH, minor flake
on base $1870.00*

A-TX 1993 *Majolica Auctions*
ETRUSCAN SARDINE BOX, cobalt w/
overlapping fish lid $1100.00*

A-MD May 1993 *C.G. Sloan & Co., Inc.*
ROYAL BAYREUTH

Back Row, left to Right
TOMATO SERVICE, 28 pcs., (8 illus.), bowl, teapot, creamer, covered sugar, 3 covered
mustard pots, mustard spoon, 3 shakers, 5 saucers, 4 cups, 2 shallow bowls, 6
nappies $850.00*

Row 2, Left to Right
FRUIT CONDIMENT SET, 7 pcs., porcelain, 2 leaf nappies, leaf & flamingo nappy, 2 pear
covered dishes, apple covered dish, apple dish $600.00*
POPPY SERVICE, 7 pcs., (3 illus.), porcelain, pitcher, creamer, cup and saucer, 2-handled
cup, 2 mustard pots $475.00*

A-TX 1993 *Majolica Auctions*
MINTON CHINAMAN TEAPOT, re-
pair $1925.00*

A-TX 1993 *Majolica Auctions*
**GEORGE JONES PHEASANT
COVERED GAME DISH,** re-
pair $1980.00*

A-TX 1993 *Majolica Auctions*
**MINTON HARE AND DUCK GAME
DISH,** repair $2310.00*

A-PA May 1993 *Conestoga Auction Co.*
ROSEVILLE
MING TREE BASKET, green . . $150.00*
WINCRAFT PANTHER VASE, char-
treuse $250.00*
VISTA BASKET, flake, 9½" T . . $170.00*
PINECONE VASE, blue $170.00*

A- OH Nov. 1992   *Garth's Auctions, Inc.*
STAFFORDSHIRE, *all are historical blue.*

Row 1, Left to Right

PLATE, med. blue transfer, "King's Weston, Glouchestershire, Riley," 8¾" $82.50
PLATE, dk. blue transfer, "Hospital Boston," "Stevenson," scratches, 8⅞" $77.00
PLATE, med. blue transfer, "The Landing of the Fathers at Plymouth . . .," wear, hairline, 7⅝" $60.50

PLATE, dk. blue, "Christmas Eve, From Wilkie's designs," impressed "Clews," 9" $159.50
PLATE, dk. blue transfer, fruit, impressed "Stubbs," flakes, 10" $132.00

Row 2, Left to Right

PLATE, dk. blue transfer, "Palestine, R. Stevenson," 10½" $82.50
PLATE, lt. med. blue transfer, Boston state house, unmarked, 10" $110.00
PLATE, med. blue and black transfer, "Sulpher Springs, Delaware, Ohio," wear, 9½" $198.00
PLATE, dk. blue transfer, "American Villa," edge flakes, stains, 10" $93.50
PLATE, dk. blue transfer, "Pains Hill, Surrey, R. Hall's Select Views," flakes, 10" $82.50

A-OH Nov. 1992   *Garth's Auctions, Inc.*
NOTE: *All Pearlware unless noted.*

Row 1, Left to Right

SUGAR BOWL, Leeds tulip in yellow, green, brown and orange, minor flakes and chips 4¼" D, 4¾" H $412.50
CREAMER, Oriental export, molded design with blue and black grisaille decoration under glaze, traces of gilt, 5½" H $440.00
HANDLESS CUP AND SAUCER, oriental export, blue and white, paper label "Christies, the Nanking Cargo," hairline $55.00
TEA CADDY, divided interior, Leeds floral decoration in green, dk. brown and yellow ochre, wear, damage, 5¼" H $1017.50
SAUCER, Leeds gaudy floral in blue, green, brown, and orange, 4¼" D $82.50
SUGAR BOWL, Leeds gaudy floral in blue, green and yellow ochre, stains and wear, 4½" H $330.00

Row 2, Left to Right

TEAPOT, Leeds gaudy floral, blue, yellow, tan, damage, repair, 7⅝" H $385.00

SUGAR BOWL, Leeds gaudy floral in blue and white, flakes, chip and crow's foot on bottom, 5¼" H $165.00
HANDLESS CUP AND SAUCER, Leeds gaudy floral in blue and white, wear, flakes, stains $104.50
PITCHER, Leeds gaudy floral in blue and orange, leaf handle, wear, flakes, 6⅛" H $330.00

A-MD May 1993   *C.G. Sloan & Co., Inc.*

HUMMELS

PUPPY LOVE, TO MARKET, MEDITATION, (2 illus.), each w/full bee mark in incised circle, up to 5¼" T $175.00*
WAYSIDE HARMONY, JUST RESTING, (1 illus.), full bee mark, up to 5½" T .. $175.00*
CULPRITS, OUT OF DANGER, each w/full bee mark in incised circle, up to 6¾" T $175.00*
CHICK GIRL BOX, old style, West Germany stylized incised circle, 5⅞" T $130.00*
HOME FROM MARKET, MERRY WANDERER, TRUMPET BOY, LITTLE SHOPPER, SCHOOL GIRL, (2 illus.), all w/"Goebel W Germany" mark, up to 4⅝" T $200.00*

A-OH Nov. 1992   *Garth's Auctions, Inc.*

SPATTERWARE

Row 1, Left to Right
HANDLESS CUP AND SAUCER, red, blue, green, impressed "Adams," flakes, hairline $275.00
HANDLESS CUP AND SAUCER, red, blue, green, impressed "Harvey" $220.00
HANDLESS CUP, green, red, yellow, black, flakes, hairlines $148.50
HANDLESS CUP AND SAUCER, green, blue, red, yellow, black, repair $330.00
HANDLESS CUP AND SAUCER, green, purple $93.50
Row 2, Left to Right
PLATE, red, green, blue, black, 8½" D $247.50
CREAMER, green, black, red, chips, 6" T $336.00
PLATE, bull's eye, swag rim, purple, white, 9" D $423.50
SAUCER, peafowl, blue, yellow, red, black, 4⅜" D $330.00
PLATE, green, pink, 8⅜" D $71.50
CREAMER, brown, stains, crazing, 4⅜" T $104.50
PLATE, red, white, bull's eye, wear, 8⅝" D $82.50
CREAMER, blue, pink, chips, hairline, 5¾" T $275.00

A-PA May 1993   *Conestoga Auction Co.*

FULPER

VASE, pink, green, ink stamp, 7½" T $110.00*
VASE, mirror black over butterscotch, ink stamp, 8" T $130.00*
VASE, chartreuse, aqua, incised mark, 9" T $130.00*
VASE, rose w/aqua drip, 8" T .. $190.00*

A-IL Apr. 1993   *Leslie Hindman Auction*
STAFFORDSHIRE FIGURINE, pottery, 19th c., courting couple, 14" H .. $475.00*
STAFFORDSHIRE WATCH HOLDER, pottery, 19th c., 12" H $400.00*

A-IL Apr. 1993   *Leslie Hindman Auction*
STAFFORDSHIRE COW CREAMERS, pr., pottery, 19th c., 4" H $850.00*

A-IL Apr. 1993   *Leslie Hindman Auction*
STAFFORDSHIRE HUNTERS, pr., 19th c., 14½" H $750.00*

A-OH Dec. 1992   *Garth's Auctions, Inc.*

Row 1
PITCHER AND COFFEE POT, paneled ironstone, lt. blue transfer, mismatched lid, 8" H, 9½" H $115.50
"WEDGWOOD" TEAPOT, blue transfer, hairline, 7" H. $187.00
"WEDGWOOD" PLATE, blue transfer, "Faneuil Hall," stains 9¼" D $22.00
STAFFORDSHIRE COVERED VEGETABLE, blue willow transfer, lion finial, stains, hairline, chip, 9½" x 10¾" $49.50

Row 2
IRONSTONE PLATE, (center), blue transfer, impressed "Ashworth," 9¼" D . . . $49.50
COPELAND SPODE, 54 pc. set, service for 12, drk. blue transfer $632.50

A-OH Dec. 1992   *Garth's Auctions, Inc.*

Row 1
STAFFORDSHIRE DOGS, , pr., white, gold luster, polychrome, 9¾" H $275.00
CANDLESTICKS, pr., brass, porcelain stems, polychrome enamel, 8⅜" H $99.00
STAFFORDSHIRE CHIMNEY PIECE, "Burns and his Mary," polychrome, gilt, wear, 12⅜" H $137.50

ROW 2
APOTHECARY JARS, pr., porcelain, "Ginori," black, gilt, 11¾" H $385.00
APOTHECARY JARS, pr., pottery, "Luneville, France," damage, 10¼" H $297.00
APOTHECARY JAR, blue blown glass, worn label, gilded tin lid, 9¼" H $165.00

A-OH Apr. 1993   *Garth's Auctions, Inc.*
CANARY
Row 1, Left to Right
CUP AND SAUCER, red transfer, impressed Sewell, poor repair $110.00
CREAMER, red, green enamel, chips, hairlines, 4" T $71.50
WASTE BOWL, red transfer, Leo Kaplan and Millie Manheim stickers, wear, hairline, 3" H, 5⅞" D $302.50
SUGAR BOWL, silver luster, impressed "Leeds Pottery," chips, 4½" T $577.50
SAUCER, black transfer, impressed Adams, hairlines $214.50
Row 2, Left to Right
PLATE, black transfer, impressed L.L. & T., scratches, 8½" D $27.50
CREAMER, black transfer, hairlines, wear, 4½" T $82.50
JUG, molded basketweave, polychrome enamel, wear, professional repair, 6" T $115.50
JUG, black transfer, polychrome enamel, wear, chips, hairlines, repair, 4⅞" T $137.50
PLATE, black transfer, wear, 8½" D $49.50

A-MA Nov. 1992   *James D. Julia, Inc.*
Row 1, Left to Right
CHOCOLATE SET, 13 pcs, (3 illus.), signed Handel, pot, 5 cups, 5 saucers, sugar w/cover, creamer, art china, gold accents on beige $1500.00*
VASE, signed Handel, art china, shades of green, brown, white, yellow, green enamel ground, wear, 13" T $1050.00*
CHOCOLATE POT, signed Handel, green, gold, grey on beige, 11½" T $450.00*
Row 2, Left to Right
ASHTRAY, signed Handel, shades of brown, green, tan opal glass . . . $750.00*
NAPPY, signed Handel, art china, pink, green, gold on beige, 7" D $175.00*

A-OH Jan. 1993   *Garth's Auctions, Inc.*
Row 1, Left to Right
STAFFORDSHIRE PLATES, pr., (1st & last illus.), blue transfer "Quadrupeds" by Hall, flakes, scratches, 8⅝" D $302.50
PEARLWARE CREAMER, dk. brown, lt. blue, green, ochre, wear, 4⅜" H . . $115.50
WHIELDON PLATTER, embossed, brown tortoise shell glaze, blue, green, repair, 10⅜" L $302.50
HANDLED BOWL, grey, orange, white, brown, blue, green, chips, stains, hairline, 4¼" D $522.50
Row 2, Left to Right
WHIELDON PLATE, embossed, tan, green, brown, scratches, 9⅝" D . . $214.50
MOCHA MUG, embossed, tan, green, brown, chips, stains, hairline, 6" H $220.00
MOCHA MUG, grey, black, blue, chips, hairline, 5⅝" H $412.50
MOCHA MUG, blue, brown, white, broken, 4⅝" H $137.50
PEARLWARE PLATE, embossed, blue, white, wear, stains, 4¾" D $165.00

A-OH Nov. 1992   *Garth's Auctions, Inc.*
NOTE: *All cast iron unless noted.*
Row 1, Left to Right
DOG DOORSTOP, original black and greyish tan paint, 7" H $110.00
DOG DOORSTOP, Boston bull, original black and grey paint, 4⅝" H $93.50
CLOWN, wood body, articulated cast iron limbs and head, polychrome paint, 10½" H $385.00
CAT DOORSTOP, original black, beige, green, blue, pink and white paint, 8" H $247.00
SHOE, original black and gold paint, marbleized base, 5" H $22.00
BIRD, polychrome, 7" H $808.50
Row 2, Left to Right
MONKEY DOORSTOP, worn brown paint, rust, 8½" H $275.00
PENGUIN DOORSTOP, worn original white and black paint, flaking, yellow re-paint, 10" H $110.00
ELEPHANT DOORSTOP, worn original platinum paint, flaking 8" H $93.50
HORSE DOORSTOP, original brown, white and black paint, 8" H . . . $214.50

A-OH May 1993   *Garth's Auctions, Inc.*
Row 1, Left to Right
FLOWER POT, redware, green amber glaze, wear, chips, 5½" H $136.50
SUGAR BOWL, redware, dk. glaze, black splotches, chips, 5½" H $137.50
BURL BOWL, ash, cracks, 4½" H, 10¾" D $385.00
BUTTER SCOOP, maple, 11½" L $60.50
PITCHER, amber glaze, brown swirls, wear, flakes, 7¾" H $82.50
Row 2, Left to Right
CHARGER, redware, yellow, orange, brown slip dec., wear, flakes, hairlines, repairs, 11½" D $632.50
PITCHER, Sewerpipe, tan amber glaze, impressed "U.S. Stoneware Co. Akron, Oh. 1G," hairlines, 12" H $38.50
JUG, southern pottery, brown green ash glaze, flakes, 9½" H $45.00
CHARGER, redware, coggled rim, yellow slip dec., wear, chips, hairline, 12" D $385.00

A-OH Nov. 1992   *Garth's Auctions, Inc.*
Row 1, Left to Right
CANDLESTICK, Bennington w/Rockingham glaze, 8⅜" T $368.50
NAME PLATE, Bennington w/Rockingham glaze, chips, 3⅜" x 7¼" $308.00
COACHMAN'S BOTTLE, Rockingham glaze, 8⅞" T $115.50
NAME PLATE, Bennington w/Rockingham glaze, chips, 3⅜" x 7¼" $198.00
CANDLESTICK, Bennington w/flint enamel glaze, 7¾" T $385.00
Row 2, Left to Right
PITCHER, Rockingham, molded animals, 10" T $99.00
BOTTLE, Rockingham, molded floral dec., 10⅜" T $352.00
PITCHER, Rockingham, molded hunt scene, 9⅞" T $115.50

A-MA Mar. 1993   *Skinner, Inc.*
LEEDS POTTERY, 2 pcs., vase, pitcher, imperfections, 7" H $357.50
STAFFORDSHIRE WINDOW STOP, polychromed, 4½" H $440.00
ABC PLATE, "Gathering Cotton" vignette, 6" D $550.00
STAFFORDSHIRE POTTERY, 5 pcs., child's mug (illus.), ABC plate, motto plate, 2 small plates, imperfections $412.50
DALMATIONS, pr., 7½" H $440.00
EARTHENWARE FIGURES, 4 pcs., (3 illus.), Bennington lion head inkwell, Staffordshire cat, pig and cat banks, imperfections, 1½" to 3¾" H $660.00

A-OH Nov. 1992   *Garth's Auctions, Inc.*

Row 1, Left to Right
MOCHA MUG, brown, orange and white stripes, flaking glaze, 5½" H $82.50
STAFFORDSHIRE PLATE, dark blue transfer of cupid and maiden, impressed "Adams," 9" $159.50
MOCHA MUG, marbelized brown and white, firing crack in handle, 4¼" H.. $220.00
STAFFORDSHIRE PLATTER, dark blue transfer, "Clarence Terrace. Regents Park," 10¾" L $412.50
MOCHA MUG, olive with black and white bands, damage, repair, 3¾" H $82.50
STICK SPATTER PLATE, gaudy floral rim, rabbit transfer in center, 9⅛" ... $330.00
MOCHA MUG, light blue, orange, brown and medium blue stripes, leaf handle, flaking, minor hairlines, 5¾" H $104.50

Row 2, Left to Right
STAFFORDSHIRE SOUP PLATE, dark blue transfer, "Sancho Panza at the Boar Hunt," 9¾" $192.50
STAFFORDSHIRE TODDY, Black transfer with enamel, "Robinson Crusoe," edge flakes, 5⅛" $93.50
MOCHA PITCHER, white black, blue and orange stripes, embossed green bowl, leaf handle, badly damaged and repaired, 8" H $60.50
CUP AND SAUCER, english porcelain, polychrome floral design, stains $44.00
STAFFORDSHIRE SOUP PLATE, dark blue transfer, "Doctor Syntax mistakes a gentleman's house for an Inn," impressed "Clews," 9⅞" 165.00

A-OH Apr. 1993   *Garth's Auctions, Inc.*
NOTE: Gaudy Welsh with underglaze blue and polychrome enameling.

Row 1, Left to Right
CUPS AND SAUCERS, 2 sets, (1 illus.), hexagon, luster trim, hairlines $33.00
CUPS AND SAUCERS, 3 sets, (1 illus.), tulip, luster trim, hairlines $24.75
CUP AND SAUCER, oversize, porcelain, hexagon, luster trim $82.50
CUPS AND SAUCERS, 6 sets, (1 illus.), rainbow, luster trim, chips, hairlines $231.00
CUPS AND SAUCERS, 6 sets, (1 illus.), buckle, luster trim, hairlines $99.00

Row 2, Left to Right
PITCHER, pottery, dragon handle, wear, crazing, 5¾" T $203.50
TUREEN W/UNDERTRAY, porcelain, gilt trim, hairline, 7" T $165.00
SUGAR BOWL, porcelain, tulip, luster trim, stains, 7" T $209.00
TUREEN W/UNDERTRAY, ironstone, stains, worn gilt, 6½" T $192.50
PITCHER, molded pottery, luster trim, wear, stains, hairlines, 7½" T $137.50

Row 3, Left to Right
PORCELAIN TEA SET, 14 pcs., peppermint, luster trim, stains, hairlines, no sugar bowl $764.50

A-MA Apr. 1993   *Skinner, Inc.*
FIGURAL MANTEL CLOCK, Meissen, porcelain, 19th c., damage, 9" H, 9½" L $1980.00
MEISSEN FIGURINE, Europa and the Bull, porcelain, restored, 8½" H $825.00
MEISSEN FIGURINE, Europa and the Bull, porcelain, restored, 9½" H $825.00

A-MA Jan. 1993   *Skinner, Inc.*
FIGURE OF AUTUMN, Prattware-type, 19th c., 9" H $357.50
FIGURAL STAFFORDSHIRE, 5 pcs., 19th c., cottage figures, house pastille burner, 2¼ to 5¼" H $1100.00

A-OH Jan. 1993   *Garth's Auctions, Inc.*

Row 1, Left to Right

HANDLESS CUP & SAUCER, Staffordshire, dk. blue transfer, impressed "Clews" $137.50

HANDLESS CUP & SAUCER, Gaudy Staffordshire, Adam's Rose, impressed "A," rough $165.00

HANDLESS CUP & SAUCER, pearlware, blue, white, flakes $104.50

HANDLESS CUP & SAUCER, gaudy Staffordshire, cabbage rose, flakes $143.00

HANDLESS CUP & SAUCER, gaudy Dutch, carnation, flakes, hairlines $357.50

Row 2, Left to Right

PITCHER, gaudy Staffordshire, blue, green, yellow, ochre, black, flakes, hairline, 8" H......................... $132.00

PLATE, King's Rose, green, flakes, 8¼" D $93.50

CREAMER, silver luster resist, bird in tree, wear, 4⅝" H $132.00

PLATE, pearlware, wear, 8¼" D $115.50

PITCHER, gaudy Staffordshire, red, green, blue, black, hairline, damage, stains, chips, 7" H $176.00

Row 3, Left to Right

MOCHA PITCHER, ironstone, lt. green, blue, black, hairline, damage, 7" H........................... $165.00

PLATE, gaudy Staffordshire, Adam's Rose, 9¾" D $110.00

PLATE, gaudy Staffordshire, Adam's Rose, impressed "Adams," chip, 7½" D ... $71.50

MOCHA PITCHER, yellowware, blue, white, brown, hairlines, 7½" T ... $440.00

A-NY Nov. 1992   *David Rago Gallery*

TEA SET FOR SIX, clear speckled brown glaze over dk. brown clay, each pc. marked "Master Potter Ben Owen," teapot 7¼" T, candlesticks 6½" T $375.00*

A-OH July 1993   *Garth's Auctions, Inc.*

SPATTERWARE

Row 1, Left to Right

CREAMER, brown, black, red, green, 4" T......................... $247.50

HANDLESS CUP AND SAUCER, blue, red, impressed "Tunstall," stains .. $71.50

SAUCER, purple, green, red, black, stains $181.50

CREAMER, red, blue, green, black, stains, hairlines, 5⅜" T $143.00

SUGAR BOWL, blue, purple, stains, mismatched lid, 4" T $71.50

Row 2, Left to Right

PITCHER, white reserves w/blue, black, green, pink, yellow, black, stains, wear, 7⅝" T $330.00

OBLONG DISH, impressed "Wedgwood," mauve, green, red, yellow, black, flakes, chip, 8½" x 11" $192.50

PLATE, red, blue, green, chip, 7¾" D $104.50

A-IL Apr. 1993   *Leslie Hindman Auction*

LEEDS PLATES, creamware pottery, ships, 10" D $750.00*

A-PA May 1993   *Alderfer Auction Co.*

URN, Shenandoah Valley, multiple glazed, 5" T......................... $400.00

TART PLATES, 2 pcs., slip dec., 4" D $560.00

PLATE, redware, yellow slip dec., 8¼" D $375.00

A-PA May 1993   *Alderfer Auction Co.*

PITCHER, New Geneva, PA, 6" T......................... $575.00

PITCHER, redware, 9" T $250.00

POSSUM ON LOG CABIN, redware, by William H. Christman, 1846, chip $2250.00

MEDINGER VASE, coggle lines, green/brown glaze, 8" T $225.00

A-MA Mar. 1993   *Skinner, Inc.*

WHEILDON TYPE PLATES, 2 pcs., imperfections, 9¼" D $330.00

WHEILDON TEAPOT, clouded ware, brown, yellow, green tortoiseshell glaze, 5¼" H $385.00

EARTHENWARE, 11 pcs., (1 illus.), 19th c., England, imperfections $935.00

A-NY Nov. 1992   *David Rago Gallery*

CLARICE CLIFF POTTERY. All hand painted w/vibrant multi-colors of red, blue, green, yellow, orange, black.

Row 1, Left to Right

VASES, pr., Red Autumn, 8½" T ..... NS

VASE, Blue Chintz, 8" T $1100.00*

IRIS JUG, Farmhouse, 9¾" T .. $1500.00*

Row 2, Left to Right

PLATE, Pansies Delicia, 10" D .... NS

BOWL, Geometric, 5" H, 10" D ...... NS

LOTUS JUG, Gardenia, 11¾" T $1500.00*

A-IL Apr. 1993   *Leslie Hindman Auction*
STONEWARE JUGS, 2 pcs., salt glazed, 19th c., blue dec., by Frank B. Norton, 13" H......................... $800.00*

A-IL Apr. 1993   *Leslie Hindman Auction*
STONEWARE JUGS, 2 pcs., salt glazed, 19th c., blue dec., 1 by J. and E. Norton, 13½" H......................... $750.00*

A-PA May. 1993   *Alderfer Auction Co.*
SPITTOON, stoneware, Remy, chip $315.00
CROCK, blue dec., stoneware, 10½" T........................... $270.00
CANNING JAR, blue dec., stoneware....................... $200.00

A-MA Aug. 1993   *Skinner, Inc.*
STONEWARE
JUG, 19th c., inscribed "Geo. Washington," cobalt dec., 13" T............. $990.00
JUG, 19th c., cobalt dec., imperfections, 16" T $357.50
BELLERMINE JUG, Germany, 19th c., 8½" T......................... $770.00
BELLARMINE JUG, Germany, 19th c., 8½" T $412.50
CROCK, 19th c., cobalt dec., 3 gal., imperfections, 10" T $467.50

A-PA May 1993   *Glass Works Auctions*
STONEWARE BOTTLES
BEER, stamped J. Chester - Root Beer, ca. 1840-1860, cream glaze, 9¾" T .. $80.00*
BEER, stamped P. Mansfield - Lemon Beer, ca. 1840-1860, grayish glaze, 9" T......................... $80.00*
BEER, stamped B.F. Haley, California Pop Beer, ca. 1840-1860, greyish glaze w/ cobalt across lettering, 10⅜" T .. $80.00*

A-PA May 1993   *Alderfer Auction Co.*
BATTER JUG, Cowden and Wilcox, blue dec. stoneware $575.00
STONEWARE BOTTLES, Hancock & Melvins and E. Ferris........... $250.00

A-ME Feb. 1993   *James D, Julia, Inc.*
ETAGERE, mahogany, 19th c., 52" H, 19" W, 19" D.................... $400.00*
PITCHER, stoneware, cobalt, gray splotches, 7½" T $90.00*
JUG, stoneware, 1 gal., cobalt dec., chips, hairline.................... $175.00*
JUG, stoneware, stamped "White Utica," 3 gal., cobalt dec., chips $300.00*

A-PA May 1993   *Alderfer Auction Co.*
YELLOWWARE, 3 pcs., syrup, pitcher, blue/white tub $455.00

A-MA Oct. 1992   *Skinner, Inc.*
REDWARE
POODLE, 4½" T .... NS
PRESERVE JAR, 19th c., glazed, mottled green, brown dec., 4⅝" T $935.00
JAR, 19th c., glazed, manganese splotches, damage, 9½" T $522.50
HERB POT, 19th c., ochre glaze w/brown splotches, damage, 4¼" T $522.50

A-MA Mar. 1993   *Skinner, Inc.*

STONEWARE
FOUR GALLON CROCK, cobalt dec., impressed "BC Millburn, 14" H $412.50
CROCK, JUG, 2 pcs., " A.E. Allen Massena Springs," flakes, 15" H, 17½" H $467.50
CROCK, cobalt dec., impressed "John B. Caire & Co. Main St. Pokeepsie NY," flakes, 10½" H $330.00
THREE GALLON JUG, cobalt dec., impressed "3 John Young, & Co. Harrisburg PA.," 17" H $935.00
INCISED JUG, cobalt dec., chips, abrasions, 15" H $1540.00
PRESENTATION JUGS, cobalt dec., 2 impressed "made for Wright Smith R. Pearsall No. 5 North Philadelphia," 1 impressed "John C. Hopkins & Co. Importers & Dealers in China, glass and Queensware no. 612 Market St. Philadelphia," chips, flakes, 9¼" to 15" H . . . $1980.00

A-MA Aug. 1993   *Skinner, Inc.*

LIVERPOOL TRANSFER PRINTED CREAMWARE PITCHERS

PITCHERS, 2 pcs., 19th c., 1 w/Washington, map, Independence, eagle, 1 w/Masonic dec., each w/cracks, flakes, 9½" T, 11¼" T $522.50
PITCHER, 19th c., Washington, map, Independence, repair, 10" T $935.00
PITCHER, 19th c., ship flying American flag, reverse w/pastoral scene, imperfections, 6¾" T $660.00

A-MA Aug. 1993   *Skinner, Inc.*

REDWARE
4 ITEMS, 19th c., 3 jars, pitcher, manganese splotches, 8½" to 11" T $990.00
PITCHER, (center of illus.), glazed, 19th c., manganese splotches, 10½" T $357.50

A-OH Nov. 1992   *Garth's Auctions, Inc.*
NOTE: *Jugs and Jars are all miniatures.*
Row 1, Left to Right
STONEWARE JUG, brown Albany slip, sgraffito label "Compliments of Geo. Kuntz 1113 E. Third St. Dayton, Ohio," chip, 3⅜" H $71.50
SHENANDOAH JUG, clear glaze, brown and green sponging, edge flakes, 2¾" H $49.50
GROTESQUE JUG, southern stoneware, greenish ash glaze, damage, chips, 4" H $5170.00
STONEWARE JAR, brown glaze, chips, 3¼" H $5.50
STONEWARE PITCHER, greenish black glaze 2⅝" H $38.50
Row 2, Left to Right
REDWARE JUG, green glaze, flecks and brown splotches, 4⅛" H $82.50
REDWARE JAR, interior glaze, 3⅛" H $33.00
STONEWARE DOG, mottled tan and white glaze, chips, 4¼" H $104.50
STONEWARE JAR, brown glaze, greenish highlights, chips, 3½" T $38.00
STONEWARE JUG, grey salt glaze w/blue, flakes, 4½" T $357.50
Row 3, Left to Right
SHENANDOAH JUG, clear glaze, green circles, minor glaze flakes, short hairline, 4⅞" H $38.50
OVOID STONEWARE JUG, grey salt glaze, brown highlights, 3⅜" H . . $38.50
OVOID STONEWARE JUG, brown Albany slip, 4" H $22.00
OVOID STONEWARE JUG, grey salt glaze, brown highlights, 3⅜" H . . $49.50
STONEWARE JUGS, two, (one illus.) dark brown Albany slip, 4¾" H, 2 ¾" H . . . $33.00

A-MA Jun. 1993   *Skinner, Inc.*
STONEWARE JUG, impressed "New York Stoneware Co. Fort Edward N.Y.," dated 1876, 5 gal., flakes, 19½" H $1540.00

A-MA Aug. 1993 *Skinner, Inc.*
LOOKING GLASS CLOCK, mahogany, Munger and Benedict, NY, ca. 1825, restored, 39½" T $1870.00
MANTLE CLOCK, mahogany, gilt gesso, George March, Winchester, CT, ca. 1830, restored, 34" T $220.00
LOOKING GLASS CLOCK, carved mahogany, Henry C. Smith, Plymouth, CT, ca. 1825, imperfections, 30" T $357.50

A-MA Aug. 1993 *Skinner, Inc.*
FEDERAL PILLAR AND SCROLL CLOCK, mahogany, Seth Thomas, Plymouth CT, ca. 1818, off-center strap wood movement, 29" T $4125.00

A-MA Aug. 1993 *Skinner, Inc.*
MANTLE CLOCK, carved mahogany, Forestville Manufacturing Co., Bristol, CT, ca. 1830, imperfections, 36" T $330.00
LOOKING GLASS CLOCK, carved mahogany, Hotchkiss and Benedict, "A Munger's Patent," NY, ca. 1830, imperfections, 37¾" T $1100.00

A-IL Apr. 1993 *Leslie Hindman Auction*
FEDERAL PILLAR AND SCROLL CLOCK, mahogany, 19th c., by Eli Terry and Sons, Plymouth Connecticut, 29"H, 17" W, 4½" D $1200.00*

A-ME May 1993   *James D. Julia, Inc.*
SCHOOLHOUSE CLOCK, Coca-Cola, dial faded, label, 17" x 25" x 4" $3250.00*

A-MA Jan. 1993   *Skinner, Inc.*
ACORN SHELF CLOCK, Forestville Manufacturing Co., fusee mvm't, ca. 1850, 24" H $4125.00
DOUBLE STEEPLE MANTEL CLOCK, Birge and Fuller, fusee mvm't, ca. 1840, 27½" H $1210.00

A-MA Jan. 1993   *Skinner, Inc.*
FEDERAL PILLAR AND SCROLL CLOCK, mahogany, E. Terry and Sons, ca. 1820, 31¼" H $2200.00
FEDERAL PILLAR AND SCROLL CLOCK, Mahogany, E. Terry and Sons, ca. 1820, 31" H $1540.00

A-NH May. 1993   *Northeast Auctions*
GRAFTON-STYLE DWARF-CASE CLOCK, inlaid cherry, Simon Willard or apprentice, ca. 1800, silvered-brass dial, 8-day works, 43" H $27000.00*

CHIPPENDALE DWARF-CASE CLOCK, mahogany, Reuben Tower, Hingham, Mass., ca. 1800, dial depicting a seated boy in blue and urn spandrels, brass 8-day works, 48¾" H $55000.00*

A-MA Dec. 1992   *Skinner, Inc.*
PILLAR AND SCROLL CLOCK, mahogany, Chauncey Ives, Bristol, Connecticut, replacements, crazing, 30¼" H .. $1600.00*

A-MA Aug. 1993   *Skinner, Inc.*
GOTHIC SHELF CLOCK, mahogany, Brewster and Ingrahams, Bristol, CT, ca. 1840, imperfections, 19¾" T $935.00
COTTAGE CLOCK, rosewood, Chauncy Goodrich, ca. 1845, restored, 14¾" T ... $302.50
GOTHIC STEEPLE CLOCK W/FUSEE, mahogany, Smith and Goodrich, Bristol, CT, ca. 1840, imperfections, 19½" T $302.50

A-MA Oct. 1992   *Skinner, Inc.*
WALL MIRROR TIMEPIECE, giltwood, A. Chandler, ca. 1830, 30" H, 14" W, 4" D $1870.00

FEDERAL SHELF CLOCK, inlaid mahogany, John Gains, ca. 1800, eight-day weight driven brass movement, 41" H $22,000.00

A-MA Aug. 1993   *Skinner, Inc.*
FEDERAL PRESENTATION CLOCK,
mahogany w/gilt, New England, ca. 1820,
restored, 32" L $935.00
FEDERAL BANJO CLOCK, mahogany
w/gilt dial signed "Simon Willard, Boston,"
ca. 1815, imperfections, 41" L . . $1100.00

A-MA Mar. 1993   *Skinner, Inc.*
FEDERAL BANJO CLOCK, inlaid mahog-
any, "Willard's Patent Boston Mass," re-
stored, 33" H $2750.00
WALL CLOCK, walnut, E. Howard and
Co., Boston, 50" H $6600.00

A-MA Jun. 1993   *Skinner, Inc.*
FEDERAL BANJO CLOCK, mahogany,
gilt, dial signed "Sawin," Boston, brass
weight-driven full striking movement,
33½" L $3575.00
FEDERAL BANJO CLOCK, mahogany,
gilt, dial signed "Willard Jr. Boston, no.
3668," ca. 1815, 33½" L $1650.00

A-MA Aug. 1993   *Skinner, Inc.*
BANJO CLOCK, E. Howard and Co., Boston, walnut, ca. 1840, 44" T $1760.00

A-NH Aug. 1993   *Northeast Auctions*
BANJO CLOCK, Levi Hutchins, Concord, NH, 29" T $7500.00*
LYRE-FORM CLOCK, carved giltwood, eglomise, Joshua Seward, Boston, 37"
T $9500.00*
TIME-AND-STRIKE WALL CLOCK, mahogany, eglomise, Timothy Chandler, Concord,
NH, 38" T $9000.00*
BANJO CLOCK, giltwood, eglomise, Aaron Willard, Jr., Boston, 35" T $7000.00*

A-MA Dec. 1992   *Skinner, Inc.*
GIRANDOLE CLOCK, Elmer O. Stennes, Weymouth, Massachusetts, 47″ H........................ $3250.00*

A-MA Oct. 1992   *Skinner, Inc.*
FEDERAL BANJO CLOCK, gilt and mahogany, Aaron Willard, ca. 1815, inscribed "A.A. Cheney Brookline, Mass," 42½″ H.................... $6820.00
FEDERAL BANJO CLOCK, painted, stenciled, ca. 1830, 33½″ H .. $3410.00

A-MA Aug. 1993   *Skinner, Inc.*
FIGURE-EIGHT REGULATOR CLOCK, oak, E. Howard and Co., Boston, 19th c., imperfections, 44″ L $2640.00

A-NH May. 1993   *Northeast Auctions*
GEORGE II STICK BAROMETER, mahogany, Thomas Wright, London, 38″ L.. $10500.00*
PILLAR BAROMETER, carved walnut, brass, Daniel Quare, 39″ T $36000.00*
GIMBAL-FORM SHIP'S BAROMETER, Mahogany, brass, James Bassnett, Liverpool, ca. 1835, 38″ T $7500.00*
STANDING WHEEL BAROMETER, mahogany, Carman, London, 45″ T $9000.00*
BAROMETER, satinwood, C. Blunt, Tavistock Street, London, 36″ L........ $4000.00*

A-MA Aug. 1993   *Skinner, Inc.*
SHELF CLOCK, mahogany, George Mitchell, Bristol, CT, ca. 1830, restored, 29¼″ T........................ $385.00

A-MA Jun. 1993   *Skinner, Inc.*
TALL CASE CLOCK, inlaid cherry, Isaac Gere, Northhampton, Mass., ca. 1795, weight driven movement, restored, 89½" T $13200.00

A-MA Oct. 1992   *Skinner, Inc.*
FEDERAL TALL CASE CLOCK, inlaid mahogany, ca. 1797, 96¾" H . . $9350.00

A-MA Aug. 1993   *Skinner, Inc.*
FEDERAL TALL CASE CLOCK, inlaid mahogany, New Brunswick, 1800–1815, 94¾" T $11000.00

A-ME Mar. 1993   *James D. Julia, Inc.*
CHIPPENDALE TALL CLOCK, inlaid mahogany, "Walter H. Durfee, Providence," 99" T $4250.00*

A-ME Mar. 1993   *James D. Julia, Inc.*
CHIPPENDALE GRANDFATHER CLOCK, inlaid mahogany, 95" T $1550.00*

A-MA Jan. 1993   *Skinner, Inc.*
FEDERAL TALL CASE CLOCK, ca. 1800, 96" T $4950.00

A-IL Apr. 1993   *Leslie Hindman Auction*
FEDERAL TALL CASE CLOCK, cherry, 18th c., signed "Jacob Edy Manhein," 93½" H, 19½" W, 10" D $7000.00*

A-MA Aug. 1993   *Skinner, Inc.*
FEDERAL TALL CASE CLOCK, inlaid mahogany, PA, ca. 1815, 93" T $2860.00

A-MA Mar. 1993   *Skinner, Inc.*
FEDERAL TALL CASE CLOCK, restored, imperfections, 85" H $3630.00

A-MA Jan. 1993   *Richard A. Borne Co., Inc.*
TALL CLOCK, ca. 1800 reduced in height, replacements, 93¾" $2500.00*

A-ME Mar. 1993   *James D. Julia, Inc.*
GRANDFATHER CLOCK, mahogany, "Shreve, Crump & Lowe Co.," 101" T $3750.00*

A-NH Aug. 1993   *Northeast Auctions.*
CHIPPENDALE TALL CASE CLOCK, cherry, Asahel Cheney, East Hartford, CT, brass dial engraved w/bust of G. Washington, 7" T $12000.00*
CHIPPENDALE TALL CASE CLOCK, cherry, George W. Babcock, Providence, RI, 7' T $3000.00*

A-MA Mar. 1993   *Skinner, Inc.*
CHIPPENDALE TALL POST BED, mahogany, carved and fluted, restored, 81¾" H, 56¾" W, 76" D $3300.00

A-MA Apr. 1993   *Skinner, Inc.*
SLEIGH BED, walnut, ebonized, 19th c., 47" H, 52" W, 69" L $1540.00

A-MA Mar. 1993   *Skinner, Inc.*
TURNED POST BED, grain painted, 47½" H, 51½" W $1325.00

A-NH Mar. 1993   *Northeast Auctions*
FEDERAL TALL POST BED, mahogany, 92" H $2750.00*

A-NH May. 1993   *Northeast Auctions*
FEDERAL TESTER BED, ivory painted, Mass., decorated w/Neptune and chariot, 87" H, 56" W, 78" D $11000.00*

A-NH Mar. 1993   *Northeast Auctions*
FEDERAL BEDSTEAD, inlaid mahogany, tester w/ivory, mauve, gilt dec. 93" H, 64" W, 76" L $10000.00*

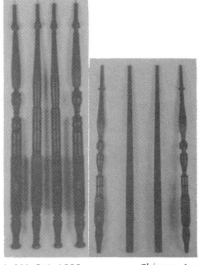

A-MA Oct. 1992   *Skinner, Inc.*
FEDERAL TALL POST BED W/ TESTER, carved mahogany, ca. 1800, 82" H $1980.00
FEDERAL TALL POST BED, painted red, ca. 1810, 78½" H $1760.00

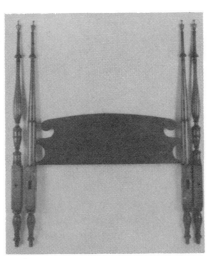

A-MA Jan. 1993   *Skinner, Inc.*
FEDERAL TALL POST BED, carved maple, ca. 1810, 71" H $1320.00

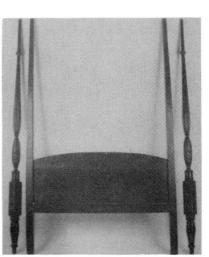

A-MA Jan. 1993   *Skinner, Inc.*
FEDERAL TALL POST BED, carved mahogany and veneer, ca. 1820, 90½" H, 52" W, 74" D $1980.00

A-MA May 1993   *Skinner, Inc.*
SETTLE BED, Canada, ca. 1800, brown
paint, 33″ H, 66½″ L $880.00

A-NY Nov. 1992   *David Rago Gallery*
FULL-SIZE BED, unmarked L. and J.G.
Stickley, headboard 44″ H, 57½″ W, rails
74″ L. $3800.00*

A-ME Feb. 1993   *James D, Julia, Inc.*
TURNED POST BED, tiger maple, 59″
T $1000.00*

A-NH Aug. 1993   *Northeast Auctions*
SHERATON TESTER BED, carved mahogany, 85″ H, 79″ L $3000.00*

A-IL Apr. 1993   *Leslie Hindman Auction*
FOUR POSTER BED, walnut, 19th c.,
75″ H $1400.00*

A-NH Aug. 1993   *Northeast Auctions*
SHERATON TESTER BED, original red,
New England, 51″ W, 75″ L $2250.00*

A-MD May 1993   *C.G. Sloan & Co., Inc.*
SHERATON TESTER BEDSTEAD,
cherry, 78½″ H, 56″ W. 82″ L . . $2723.00*

A-NY Nov. 1992   *David Rago Gallery*
CRIB SETTLE, unmarked Gustav Stickley, refinished, 39″ H, 79¾″ L $2500.00*

A-MA Oct. 1992　　　*Skinner, Inc.*
CHIPPENDALE SIDE CHAIRS, pair, carved birch, ca. 1780, 37" H . . $2420.00

A-NH Mar. 1993　　　*Northeast Auctions*
CHIPPENDALE CORNER CHAIR, maple $1000.00*

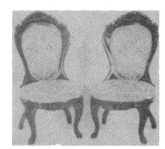

A-ME Mar. 1993　　　*James D, Julia, Inc.*
CHAIRS, pr., rosewood, by John Belter, 35" H $4150.00*

A-NH May. 1993　　　*Northeast Auctions*
CHIPPENDALE CHAIRS, pr., carved walnut, Newport Rhode Island, ca. 1775, 38" T $18000.00*

A-MA Oct. 1992　　　*Skinner, Inc.*
CHIPPENDALE CHAIR, carved cherry, c. 1780, 37" H $3630.00

A-MA Mar. 1993　　　*Skinner, Inc.*
QUEEN ANNE SIDE CHAIR, maple, ca. 1760, refinished, repair, 40" H . . $2640.00

A-NH May. 1993　　　*Northeast Auctions*
QUEEN ANNE CHAIR, carved walnut, Newport, Rhode Island, ca. 1750, Attributed to Townsend and Goddard Workshops, 39" T $21000.00*

A-MA Jan. 1993　　　*Skinner, Inc.*
CHIPPENDALE LADDER—BACK CHAIRS, pr., carved mahogony, ca. 1775, 37" H, seat 17" $1870.00

A-MA Oct. 1992　　　*Skinner, Inc.*
QUEEN ANNE CHAIR, walnut, ca. 1760, 39" H $1320.00

A-MA Oct. 1992　　　*Skinner, Inc.*
WINDSOR CHAIR, knuckle arm, ca. 1780 . . . . $990.00

A-MA Mar. 1993   *Skinner, Inc.*
WINDSOR ARMCHAIR, old black paint,
39″ H $4400.00

A-MA May 1993   *Skinner, Inc.*
SIDE CHAIR, New Hampshire, 18th
c., ... $935.00
SIDE CHAIR, carved, turned maple, 17th
c $1210.00
SIDE CHAIR, carved, 18th c. ... $605.00

A-MA Jan. 1993   *Skinner, Inc.*
**SHAKER NO. 6 ARM ROCKING
CHAIR,** 1880–1920 .... $880.00
SHAKER NO. 6 ARM CHAIR, 1880–
1920 .... $880.00
SHAKER NO. 7 ROCKING CHAIR,
1880–1920 .... $825.00

A-MA May 1993   *Skinner, Inc.*
WINDSOR ARM CHAIR, 18th
c. $880.00
WINDSOR ARM CHAIR, carved, Pen-
nsylvania, 18th c. $1760.00
WINDSOR CONTINUOUS ARM CHAIR,
England, 18th c., 42″ H $935.00

A-MA Dec. 1992   *Skinner, Inc.*
HITCHCOCK CHAIRS, set of 6, (1 illus.),
2 armchairs, 4 side chairs, some refinished $600.00*
HITCHCOCK SIDE CHAIR, original dec.,
new seat $85.00*

CHIPPENDALE DINING CHAIRS, set of
12, (3 illus.), carved mahog—
any $4250.00*

A-MA May 1993   *Skinner, Inc.*
QUEEN ANNE SIDE CHAIRS, set of 4,
New York, 18th c., refinished ... $1980.00

A-MA Oct. 1992   *Skinner, Inc.*
CHIPPENDALE ARMCHAIR, mahogany, ca. 1780, 38″ H $1650.00

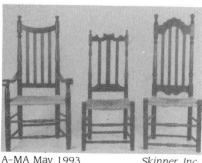

A-MA May 1993   *Skinner, Inc.*
ARM CHAIR, painted, decorated, New
England, 18th c. $522.50
SIDE CHAIR, painted, New England,
18th c. $165.00
SIDE CHAIR, New England, 18th
c. $330.00

A-MA May 1993   *Skinner, Inc.*
SIDE CHAIR, carved, painted, New Eng-
land, 18th c. $550.00
ARM CHAIR, painted, Connecticut, 18th
c. $770.00
SIDE CHAIR, carved, turned, New Haven
Colony, ca. 1800 .... $990.00

A-MA Oct. 1992   *Skinner, Inc.*
WINDSOR SIDE CHAIR, ca. 1780, 38"
H $715.00
WINDSOR CHAIR, continuous arm
brace-back, labeled "W. MacBride N. York,"
ca. 1790, 37" H $2090.00
WINDSOR CHAIR, continuous arm
brace-back, ca. 1780, 35¼"H . . $880.00

A-NH Mar. 1993   *Northeast Auctions*
SHAKER ROCKER, bird's-eye
maple $4500.00*

A-MA Mar. 1993   *Skinner, Inc.*
QUEEN ANNE ROUNDABOUT CHAIR,
mahogany, restored, 32½" H . . . $6600.00

A-MA Mar. 1993   *Skinner, Inc.*
SHAKER SIDE CHAIR, cherry, tiger
maple, old finish, 41½" H $880.00

A-MA Mar. 1993   *Skinner, Inc.*
HIGH CHAIR, 34" H $1210.00

A-MA Jun. 1993   *Skinner, Inc.*
TURNED CORNER CHAIR, maple, ash,
New England, ca. 1750, old refinish, 32"
H $770.00

A-NH May. 1993   *Northeast Auctions*
CHIPPENDALE ARMCHAIR, mahog-
any, Massachusetts, ca. 1775, 43"
H $145000.00*

A-MA Oct. 1992   *Skinner, Inc.*
CHIPPENDALE CHAIR, mahogany, ca.
1780, 44½" T $11000.00

A-MA Jun. 1993   *Skinner, Inc.*
ARMCHAIR, painted, New England, 18th
c., dark varnish, 47" H $1430.00
WILLIAM AND MARY ARMCHAIR,
Connecticut, 18th c., damage, 49"
H $880.00

A-MA Jun. 1993   *Skinner, Inc.*
CHIPPENDALE SIDE CHAIRS, mahogany, New England, ca. 1780, imperfections, 37½" H $2200.00

A-NY Nov. 1992   *David Rago Gallery*
HIGH-BACK PRAIRIE SCHOOL DINING CHAIRS, by Stickley brothers, 1 w/ paper label, 41¾" H, 18½" W, 18" D $650.00*

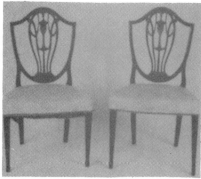

A-MA Aug. 1993   *Skinner, Inc.*
SIDE CHAIRS, pr., mahogany, George III style, 36½" H $825.00

A-NH May. 1993   *Northeast Auctions*
CHIPPENDALE ARMCHAIR, mahogany, Newport, Rhone island, ca. 1775, 42" H $15000.00*

A-MA Jan. 1993   *Skinner, Inc.*
FEDERAL EASY CHAIR, c. 1790, 46" H $2750.00

A-MA Aug. 1993   *Skinner, Inc.*
QUEEN ANNE EASY CHAIR, walnut, 1730–1750, refinished, imperfections, 45" H $26400.00

A-NH May. 1993   *Northeast Auctions*
QUEEN ANNE WING CHAIR, carved walnut, Newport or Boston, ca. 1750–1775, 47" H $27500.00*

A-MA May 1993   *Skinner, Inc.*
CHIPPENDALE CHAIR, cherry, attributed to Chapin, Conn. 18th c., 37" T $467.00

A-NH May. 1993   *Northeast Auctions*
QUEEN ANNE WING CHAIR, carved walnut, Newport, Rhode Island, ca. 1740–1765, 46" H $35000.00*

A-MA Aug. 1993   *Skinner, Inc.*
SIDE CHAIRS, set of 6, mahogany veneer, 1835–1845, old refinish, imperfections, 31½"
H $1760.00

A-MA Aug. 1993   *Skinner, Inc.*
WINDSOR SIDE CHAIR, New England,
19th c., old green-black paint, 34½"
H $880.00

A-MA Aug. 1993   *Skinner, Inc.*
WINDSOR SIDE CHAIR, New England,
19th c., old black paint, 26½"
H. $1045.00

A-MA Aug. 1993   *Skinner, Inc.*
SHAKER LADDERBACK SIDE CHAIRS, set of 6, Kentucky, ca. 1870, refinished, 36"
H $770.00

A-MA Aug. 1993   *Skinner, Inc.*
WINDSOR SIDE CHAIRS, 4 pcs., New England, 19th c., refinished, 36½" H $880.00

A-MA Aug. 1993   *Skinner, Inc.*
WINDSOR SIDE CHAIR, New England,
19th c., old green paint, 36" H . . . $880.00

A-MA Aug. 1993   *Skinner, Inc.*
QUEEN ANNE CHAIR, New England, red paint, 18th c., 39" H $1100.00

A-MA Aug. 1993   *Skinner, Inc.*
ARROW-BACK SIDE CHAIRS, set of 7, PA, ca. 1830, later yellow paint w/polychrome stencil, 34" H $1760.00

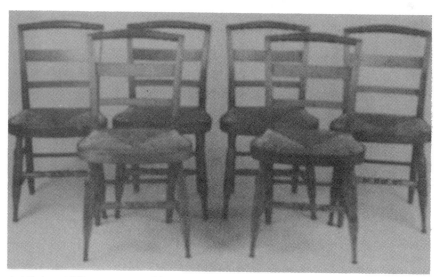

A-MA Aug. 1993   *Skinner, Inc.*
SHERATON SIDE CHAIRS, set of 6, maple, New England, ca. 1820, refinished, imperfections, 33½" H $1045.00

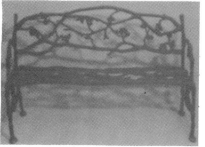

A-OH Sep. 1993   *Garth's Auctions, Inc.*
GARDEN BENCH, cast iron, 41½" H, 45" L $1760.00
GARDEN BENCH, cast iron, "Mfg. by the Kramer Bros. Fdy Co, Dayton, O," repairs, 35" H, 58" L $880.00
GARDEN BENCH, cast iron, rust, 32" H, 47h" L $1155.00

A-MA Aug. 1993   *Skinner, Inc.*
WINDSOR SIDE CHAIRS, set of 4, New England, 19th c., 36" H $2530.00

A-NH May. 1993   *Northeast Auctions*
CHIPPENDALE SIDE CHAIRS, 6 pcs., grain-painted maple, provincial Rhode Island $7000.00*

A-MA Jan. 1993   *Skinner, Inc.*
CHIPPENDALE CHAIRS, eight, mahogany, 18th c., 37" H, seat 17" $16500.00

A-MA Jun. 1993   *Skinner, Inc.*
SIDE CHAIRS, assembled set of 6, Mass., 19th c., restored, 42¼" H $990.00

A-MA Mar. 1993   *Skinner, Inc.*
CHIPPENDALE SIDE CHAIRS, 3 pcs., mahogany, underside stamped "W. Simes," old refinish, repairs, 35½" H $2200.00

A-MA Jan. 1993   *Skinner, Inc.*
WINDSOR CHAIRS, set of 6, painted yellow, polychromed, ca. 1820, 33" H $1650.00

A-MA Mar. 1993   *Skinner, Inc.*
WINDSOR SIDE CHAIR, red-brown paint, 37½" H $3190.00
WINDSOR KNUCKLE ARM CHAIR, black paint, gilt striping, restored, 44½" $2420.00
WINDSOR SIDE CHAIR, brown paint, 40" H $2200.00

A-MA Mar. 1993   *Skinner, Inc.*
WINDSOR SIDE CHAIRS, pr., stamped "H. McFall," 37½" H $467.50

A-MA Jan. 1993   *Skinner, Inc.*
CHAIRS, set of 12, polychrome decorated, ca. 1820, 33¾" H $990.00

A-MA Jun. 1993   *Skinner, Inc.*
CHIPPENDALE CHAIRS, set of 5, ca. 1780, imperfections, 36½" H . . . $1650.00

A-MA Oct. 1992   *Skinner, Inc.*
FEDERAL CHAIRS, set of 8, inlaid mahogany, ca. 1790, 37½" H, seat 17½" H $13200.00

A-MA Jan. 1993   *Skinner, Inc.*
ROD-BACK WINDSOR SIDE CHAIRS, set of 6, impressed "I.C. Tuttle," 34¼" H, seat 17¼" H $8250.00

A-MA Jun. 1993　　*Skinner, Inc.*
CHIPPENDALE ARMCHAIR, mahogany, walnut, 31½" H $1980.00

A-NH Aug. 1993　　*Northeast Auctions*
QHEEN ANNE SIDE CHAIR, Hudson River Valley, red paint $4000.00*

A-NY Nov. 1992　　*David Rago Gallery*
ROCKER AND ARMCHAIR, leather seats, wear, "Work of L. and J.G. Stickley" decal, 38" H $1600.00*

A-NY Nov. 1992　　*David Rago Gallery*
HIGH-BACK CHAIR, Gustav Stickley decal, designed by Harvey Ellis, restored, 46" H, 19" W, 18" D $1800.00*

A-NH May. 1993　　*Northeast Auctions*
QUEEN ANNE ROUNDABOUT CHAIR, walnut, Mass., ca. 1740-1765, 30¾" H $42500.00*

A-MA Aug. 1993　　*Skinner, Inc.*
CLASSICAL SOFA, carved mahogany veneer, New England, ca. 1835, imperfections, 36½" H, 16" D, 48" L $1320.00

A-MA Aug. 1993　　*Skinner, Inc.*
WINDSOR CHAIRS, 2 pcs., New England, 19th c., 1 signed Jos. Tracy, refinished, 34" H, 35" H $1210.00

A-IL Apr. 1993　　*Leslie Hindman Auction*
WINDSOR SIDE CHAIRS, painted wood, 19th c. $1800.00*

A-MA Oct. 1992　　*Skinner, Inc.*
WINDSOR CHAIR, knuckle arms, old red varnish, ca. 1980, 28" H .. $3850.00

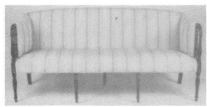

A-MA Mar. 1993   Skinner, Inc.
FEDERAL SOFA, inlaid mahogany, 35" H,
71" L, 24" D $4125.00

A-IL Apr. 1993   Leslie Hindman Auction
SETTEE, mahogany, 19th c., 90"
L $3800.00*

A-NH Mar. 1993   Northeast Auctions
SOFA, carved mahogany, classical revival,
92" L $1300.00*

A-MA Jan. 1993   Skinner, Inc.
FEDERAL SOFA, inlaid maple, ca. 1810,
33" H, 76" W, 28" D $1540.00

A-PA May 1993   Alderfer Auction Co.
SETTEE, 19th c., floral dec., 70¾"
T $1800.00

A-IL Apr. 1993   Leslie Hindman Auction
SETEE, carved mahogany, 19th
c. $4600.00*

A-MA Jan. 1993   Skinner, Inc.
WINDSOR SETTEE, painted, 1760-
1780, 28" H, 47" W, seat 17½"
H $1540.00

A-PA May 1993   Alderfer Auction Co.
WINDSOR SETTEE, bamboo turned,
New England, 19th c., alligatored red over
green, repairs, 64" L $2150.00

A-IL Apr. 1993   Leslie Hindman Auction
CHILD'S BENCH, pine, 19th c., 33½"
L $3000.00*

A-IL Apr. 1993   Leslie Hindman Auction
WINDSOR BENCH, birch, 19th c., bamboo spindles and legs, 79" L ... $4800.00*

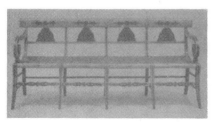

A-IL Apr. 1993   Leslie Hindman Auction
FOUR CHAIR BACK SETTEE, painted
wood, 72" L $2600.00*

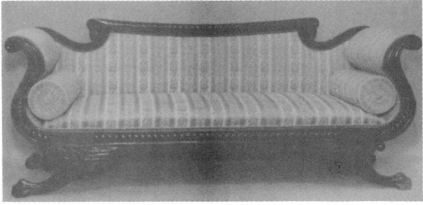

A-OH July 1993   Garth's Auctions, Inc.
EMPIRE SOFA, carved mahogany, refinished, reupholstered in blue, ivory, gold, pink, green
silk brocade, 81" L $2310.00

A-MA Dec. 1992   *Skinner, Inc.*
CHIPPENDALE CHEST, curly maple, old refinish, replacements, 54½" H, 39" W, 18" D $2500.00*

A-OH March. 1993   *Garth's Auctions, Inc.*
HEPPLEWHITE CHEST, inlayed curly walnut, poplar, refinished, 38½" W, 18¼" D, 38" H $2530.00

A-IL Apr. 1993   *Leslie Hindman Auction*
EMPIRE MINIATURE CHEST, tiger maple, maple, 19th c., 24" H, 15" W, 8" D $2800.00*
MINIATURE CHEST, grain painted, 10" H, 14" W, 14½" D $3800.00*

A-MA Jan. 1993   *Skinner, Inc.*
CHIPPENDALE TALL CHEST, maple, ca. 1780, 56" H, 36" W, 18" D .. $3300.00

A-OH Nov. 1992   *Garth's Auctions, Inc.*
FEDERAL HIGH CHEST, mahogany, figured veneer, poplar, pine, replacements, losses, damage, 46¼" W, 22¼" D, 48¾" H.......................... $1045.00

A-NH Mar. 1993   *Northeast Auctions*
HIGHBOY, figured maple, 76½" H, 38" W, 22" D $18000.00*

A-MA Mar. 1993   *Skinner, Inc.*
CHIPPENDALE TALL CHEST, maple, ca. 1770, refinished, imperfections, 63" H, 35½" W, 17¼" D $4125.00

A-MA Oct. 1992   *Skinner, Inc.*
CHIPPENDALE CHEST-ON-CHEST, cherry bonnet, ca. 1770, 85" H, 38½" W, 17½" D $6600.00

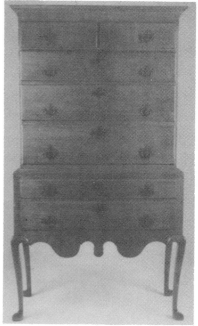

A-MA Jan. 1993   *Skinner, Inc.*
QUEEN ANNE HIGHBOY, maple and poplar, ca. 1760, 72½" H, 39½" W, 19¾" D $7150.00

A-ME Feb. 1993   *James D, Julia, Inc.*
QUEENE ANNE HIGHBOY, tiger maple, New England, 74" H, 37" W, 18" D $15500.00*

A-NH May. 1993   *Northeast Auctions*
QUEEN ANNE LOWBOY, maple, birch, New England, 31" W $4250.00*

A-ME Feb. 1993   *James D, Julia, Inc.*
QUEENE ANNE HIGHBOY, figured maple, Dunlap School, NH, 79" H, 38" W, 18" D $8000.00*

A-MA Oct. 1992   *Skinner, Inc.*
CHIPPENDALE SERPENTINE BUREAU, mahogany, ca. 1790, 33⅛" H, 38" W, 21" D $6050.00

A-MA Jun. 1993   *Skinner, Inc.*
FEDERAL SERPENTINE BUREAU, mahogany veneer, ca. 1830 refinished, repairs, 37¾" H, 46½" W, 22¼" D $1320.00

A-MA Jan. 1993   *Skinner, Inc.*
FEDERAL BOWFRONT BUREAU, cherry and mahogany veneer, ca. 1790, 33½" H, 39" W, 22" D $2750.00

A-NH May. 1993   *Northeast Auctions*
CHIPPENDALE DRESSING TABLE, mahogany, Newport Rhode, Island, ca. 1765, Attributed to Edmund Townsend, 33⅜" H, 35¾" W, 20⅜" D ... $125000.00*

A-NH May. 1993   *Northeast Auctions*
QUEEN ANNE DRESSING TABLE, carved wlnut, Massachusetts, ca. 1760, 30" H, 34" W, 21¾" D $80000.00*

A-NY Nov. 1992   *David Rago Gallery*
DRESSING TABLE, decal "Work of L. and J.G. Stickley," table 29½" H, 44" W, 22½" D $1300.00*

A-MA Jun. 1993 *Skinner, Inc.*
CHIPPENDALE SERPENTINE CHEST, cherry, Massachusetts, ca. 1780, old refinish, 34" H, 33¾" W, 18" D $26400.00

A-NH Aug. 1993 *Northeast Auctions*
CHIPPENDALE CHEST, mahogany, Penn. 34" W $5000.00*

A-IL Apr. 1993 *Leslie Hindman Auction*
CHIPPENDALE CHEST, walnut, 18th c., 65" H, 42" W, 22" D $4600.00*

A-MA Jun. 1993 *Skinner, Inc.*
CHIPPENDALE TALL CHEST, maple, Southern New England, 18th c., old refinish, repairs, 57" H, 36¼" W, 17" D . . . $2420.00

A-NH May. 1993 *Northeast Auctions*
CHIPPENDALE SERPENTINE-BOMBE CHEST, mahogany, Boston, ca. 1770, 32¾" H, 36" W, 19" D $300000.00*

A-OH July 1993 *Garth's Auctions, Inc.*
CHIPPENDALE HIGH CHEST, walnut, poplar, Pennsylvania, repairs, replacements, 68½" H, 44½" W, 23¾" D $4125.00

A-NH May. 1993 *Northeast Auctions*
CHIPPENDALE BLOCK-FRONT CHEST, mahogany, Mass., 1760-1775, 31¾" H, 36" W, 21⅝" D $65000.00*

A-NH Aug. 1993 *Northeast Auctions*
CHIPPENDALE CHEST ON CHEST, carved mahogany, English, 75" T $4500.00*

A-NH May. 1993 *Northeast Auctions*
CHIPPENDALE BLOCK-FRONT CHEST, cherry, 41¼" H, 39" W, 19" D $16000.00*

A-OH July 1993 *Garth's Auctions, Inc.*
CHIPPENDALE HIGH CHEST, walnut, pine, old refinish, replaced feet/brasses, repairs, 63¼" H, 42¾" W, 22½" D $3190.00

A-NY Nov. 1992 *David Rago Gallery*
CHEST, unmarked L. and J.G. Stickley, 38½" H, 38" W, 19" D $1200.00*

A-MA Jun. 1993 *Skinner, Inc.*
CHIPPENDALE BOW-FRONT CHEST, ca. 1780, old refinish, 33" H, 38" W, 22" D $4125.00

A-NH Aug. 1993 *Northeast Auctions*
CHIPPENDALE CHEST, carved birch, Newburyport, original brasses and finish, 37" W $4250.00*

A-NH Aug. 1993 *Northeast Auctions*
CHIPPENDALE CHEST, tiger maple, New England, original brasses and finish, 36" W $12000.00*

QUENE ANNE HIGHBOY, tiger maple, Massachusetts North Shore, 74" H, 38" W $23000.00*

A-NH Aug. 1993 *Northeast Auctions*
QUEEN ANNE HIGHBOY, tiger maple, New England, 74" H, 40" W ... $4000.00*

A-NH Aug. 1993 *Northeast Auctions*
SHERATON CHEST, tiger maple, labeled Ephraim Blanchard, Amherst, NH, 40" W $1300.00*

A-MA Jan. 1993   *Skinner, Inc.*
WORK TABLE, tiger maple w/mahogany veneer, ca. 1810, 28½" H, top 16½" x 20" $715.00

A-MA Oct. 1992   *Skinner, Inc.*
FEDERAL BOW-FRONT BUREAU, mahogany, ca. 1800 . . . . $1650.00

A-MA Jan. 1993   *Skinner, Inc.*
FEDERAL BOWFRONT BUREAU, inlaid mahogany and veneer, ca. 1790, 40½" H, 40" W, 17½" D $2475.00

A-NH Mar. 1993   *Northeast Auctions*
CHIPPENDALE CHEST, maple, 36" W $5750.00*

A-MA Mar. 1993   *Skinner, Inc.*
QUEEN ANNE CHEST OVER DRAWERS, painted pine, 36¼" H, 34½" W, 17½" D $1540.00

A-MA Mar. 1993   *Skinner, Inc.*
CHEST OVER DRAWERS, pine paneled, 17th c., MA, old refinish, 43" H, 41½" W, 19" D $4125.00

A-MA Jan. 1993   *Skinner, Inc.*
FEDERAL CHEST, cherry, 42¼" H, 39¾" W, 19" D $1210.00

A-MA Mar. 1993   *Skinner, Inc.*
FEDERAL BUREAU, cherry, tiger maple veneer, refinished, repairs, 38½" H, 41¼" W, 18½" D $1870.00

A-MA Mar. 1993   *Skinner, Inc.*
CHEST OVER DRAWERS, pine, raised panels, old refinish, 43" H, 41½" W, 19½" D $4125.00

A-MA Mar. 1993   *Skinner, Inc.*
FEDERAL BOWFRONT BUREAU, inlaid cherry, refinished, 37½" H, 39" W, 21" D $2750.00

A-MA Jan. 1993   *Skinner, Inc.*
FEDERAL CHEST OF DRAWERS, birch and pine, ca. 1800, 41" H, 36" W, 18" D $2350.00

A-NH May. 1993   *Northeast Auctions*
SHERATON TWELVE-PANEL CHEST,
mahogany, flame birch, New Hampshire,
41″ W $2500.00*

A-NH May. 1993   *Northeast Auctions*
HEPPLEWHITE DROP-PANEL CHEST,
inlaid mahogany, Portsmouth, 37½″ H, 38″
W $5250.00*

A-ME Feb. 1993   *James D, Julia, Inc.*
FEDERAL BOW FRONT CHEST, maho-
gany, flame birch, 41″ H, 43″ W, 20″
D $6500.00*

A-MA Oct. 1992   *Skinner, Inc.*
FEDERAL BOMBE FRONT CHEST,
cherry, ca. 1800, 32½H, 37″ W, 20″
D $5060.00

A-MA Dec. 1992   *Skinner, Inc.*
TALL CHEST, pine, old refinished, replace-
ments, 43″ H, 36⅞″ W, 16½″
D $1300.00*

A-OH Nov. 1992   *Garth's Auctions, Inc.*
SHERATON CHEST, cherry, walnut inlay,
poplar, old refinish, age cracks, stains,
repairs, 40¾″ W, 19″ D, 47¾ H . . $1210.00

A-MA May 1993   *Skinner, Inc.*
SIX-BOARD CHEST, pine, New England,
ca. 1710 . . . . $440.00

A-MA Jun. 1993   *Skinner, Inc.*
SHAKER CASE OF DRAWERS, walnut,
19th c., varnish, imperfections, 55″ H, 43½″
W, 23″ D $9350.00

A-IL Apr. 1993   *Leslie Hindman Auction*
FEDERAL CHEST, inlaid mahogany, 19th
c., 35½″ H, 39½″ W, 22″ D $3600.00*

A-IL Apr. 1993   *Leslie Hindman Auction*
CHEST, 19th c., brown/gold grain painting, 25″ H, 50″ W, 22″ D $1000.00*

A-NH Mar. 1993   *Northeast Auctions*
HEPPLEWHITE SIDEBOARD, inlaid mahogany, 41" H, 54" W, 25" D . . . $4250.00*
HEPPLEWHITE SIDEBOARD, inlaid mahogany, 29½" H, 70" W $4750.00*

A-MA Nov. 1992   *Skinner, Inc.*
FEDERAL SIDEBOARD, wavy birch and carved mahogany, MA, ca. 1780, restored, 39" H, 69" L, 21½" D $3025.00

A-MA Jun. 1993   *Skinner, Inc.*
FEDERAL SIDEBOARD, inlaid mahogany, ca. 1790, refinished, imperfections, 40" H, 69½" W, 26" D $4950.00

A-MA Oct. 1992   *Skinner, Inc.*
FEDERAL SIDEBOARD, mahogany and veneer, ca. 1815, 42½" H, 55" W, 19½" D $3575.00

A-MA Jun. 1993   *Skinner, Inc.*
CELLARETTE, cherry, 19th c., old refinish, 29" H, 31" W, 19½" D $2860.00

A-NH Aug. 1993   *Northeast Auctions*
SHERATON SIDEBOARD, inlaid mahogany, Massachusetts, 42" H, 69" W, 27" D $16000.00*

A-MA Jun. 1993   *Skinner, Inc.*
FEDERAL BOW-FRONT BUREAU, maple, New England ca. 1800, old refinish, 35½" H, 40" W, 22" D $1430.00

A-ME Feb. 1993   *James D, Julia, Inc.*
PIE SAFE, walnut, pierced tins dated 1868, 58" H, 47" W, 14" D $2600.00*

A-NY Nov. 1992   *David Rago Gallery*
CHINA CABINET, oak, Limbert branded mark, original dk. finish, replaced glass, 58" H, 45" W, 16" D $3300.00*

A-MA Aug. 1993   *Skinner, Inc.*
FEDERAL BOOKCASE, grain painted pine, MA, ca. 1790, 91" H, 40" W, 18½" D $22000.00

A-OH Nov. 1992   *Garth's Auctions, Inc.*
JELLY CUPBOARD, poplar, cleaned to old red, dovetailed case, wrought iron hinges, four shelves, water damage, replacements, repairs, 20¼" x 45¾", 65½" H $2640.00

A-MA Oct. 1992   *Skinner, Inc.*
FEDERAL CORNER CUPBOARD, inlaid walnut, 90¾" H, 41¼" W $3025.00

A-OH Nov. 1992   *Garth's Auctions, Inc.*
CORNER CUPBOARD, yellow pine, refinished, originally built in, beveled sides added to make it freestanding, repairs, replacements, three butterfly shelves, 58" W, 96" H $3520.00

A-OH Nov. 1992   *Garth's Auctions, Inc.*
CORNER CUPBOARD, cherry, poplar, two piece, old refinishing, dovetailed drawer, 45" W, 87½" H $5500.00

A-MA Jun. 1993 *Skinner, Inc.*
SHAKER CUPBOARD, walnut, attributed to Daniel Baird, Union Village, Ohio, ca. 1832, 96½" H, 39½" W, 19" D . . . $11000.00

A-MA Aug. 1993 *Skinner, Inc.*
SIDEBOARD, carved mahogany, wavy birch veneer, MA, ca. 1825, 50" H, 46½" W, 21½" D $1320.00

A-MA Jun. 1993 *Skinner, Inc.*
WILLIAM & MARY SPICE CHEST, grain painted, Mass. 18th c., 18" H, 18¾" W, 12½" D $10450.00

A-MA Jun. 1993 *Skinner, Inc.*
SHAKER CUPBOARD W/DRAWERS, pine, signed and dated, Levi Swain, 1845, old refinish, 78" H, 43½" W $2860.00

A-MA Oct. 1992 *Skinner, Inc.*
CUPBOARD, pine, 18th c., 89" H, 35" W, 17½" D $1650.00

A-MA Oct. 1992 *Skinner, Inc.*
FEDERAL TWO-PART CORNER CUP-BOARD, cherry, ca. 1800, 97½" H, 46" W, 23½" D $4950.00

A-OH Sep. 1993 *Garth's Auctions, Inc.*
CUPBOARD, walnut, poplar, old glass, refinished, replacements, 91" H, 50¾" W, 19¼" D $2420.00
PLATE, pewter, Parks Boyd eagle touch, battered, split, 7⅞" D $55.00
TANKARD MEASURE, pewter, "England," 5½" T $104.50
PITCHER, pewter, battered, 7½" T $71.50
BASIN, pewter, "Love" touch, wear, corroded, 2" H, 8" D $165.00

A-PA May 1993   *Alderfer Auction Co.*
HANGING SPICE CUPBOARD, red
paint, 19th c., 20½" T $850.00
CHILDS CUPBOARD, blue, 19th c., PA,
28¾" T $600.00

A-MA May 1993   *Skinner, Inc.*
PEWTER CUPBOARD, pine, New England, 18th c., 78" H $1430.00

A-MA Jun. 1993   *Skinner, Inc.*
SHAKER CUPBOARD, pine, 19th c., old
varnish, imperfections, 84" H, 52½" W, 20"
D $6050.00

A-ME Feb. 1993   *James D, Julia, Inc.*
CORNER CUPBOARD, pine, 83" H, 58"
W, 32" D $1500.00*

A-ME Mar. 1993   *James D, Julia, Inc.*
HEPPLEWHITE CORNER CABINET,
mahogany, string and shell inlay, 74" H,
34" W $725.00*

A-ME Mar. 1993   *James D, Julia, Inc.*
CHINA CABINET, carved oak, 72" H, 47"
W, 16" D $1350.00*

A-OH Nov. 1992   *Garth's Auctions, Inc.*
JELLY CUPBOARD, yellow pine, old blue
repaint, repair, 47½" W, 17½" D, 53¼"
H $1100.00
NOAH'S ARK, pine, handmade, worn
paint, incomplete set of 14 animals, repairs,
19½" L $137.50

A-OH Nov. 1992   *Garth's Auctions, Inc.*
SOUTHERN CUPBOARD, pine, refinished, 50¾" W, 20" D, 53" H $687.50

A-ME Feb. 1993   *James D, Julia, Inc.*
CABINET, carved teakwood, applied
ivory, MOP inlay, 60" H, 36" W, 12"
D $2000.00*

A-MA Jun. 1993   *Skinner, Inc.*
DESK, walnut, New England, 19th c., old refinish, 45¾" H, 37¼" W, 24" D . . . $495.00

A-MA Mar. 1993   *Skinner, Inc.*
CHIPPENDALE SLANT LID DESK, maple, refinished, 44" H, 36¼" W, 17¼" D $3575.00

A-MA Mar. 1993   *Skinner, Inc.*
CHIPPENDALE SLANT LID DESK, tiger maple, restored, 44¾" H, 36¾" W, 17¼" D $3575.00

A-MA Jan. 1993   *Skinner, Inc.*
CHIPPENDALE SLANT-LID DESK, maple, ca. 1780, 42½" H, 38" W, 18¾" D $3575.00

A-MA Jun. 1993   *Skinner, Inc.*
CHIPPENDALE SERPENTINE DESK, carved mahogany, Mass., ca. 1770, refinished, 43" H, 41½" W, 22" D $9350.00

A-NH May. 1993   *Northeast Auctions*
CHIPPENDALE SLANT-LID DESK, walnut, Virginia, 34½" W $4000.00*

A-MA Oct. 1992   *Skinner, Inc.*
FEDERAL DESK/BOOKCASE, tiger maple, ca. 1820, 70" H, 39½" W, 19" D $3960.00

A-MA Oct. 1992   *Skinner, Inc.*
QUEEN ANNE SLANT-LID DESK/ DRESSING TABLE, maple, ca. 1760, 66¾" H, 35¼" W, 19" D $9350.00

A-MA Jan. 1993   *Skinner, Inc.*
SECRETARY DESK, painted poplar, ca. 1850, 62" H, 53" W, 19" D $2750.00

A-ME Mar. 1993   *James D, Julia, Inc.*
SECRETARY, carved walnut, 105″ H, 47″ W, 26″ D $21,000.00*

A-ME Feb. 1993   *James D, Julia, Inc.*
SLANT LID DESK, cherry, 18th c., Penn., 41″ H, 36″ W, 17½″ D $3000.00*

A-OH July 1993   *Garth's Auctions, Inc.*
CHIPPENDALE SLANT FRONT DESK, walnut, pine, repairs, replacements, 41″ H, 37¾″ W, 17¾″ D $3960.00

A-ME Mar. 1993   *James D, Julia, Inc.*
ROLLTOP DESK, oak, Derby Desk, Co., 66″ W $2250.00*

A-NH May. 1993   *Northeast Auctions*
CHIPPENDALE OXBOW SLANT-LID DESK, mahogany, Mass. ca 1780, 43¾″ H, 40¼″ W, 21⅝″ D $14500.00*

A-NY Nov. 1992   *David Rago Gallery*
WRITING DESK, Limbert branded mark, refinished, 35″ H, 32″ W, 20″ D . . $800.00*

A-MD May 1993   *C.G. Sloan & Co., Inc.*
WILLIAM AND MARY FLAT-TOP HIGHBOY, maple, MA, ca. 1720, orig. brasses, 63″ H, 40″ W, 20″ D . . . $3200.00*

A-MA Oct. 1992   *Skinner, Inc.*
CHIPPENDALE OX BOW SLANT LID DESK, mahogany, ca. 1780, 44″ H, 42″ W, 24″ D $2750.00

A-MA Jun. 1993   *Skinner, Inc.*
SLANT LID DESK, cherry, Connecticut, ca. 1780, restored, imperfections, 43″ H, 42″ W, 19″ D $2530.00

A-MA Jan. 1993   *Skinner, Inc.*
HUTCH TABLE, pine and maple, 18th c.,
27⅛" H, 45¾" D $2090.00

A-MA Oct. 1992   *Skinner, Inc.*
TAVERN TABLE, pine and maple, red
stained, 18th c., 24" H, 41" W, 23"
D $1430.00

A-MA Jan. 1993   *Skinner, Inc.*
CARD TABLE, carved mahogany and
veneer, ca. 1820, 30" H, 38¼" W, 19"
D $1760.00

A-MA Jun. 1993   *Skinner, Inc.*
FEDERAL CARD TABLE, inlaid mahogany, ca. 1815, old refinish, imperfections,
29¼" H, 36½" W, 17½" D $2090.00

A-MA Mar. 1993   *Skinner, Inc.*
FEDERAL CARD TABLE, inlaid mahogany, ca. 1810, old refinish, 28½" H, 34½" W,
17" D $1760.00

A-MA Jan. 1993   *Skinner, Inc.*
FEDERAL CARD TABLE, inlaid cherry,
ca. 1820, 28" H, 36⅛" W, 17" D .. $550.00

A-MA Jan. 1993   *Skinner, Inc.*
CARD TABLE, carved mahogany, brass
and mahogany veneer inlaid, ca. 1820,
28½" H, 37" W, 18½" D $1320.00

A-MA Oct. 1992   *Skinner, Inc.*
FEDERAL CARD TABLE, inlaid mahog-
any, ca. 1790, 28¼" H, 36" W, 17"
D $6050.00

A-MA Oct. 1992   *Skinner, Inc.*
CARD TABLES, pair, mahogany and
veneer, ca. 1820, 29¼" H, 38" W, 17"
D $2200.00

A-MA Jan. 1993   *Skinner, Inc.*
CARD TABLES, pr., mahogany w/inlay,
ca. 1800, 29" H, 36" W, 16¾"
D $12100.00

A-MA Oct. 1992   *Skinner, Inc.*
FEDERAL CARD TABLE, inlaid mahog-
any, ca. 1800, 29¼" H, 36" W, 17¾"
D $2310.00

A-NH May. 1993   *Northeast Auctions*
CHIPPENDALE CARD TABLE, carved
mahogany, Newport, Rhode Island, ca. 1790,
attributed to Townsend and Goddard Workshops, 29" H, 32" W, 15" D ... $23000.00*

A-MA Dec. 1992 *Skinner, Inc.*
CONSOLE TABLES, pr., inlaid mahogany, George III style $3630.00

A-MA Aug. 1993 *Skinner, Inc.*
FEDERAL CARD TABLE, mahogany veneer, carved, MA, ca. 1820, old refinish, 30½" H, 36¾" W, 18¼" D $1100.00

A-MA Aug. 1993 *Skinner, Inc.*
CLASSICAL CARD TABLE, carved mahogany, MA, ca. 1820, imperfections, 29" H, 36" W, 18" D $990.00
CLASSICAL CARD TABLE, carved mahogany, MA Ca. 1820, imperfections, 29" H, 37" W, 17¾" D $1045.00

A-IL Apr. 1993 *Leslie Hindman Auction*
HEPPLEWHITE FOLD-TOP TEA TABLE, inlaid mahogany, 18th c., 28" H, 36" W, 16½" D $3000.00*

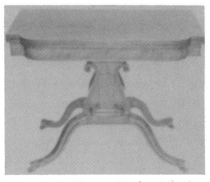

A-NH Aug. 1993 *Northeast Auctions*
CARD TABLE, brass inlaid, Boston, 36" L $2500.00*

A-NH Aug. 1993 *Northeast Auctions*
QUEEN ANNE TEA TABLE, mahogany, Rhode Island, 34" L $15500.00*

A-IL Apr. 1993 *Leslie Hindman Auction*
SHERATON FOLD-TOP CARD TABLE, mahogany, 19th c., 29½" H, 36½" W, 18" D $800.00*

A-NY Nov. 1992   *David Rago Gallery*
OCTAGONAL TABOURET, L. and J.G. Stickley decal, original color, added finish, 20½" H, 18" sq. $600.00*
LAMP TABLE, by Stickley brothers, refinished, 30" H, 26" W, 20" D $950.00*
PLANT STAND, by Gustav Stickley, unmarked, 27¾" H, 14¾" sq. $800.00*

A-MA Jun. 1993   *Skinner, Inc.*
SHAKER TABLE, birch, ca. 1800, old shellac, 24½" H, 27½" W, 17¼" D . . . $9350.00

A-MA May 1993   *Skinner, Inc.*
UTILITY TABLE, inlaid walnut, 18th c., 28" H, 36½" W $495.00

A-NH Aug. 1993   *Northeast Auctions*
TABLE, grained finish, New England, 37" L $5000.00*

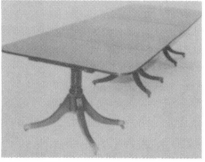

A-NH Aug. 1993   *Northeast Auctions*
HEPPLEWHITE DINING TABLE, 3-part, mahogany, 48" W, 120" L $8500.00*

A-NH Aug. 1993   *Northeast Auctions*
QUEEN ANNE TEA TABLE, mahogany, Rhode Island, 26" H, 36" W $3750.00*

A-MA Jun. 1993   *Skinner, Inc.*
REGENCY DINING TABLE, mahogany, England, 19th c., restored $3520.00

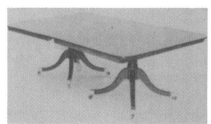

A-NH Aug. 1993   *Northeast Auctions*
REGENCY PEDESTAL DINING TABLE, mahogany, English, 54" W, 88" L $4750.00*

A-MA Aug. 1993   *Skinner, Inc.*
WORK TABLE, mahogany veneer, carved, NY, ca. 1820, old refinish, loss, 29½" H, 22½" W, 18" D $770.00

A-NH Aug. 1993   *Northeast Auctions*
TRIPLE-PEDESTAL DINING TABLE, mahogany, English, 46" W, 124" L . . $4750.00

A-NH Aug. 1993   *Northeast Auctions*
WORK TABLE, brass inlaid mahogany, game board top, Phila., 29" H, 30" L $2500.00*

A-MA Mar. 1993   *Skinner, Inc.*
FEDERAL DRESSING TABLE, tiger
maple, old refinish, imperfections, 30" H, 37"
W, 16" D $2200.00

A-MA Jan. 1993   *Skinner, Inc.*
HUTCH TABLE, cherry, 18th c., 29" H,
47½" D $2970.00

A-MA Jun. 1993   *Skinner, Inc.*
SHAKER TABLE, cherry, 19th c., imperfections, drawer initialed "E.B.K." in chalk,
28" H, 22" W, 30" D $7700.00

A-MA Oct. 1992   *Skinner, Inc.*
SHAKER WORK TABLE, cherry and
pine, 19th c., 29¼" H, top 36¼" x
25" $3850.00

A-MA Oct. 1992   *Skinner, Inc.*
**CHIPPENDALE BIRDCAGE TEA
TABLE,** mahogany, New England, 28" H,
34" D $1650.00

A-MA Jan. 1993   *Skinner, Inc.*
CHIPPENDALE TEA TABLE, walnut,
ca. 1780, 29½" H, 33" D $1320.00

A-MA Oct. 1992   *Skinner, Inc.*
FEDERAL DRESSING TABLE, Mahog-
any, ca. 1825, 38½" H, 33" W, 18"
D $605.00

A-IL Apr. 1993   *Leslie Hindman Auction*
SHERATON WORK TABLE, tiger maple,
19th c., 29" H, 21½" W, 20½"
D $2600.00*

A-MA Oct. 1992   *Skinner, Inc.*
CHIPPENDALE TEA TABLE, cherry,
27¾" H, top 33" x 30½" $935.00

A-MA Oct. 1992   *Skinner, Inc.*
CHIPPENDALE TEA TABLE, cherry
and pine, carved, ca. 1780, 28" H, top
35½" D $550.00

A-MA Jun. 1993   *Skinner, Inc.*
QUEEN ANNE DINING TABLE, maple, New England, ca. 1760, old refinish, imperfections, 27" H, 40" W, 41" D $1970.00

A-MA May 1993   *Skinner, Inc.*
BUTTERFLY TABLE, birch, New England, 18th c., 44" W, 49½" D $825.00

A-MA May 1993   *Skinner, Inc.*
QUEEN ANNE DINING TABLE, cherry, New England, 42" W, 51¾" D . . . $1760.00

A-MA May 1993   *Skinner, Inc.*
TAVERN TABLE, birch, 18th c., 26½" H $1100.00

A-MA Aug. 1993   *Skinner, Inc.*
WILLIAM AND MARY TABLE, New England, ca. 1740, old surface, restored, 29¼" H, 41¾" W, 47½" D $2860.00

A-IL Apr. 1993   *Leslie Hindman Auction*
PEMBROKE TABLE, cherry, burl elm, 19th c., turned and carved legs, 28" H, 20" W, 14" D $1400.00*

A-MA May 1993   *Skinner, Inc.*
QUEENE ANNE DROP LEAF TABLE, maple, 18th c., 26½" H $935.00

A-MA Dec. 1992   *Skinner, Inc.*
EXTENSION TABLE, cherry, ca. 1800, 28" H, 39" W, 23½" D $1500.00*

A-IL Apr. 1993   *Leslie Hindman Auction*
QUEEN ANNE DROP LEAF TABLE, walnut, 18th c., 28" H, 42" W, 15½" D $1600.00*

A-MD May 1993   *C.G. Sloan & Co., Inc.*
TAVERN TABLE, pine, maple, PA, red washed, 22" H, 27" W, 23" D . . . $1100.00*

A-MA Jun. 1993   *Skinner, Inc.*
FEDERAL PEMBROKE TABLE, inlaid mahogany, New England, ca. 1800, old refinish, 28" H, 15½" W, 32" D . . $1980.00

A-MA Jun. 1993   *Skinner, Inc.*
FEDERAL CHAMBER STAND, mahogany, Mass. ca. 1790, old refinish, 42" H, 22½" W, 15¾" D $935.00

A-NY Nov. 1992   *David Rago Gallery*
NIGHTSTAND, J.G. Stickley, 29½" H, 20" W, 18" D $1300.00*

A-MA Oct. 1992   *Skinner, Inc.*
CHIPPENDALE TILT-TOP TEA TABLE, mahogany, ca. 1780, 28½" H, top 32¾" D $1650.00

A-NH Aug. 1993   *Northeast Auctions*
HUTCH TABLE, maple, New England, 43" D $5500.00*

A-NH Aug. 1993   *Northeast Auctions*
SHERATON WORK TABLE, mahogany, Salem, 20" L $2500.00*
STAND, inlaid mahogany, New Hampshire, 21" L $1600.00*
SHERATON WORK TABLE, mahogany, New England, 22" L $3100.00*

A-MA Mar. 1993   *Skinner, Inc.*
FEDERAL WORK TABLE, mahogany, mahogany veneer, old refinish, imperfections, 26½" H, 19" W, 17¾" D $880.00

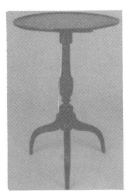

A-MA Mar. 1993   *Skinner, Inc.*
FEDERAL WORK TABLE, inlaid mahogany, old refinish, imperfections, 27¾" H, 19" W, 15" D $1870.00

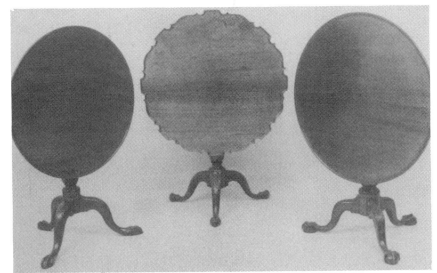

A-NH May. 1993   *Northeast Auctions*
CHIPPENDALE TILT-TOP TABLE, carved mahogany, 31" D $700.00*
CHIPPENDALE TILT-TOP TEA TABLE, 34" D $2700.00*
CHIPPENDALE BIRDCAGE TEA TABLE, carved mahogany, 34" D $1100.00*

A-MA Oct. 1992   *Skinner, Inc.*
FEDERAL TILT-TOP CANDLESTAND, cherry, ca. 1810, 29½" H, 19¾" D $1320.00

A-MA Oct. 1992   *Skinner, Inc.*
FEDERAL PEMBROKE TABLE, tiger
maple, ca. 1800, 28¼" H, 35" L, 17½"
D $5500.00

A-MA Oct. 1992   *Skinner, Inc.*
QUEEN ANNE DINING TABLE, mahog-
any, ca. 1770, 27" H, 47¾" L, 46½"
W $5500.00

A-MA Oct. 1992   *Skinner, Inc.*
QUEEN ANNE DINING TABLE, cherry,
ca. 1760, 28" H, 54" L, 54" W .. $7150.00

A-MA Oct. 1992   *Skinner, Inc.*
FEDERAL PEMBROKE TABLE, inlaid
cherry, ca. 1800, 28¾" H, 36" L, 18½"
D $1980.00

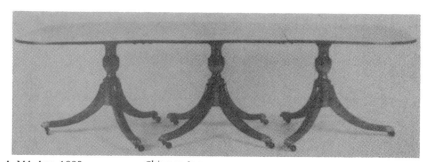

A-MA Apr. 1993   *Skinner, Inc.*
REGENCY THREE-PEDISTAL DINING TABLE, mahogany, 28½" H, 47½" W, 100½"
L $4400.00

A-MA Dec. 1992   *Skinner, Inc.*
REGENCY TWO-PEDESTAL DINING TABLE, mahogany, 2 leaves $3960.00

A-MA Oct. 1992   *Skinner, Inc.*
FEDERAL PEMBROKE TABLE, mahogany, ca. 1785, inlaid flutes, shaded
husks, overlapping ovals, 28½" H, 19⅛"
W, 31½" D $14300.00

A-MA Dec. 1992   *Skinner, Inc.*
REGENCY THREE-PEDESTAL DINING TABLE, ... $6050.00

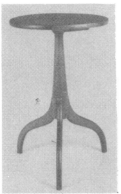

A-MA Jun. 1993   *Skinner, Inc.*
SHAKER STAND, cherry, old shellac, Thomas Hammond, Jr., Harvard, Mass., 17" H, 27" D $5500.00

A-MA Jan. 1993   *Skinner, Inc.*
CHIPPENDALE DISH-TOP TIP TABLE, mahogany, ca. 1780, 27¾" H, 19" D $550.00
CHIPPENDALE DISH-TOP TEA TABLE, mahogany, ca. 1780, 28" H, 25⅛" D $2090.00

A-MA Dec. 1992   *Skinner, Inc.*
QUEEN ANNE CANDLESTAND, cherry, stains, 28½" H $1600.00*

A-MA Dec. 1992   *Skinner, Inc.*
QUEEN ANNE CANDLESTAND, pine, oak, old refinish, wear, 27" H . . . $400.00*
HEPPLEWHITE CANDLESTAND, mahogany, refinished, repairs, warped, 28⅝" H $350.00*

A-MA Mar. 1993   *Skinner, Inc.*
CHIPPENDALE TIP-TOP TEA TABLE, walnut, refinished, repairs, 31" H, 22" D $605.00

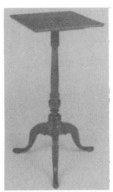

A-MA Oct. 1992   *Skinner, Inc.*
FEDERAL CANDLESTAND, inlaid cherry, ca. 1800, 27¼" H, top 12½" x 12¼" $3190.00

A-MA Oct. 1992   *Skinner, Inc.*
FEDERAL BANQUET TABLE, inlaid walnut, 29" H, 46 W, 92" L . . . $3025.00

A-MA Mar. 1993   *Skinner, Inc.*
WILLIAM AND MARY BUTTERFLY TABLE, birch, old refinish, imperfections, losses, 25" H, 27" W, 27" D $1210.00

A-NH May. 1993   *Northeast Auctions*
QUEEN ANNE DROP-LEAF TABLE, mahogany, Mass. 26" H, 29" D . . . $38000.00*

A-MA Oct. 1992   *Skinner, Inc.*
FEDERAL PEMBROKE TABLE, inlaid mahogany and veneer, ca. 1800, 28" H, 32" W, 38" D $1980.00

A-MD May 1993   *C.G. Sloan & Co., Inc.*
CANAPE AND PAIR FAUTEUILS, green silk upholstery $1200.00*
JARDINIERE STANDS, pr., oval marble-top inset, 37″ H, 18½″ W, 14″ D $1050.00*

A-MD May 1993   *C.G. Sloan & Co., Inc.*
SIDE CHAIRS, 4 pcs., (2 illus.), green silk $600.00*
CENTER TABLE, oval marble-top inset, 29½″ H, 29½″ W, 18½″ D $600.00*

A-NY Nov. 1992   *David Rago Gallery*
DROP-ARM MORRIS CHAIR, unmarked L. and J.G. Stickley, seat missing, refinished, 42½″ H, 32½″ W, 38½″ D $4500.00*
OCTAGONAL TABOURET, branded "Work of L. and J.G. Stickley," 17½″ H, 15″ sq. $600.00*

A-MA Jun. 1993   *Skinner, Inc.*
SHAKER ROCKER, maple, Enfield, 19th c., red stain, 39½″ H $3575.00
SHAKER TABLE, maple, birch, Canterbury, 19th c., old refinish, 26″ H, 30″ W, 18½″ D $2420.00

A-NY Nov. 1992   *David Rago Gallery*
CHAIR, by Gustav Stickley, leather seat, 37½″ H $2900.00*
BROOKS TABOURET, refinished, unmarked, 28½″ H, 18″ sq. $900.00*

A-NY Nov. 1992   *David Rago Gallery*
HIGH-BACK CHAIR, marked Ford/ Johnson, early restoration, 23½″ H $700.00*
JAR, hammered copper, original patina, 17¼″ H, 21½″ D $950.00*

A-NH Aug. 1993   *Northeast Auctions*
SIDE CHAIRS, 2 pcs., old finish, 1 carved $3750.00*
CHIPPENDALE TAVERN TABLE, New England, grain painted, 40″ L $2000.00*
PEG LAMPS, pr., Sheffield plated $250.00*
FOOT STOOLS, pr., Rhode Island, black paint, inscribed "Pew 96," 19″ L $3000.00*

A-NH Mar. 1993   *Northeast Auctions*
CHAIRS, 4 pcs., (3 illus.), windsor armchair, 3 ladderback chairs $650.00*
SAWBUCK TABLE, pine, scrubbed top, mustard painted base, 82" L $4500.00*

A-MA Dec. 1992   *Skinner, Inc.*
FLUID LAMP, blue Sandwich, brass font, 21" H $250.00*
SEWING TABLE,, mahogany, 28¾" H $525.00*
EMPIRE CHAIRS, set of 4, (1 illus.), mahogany $500.00*
FLUID LAMP, brass standard, brass font, marble base, electrified, 23¼" H $150.00*
SEWING TABLE, mahogany, satinwood facings, bag torn, 28⅝" H $1015.00*

A-ME Feb. 1993   *James D, Julia, Inc.*
RECEIVING HALL SET, 3 pc., MOP inlay, carved, laquered, labeled "Pekin," pr. carved armchairs, 38" H, marble-top demilune table, 34" H, 39" W, 19" D $1200.00*

A-NY Nov. 1992   *David Rago Gallery*
ROCKER AND ARMCHAIR, leather seats, wear, "Work of L. and J.G. STICKLEY" decals, 38" H $1600.00*

A-MA Jun. 1993   *Skinner, Inc.*
BLANKET BOX, painted, 19th c., imperfections, 20½" L, 15" W, 12" D . . . $1100.00

A-MA Dec. 1992   *Skinner, Inc.*
CHAIR TABLE, maple, refinished, 27½" H, 39½" W, 29½" D $600.00*
WALL BOX, pine, 19½" H, 13" W, 9½" D $600.00*
SETTLE, pine, old refinish, 64" H, 24" W, 14" D $950.00*
CANDLE TABLE, traces of red paint, 23½" H, 13" sq. $400.00*
WALL BOX, pine, green paint, wear, replacement, loss, 14¾" H, 13½" W, 9¼" D $450.00*

A-MA Jun. 1993 *Skinner, Inc.*
SHAKER WASH STAND, pine, chrome
yellow wash, ca. 1850, 38" H, 45¼" W, 16"
D $6050.00

A-MA Jun. 1993 *Skinner, Inc.*
SHAKER WOOD BOX W/DRAWER,
pine, poplar, 19th c., red stain, 30⅞" H, 34⅝"
W, 18½" D $1100.00

A-OH July 1993 *Garth's Auctions, Inc.*
EMPIRE CUPBOARD, grain painted wal-
nut, poplar, labeled "JAN HART JAN THE 4,
1847," 57¾" H, 39" W, 24" D . . . $1705.00
EAGLE, cast iron, gold repaint, 14"
H $220.00

A-NH Mar. 1993 *Northeast Auctions*
TILT-TOP TEA TABLE, mahogany, 34" D $3500.00*
CHIPPENDALE SIDE CHAIRS, pr. $1500.00*

A-MA Jun. 1993 *Skinner, Inc.*
SHAKER TILTING CHAIR, maple, birch,
19th c., refinished, 40¾" H $550.00
SHAKER STAND, birch, maple, 19th c.,
old refinish, 24½" H, 19¼" D $2310.00
SHAKER CHAIR, maple, 19th c., old refinish, imperfections, 40½" H $412.50

A-MA Dec. 1992 *Skinner, Inc.*
SHERATON BUREAU, maple, bird's eye maple, crack, replacements, 40" L $500.00
ROPE-LEG WASHSTAND, mahogany, 37¼" H, 18⅛" W, 16" D $325.00

A-MA Jun. 1993 *Skinner, Inc.*
CHIPPENDALE SIDE CHAIR, ca. 1790,
40½" H $605.00
CHIPPENDALE CANDLESTAND, maple,
New England, 18th c., refinished, 26" H,
18" D $440.00
CHIPPENDALE CHAIRS, 2 pcs., (1 illus.),
New England, 18th c., refinish . . . $220.00

A-MD May 1993   *C.G. Sloan & Co., Inc.*
WASHSTAND, bird's eye maple, 29″ H,
25¼″ W, 17″ D $1100.00*

A-MA Aug. 1993   *Skinner, Inc.*
FOUR PANEL SCREEN, Japanese, inlaid lacquer, 19th c., 73″ H, 97″ W $1100.00

A-MD May 1993   *C.G. Sloan & Co., Inc.*
ART NOUVEAU DINING TABLE, carved walnut, by Diot, one leaf, 29″ H, 46″ W, 51″
L $1250.00*

A-OH Nov. 1992   *Garth's Auctions, Inc.*
**CHIPPENDALE PENNSYLVANIA
WALL CUPBOARD,** pine, worn brown
finish, two piece, dovetailed drawers, wavy
glass, chamfered corners, shelf notched
for spoons, edge damage, replacements,
one cracked glass, 47″ W, 20″ D, 78½″
H $3025.00
CHALK GARNITURE, fruit and foliage,
original black, green, yellow and red paint,
14″ H $962.50

A-ME Feb. 1993   *James D, Julia, Inc.*
LIFT TOP BAKER'S TABLE, tiger maple, 19th c., 30" H, 44" W, 24" D ... $1450.00*
GAME BOARD, 2 sides, inlaid checker board, painted Parcheesi board, 19" x 28" $2350.00*

A-ME Feb. 1993   *James D, Julia, Inc.*
CHAIR TABLE, red paint, 30" H, 51" D $3000.00*
CHAIR TABLE, green paint, 29" H, 42" W $2750.00*

A-MA July 1993   *Skinner, Inc.*
VICTORIAN SPOOL CABINET, walnut, "Brainerd & Armstrong Co.," glass drawer fronts, mirror sides $990.00

A-NY Nov. 1992   *David Rago Gallery*
DROP LEAF TABLE, paper label Gustav Stickley, refinished, 29¾" x 32" $1100.00*
MAGAZINE STAND, L. and J.G. Stickley decal, 42" H, 18" W, 15" D $1300.00*

A-ME Feb. 1993   *James D, Julia, Inc.*
BENCH TABLE, pine, 18th c., refinished, 29" H, 34" W, 59" L $800.00*

A-NH Aug. 1993   *Northeast Auctions*
CARD TABLE, stenciled mahogany, Boston, 36" L $2000.00*
CANTERBURY, mahogany, stamped "T. W. Boston," 18" L $1500.00*

A-MA Dec. 1992   *Skinner, Inc.*
HEPPLEWHITE CANDLESTAND, walnut, old repair $325.00*
EMPIRE DROP-LEAF TABLE, mahogany, old refinish, 28¾" H, 39⅝" W, 22" D $400.00*

-MA Jan. 1993   *Skinner, Inc.*
CLASSICAL REVIVAL CELLARETTE, mahogany and veneer, ca. 1825, 33" H, 16½" W, 15" D $1045.00

A-IL Apr. 1993   *Leslie Hindman Auction*
GEORGE III STOOL, mahogany, 18th c., needlepoint seat, 17" H, 21½" W, 15" D $2200.00*

A-NH Aug. 1993   *Northeast Auctions*
LADY'S WINDSOR CHAIRS, pr., old green paint, New England $6000.00*
WORK TABLE, inlaid tiger maple, New England, 20″ L $18500.00*

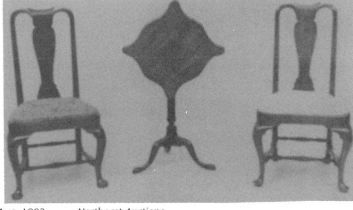

A-NH Aug. 1993   *Northeast Auctions*
QUEEN ANNE SIDE CHAIR, walnut, MA, balloon seat $8000.00
TILT-TOP CANDLESTAND, mahogany, MA, 17″ W $3750.00
QUEEN ANNE SIDE CHAIR, walnut, New England, balloon seat $1100.00

A-MA Jun. 1993   *Skinner, Inc.*
SHAKER ROCKER, maple, Canterbury, refinished, 33½″ H $330.00
SHAKER TABLE, cherry, birch, Canterbury, 19th c., old shellac, imperfections, 26″ H, 26″ W, 18″ D $1650.00
SHAKER ROCKER, maple, 19th c., 40½″ H $440.00

A-NH Aug. 1993   *Northeast Auctions*
FEDERAL MIRROR, Giltwood, Eglomise, Boston, labeled John Doggett, 34″ T $2000.00*

A-NH May. 1993   *Northeast Auctions*
QUEEN ANNE MIRROR, burl walnut, parcel-gilt, ca. 1750, 41″ H, 25″ W $16000.00*

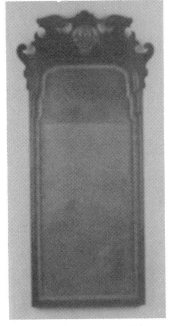

A-MA Oct. 1992   *Skinner, Inc.*
QUEEN ANNE MIRROR, walnut, gilt, ca. 1750, 48″ H, 22″ W $2200.00

A-NH May 1993   *Northeast Auctions*
AMERICAN DRESSING GLASS, mahogany, parcel-gilt, 25″ H, 14″ W . . $7000.00*

A-NH May. 1993   *Northeast Auctions*
CHIPPENDALE DRESSING GLASS, mahogany, American, 29″ H . . $1500.00*
HEPPLEWHITE BOWFRONT CHEST, mahogany, 32½″ H, 39½″ W . . $4000.00*

AGATA GLASS was patented by Joseph Locke of the New England Glass Company of Cambridge, Massachusetts, in 1877. The application of a metallic stain left a mottled design characteristic of agata, hence the name.

AMBER GLASS is the name of any glassware having a yellowish-brown color. It became popular during the last quarter of the 19th century.

AMBERINA GLASS was patented by the New England Glass Company in 1833. It is generally recognized as a clear yellow glass shading to a deep red or fushcia at the top. When the colors are opposite, it is known as reverse amberina. It was machine-pressed into molds, free blown, cut and pattern molded. Almost every glass factory here and in Europe produced this ware; however, few pieces were ever marked.

AMETHYST GLASS — The term identifies any glassware made in the proper dark purple shade. It became popular after the Civil War.

ART GLASS is a general term given to various types of ornamental glass made to be decorative rather than functional. It dates primarily from the late Victorian period to the present day and, during the span of time, glassmakers have achieved fantastic effects of shape, color, pattern, texture and decoration.

AVENTURINE GLASS — The Venetians are credited with the discovery of aventurine during the 1860s. It was produced by various mixes of copper in yellow glass. When the finished pieces were broken, ground or crushed, they were used as decorative material by glassblowers. Therefore, a piece of aventurine glass consists of many tiny glittering particles on the body of the object, suggestive of sprinkled gold crumbs or dust. Other colors in aventurine are known to exist.

BACCARAT GLASS was first made in France in 1756 by La Compagnie des Cristelleries de Baccarat—until the firm went bankrupt. Production began for the second time during the 1820s and the firm is still in operation, producing fine glassware and paperweights. Baccarat is famous for its earlier paperweights made during the last half of the 19th century.

BOHEMIAN GLASS is named for its country of origin. It is ornate, overlay, or flashed glassware, popular during the Victorian era.

BRISTOL GLASS is a lightweight opaque glass, often having a light bluish tint, and decorated with enamels. The ware is a product of Bristol, England—a glass center since the 1700s.

BURMESE — Frederick Shirley developed this shaded art glass at the now-famous old Mt. Washington Glass Company in New Bedford, Massachusetts, and patented his discovery under the name of "Burmese" on December 15, 1885. The ware was also made in England by Thomas Webb & Sons.

Burmese is a hand-blown glass with the exception of a few pieces that were pattern molded. The latter are either ribbed, hobnail or diamond quilted in design. This ware is found in two textures or finishes: the original glazed or shiny finish, and the dull, velvety, satin finish. It is a homogeneous glass (singlelayered) that was never lined, cased or plated. Although its color varies slightly, it always shades from a delicate yellow at the base to a lovely salmon-pink at the top. The blending of colors is so gradual that it is difficult to determine where one color ends and the other begins.

CAMBRIDGE glasswares were produced by the Cambridge Glass Company in Ohio from 1901 until the firm closed in 1954.

CAMEO GLASS can be defined as any glass in which the surface has been cut away to leave a design in relief. Cutting is accomplished by the use of hand-cutting tools, wheel cutting and hydrofluoric acid. This ware can be clear or colored glass of a single layer, or glass with multiple layers of clear or colored glass.

Although cameo glass has been produced for centuries, the majority available today dates from the late 1800s. It has been produced in England, France and other parts of Europe, as well as the United States. The most famous of the French masters of cameo wares was Emile Gallé.

CANDY CONTAINTERS were used for holding tiny candy pellets. These were produced in a variety of shapes—locomotives, cars, boats, guns, and such, for children.

CARNIVAL GLASS was an inexpensive, pressed iridescent glassware made from about 1900 through the 1920s. It was made in quantitites by Northwood Glass Company, Fenton Art Glass Company and others, to compete with the expensive art glass of the period. Originally called "taffeta" glass, the ware became known as "carnival" glass during the 1920s when carnivals gave examples as premiums or prizes.

CORALENE — The term coralene denotes a type of decoration rather than a kind of glass—consisting of many tiny beads, either of colored or transparent glass—decorating the surface. The most popular design used resembled coral or seaweed, hence the name.

CRACKLE GLASS — This type of art glass was an invention of the Venetians that spread rapidly to other countries. It is made by plunging red-hot glass into cold water, then reheating and reblowing it, thus producing an unusual outer surface which appears to be covered with a multitiude of tiny fractures, but is perfectly smooth to the touch.

CRANBERRY GLASS — The term "cranberry glass" refers to color only, not to a particular type of glass. It is undoubtedly the most familiar colored glass known to collectors. This ware was blown or molded, and often decorated with enamels.

CROWN MILANO glass was made by Frederick Shirley at the Mt. Washington Glass Company, New Bedford, Massachusetts, from 1886-1888. It is ivory in color with a satin finish, and was embellished with floral sprays, scrolls and gold enamel.

CROWN TUSCAN glass has a pink-opaque body. It was originally produced in 1936 by A.J. Bennett, president of the Cambridge Glass Company of Cambridge, Ohio. The line was discontinued in 1954. Occasionally referred to as Royal Crown Tuscan, this ware was named for a scenic area in Italy, and it has been said that its color was taken from the fresh-colored sky at sunrise. When transilluminated, examples do have all of the blaze of a sunrise—a characteristic that is even applied to new examples of the ware reproduced by Mrs. Elizabeth Degenhart of Crystal Art Glass, and Harold D. Bennett, Guernsey Glass Company of Cambridge, Ohio.

CUSTARD GLASS was manufactured in the United States for a period of about 30 years (1885-1915). Although Harry Northwood was the first and largest manufacturer of custard glass, it was also produced by the Heisey Glass Company, Diamond Glass Company, Fenton Art Glass Company and a number of others.

The name custard glass is derived from its "custard yellow" color which may shade light yellow to ivory to light green—glass that is opaque to opalescent. Most pieces have fiery opalescence when held to the light. Both the color and glow of this ware came from the use of uranium salts in the glass. It is generally a heavy type pressed glass made in a variety of different patterns.

CUT OVERLAY — The term identifies pieces of glassware usually having a milk-white exterior that have been cased with cranberry, blue or amber glass. Other type examples are deep blue, amber or cranberry on crystal glass, and the majority of pieces has been decorated with dainty flowers. Although Bohemian glass manufacturers produced some very choice pieces during the 19th century, fine examples were also made in America, as well as in France and England.

DAUM NANCY is the mark found on pieces of French cameo glass made by August and Antonin Daum after 1875.

DURAND ART GLASS was made by Victor Durand from 1879 to 1935 at the Durand Art Glass Works in Vineland, New Jersey. The glass resembles Tiffany in quality. Drawn white feather designs and thinly drawn glass threading (quite brittle) applied around the main body of the ware, are striking examples of Durand creations on an iridescent surface.

FLASHED WARES were popular during the late 19th century. They were made by partially coating the inner surface of an object with a thin plating of glass or another, more dominant color—usually red. These pieces can readily be identified by holding the object to the light and examining the rim, as it will show more than one layer of glass. Many pieces of "rubina crystal" (cranberry to clear), "blue amberina" (blue to amber), and "rubina verde" (cranberry to green), were manufactured in this way.

FINDLAY or ONYX art glass was manufactured about 1890 for only a short time by the Dalzell Gilmore Leighton Company of Findlay, Ohio.

FRANCISWARE is a hobnail glassware with frosted or clear glass hobs and stained amber rims and tops. It was produced during the late 1880s by Hobbs, Brockunier and Company.

FRY GLASS was made by the H.C. Fry Company, Rochester, Pennsylvania, from 1901, when the firm was organized, until 1934 when operations ceased. The firm specialized in the manufacturing of cut glassware. The production of their famous "foval" glass did not begin until the 1920s. The firm also produced a variety of glass specialties, oven wares and etched glass.

GALLÉ glass was made in Nancy, France, by Emile Gallé at the Gallé Factory founded in 1874. The firm produced both enameled and cameo glass, pottery, furniture and other art nouveau items. After Gallé 's death in 1904, the factory continued operating until 1935.

GREENTOWN glass was made in Greentown, Indiana, by the Indiana Tumbler and Goblet Company from 1894 until 1903. The firm produced a variety of pressed glasswares in addition to milk and chocolate glass.

GUNDERSON peachblow is a more recent type art glass produced in 1952 by the Gunderson-Pairpoint Glass Works of New Bedford, Massachusetts, successors to the Mt. Washington Glass Company. Gunderson pieces have a soft satin finish shading from white at the base to a deep rose at the top.

HOBNAIL — The term hobnail identifies any glassware having "bumps"—flattened, rounded or pointed—over the outer surface of the glass. A variety of patterns exists. Many of the fine early examples were produced by Hobbs, Brockunier and Company, Wheeling, West Virginia, and the New England Glass Company.

HOLLY AMBER, originally known as "golden agate," is a pressed glass pattern which features holly berries and leaves over its glossy surface. Its color shades from golden brown tones to opalescent streaks. This ware was produced by the Indiana Tumbler and Goblet Company for only 6 months, from January 1 to June 13, 1903. Examples are rare and expensive.

IMPERIAL GLASS — The Imperial Glass Company of Bellaire, Ohio, was organized in 1901 by a group of prominent citizens of Wheeling, West Virginia. A variety of fine art glass, in addition to carnival glass, was produced by the firm. The two trademarks which identified the ware were issued in June 1914. One consisted of the firm's name, "Imperial," and the other included a cross formed by double-pointed arrows.

The latter ll of their present production—including reproduced carnival glass.

LATTICINO is the name given to articles of glass in which a network of tiny milk-white lines appear, crisscrossing between two walls of glass. It is a type of filigree glassware developed during the 16th century by the Venetians.

LEGRAS GLASS, cameo, acid cut and enameled glasswares were made by August J.F. Legras at Saint-Denis, France, from 1864-1914.

LOETZ GLASS was made in Austria just before the turn of the century. As Loetz worked in the Tiffany factory before returning to Austria, much of his glass is similar in appearance to Tiffany wares. Loetz glass is often marked "Loetz" or "Loetz-Austria."

LUTZ GLASS was made by Nicholas Lutz, a Frenchman, who worked at the Boston and Sandwich Glass Company from 1870 to 1888 when it closed. He also produced fine glass at the Mt. Washington Glass Company. Lutz is noted for two different types of glass—striped and threaded wares. Other glass houses also produced similar glass and these wares were known as Lutz-type.

MARY GREGORY was an artist for the Boston and Sandwich Glass Company during the last quarter of the 19th century. She decorated glassware with white enamel figures of young children engaged in playing, collecting butterflies, etc., in white on transparent glass, both clear and colored. Today the term "Mary Gregory" glass applies to any glassware that remotely resembles her work.

MERCURY GLASS is a double-walled glass that dates from the 1850s to about 1910. It was made in England as well as the United States during this period. Its interior, usually in the form of vases, is lined with flashing mercury, giving the items an all over silvery appearance. The entrance hole in the base of each piece was sealed over. Many pieces were decorated.

MILK GLASS is an opaque pressed glassware, usually of milk-white color, although green, amethyst, black, and shades of blue were made. Milk glass was produced in quantity in the United States during the 1880s, in a variety of patterns.

MILLEFIORI — This decorative glassware is considered to be a specialty of the Venetians. It is sometimes called "glass of a thousand flowers," and has been made for centuries. Very thin colored glass rods are arranged in bundles, then fused together with heat. When the piece of glass is sliced across, it has a design like that of many small flowers. These tiny wafer-thin slices are then embedded in larger masses of glass, enlarged and shaped.

MOSER GLASS was made by Kolomon Moser at Carlsbad. The ware is considered to be another type of art nouveau glass as it was produced during its heyday—during the early 1900s. Principal colors included amethyst, cranberry, green and blue, with fancy enameled decoration.

MOTHER-OF-PEARL, often abbreviated in descriptions as M.O.P., is glass composed of two or more layers, with a pattern showing through to the other surface. The pattern, caused by internal air traps, is created by expanding the inside layer of molten glass into molds with varying design. When another layer of glass is applied, this brings out the design. The final layer of glass is then acid dipped, and the result is mother-of-pearl satinware. Patterns are numerous. The most frequently found are the diamond quilted, raindrop and herringbone. This ware can be one solid color, a single color shading light to dark, two colors blended or a variety of colors which include the rainbow effect. In addition, many pieces are decorated with colorful enamels, coralene beading, and other applied glass decorations.

NAILSEA GLASS was first produced in England from 1788 to 1873. The characteristics that identify this ware are the "pulled" loopings and swirls of colored glass over the body of the object.

NEW ENGLAND PEACHBLOW was patented in 1886 by the New England Glass Company. It is a single-layered glass shading from opaque white at the base to deep rose-red or raspberry at the top. Some pieces have a glossy surface, but most were given an acid bath to produce a soft, matte finish.

NEW MARTINSVILLE PEACHBLOW GLASS was produced from 1901-1907 at New Martinsville, Pennsylvania.

OPALESCENT GLASS — The term refers to glasswares which have a milky white effect in the glass, usually on a colored ground. There are three basic types of this ware. Presently, the most popular includes pressed glass patterns found in table settings. Here the opalescence appears at the top rim, the base, or a combination of both. On blown or mold-blown glass, the pattern itself consists of this milky effect—such as Spanish lace. Another example is the opalescent points on some pieces of hobnail glass. These wares are lighter weight. The third group includes opalescent novelties, primarily of the pressed variety.

PEKING GLASS is a type of Chinese cameo glass produced from the 1700s, well into the 19th century.

PHOENIX GLASS — The firm was established in Beaver County, Pennsylvania, during the late 1800s, and produced a variety of commercial glasswares. During the 1930s the factory made a desirable sculptured gift-type glassware which has become very collectible in recent years. Vases, lamps, bowls, ginger jars, candlesticks, etc., were made until the 1950s in various colors with a satin finish.

PIGEON BLOOD is a bright reddish-orange glassware dating from the early 1900s.

POMONA GLASS was invented in 1884 by Joseph Locke at the New England Glass Company.

PRESSED GLASS was the inexpensive glassware produced in quantity to fill the increasing demand for tablewares when Americans moved away from the simple table utensils of pioneer times. During the 1820s, ingenious Yankees invented and perfected machinery for successfullly pressing glass. About 1865, manufacturers began to color their products. Literally hundreds of different patterns were produced.

QUEZAL is a very fine quality blown iridescent glassware produced by Martin Bach, in his factory in Brooklyn, New York, from 1901-1920. Named after the Central American bird, quezal glassware has an iridescent finish featuring contrasting colored glass threads. Green, white and gold colors are most often found.

ROSALINE GLASS is a product of the Steuben Glass Works of Corning, New York. The firm was founded by Frederick Carter and T.C. Hawkes, Sr. Rosaline is a rose-colored jade glass or colored alabaster. The firm is now owned by the Corning Glass Company, which is presently producing fine glass of exceptional quality.

ROYAL FLEMISH ART GLASS was made by the Mt. Washington Glass Works during the 1880s. It has an acid finish which may consist of one or more colors, decorated with raised gold enameled lines separating into sections. Fanciful painted enamel designs also decorate this ware. Royal Flemish glass is marked "RF," with the letter "R" reversed and backed to the letter "F," within a four-sided orange-red diamond mark.

RUBINA GLASS is a transparent blown glassware that shades from clear to red. One of the first to produce this crystal during the late 1800s was Hobbs, Brocunier and Company of Wheeling, West Virginia.

RUBINA VERDE is a blown art glass made by Hobbs, Brocunier and Company, during the late 1800s. It is a transparent glassware that shades from red to yellow-green.

SABINO GLASS originated in Paris, France, in the 1920s. The company was founded by Marius-Ernest Sabine, and was noted for art deco figures, vases, animals, nudes and animals in clear, opalescent and colored glass.

SANDWICH GLASS — One of the most interesting and enduring pages from America's past is Sandwich glass produced by the famous Boston and Sandwich Glass Company at Sandwich, Massachusetts. The firm began operations in 1825, and the glass flour-ished until 1888 when the factory closed. Despite the popularity of Sandwich Glass, little is known about its founder, Deming Jarvis.

The Sandwich Glass house turned out hundreds of designs in both plain and figured patterns, in colors and crystal, so that no one type could be considered entirely typical—but the best known is the "lacy" glass produced there. The variety and multitude of designs and patterns produced by the company over the years is a tribute to its greatness.

SILVER DEPOSIT GLASS was made during the late 19th and early 20th centuries. Silver was deposited on the glass surface by a chemical process so that a pattern appeared against a clear or colored ground. This ware is sometimes referred to as "silver overlay."

SLAG GLASS was originally known as "mosaic" and "marble glass" because of its streaked appearance. Production in the United States began about 1880. The largest producer of this ware was Challinor, Taylor and Company, The various slag mixtures are: purple, butterscotch, blue, orange, green and chocolate. A small quantity of pink slag was also produced in the inverted fan and feather pattern. Examples are rare and expensive.

SPANISH LACE is a Victorian glass pattern that is easily identified by its distinct opalescent flower and leaf pattern. It belongs to the shaded opalescent glass family.

STEUBEN — The Steuben Glass Works was founded in 1904 by Frederick Carter, an Englishman, and T.G. Hawkes, Sr., at Corning, New York. In 1918 the firm was purchased by the Corning Glass Company. However, Steuben remained with the firm, designing a bounty of fine art glass of exceptional quality.

STIEGEL-TYPE GLASS — Henry William Stiegel founded America's first flint glass factory during the 1760s at Manheim, Pennsylvania. Stiegel glass is flint or crystal glass; it is thin and clear, and has a bell-like ring when tapped. The ware is quite brittle and fragile. Designs were painted free-hand on the glass—birds, animals and architectural motifs, surrounded by leaves and flowers. The engraved glass resulted from craftsmen etching the glass surface with a copper wheel, then cutting the desired patterns.

It is extremely difficult to identify, with certainty, a piece of original Stiegel glass. Part of the problem resulted from the lack of an identifying mark on the products. Additionally, many of the craftsmen moved to other areas after the Stiegel plant closed—producing a similar glass product. Therefore, when one is uncertain about the origin of this type ware, it is referred to as "Stiegel-type" glass.

TIFFANY GLASS was made by Louis Comfort Tiffany, one of America's outstanding glass designers of the art nouveau period, from about 1870 to the 1930s. Tiffany's designs included a variety of lamps, bronze work, silver, pottery and stained glass windows. Practically all items made were marked "L.C. Tiffany" or L.C.T." in addition to the word "Favrile"—the French word for color.

TORTOISESHELL GLASS — As its name indicates, this type glassware resembles the color of tortoiseshell and has deep rich brown tones combined with amber and cream-colored shades. Tortoiseshell glass was originally produced in 1880 by Francis Pohl, a German chemist. It was also made in the United States by the Sandwich Glass Works and other glass houses during the late 1800s.

VAL ST. LAMBERT Cristalleries, located in Belgium, was founded in 1825 and the firm is still in operation.

VASA MURRHINA glassware was produced in quantity at the Vasa Murrhina Art Glass Company of Sandwich, Massachusetts, during the late 1900s. John C. DeVoy, assignor to the firm, registered a patent on July 1, 1884, for the process of decorating glassware with particles of mica flakes (coated with copper, gold, nickel or silver) sandwiched between an inner layer of clear or transparent colored glass. The ware was also produced by other American glass firms and in England.

VASELINE GLASS — The term "vaseline" refers to color only, as it resembles the greenish-yellow color typical of the oily petroleum jelly known as Vaseline. This ware has been produced in a variety of patterns both here and in Europe—from the late 1800s. It has been made in both clear and opaque yellow, vaseline combined with clear glass, and occasionally the two colors are combined in one piece.

VERLYS GLASS is a type of art glass produced in France after 1931. The Heisey Glass Company, Newark, Ohio, produced identical glass for a short time, after having obtained the rights and formula from the French factory. French-produced ware can be identified from the American product by the signature, the French is mold marked, whereas the American glass is etched script signed.

WAVECREST GLASS is an opaque white glassware made from the late 1890s by French factories and the Pairpoint Manufacturing Company at New Bedford, Massachusetts. Items were decorated by the C.F. Monroe Company of Meriden, Connecticut, with painted pastel enamels. The name wavecrest was used after 1898 with the initials for the company "C.F.M. Co." Operations ceased during World War II.

WEBB GLASS was made by Thomas Webb & Sons of Stourbridge, England, during the late Victorian period. The firm produced a variety of different types of art and cameo glass.

WHEELING PEACHBLOW — With its simple lines and delicate shadings, Wheeling Peachblow was produced soon after 1883 by J.H. Hobbs, Brockunier and Company at Wheeling, West Virginia. It is a two-layered glass lined or cased inside with an opaque, milk-white type of plated glassware. The outer layer shades from a bright yellow at the base to a mahogany red at the top. The majority of pieces produced are in the glossy finish.

A-MA Nov. 1992   *James D. Julia, Inc.*
VASE, mulberry cameo on frosted glass, signed "CV Esgiere Nancy," 14" T $600.00
DAUM-NANCY DECANTER, enameled lake scene on white opalescent ground, signed, 9½" T $2200.00
GALLE VASE, fire polished cameo glass, purple iris on frosted, shaded purple ground, 13½" T $2200.00

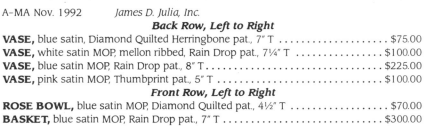

A-MA Nov. 1992   *James D. Julia, Inc.*

Back Row, Left to Right
VASE, blue satin, Diamond Quilted Herringbone pat., 7" T $75.00
VASE, white satin MOP, mellon ribbed, Rain Drop pat., 7¼" T $100.00
VASE, blue satin MOP, Rain Drop pat., 8" T $225.00
VASE, pink satin MOP, Thumbprint pat., 5" T $100.00

Front Row, Left to Right
ROSE BOWL, blue satin MOP, Diamond Quilted pat., 4½" T $70.00
BASKET, blue satin MOP, Rain Drop pat., 7" T $300.00
VASE, blue satin MOP, Diamond Quilted pat., 5" T $75.00

A-MD May 1993   *C.G. Sloan & Co., Inc.*
GLASS BASKETS

Pictured Left to Right
CASED GLASS, 2 pcs., blue, white, clear handles, up to 7" T $150.00*
PEACH BLOW, 2 pcs., up to 6¾" T $160.00*
MOTTLED GLASS, 2 pcs., Czech, molded, clear "thorny" handles, up to 9¾" T $200.00*
OPALESCENT GLASS, cranberry to yellow, clear handle, 6¾" T $140.00*
CASED GLASS, 2 pcs., Czech, green/white mottled body encased in clear melon ribbed glass, twisted clear handle, 6" T $140.00*
BASKETS, 2 pcs., Czech, cranberry/white striped, clear handles, up to 5½" T .. $200.00*
FLAME GLASS, 2 pcs., red to yellow interior, yellow exterior, clear "thorny" handles, up to 5¾" T $270.00*

A-MA Nov. 1992   *James D. Julia, Inc.*
LAVERRE FRANCAIS EWER, brown, orange cameo on mottled yellow ground, orange foot, 12" T $800.00
A. DELATTE NANCY VASE, gourd form, red cased glass, enameled dec., 11" T $475.00
LAVERRE FRANCAIS VASE, brown, orange cameo on mottled yellow ground, 14" T $850.00
GALLE ATOMIZER, lavendar cameo on shaded yellow and frosted ground, 8" T $1250.00

N-229   150   197   145   339   130   227   154   61   316

338   118   186   51   187   65   236   334

73   231   139   256   234   373   297   239   168

274   203   110   68   220   142   132   136   290

A-OH Apr. 1993 *Early Auction Co.*

Row 1, Left to Right
N-229 STEUBEN VASE, mkd. w/fleur-de-lis, 9½" T $800.00*
150 HANDEL LAMP, green, red, yellow, leaded shade, bronzed base, 29" T . . . NS
197 BURMESE VASE, acid finish, blue & white enamel dec., 11¾" T $750.00*
145 STEVENS & WILLIAMS VASE, blue satin hobnail, w/camphor Matsu-no-ke vine $400.00*
339 QUEZAL VASE, gold, random King Tut pat., by Larson, 13" T $1150.00*
130 CAMEO VASE, French, signed Le Vez, 11¾" T $1100.00*
277 IMPERIAL VASE, cobalt, opal hearts, vines, 6½" T $375.00*
154 TIFFANY FAVRILE VASE, iridescent gold, signed, 19" T $1900.00*
61 FAIRY LAMP, cream, pink, 2½" T $775.00*
316 STEUBEN CLUTHRA VASE, white, signed w/fleu-de-lis, 10½" T . . $1000.00*

Row 2, Left to Right
338 V. DURAND VASE, gold, signed, 6" T $375.00*
118 WEBB PEACHBLOW CORALENE PITCHER, 4¾" T $500.00*
186 WHEELING PEACHBLOW MORGAN VASE, amber Griffin holder, 7¾" T $1000.00*

51 BURMESE VASE, acid finish, enamel dec., 4¼" T $250.00*
187 STEUBEN ALABASTER ACB VASE, mkd w/fleur-de-lis, lt. blue dec., 8" D, 7" T $1000.00*
65 BURMESE VASE, acid finish, 4¾" T $1050.00*
236 DAUM NANCY CAMEO VASE, French, signed, mold blown, green on marmalade, 11" T $5000.00*
334 NASH VASE, signed, tomato red, 9" T $675.00*

Row 3, Left to Right
73 MT. WASHINGTON PEACHBLOW VASE, acid finish, 9" T $2700.00*
231 DAUM NANCY CAMEO SCENT BOTTLE, signed, brown on citron, 4½" T $1900.00*
139 BURMESE FAIRY LAMP, acid finish, in 4-arm metal stand w/4 Burmese holders w/camphor berry pontils, 9½" D, 5½" T $1200.00*
234 FINDLAY MUSTARD POT, onyx, hinged metal top, 3" T $650.00*
256 LOETZ AUSTRIA VASE, signed, iridescent pink, 9" T $400.00*
373 HELMSCHMIED SWIRL HINGED BOX, pink morning glories on grey-green ground, overlaid w/grey web design outlined w/raised pink enamel, 6" D, 4" T $650.00*

297 STEUBEN BASKET, calcite, gold interior and handle, 7½" T $750.00*
239 PAIRPOINT LOTUS LAMP, green, white, pink, 16" T . . . . NS
168 WEBB VASE, blue satin MOP, 8" T $400.00*

Row 4, Left to Right
274 IMPERIAL VASE, marigold w/ textured cobalt leaves & vines, 7" T $400.00*
203 BURMESE VASE, acid finish, 3½" T $200.00*
110 CROWN MILANO ROSE BOWL, mkd., floral dec. on pink to white satin ground, 5½" D $425.00*
220 BURMESE TOOTHPICK, acid finish, enamel dec., 2¾" T $450.00*
68 BURMESE LEMONADE, shiny, 5" T $275.00*
142 MT. WASHINGTON COCKLE-SHELL SALT & PEPPER, frosted w/ enamel dec., in figural donkey holder, 5" T $3250.00*
132 TIFFANY FAVRILLE CENTER BOWL W/FROG, iridescent gold, signed, 13" D $800.00*
136 CROWN MILANO BISCUIT JAR, floral and gold dec. on cream ground, 7½" D $700.00*
290 TIFFANY FAVRILE VASE, black w/platinum dec., 5½" T . . . . NS

A-MA Nov. 1992 *James D. Julia, Inc.*

Back Row, Left to Right
VASE, yellow satin shading to white MOP, Diamond Quilted pat., 8¾" T $125.00
VASE, pink satin MOP, Thumbprint pat., 12½" T $240.00
VASE, pastel rainbow satin MOP, Herringbone pat., 13" T . . . . NS
VASE, yellow shading to white satin MOP, Herringbone pat., 7¼" T $50.00
SPOONER, rainbow satin MOP, Diamond Quilted pat., 6¼" T $275.00

Front Row, Left to Right
VASE, lt. blue satin MOP, Diamond Duilted pat., 4½" T . . . . NS
CANDY DISH, jewel and enamel dec. rainbow satin MOP, jewel loss, 6" D . . . . NS
ROSE BOWL, pink satin MOP, Thumbprint pat., 2¾" T, 4¼" D $150.00

A-PA May 1993 *Glass Works Auctions*
FLASKS

SCROLL, ca. 1840-1850, amber pint $225.00*
SCROLL, ca. 1830-1850, gold pint, chip $225.00*
SCROLL, 1840-1850, deep amber pint $350.00*

A-OH Apr. 1993   *Early Auction Co.*

Row 1, Left to Right
159 KIMBALL CLUTHRA VASE, mottled yellow and opal, mkd., 11" T $350.00*
215 BURMESE WINE, shiny, green vine & berries, 4½" T $800.00*
250 PAIRPOINT LAMP, Stratford shade w/pink & blue flowers, silver base, mkd., 14½" T $2800.00*
337 DURAND COMPOTE, iridescent royal blue w/lt. blue dec., amber base, 4½" T $1000.00*
176 TIFFANY FAVRILE VASE, iridescent gold, 15½" T $1100.00*
43 CAMEO VASE, French, plum, signed Le Verre Francais, 10¾" T $650.00*
122 WHEELING PEACHBLOW CREAMER, shiny, amber handle, 3" T $575.00*
295 STEUBEN VASE, ivorene, signed, 12" T $900.00*
179 WEBB PEACHBLOW VASE, shiny, raised gold dec., 7¼" T $250.00*
138 NAILSEA FAIRY LAMP, chartreuse satin, pressed clear Clarke's holder, 5¾" T $600.00*
47 HANDEL LAMP, signed rev. painted shade, labeled bronzed base . . $1900.00*

Row 2, Left to Right
335 DURAND VASE, ribbed, blue, 12" T $950.00*
140 BURMESE FAIRY LAMP, acid finish, clear pressed Eden holder, Thomas Webb & Sons & S. Clarke's Patent . . . $1100.00*
104 WHEELING PEACHBLOW LIN-COLN DRAPE PITCHER, shiny, clear handle, 4" T $500.00*

79 QUEZAL VASE, signed, green pulled feathers on opal, gold interior, 6" T $825.00*
50 WEBB CAMEO VASE, English, white on golden amber ground, 5" T . . $750.00*
180 CROWN MILANO CRACKER JAR, yellow & maroon on shaded apricot ground, 5½" D $800.00*
189 GALLE CAMEO VASE, French, frosted apricot dec. on lt. apricot ground, signed, 3¾" T $675.00*
131 TIFFANY FAVRILE BASE, iridescent lavender, signed, 12" T $850.00*

Row 3, Left to Right
198 BURMESE VASE, ornate de. w/ raised gold scrolls, white enamel flowers, acid finish, 11" T $4000.00*
218 BURMESE VASE, acid finish, raspberry dec., chips, 3½" T $475.00*
164 STEUBEN AURENE BOWL, iridescent gold, signed, 11½" D $350.00*
209 BURMESE VASE, acid finish, 13¾" T $600.00*
13 TOOTHPICK, amber, Holly pat., 2¼" T $425.00*
165 STEUBEN VASE, gold calcite, 6¼" T $300.00*
194 VASE, translucent red w/iridescent gold, 3½" T . . . . NS
288 TIFFANY FAVRILE CANDLE LAMP, iridescent green w/blue shade, iridescent gold base, 11¾" T $1100.00*
81 TARTAN FAIRY LAMP, rainbow pastel plaid, w/ orig. candle, roughness $1650.00*
287 TIFFANY VASE, iridescent gold, signed, 12" T $700.00*
92 AGATA TOOTHPICK, New England, 2" T $700.00*

257 DURAND VASE, Lady Gay Rose ground w/iridescent King Tut design, orange interior, 8" T $2000.00*
230 BACCARAT VASE, mkd., dk. snake in opalescent stalk, 9" T . . . . NS

Row 4, Left to Right
167 WEBB SWEETMEAT, chartreuse satin MOP, silver cover, 5" D $500.00*
219 BURMESE VASE, raised painted dec., shiny, 2½" T $875.00*
129 DAUM NANCY CAMEO VASE, blue on frost, 4¾" T . . . . NS
369 KELVA TRAY, blue daisies, mottled maroon ground, 3½" D $300.00*
91 VASE, alexandrite, 16" T . . $1550.00*
96 CROWN MILANO CUP & SAUCER, paper labels, raised gold and floral dec. $2400.00*
99 WEBB PEACHBLOW COLOGNE, shiny, raised gold netting dec., gold wash top, mkd., 4½" T $500.00*
184 DURAND COVERED DRESSER JAR, transparent iridescent amber, cut w/feathered flowers and leafy stems, 4½" D, 3" T $255.00*
285 TIFFANY FAVRILE BOWL, Tel El Armana dec., signed, 11" D . . . $1250.00*
116 AGATA PUNCH CUP, New England, 2¼" T $625.00*
80 VASE, ribbed, rose, dut velvet, camphor edge, 5" T $325.00*
88 MILLEFIORI FINGER BOWL & UNDERPLATE, iridescent gold, mkd., signed L.C.T. $1250.00*
228 STEUBEN PERFUME, iridescent blue-gold, signed Aurene, 8" T . . $450.00*
49 GALLE CAMEO VASE, citron & lavender ships on blue, brown, citron sky & water, signed, 4½" T $850.00*

A-PA May 1993   *Glass Works Auctions*
BEER BOTTLES

SWAN BREWERY, ca. 1870–1875, yellow-green, stain, 6¼" T $650.00*
W.B. CO., ca. 1870–1875, deep aqua, bruise, 6⅛" T $575.00*
D. TWEDIE, ca. 1890–1900, olive, 7⅝" T $100.00*

A-PA May 1993   *Glass Works Auctions*
VELVET CREAM & DAIRY PRODUCTS, ca. 1940–1950, clear quart, red paint $60.00*
SELTZER BOTTLE, ca. 1920–1930, clear glass, blue paint, 11⅞" T $30.00*
SELTZER BOTTLE, ca. 1920–1930, acid etched clear glass, colored transfer label, 11⅜" T $190.00*

A-PA May 1993   *Glass Works Auctions*
BOTTLES

EAGLE, ca. 1820–1840, amber pint $100.00*
EAGLE, ca. 1830–1840, yellow-olive pint $180.00*
EAGLE, ca. 1850–1860, Granite Glass Co., amber pint $190.00*

A-MA Nov. 1992   *James D. Julia, Inc.*
LOETZ STERLING SILVER OVERLAY VASES

Row 1, Left to Right
VASE, blue art glass, 4¼" T $750.00
VASES, 2 pcs., (1 illus.), 1 grey-green, internally decorated, rough edge, 4¾" T, 1 cranberry cased white glass, 3½" T $400.00
VASE, Gold Raindrop irridescent, 2½" W, 4½" T $550.00

Row 2, Left to Right
VASE, gold iridescent w/bronze raindrop and blue highlights, 5" T $500.00
VASE, green w/blue iridescence, counterfeit Tiffany signature, 3½" T $400.00
VASE, shades of pink, green gold iridescence cased in white, 7¼" T $500.00
VASE, pink, green, yellow stripes and swirls w/white lining, iridescent, 5½" T $550.00

A-MA Nov. 1992   *James D. Julia, Inc.*
LOETZ STERLING SILVER OVERLAY VASES

Row 1, Left to Right
VASES, 2 pcs., iridescent green, oyster finish w/pink and purple, 3" and 4" T $600.00
VASES, 2 pcs., 1 lt. green w/gold iridescence, "For Auntie Kate from Luke 1905," mkd. Alvin, numbered, 3¾" T; other iridescent amethyst, repair, 4" T $525.00
VASE, gold w/green, pink, purple iridescence, 3½" T $450.00

Row 2, Left to Right
VASE, pink Rosaline glass w/oyster iridescence, 4" W, 3" T $453.00
VASE, chartruese shaded to brown w/silver feathered iridescence, 4" T $1500.00
VASE, lt. brown glass w/blue iridescence, "1123," 5" T $175.00
VASE, rosaline glass, oyster finish w/pink, green iridescence, 4½" T $425.00

A-MA Nov. 1992   *James D. Julia, Inc.*
D'ARGENTAL VASE, brown cameo on gold ground, 14" T . . . . NS
GALLE VASE, pink cameo on yellow and frosted white ground, 6½" T $1100.00
GALLE VASE, brown cameo on yellow frosted ground, 6½" T $1050.00
DEGUE PLANTER, mottled brown, orange cameo on frosted clear ground, 7" T $400.00

A-MA Nov. 1992   *James D. Julia, Inc.*
**STERLING SILVER OVERLAY ON
EMERALD GREEN GLASS**
Row 1, Left to Right
CRUET, cut green over crystal, signed "patented 999/1000 fine," mkd. Alvin, numbered, 7¼" T $750.00
BUD VASES, pr., crystal, different floral designs, 7" T $200.00
PERFUME BOTTLE, signed "Sterling Silver Deposit," numbered, 4" W, 6" T $600.00
ROSE BOWL, signed "999/1000 fine," mkd. Alvin, "G276," 4½" T $725.00
Row 2, Left to Right
VASE, flake, 3" W, 8¼" T $600.00
VASES, 2 pcs., 1 w/monogram and date of 07, 6½" T $400.00
VASE, mkd. Alvin, signed patented 999/1000 fine," "G308," 7" T $500.00

A-MA Nov. 1992   *James D. Julia, Inc.*
STERLING SILVER OVERLAY
BATH SALTS JARS, 3 pcs., hinged and covered, 2 clear, 1 emerald, to 3" T $450.00
VASE, emerald, monogrammed, signed "patented, sterling," 5½" W, 3½" T $725.00
BOTTLES, 2 pcs., emerald, 1 for perfume, 1 for bath salts, to 4¼" T $350.00
VASE, emerald, 2½" W, 3" T $275.00
Row 2, Left to Right
VIOLET BOWLS, 2 pcs., 1 cranberry, 1 emerald, 3" W, 3" T $750.00
INK WELL, bright green, monogrammed "E," 3" W, 3¼" T $650.00
PERFUME BOTTLES, 2 pcs., emerald, 3¾" and 4½" T $500.00

A-MA Nov. 1992   *James D. Julia, Inc.*
TIFFANY FAVRILE VASE, opalescent w/ green feathering, amber interior, inscribed "LCT M7493," wear, 13½" T $2500.00
TIFFANY FAVRILE VASE, inscribed "LC Tiffany Favrile #9459J," .... NS
QUEZAL VASE, gold iridescent w/purple-blue highlights, 12" T $1650.00

Photo V

A-OH Apr. 1993   *Early Auction Co.*

Row 1, Left to Right

707 CAKE TRAY, 3-color cut glass, amethyst, chartreuse, clear, 9½" D $475.00*

N-235 WEBB ROSE BOWL, propeller mark, gold leaves on cream ground, 3½" T $750.00*

71 VASE, iridescent gold, signed V. Durand, 9½" T $450.00*

N-223-B LOTUSWARE EWER, melon ribbed reticulated body, beaded slender neck, 10" T $1850.00*

233 MT. WASHINGTON EGG MUFFINEER, satin peachblow w/blue & white enamel dec., 4" T $250.00*

44 VASE, mottled yellow & white to mottled grey-brown foot, signed Kimball, 12" T $50.00*

N-223-C LOTUSWARE VASE, pastel reticulated melon ribbed lower body, painted floral dec., gold ball feet, 8" T $750.00*

N-67 VASE, iridescent gold, opal leaves & vines, 10" T $500.00*

209-C ROOKWOOD PITCHER, yellow-brown glaze, "The Great Seal of the State of Ohio 1788," "City of Cincinnati, Ohio-1888," 6½" T $475.00*

171 TIFFANY VASE, iridescent gold ribbed, bluish edged rim, bronze pod base, 17" T $600.00*

N-245 NORTHWOOD OVERLAY VASE, white exterior, pink interior w/amber edge and handle, 10½" T $160.00*

N-39 FINDLAY ONYX CELERY, hairline, open bubble, 6" T $325.00*

CLEAR CUT GLASS

Row 2, Left to Right

795 TANKARD PITCHER, hobstars, fans, cross-cut diamonds, 11" T $250.00*

776 CHAMPAGNES, 6 pcs., (1 illus.), strawberry-diamonds, fans, pyramidal stars, 4½" T $225.00*

779 EGG NOG COMPOTE, strawberry-diamond vesicas, hobstars, bars of cane, 8" D $500.00*

799 2 PCS., bowl, (illus.), fans, triangles, beaded bars, chip 7" D; relish, reflecting fans, diamonds, chips, 13½" L . . $150.00*

794 COMPOTE, flashed stars & cane, beaded cut stem, star base, 10¾" T $60.00*

Row 3, Left to Right

770 CRUET, notched prism hobstars & fans, notched fluted neck and spout, faceted stopper, 8" T $100.00*

777 BOWL, Alhambra pat., 9" D $950.00*

786 CARAFE, Russian pat., 7" T $150.00*

790 PUNCH BOWL, 2 pc., hobstars, fans of cane, Russian patterns connected w/beaded bars, faceted collar, chip, 13" D, 15½" T $2250.00*

778 TANKARD PITCHER, Alhambra pat., 10" T $1550.00*

785 ICE BUCKET, Russian pat., 6½" D, 5¼" T $350.00*

Row 4, Left to Right

789 SQUATTY PITCHER, fans, hobstars, buttons w/stars, 6½" T $365.00*

749 CLOVER LEAF BOWL, mkd. Maple City, encircled notched flashed prisms, flashed hobstars, 8½" D $160.00*

796 WHISKEY JUG, clear tusks vesicas around hobstars, fans, relief diamond vesicas, notched neck, faceted rim, 9½" T $700.00*

771 SPOONER, stars, fans, 4½" T $95.00*

782 CHAMPAGNE PITCHER, bullseyes, lattice, hobstars, fans, signed Hawkes, 16" T $825.00*

780 CELERY, signed J. Hoare, bars of cane, hobstars, beading, 1½" L $300.00*

Row 5, Left to Right

706 3 PCS., mustard jar, (illus.), prism rim, pyramidal stars & fans, mkd. sterling spoon, 4" T; sugar & creamer, hobstars, fans, signed Libbey, repair, 3" T $105.00*

775 ICE CREAM TRAY, Stratford pat., 10½" W, 17½" L $600.00*

798 COVERED BUTTER, hobstars, cross-cut diamonds, fans, 9" D, 7" T $225.00*

709 JUG, pinwheels, hobstars, fans, crescent prisms, faceted stopper, internal bruise, 8" T $150.00*

772 MAYONNAISE W/UNDERTRAY, Harvard pat., 4" W, 6" L $295.00*

747 SUGAR & CREAMER, signed J. Hoare, hobstars, crosshatches, 4" T . . . NS

A-MA Nov. 1992   *James D. Julia, Inc.*
AMERICAN BRILLIANT PERIOD CUT GLASS
Row 1, Left to Right
ICE BUCKET, expanding star design, 6″ W, 6″ T $125.00
BUTTERMILK JUG, 8″ T $300.00
CRUET, Harvard and Band pat., 8½″ T $75.00
TUMBLERS, set of 7, strawberry diamond, signed Hawkes, flakes, 4″ T $85.00
Row 2, Left to Right
SALAD FORK, metal w/hobstar cut bottom, 12″ L $100.00
SALAD FORK, silver mkd. "Gorham & Company," 12″ L . . . . NS
SERVING PLATE, expanding star, 10″ D $100.00
WATER CARAFE, expanding stars, notched prism neck, 6″ D, 7″ T $105.00

A-MA Nov. 1992   *James D. Julia, Inc.*
VASE, American Brilliant cut glass, Hobstar and Sunburst pat., 8¼″ T . . . $1000.00
TANKARD PITCHER, American Brilliant cut glass, Harvard pat., 14″ T $625.00

A-MA Nov. 1992   *James D. Julia, Inc.*
AMERICAN BRILLIANT PERIOD CUT GLASS unless noted.
TAZZAS, pr., (1 illus.), expanding star, fan, strawberry diamond pat., 6″ D, 7½″
T $300.00
TRAY, wild rose pat., signed Tuthill, 5″ W, 8″ L $250.00
PLATE, signed Hawkes, Gladys pat., 8″ D $85.00
PYREX TEA POT, signed, floral and lined engraving, underplate, 6½″ T $250.00

A-MA Nov. 1992   *James D. Julia, Inc.*
FLOWER CENTER, American Brilliant cut glass, signed Strauss, Pinwheel pat., 8½″
T $800.00
PEDESTAL NAPPIE, American Brilliant cut glass, Harvard pat., 8½″ T . . . $400.00

A-MA Nov. 1992   *James D. Julia, Inc.*
AMERICAN BRILLIANT PERIOD CUT GLASS
BUTTER DISH, star and punty design, 5″ H, 8″ D $150.00
BASKET, geometric floral cutting, twisted glass handle, 6½″ T, 7″ D $145.00
ICE CREAM TRAY, 10″ W, 18″ L $650.00

A-MA Dec. 1992   *Skinner, Inc.*

FLINT GLASS CLEAR BELLFLOWER PATTERN

Row 1, Left to Right

TUMBLER, ... $20.00*
GOBLETS, 11 assorted, (1 illus.) $225.00*
EGG CUPS, 4 nonmatching, (1 illus.) $125.00*
SPOONHOLDERS, pr., (1 illus.) $50.00*
MASTER SALT, ... $15.00*
BUTTER DISH, rough edge $25.00*

Row 2, Left to Right

WATER PITCHER, ... $300.00*
BAR LIP DECANTER, discolored $30.00*
COMPOTE, chips, 4½" H, 8" D $25.00*

A-MA Nov. 1992   *James D. Julia, Inc.*

BOWLS, 3 pcs., (1 illus.), cut glass, some roughness $110.00*
VASE, cut glass, 11½" T $55.00*
BOWLS, 3 pcs., (1 illus.), cut glass, heart shaped, some roughness $110.00*

A-MA Nov. 1992   *James D. Julia, Inc.*

BOWLS, pr., cut glass, 10" D ... $385.00*
COMPOTE, signed Tuthill, cut glass, 5½" T, 11½" D $880.00*
FLOWER CENTER, signed Libby, cut glass, 6½" T, 10" D $495.00*

A-MA Dec. 1992   *Skinner, Inc.*

QUART DECANTERS, pr., Sandwich Glass Star pat., chip $200.00
COMPOTE, Flint Glass Sawtooth pat., 10½" T, 7" D $80.00
CONDIMENT SET, 3 pc., clear Daisy & Button pat., replacement $75.00

A-MA Nov. 1992   *James D. Julia, Inc.*

Row 1, Left to Right

STICK VASE, signed Stueben Aurene, gold, 12" T $225.00*
VASE, signed Quezal, gold, blue swirls on oyster ground, iridescent, 8¼" T ... $1000.00*
VASE, Fostoria, green, gold on opal, iridescent gold interior, 12" T............ $625.00*
VASE, maroon, red swirls on oyster, iridescent, 14" T .... NS
VASE, Fostoria, green, gold on opal, iridescent gold interior, 12" T............ $625.00*
VASE, Imperial, orange, black on opal, iridescent, 8½" T.................... $200.00*
VASE, signed Quezal, green on opal, interior is iridescent w/purple, blue, 6" T ...... NS

Row 2, Left to Right

BULB BASE, signed Steuben Aurene, gold w/red, iridescent, 4¼" T......... $400.00*
BOWL, unsigned Tiffany Favrile, white on oyster w/gold-bronze, 2" T, 4½" D .. $225.00*

A-MA Nov. 1992   *James D. Julia, Inc.*

VASE, signed Handel Teroma, artist signed "Bedigie," 11" T 2400.00*

A-MA Nov. 1992   *James D. Julia, Inc.*

VASE, signed R. Lalique France, opalescent white, flake, repair, 8″ T, 8½″ D $450.00*
VASE, unsigned Stevens & Williams, pink, green, amber on opalescent blue, rim grinding, 8½″ T $400.00*

A-MA Nov. 1992   *James D. Julia, Inc.*

Row 1, Left to Right

VASE, blue opalescent glass, pink, green, amber dec., 8½″ T $400.00*
DAUM NANCY CAMEO GLASS VASE, signed, 3¾″ T $1000.00*
QUEZAL VASE, signed, gold, blue on white, iridescent, 8¼″ T $1000.00*
TIFFANY VASE, glass, platinum base, signed, 10″ T $650.00*
LE GRAS VASE, Cameo Glass, signed, shades of brown, green, clear, 11″ T . . . . NS
TIFFANY VASE, gold, signed $1600.00*
TEAPOT, pink, peach, green, signed "Rookwood 554W, H.E.W.," 4½″ T $320.00*
QUEZAL VASE, opal white, green, purple, blue, iridescent, signed, 6″ T . . . . NS
AURENE VASE, iridescent gold, red, signed, 4¼″ T. $400.00*

Row 2, Left to Right

EWER, brown, yellow, green on green, signed "Owens Utopian," 10½″ T $150.00*
WELLER FLUID LAMP, artist signed "K.U.T.," 11½″ T, 13″ W $3000.00*
TIFFANY CANDLESTICK, holder set w/peacock glass jewels, iridescent amber Favrile shade, base stamped, 11½″ T $2750.00*
VASE, iridescent, maroon, red on white, 14″ T . . . . NS
VASE, white, yellow, on brown, signed "Handelware, JPL France," 13″ T $1050.00*
TIFFANY VASE, Favrile, bronze base, signed, 12″ T $1200.00*

A-MA Nov. 1992   *James D. Julia, Inc.*

AMBERINA WASH BOWL AND PITCHER, signed Baccarat, pitcher base bruised, 15″ T, bowl 15″ D $110.00*
OYSTER PLATES, set of 6, signed Pairpoint Limoges, gold on white . . . $650.00*

A-MA Nov. 1992   *James D. Julia, Inc.*

CUT GLASS

Row 1, Left to Right

BOWL, signed Hawkes Gravic Glass, Carnation pat., 8″ D. $250.00*
TRAY, signed Hawkes Gravic Glass, Carnation pat., 9″ x 12″. $825.00*
BOWL, signed Hawkes Gravic Glass, Carnation pat., 9¼″ D $165.00*

Center

TUMBLERS, set of 6, Battleship Olympia pat., silverplated holder $150.00*

Row 2, Left to Right

BUTTER TUB, American Brilliant, 5½″ T, 5½″ D $75.00*
NAPPY, American Brilliant, 6″ D $50.00*
BOWL, signed Hawkes Gravic Glass, 8″ D $1250.00*

A-MA Nov. 1992   *James D. Julia, Inc.*

TIFFANY GLASS

VASE, cameo, shades of green, red on opalescent white, gold/bronze iridescent interior, 5″ T $5900.00*
VASE, signed Favrile, gold platinum base, 10″ T $650.00*
VASE, opalescent white, mint green interior, 12″ T $1200.00*
VASE, green, white, orange on clear iridescent, 6″ T $4150.00*
VASE, green, white on iridescent gold/bronze, 6″ T $1400.00*

FRONT

VASE, pastel gold and Favrile, 3½″ T. $500.00*

A-MA Nov. 1992   *James D. Julia, Inc.*
TIFFANY FAVRILE GLASS
    Row 1, Left to Right
VASE, iridescent gold w/blue, bronze foot, 12" T $1200.00*
VASE, iridescent gold, mirror finish base $1600.00*
VASE, bronze dore' finish w/blue enameled des., 17" T $1700.00*
VASE, iridescent gold w/blue, 12½" T $1350.00*
    Row 2, Left to Right
FINGER BOWLS W/UNDERPLATES, 2 sets, iridescent gold w/purple, blue, 4¾" T, 6½" D $950.00*
BOWL, iridescent gold w/purple, blue, wear, 7" D $500.00*
COMPOTE, iridescent gold w/ blue, mirrored base, 4" T, 7" D $600.00*
CANDLE LAMP, irridescent gold, orange bronze interior, base drilled, 13" T $1250.00*
    Row 3, Left to Right
BOWL, scratches, 10" D $1600.00*
COMPOTE, iridescent gold w/ blue, cut des., 2½" T, 7¾" D $900.00*

A-MA Nov. 1992   *James D. Julia, Inc.*
    Row 1, Left to Right
GRAVY BOAT, signed E. Galle Nancy, blue delft on pale blue, 4" T, 10" L $150.00*
VASE, Schneider Glass, orange, green, black, 10" T $175.00*
VASE, Phoenix Glass, rose, green, brown on custard glass, 11" T $100.00*
LAMP BASE, signed Stevens & Williams, cameo, opaque pink dec., 8" T $125.00*
VASE, Mont Joye glass w/enameled tulips, 5" T $150.00*
VASE, Cameo Glass, purple on white, lavendar, signature, 5½" T $150.00*
    Row 2, Left to Right
DESERT SERVICE, 10 bowls, 10 plates, (1 illus.), signed Val St. Lambert, crystal . . . . NS
BOWL, Mosier, green w/applied dec., 7" T $100.00*
SNUFF BOTTLE, Peking glass, cranberry over crystal, green stopper, 3" T $75.00*

A-MA Nov. 1992   *James D. Julia, Inc.*
    Row 1, Left to Right
EGG CRATE FERNER, Wavecrest . . NS
TRINKET BOXES, 2 pcs. $200.00*
BOWL, Pomona Glass, 9" D . . . . NS
    Row 2, Left to Right
VASES, pr., Victorian, 3 layered glass, ruby w/opal, plum linings, 5" T $250.00*
    Row 3, Left to Right
TOOTHPICK HOLDER, fushia amberina, 2½" T $247.50*
INKWELL, Laticino, pewter cover, pink, white swirls, 2½" T, 3" D $715.00*

A-MA Nov. 1992   *James D. Julia, Inc.*
    Row 1, Left to Right
VASE, Steuben, red glass w/lighter stripes, 8" T $150.00*
VASE, signed Steuben, Bristol green glass, 14" T $120.00*
SHERBERT AND UNDERPLATES, set of 4, (1 illus.), signed Steuben Aurene, gold aurene on calcite $160.00*
    Row 2, Left to Right
SHADES, set of 4, signed Quezal, white, green on iridescent gold, 5½" T $525.00*
SHADES, set of 4, (1 illus.), signed Steuben, gold aurene on calcite, 4¾" T $350.00*
BOWL, Steuben, Bristol yellow, scratches, 14" D $50.00*
DOUGHNUT HOLDER, Steuben, jade, 5½" T, 9" D $175.00*

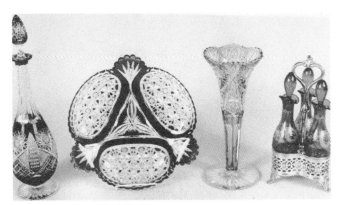

A-MA Nov. 1992　　　*James D. Julia, Inc.*
DECANTER, American Brilliant, amethyst cut to clear, 16½″ T $1760.00*
TRAY, American Brilliant, cut glass, blue cut to clear, 12″ D . . . . NS
VASE, American Brilliant, cut glass, cranberry cut to clear, 12″ T $1540.00*
CASTOR SET, engraved amber over clear, silverplated holder, 9½″ T $125.00*

A-MA Nov. 1992　　　*James D. Julia, Inc.*
PEDESTAL PUNCH BOWL, American Brilliant cut glass, by Ideal Glass Co. of NY, ca. 1902, Hobstar pat., 2-pc., 14″ T, 15″ D $2250.00

A-MA Mar. 1993　　　*Skinner, Inc.*
ALL MADE BY SANDWICH GLASS COMPANY
BLOWN THREE-MOLD LAMP, pressed base, brass collar 10¼″ H $1100.00
OINTMENT BOXES, 3 pcs., canary concave faceted, brown concave faceted, opalescent circular, 2½″ D $550.00
BLOWN THREE-MOLD LAMP, blue-green, whale oil burner, 7½″ H $880.00
PRESSED GLASS CANDLESTICKS, 2 pcs., 9½″ H, 7½″ H $275.00
PRESSED GLASS, turquoise basket match holder, blue rectangular dish, and opalescent footed pomade which is not illus. $880.00
BLOWN COLOGNE BOTTLES, 2 pcs., 8″ H, 6½″ H $1320.00

A-MA Nov. 1992　　　*James D. Julia, Inc.*
TIFFANY FAVRILE GLASS
CANDLE LAMP, gold iridescent shade, stick and candle, signed "LCT," paper label, chip, 14″ T $1300.00
VASE, gold-green opalescent, signed "LCT L368," 6″ T $1300.00
VASE, purple to white opalescent w/ stripes, clear base, signed "LCT Favrille, 1888," labeled, 12″ T $1500.00

A-MA Nov. 1992　　　　　　　　　　　　　　　*James D. Julia, Inc.*
Row 1, Left to Right
PLANTER, C.F. Monroe Co. signed Nakara, pale green, pink, 5½″ T, 8″ D $175.00*
BURMESE EPERGNE, Webb, 4 piece, bronzed holder, 5½″ T, 8″ D $700.00*
VASE, signed Wavecrest, pale green, pink, white, 17″ T $600.00*
GOURD VASES, pr., Mt. Washington, acid finished Burmese, 8″ T $300.00*
Row 2, Left to Right
COMPOTE, Pairpoint, acid finish Burmese, 4½″ T, 7½″ D . . . . NS
TRINKET BOWL, signed Wave Crest, white, blue floral on yellow, 3″ D $100.00*
JEWEL BOX, signed Nakara, satin lining, pink, green, white on green, 5″ D $350.00*

A-MA Nov. 1992   *James D. Julia, Inc.*

Back Row, Left to Right

STEVENS & WILLIAMS VASE, yellow to white satin glass, 4½" T $70.00

GUNDERSON TUMBLER, peachblow, 3¾" T $140.00

MT. WASHINGTON BURMESE VASE, pink shading to yellow, 16" T $300.00

STEVENS & WILLIAMS VASE, swirled lime green satin glass, 10½" T ... $300.00

Front Row, Left to Right

NEW ENGLAND GLASS BOWL, pink, white cased, 3" T, 8¼" D .... NS

STEVENS & WILLIAMS VASE, gilt dec. green satin glass, 3" T $250.00

NEW ENGLAND BRIDE'S BOWL, enamel dec. pink satin glass, 10½" D $100.00

A-MA Nov. 1992   *James D. Julia, Inc.*

CAMEO GLASS VASES

Row 1, Left to Right

VASE, signed Galle, 6½" T .... NS

VASE, signed Galle, purple on yellow, 7" T $1000.00*

VASE, signed Charder, "Ovington France," orange, brown on yellow, 9" T...... $250.00*

VASE, signed LeGras, maroon, green on opaque beige, 11" T $500.00*

VASE, signed LeGras, brown, green .... NS

VASE, signed Muller Freres, brown, green on frosted yellow, purple, 8" T $950.00*

VASE, signed Muller, green, yellow, purple, 5¾" T $950.00*

Row 2, Left to Right

CREAMER, signed Daum Nancy, amethyst glass, crystal handle, 3½" T $300.00*

VASE, yellow, red, 3½" T $100.00*

VASE, signed Galle, gold, brown on frosted pale blue, 4" T $550.00*

VASE, signed Daum Nancy, white amethyst, yellow, 3¾" T $1000.00*

A-MA Nov. 1992   *James D. Julia, Inc.*

DAUM-NANCY VASE, orange on mottled white and clear cluthra glass, signed, 12" W, 16" T $3000.00

GALLE VASE, red rose cameo on citron yellow to clear glass, 8" T $4000.00

A-MA Dec. 1992   *Skinner, Inc.*

CANDY CONTAINERS

GLASS CANDY CONTAINERS, 18 pcs., (5 illus.), battleship. Independence Hall, eagle drum, mug, Penny Trust Company, safe, kewpie doll, 2 locomotives, 2 bunnies, nursing bottle, revolver, tank, Scottie dog, suitcase, fire pumper, bulldog, lantern, anchor condiment set, some w/candy and covers $522.50

CHARLIE CHAPLIN, glass, George Borgfeldt, #2892, paint loss, 3¾" H $165.00

TWO FIGURAL CONTAINERS, George Borgfeldt kewpie w/drum, serial #2862, 3⅛" H; Avon top w/wooden spring-top, metal stand, 3¾" L $110.00

A-MA Nov. 1992   *James D. Julia, Inc.*

Row 1, Left to Right

GALLE COUPE, opaque pink to clear to pink w/yellow, yellow, orange dec., 400.00
DAUM-NANCY BOWL, purple shaded to white cameo glass, green, brown, fuchsia enameled dec., signed, 5½" W, 2½" T $1750.00

Row 2, Left to Right

VASE, French cameo glass, shades of green on white opalescent, signed "D'Argental," 8" T $850.00
GALLE VASE, green cameo on green, orange, clear glass, signed, chip, 4½" T . . . $75.00
DAUM-NANCY VASE, lt. opalescent blue shaded to frosted clear ground, blue, white, green dec., signed, flake, 9¾" T $850.00
GALLE VASE, cameo of brown fuchsias on yellow-brown ground, 6½" T $525.00
DAUM-NANCY VASE, lt. cranberry to white cameo glass, 3¼" W, 7½" T $525.00

A-MA Nov. 1992   *James D. Julia, Inc.*
LAVERRE FRANCAIS VASE, cameo on mottled orange ground, 15" T . . . $700.00
GALLE VASE, lt. brown cameo on frosted white ground, 6½" T $600.00
MONT JOYE VASE, enameled dec. on opalescent white, signed, 10¼" T . . . . NS
A. DELATTE LAMP, dk. blue cameo on shaded olive ground, 17" T $2000.00

A-MA Nov. 1992   *James D. Julia, Inc.*

Row 1, Left to Right

VASE, Loetz, blue, green, white on iridescent purple, 13" T . . . . NS
VASE, Loetz, blue, white, silver on iridescent aqua, 11½" T . . . . NS
VASE, Loetz, blue-green oil skin on green glass, 9½" T $175.00*
VASES, pr., (1 illus.), Loetz, green oil skin, silver overlay handles, foot, 10¾" T . . $350.00*
VASE, Lundburg Studios, 16" T . . . . NS

Row 2, Left to Right

GLASS BASKET, green w/clear handle, iridescent blue, purple dec., 9½" T $95.00*
VASE, Loetz, gold glass w/iridescent blue-green oil skin dec. . . . . NS
CRACKER JAR, iridescent w/green glass dec., replaced cover, 7" T $80.00*
CENTERPIECE, silverplated base, iridescent green glass bowl, 10½" T $60.00*
BOWL, Loetz, iridescent glass w/gold, pink highlights, 3½" T . . . . NS

A-MA Nov. 1992   *James D. Julia, Inc.*
GALLE BUD VASE, purple cameo on shaded-frosted pink, 4½" T $800.00
GALLE VASE, brown, yellow cameo on rose to frosted clear ground, 15" T $2350.00
DAUM-NANCY VASE, blue, green cameo on mottled frosted and blue ground, signed, 15" T $3400.00
GALLE BUD VASE, cinnamon cameo on shaded-frosted yellow ground, 4¼" T $800.00

A-MA Nov. 1992   *James D. Julia, Inc.*

TIFFANY FAVRILE GLASS

Row 1, Left to Right

PITCHER, iridescent gold w/blue, inscribed, 5480J, 2¾" T $350.00*
SHADES, set of 5, (1 illus.), green, bronze, gold on opalescent white, 5½" T $2500.00*
VASE, inscribed, B387, silver blue on iridescent green, 4½" T $500.00*

Row 2, Left to Right

CORDIALS, pr., inscribed, iridescent gold w/purple, pink, 4¾" T $250.00*
BOWL, signed, 599V15785-LCT, opalescent aqua marine, 8" D .... NS
WINE GLASS, bright turquoise blue to opalescent white, 5½" T $250.00*

Row 3, Left to Right

VASE, inscribed, W2375, iridescent gold w/blue, pink, 2" T $350.00*
PLATE, iridescent gold w/purple, blue $300.00*
SALTS, 2 pcs., inscribed, iridescent gold w/blue, pink, 1" to 1½" T $300.00*

A-MA Nov. 1992   *James D. Julia, Inc.*

Row 1, Left to Right

PITCHER, inverted thumbprint amberina, cranberry to amber, 8½" T $175.00
PEAR, peach blow, glossy finish, 4½" T $100.00
ATOMIZER, Flagilo-type, diamond quilted, enamel dec., 7" T $110.00
VASE, amberina, red to amber, 8½" T $325.00

Row 2, Left to Right

NEW ENGLAND GLASS TUMBLER, plated amberina, fuchsia to ruby to amber, opalescent white lining, ribbed, 4" T $800.00
BASKET, Sandwich, peach blow, amber handle, 6" W, 6½" T $250.00
HOBBS BROCKUNIER TUMBLER, wheeling peach blow, glossy finish, 4" T... $250.00
HOBBS BROCKUNIER TUMBLER, wheeling peach blow, glossy finish, 4" T... $250.00

Row 3, Left to Right

NEW ENGLAND GLASS SPOONER, wild rose peach blow, worn agata staining, 4½" T $350.00
SANDWICH VASE, swirled peach blow, camphor frosted edge, pink to white, 5" T $75.00
SUGAR & CREAMER, enameled dec., blue, yellow, pink, fglake, 2½" & 3¼" T ... $25.00

Row 4, Left to Right

GREENTOWN BERRY BOWL, opalescent amber, Holly pat., rough edge, 3" H, 7½" D $200.00
BOWL, green opaque w/agate stain, gold etching, wear, 4" H, 8" D $300.00
GREENTOWN NAPPIE, opalescent amber, Holly, rough edge, 2" H, 4½" D $200.00

A-NY Nov. 1992   *David Rago Gallery*
ROOKWOOD VASE, vellum finish by K. Shirayamadani, colorful blossoms on blue to pink ground, 1933, flame mark, 8" T $1400.00*

A-PA May 1993   *Glass Works Auctions*
BOTTLES

McKEEVER'S ARMY BITTERS, ca. 1865–1870, amber drum w/cannon balls on top, repair, 10¼" T $775.00*
NATIONAL BITTERS, ca. 1867–1875, amber ear of corn, 12¼" T $240.00*
NATIONAL TONIC BITTERS, ca. 1865–1875, aqua, 9¾" T $550.00*

A-PA May 1993   *Glass Works Auctions*
BOTTLES

INDIAN HERB BITTERS, ca. 1868–1875, amber Indian Queen, 12¼" T ... $475.00*
CALDWELL'S HERB BITTERS, ca. 1865–1875, iron pontil, amber, flakes, 12⅛" T $110.00*
DR. CALDWELL'S HERB BITTERS, ca. 1865–1875, amber, 12½" T $110.00*

A-PA May 1993   *Glass Works Auctions*
FLASKS

SUNBURST, ca. 1810–1830, yellow-amber ½ pint, seed bubbles $325.00*
SUNBURST, ca. 1820–1830, deep aqua ¾ pint $70.00*
SUNBURST, ca. 1820–1830, deep aqua ¾ pint, flakes .... NS

A-PA May 1993   *Glass Works Auctions*
BOTTLES

WM PFUNDER BLOOD PURIFIER, ca. 1890–1900, amber, 7⅝" T $70.00*
FARMER'S HORSE MEDICINE, ca. 1865–1875, aqua, 8⅜" T $60.00*
SACRAMENTO CHEMICAL CO., Entomocide, ca. 1890–1905, amethyst tinted clear, 5⅝" T .... NS

A-PA May 1993   *Glass Works Auctions*
BOTTLES

CARTER, ca. 1910–1930, cobalt quart, cathedral master ink, chip, 9¾" T .. $60.00*
CARTER, ca. 1910–1930, cobalt pint, cathedral master ink, 7⅞" T $170.00*
CARTER, ca. 1910–1930, cobalt pint+, cathedral master ink, 8" T $150.00*

A-PA May 1993   *Glass Works Auctions*
BOTTLES

PERUVIAN BITTERS, ca. 1878–1883, amber, 9" T .... NS
MARSHALL'S BITTERS, ca. 1902–1908, amber, 8⅝" T $40.00*
OLD MAN'S STOMACH BITTERS, ca. 1876–1880, amber 7⅞" T $2800.00*

A-PA May 1993   *Glass Works Auctions*
BOTTLES

FISH BITTERS, ca. 1866–1875, amber, 11⅝" T $110.00*
GORDON'S KIDNEY AND LIVER BITTERS, ca. 1890–1910, amber, 9⅜" T $140.00*
GREELY'S BOURBON BITTERS, ca. 1865–1875, smokey greyish-puce barrel, flake, 9⅜" T $300.00*

A-PA May 1993   *Glass Works Auctions*
ST. DRAKE'S CABIN BOTTLES

PLANTATION BITTERS, ca. 1860–1870, yellow-olive-amber, 10" T $475.00*
PLANTATION BITTERS, ca. 1860–1870, burgundy glass, 9¾" T $105.00*
PLANTATION BITTERS, ca. 1860–1870, burgundy glass, 10⅛" T $100.00*

A-PA May 1993　　*Glass Works Auctions*
BOTTLES
E.J. ROSE'S MAGADOR BITTERS, ca. 1895–1900, amber, 8¾" T $85.00*
STAR KIDNEY AND LIVER BITTERS, ca. 1900–1905, amber, 8⅞" T ... $50.00*
STOCKTON'S PORT WINE BITTERS, ca. 1884–1886, amber, 9⅛" T .. $400.00*

A-PA May 1993　　*Glass Works Auctions*
DAIRY BOTTLES
GENDRON RANCH DAIRY, ca. 1940–1950, clear, maroon paint, 8⅞" T .... NS
McMURTRIE DAIRY, ca. 1940–1950, clear 1/3 pint, red paint, 7⅛" T .. $45.00*
PARAMOUNT DAIRY, ca. 1940–1950, clear quart, red paint $35.00*

A-PA May 1993　　*Glass Works Auctions*
BOTTLES
CORNUCOPIA, ca. 1820–1840, yellow-green ½ pint $200.00*
CORNUCOPIA, ca. 1820–1840, olive-amber ½ pint $80.00*

A-PA May 1993　　*Glass Works Auctions*
TARGET BALLS
IRA PAINE, ca. 1880–1890, amber, 2¾" D $230.00*
BOGARDUS, ca. 1877–1890, olive, impurities, 2¾" D $475.00*
BOGARDUS, ca. 1877–1890, amber, 2¾" D $300.00*
ILMENAU, ca. 1880–1890, German, amber, 2¾" D $425.00*
L. JONES GUNMAKER, ca. 1880–1890, English, greyish sapphire blue, 2¾" D $140.00*
TARGET BALL, ca. 1880–1890, sapphire, 2¾" D $550.00*

A-PA May 1993　　*Glass Works Auctions*
JARS
MASON, ca. 1860–1870, amber ½ gallon, zink cap $85.00*
MILLVILLE ATMOSPHERIC FRUIT JAR, ca. 1861–1870, aqua pint, domed glass lid, iron yoke $150.00*
MYER'S TEST JAR, ca. 1869–1875, aqua quart, metal lid, closure $150.00*

A-PA May 1993　　*Glass Works Auctions*
BOTTLES
D.B. NORTH & CO. DRUGGISTS, ca. 1890–1900, cobalt, 4⅜" T $70.00*
SUN DRUG CO., Poison, ca. 1890–1910, yellow-green, 2⅞" T $200.00*
SUN DRUG CO., Poison, ca. 1890–1910, yellow-green, 3⅜" T $275.00*

A-PA May 1993　　*Glass Works Auctions*
BOTTLES
NATIONAL BOTTLING WORKS, ca. 1880–1910, amber quart, 11⅝" T $35.00*
NATIONAL BOTTLING WORKS, ca. 1880–1910, amber pint, porcelain stopper, 7⅝" T $45.00*
A & R POSTEL, ca. 1883, amber, 11¾" T $1550.00*

A-PA May 1993　　*Glass Works Auctions*
BOTTLES
UMBRELLA INK, ca. 1830–1860, sapphire, 2½" T $775.00*
UMBRELLA INK, ca. 1830–1860, cobalt, 2½" T $500.00*

A-ME Feb. 1993   *James D, Julia, Inc.*

Row 1, Left to Right
BASKET, Calif., coiled, human figure dec., 6″ H, 7″ D $525.00*
PIMA BASKET, coiled, decorated, 16″ H, 13″ D $700.00*
POMO BASKET, decorated, initialed, 6½″ D $500.00*

Row 2, Left to Right
WASHOE BOWL, geometric dec., 4″ H, 11″ D $950.00*
BASKET, Calif., decorated, 5″ H, 6″ D $225.00*
ESKIMO BASKET, coiled, Yukon River, diamond dec., 3″ H, 7″ D $200.00*

A-ME Feb. 1993   *James D, Julia, Inc.*

Row 1, Left to Right
PLAINS INDIAN CHILD'S DRESS, beaded felt $275.00*
PLAINS INDIAN MOCCASINS, pr., beaded hide, 10″ L $500.00*
PLAINS INDIAN DOLL, beaded hide, 12″ H $350.00*
PLAINS INDIAN MOCCASINS, pr., beaded hide, 10″ L $550.00*

Row 2, Left to Right
PLAINS INDIAN POUCH, beaded, 5″ W, 10″ L $900.00
PLAINS INDIAN BASKET, beaded, Paiute, 3¾″ H, 5″ D $750.00
BACKPACK, beaded, multicolored $300.00
PLAINS INDIAN PIPE BAG, beaded hide, 22″ L $900.00

A-OH Nov. 1992   *Garth's Auctions, Inc.*

Row 1, Left to Right
APACHE BASKET, willow, black martynia design, 3½″ H, 13″ D $495.00
PIMA BASKET, design in willow, martynia, loss, 3″ H, 12½″ D $330.00
BASKET, martynia design, loss, 13″ D $236.50
PIMA BASKET, martynia, willow fret design, wear, loss, 3″ H, 13⅝″ D $65.00

Row 2, Left to Right
WAKESHAN BASKET, lid, green, yellow, whales, boat, birds, 7¼″ H, 7¾″ D $480.00
POTTERY BOWL, red ochre, umber on white, wear, flakes, 3¼″ H, 7⅝″ D $71.50
BASKET, oval coil, martynia design, damage, stains, 4″ H, 11¼″ L $192.50

Row 3, Left to Right
SAN ILDEFONSO POTTERY JAR, red ochre, black polychrome on cream, redware bottom, repair, 9½″ H, 10″ D $1402.50
SANTO DOMINGO JAR, black on buff over red slip, hairline, 7⅜″ H, 8¾″ D . . . $302.50
ACOMA POTTERY JAR, umber, white, wear, flakes, repairs, 7⅜″ H, 9¾″ D $368.50

A-OH Nov. 1992   *Garth's Auctions, Inc.*

Row 1, Left to Right
BLACKWARE JAR, San Ildefonso, incised signature "Maria Popovi," Avanya figure, ca. 1950 6¼″ H x 4½″ H $577.50
PIMA BASKETRY TRAY, martynia and willow, 7¼″ $137.50
HOPI KACHINA DOLL, polychrome painted "Kitten" dancer, signed "Stacy Talahytewa," 10″ H $148.50
MONACHE BOTTLE-NECKED GIFT BASKET, bracken fern and sedge, ca. 1900, 9″ D x 4¾″ H $3025.00
TOTEM POLE, Northwest coast, carved and polychromed, 9″ H $104.50

BLACKWARE BOWL, San Ildefonso, incised "Marie," label "Exhibit by Marie & Julian," wear, 7⅜″ D, 2⅜″ H $687.50
APACHE BASKETRY TRAY, 8″ $159.50

Row 2, Left to Right
TLINGIT RATTLE-TOP BASKET, bracken fern and grass on cedar, polychrome design, lid damage and repair, 7½″ x 4½″ $605.00
CALIFORNIA TRAY, two-tone, wear, edge damage, 9¼″ x 13¾″ $110.00
TOTEM POLE, Northwest coast, raven, bear, ca. 1910, good old dark patina, traces of red paint, damage, 13¾″ H . . $412.50
PIMA BASKETRY OLLA, willow and martynia, braid rim, c. 1910, 9″ D, 7″ H $1045.00
ESKIMO COILED LIDDED BASKET, red and black design, rim damage, hole in lid, 6″ D, 4¾″ H $165.00
AMERICAN INDIAN BASKET, red and black on natural ground, rim damage, 8¾″ D, 4″ H $407.00
JICARILLA APACHE BASKET, polychrome design, rim damage, 11½″ D, 14¼″ H $93.50

A-OH Nov. 1992   *Garth's Auctions, Inc.*
PLATEAU BELT, black leather, goldenrod and red beading, 36" L $27.50
PLAINS BEADED POUCH, white w/3 shades of blue, red and green, tin cone dangles on long beaded strips, bead loss, 4½" x 5" plus dangles $357.50
ESKIMO DOLL, carved wooden face, drawn features, fur costume w/beading, 12½" H $27.50
NORTHERN PLAINS TOBACCO POUCH, rawhide, blue red yellow and white beading, 20" L plus fringe $1347.50
OIL ON MAHOGANY PANEL, winter landscape w/teepees, signed "J.H. Sharp, '03," back inscribed "To Mrs. H.S. Kiskadden, this is from the window of Absarokee Teepee (Palace Studio) Crow Agency, Montana, from J.H. Sharp. Xmas 1903," letter from Mrs. Sharp to Mrs. Kiskadden included, 4" x 6½", gilt frame damage, 10½" x 13" $11000.00
ESKIMO DOLLS, 2 pcs., carved wooden face, drawn features, fur costume w/beading, 9½", 4¾" $33.00
ESKIMO CARVED SCULPTURE, grey stone, man w/seal, scratch carved "A-Kan 138523," 5⅝" L $110.00
ESKIMO CARVED CRIBBAGE BOARD, ivory, salmon shape, engraved detail, 4 original pegs, replacements, 5⅝" L $176.00
IROQUOIS BEADED PURSE, polychrome flowers and birds, 6" L $137.50
IROQUOIS BEADED PURSE, polychrome flowers, date "1929," 3¾" L..... $137.50
IROQUOIS CAPS, pr., men's red wool, beaded band and bill, wear, holes .. $253.00

A-OH Jan. 1993   *Garth's Auctions, Inc.*
NEZ PERCE CORN HUSK BAG, maroon, blue, green, loses, 9⅜" x 8¼" $165.00
NORTHERN PLAINS POUCH, Blackfoot design, maroon, green, dk. blue, yellow, pink, red beading on lt. blue ground, bead loss, 6¾" x 4¾" $297.00
PLAINS BABY MOCCASINS, red, gold, dk. blue beading, 3⅞" L $148.50
NORTHERN PLAINS PIPE BAG, dk. blue, yellow, green, red, beading on Cheyenne blue ground, wear, losses, 25" L $2420.00
PIMA/PAPAGO HORSEHAIR BASKETS, 4 pcs., miniature, 2 lided, to 1½" D $88.00
PIMA/PAPAGO HORSEHAIR BASKETS, 3 pcs., miniature, 2 lidded, to 1¾" D $148.50
PIMA BASKETRY PLAQUES, 2 pcs., 8⅛", 9½" D.................... $99.00
SOUIX KNIFE SHEATH, red, yellow beading on green ground, tin dangles, 6⅜" L........................... $357.50

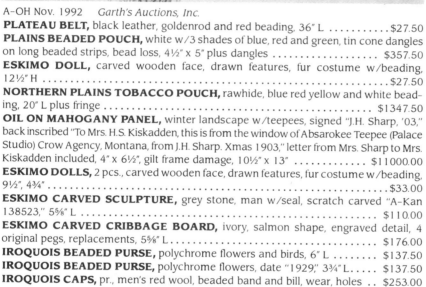

A-OH Apr. 1993   *Garth's Auctions, Inc.*
Row 1, Left to Right
NAVAHO RUG, wool, red, brown, tan, natural, selvage break, soiling, bleeding, 2'9" x 4'11" $357.50
NAVAHO RUG, red, tan, grey on cream, wear, damage, stains, 3' x 5'4" ... $330.00
NAVAHO RUG, contemporary, grey, red, black, white, brown, by Julia Francisco, 2'8" x 3'10" $132.00
Row 2, Left to Right
NAVAHO YEI RUG, polychrome figures on red ground, 2'11" x 3'6" $412.50
NAVAHO RUG, brown, tan on white, ca. 1910, wear, stains, 1'10" x 2'3" $55.00
NAVAHO-GALLUP RUG, browns, red, white, stains, 1'7½" x 3'5" $137.50
CHILKAT BLANKET, yarn on cedar bark warp, ca. 1890, damage, very frail condition, 58" x 33" $2970.00

A-MA Dec. 1992   *Skinner, Inc.*
BISQUE HEAD INDIAN DOLLS, 2 pcs., brown glass eyes, jointed composition bodys, squaw impressed "15/0," 11" H; brave impressed "14/0," 12" H .. $165.00
BISQUE HEAD INDIAN DOLL, brown glass eyes, impressed "244 O," mohair wig, jointed composition body, damage, 12" H $385.00

A-OH Apr. 1993   *Garth's Auctions, Inc.*
NAVAHO RUG, wool, tan, brown, natural, orange-red, stains, 5'2" x 6'2" $935.00

A-OH Nov. 1992   *Garth's Auctions, Inc.*

Row 1, Left to Right
WAKESHAN BASKET, purple whales, faded, 2⅛" H, 3⅝" D $165.00
WAKESHAN BASKET, analine birds, longboats, 3¼" H, 4¼" D $121.00
INUIT ESKIMO BALEEN BASKET, carved ivory walrus finial and bottom disk, loss, 2½" H, 4⅛" L $660.00
MISSION INDIAN BASKET, cat, birds, wear, loss, 3⅜" W, 10" L $495.00
ESKIMO BASKET, woven grass, red, black beading, wear, 4⅞" H, 5⅞" D $93.50
BASKET, bracken fern, grass design on red, wear, split, 2⅞" H, 5½" D $110.00

Row 2, Left to Right
PAPAGO BASKET, martynia design on yucca, 3½" H, 8⅜" D $110.00
APACHE BASKET, martynia design, damage, 2½" H, 10" D $192.50
PAPAGO BASKET, martynia on yucca, wear, 3⅝" H, 8⅝" L $137.50
THOMPSON RIVER BASKET, rim damage, 3⅝" H, 6½" D $71.50

Row 3, Left to Right
POMO BASKET, half twist overlay design, damage, 4" H, 10" D $93.50
POTTERY BOWL, umber on white, incised rim, wear, damage, 2¾" H, 7⅜" D ... $71.50
MISSION BASKET, dk. brown design, soiled, losses, 4¼" H, 7⅜" D $198.00
HOPI CORN SEED BASKET, red, green, purple, faded, loss, 4⅜" H, 4⅝" D $60.50

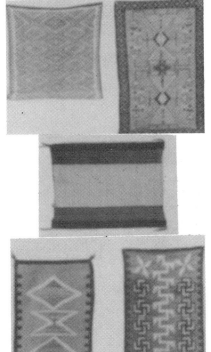

A-OH Nov. 1992   *Garth's Auctions, Inc.*
NAVAJO RUG, black, red, white, mustard and gray, 7'6" x 18' $7700.00
TES NOS PAS NAVAJO RUG, finely carded wool, black, gray, tan, red, green, orange, and natural, staining, 5' x 8'2" $4895.00
HOPI WOMEN'S MANTA, cotton, red, black, natural ground, c. 1930, staining, 3'1" x 3'11" $990.00
NAVAJO RUG, hand carded and spun wool, red, grey, tan and brown, stains, bleeding, 4'1" x 7'2" $825.00
NAVAJO RUG, hand carded and spun wool, grey, natural, gold and brown, edge repairs, 2'9" x 4'2" $247.50

A-OH Nov. 1992   *Garth's Auctions, Inc.*
NAVAHO RUGS, HAND SPUN AND CARDED WOOL

Row 1, Left to Right
SERRATE DESIGN, analine red, orange, dk. brown, breaks, 3'3" x 6' $440.00
SPIRIT LINE, ca. 1930, gold, russet, brown, black, stains, 2'10" x 4'9" $192.50
MARTHA BELEN, black, gray, white on tan, 2'6½" x 3'9" $110.00

Row 2, Left to Right
DIAMOND BANDS, red, brown, black on white, bleeding, breaks, 3'5" x 5' .. $192.50
NORTHWEST RESERVATION CROSS, dk. brown, red, tan, bleeding, wear, stains, 4'1" x 6'1" $687.50
DOUBLE SADDLE BLANKET, ca. 1915, dk. brown, red, wear, 2'7" x 5' ... $385.00

Row 3, Left to Right
YEI GALLUP, black, green, red, on natural, bleeding, 1'4½" x 2'9½" $93.50
YEI, browns, black, blue, maroon on gray, contemporary, 5' x 6'11" $440.00

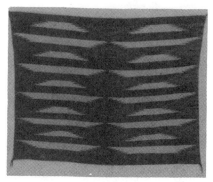

A-OH Nov. 1992   *Garth's Auctions, Inc.*
NAVAJO BLANKET, Germantown Chief pattern, dark forest green, red, natural, corner tassels, pristine condition, minor stains, 4'8" x 5'10" $10450.00

A-OH Nov. 1992   *Garth's Auctions, Inc.*

Row 1, Left to Right
PAIUTE BASKET, full beaded exterior, yellow, red, green and blue, beading damage, 3" D, 1⅝" H $110.00
TLINGIT PIPE, Northwest coast, carved for Indian's own use, polychrome, seal, raven, eagle, whale, brass bowl, hole for reed stem, 3¼" L, 2" H $1540.00
BLACKWARE BOWL, San Ildefonso, incised "Marie," paper label from 1930's World Exhibit, 4¾" D, 1½" H $797.50
BLACKWARE JAR, San Ildefonso, 1030's exhibit sticker, 2⅛" D, 1¾" H $247.50
APACHE HORSEHAIR TRAY, woven, black and white, 2½" $126.50

Row 2, Left to Right
PIMA BASKET, Martynia and willow, small break in rim, 3½" D, 2⅜" H $220.00
MAKAH LIDDED BASKET, polychrome bird and whale, 2¼" D, 2⅛" H $99.00
POPAGO LIDDED BASKET, two-tone design, 2¾" D, 2⅛" H $33.00
POPAGO LIDDED BASKET, two-tone design, 3½" D, 3" H $66.00
INDIAN BASKET, three color design, 3" D, 1¾" H $33.00

Row 3, Left to Right
MISSION BASKETRY TRAY, two-tone design, 5" $82.50
PIMA BASKET, martynia and willow, 4¼" D, 2¾" H $143.00
ACOMA POTTERY JAR, umber, ochre on white slip, wear 4⅝" D, 3¼" H $38.50
CALIFORNIA INDIAN BASKET, red design, rim damage, 4¼" D, 2⅜" H . . . $385.00

A-OH July 1993   *Garth's Auctions, Inc.*
HAND-CARDED NAVAHO RUGS
RUG, natural native dyes, mostly rabbit brush, stains, 3'11" x 5'11" $220.00
RUG, ca. 1890. Analine dye, red, orange, dk. brown, grey, faded purple, natural, bleeding, 4'7" x 6'3" $385.00
RUG, Two Grey Hills weaving, black, grey, tan, natural, Spirit Line break, ca. 1960, 2'6" x 4'10" $330.00
RUG, Two Grey Hills style, mustard, greys, black, natural, Spirit Line break, contemporary, 2'11" x 5'2" $330.00

A-ME Feb. 1993   *James D. Julia, Inc.*
NAVAJO RUG, red, black, gray, orange, 46" x 65" $400.00
NAVAJO RUG, red, black, gray, white, damage, 46" x 88" $650.00

A-ME Feb. 1993   *James D. Julia, Inc.*
NAVAJO RUG, turquoise, red, black, green, brown, 46" x 80" $1950.00
NAVAJO RUG, red, black, gray, white, 38" x 68" $300.00

A-MA Nov. 1992   *James D. Julia, Inc.*
BOUDIOR LAMP, rev. painted, basket-weave molded shade signed Handel 5609, bronze base labeled, 15″ T $2300.00*

A-MA Nov. 1992   *James D. Julia, Inc.*
Row 1, Left to Right
HANDEL FLOOR LAMP, rev. painted shade, signed, 59″ T, 10″ D $2500.00*
HANDEL TABLE LAMP, rev. painted shade, signed, 23″ T, 18″ D $2600.00*
HANDEL TABLE LAMP, rev. painted shade, signed' 23″ T, 18″ D $5500.00*
Row 2, Left to Right
HANDEL TABLE LAMP, reverse painted shade, signed, 23″ T, 18″ D $6750.00*
TIFFANY DESK LAMP, base signed, shades signed "LCT Favrile," 12¾″ H . . . . NS
HANDEL TABLE LAMP, bronzed, electrified, 20″ T $1800.00*
HANDEL BOUDOIR LAMP, rev. painted shade, signed, 15″ T, 7″ D $1900.00*
HANDEL TABLE LAMP, rev. painted shade, signed, 23″ T, 16″ D $7000.00*

A-MA Nov. 1992   *James D. Julia, Inc.*
BOUDOIR LAMP, signed Handel, bronzed base, rev. painted shade, 14″ T $4750.00*

A-MA Nov. 1992   *James D. Julia, Inc.*
TABLE LAMP, mauve, fuchsia, purple, white, green, emerald leaded shade impressed Tiffany, 1475, bronze base impressed Tiffany, 9514, 26″ T . . $31500.00*

A-MA Nov. 1992   *James D. Julia, Inc.*
SOLAR LAMP, frosted cut glass shade, embossed brass font and stem, marble base, prism loss, 20″ T $200.00*
TABLE LAMP, green cut to clear font, frosted cut glass shade, marble base, 26″ T $2050.00*

A-MA Nov. 1992   *James D. Julia, Inc.*
BOUDOIR LAMP, ribbed, painted shade signed Handel 2906 HH, bronzed base unsigned, hairline, 14″ T $350.00*
TABLE LAMP, painted cloth shade signed Handel, metal base unsigned, 24″ T $110.00*

A-MA Nov. 1992   *James D. Julia, Inc.*

Row 1, Left to Right

HANDEL TABLE LAMP, rev. painted shade, signed, bronzed base, 26″ T $7000.00*
HANDEL TABLE LAMP, signed rev. painted shade, bronzed base, 23″ T $7500.00*
HANDLE TABLE LAMP, slag glass shade overlaid w/bronzed metal fish net, bronzed base, signed, 23″ T $3000.00*

Row 2, Left to Right

HANDEL TABLE LAMP, leaded glass shade, marked bronzed base, 28″ T ... $3500.00*
HANDEL TABLE LAMP, rev. painted shade, bronzed base, signed, 23″ T .... NS
HANDEL TABLE LAMP, rev. painted shade, bronzed base, signed, 24″ T $5250.00*

A-MA Nov. 1992   *James D. Julia, Inc.*
TABLE LAMP, rev. painted Carlisle shade stamped Pairpoint Corp., copper finished base impressed Pairpoint D3034, 23½″ T $2300.00*

A-PA May 1993   *Conestoga Auction Co.*
ANEMONE LAMP, rose, lavender, yellow on lt. green, 1949–1978, 24″ T .. $300.00*
ORCHID LAMP, red, yellow, white on ivory to cobalt, 1949–1986, 24″ T $350.00*

A-MA Nov. 1992   *James D. Julia, Inc.*

Row 1, Left to Right

LAMPS, pr., embossed WMG, acorn burners, chip, 5″ T $225.00*
STUDENT LAMP, new WMG shades, brass log embossed "OCT 28 79," nutmeg burners, 12¼″ T $600.00*
LAMP, embossed WMG, painted blue, green, hornet burner, 8″ T $100.00*

Row 2, Left to Right

LAMP, ruby on white opalescent, nutmeg burner, 9¾″ T $140.00*
LAMP, red satin glass, nutmeg burner, flakes, 8½″ T $60.00*
ARTICHOKE LAMP, WMG painted pink, green, nutmeg burner, 7¾″ T ... $140.00*
LAMP, crystal upside-down cup and saucer, 3″ T $50.00*

A-MA Nov. 1992   *James D. Julia, Inc.*

Row 1, Left to Right

STEM LAMP, white clambroth font, blue clambroth base, roughness, 12″ T $1100.00*
STEM LAMP, white clambroth, flakes, 11⅛″ T $600.00*
STEM LAMP, green clambroth font, white clambroth base, drilled, 12″ T .. $325.00*

Row 2, Left to Right

STEM LAMP, blue clambroth font, white clambroth base, 11½″ T $1150.00*
STEM LAMPS, pr., white clambroth, 10⅝″ T $800.00*
STEM LAMP, blue clambroth font, brass stem, marble foot, 11¼″ T $400.00*

A-MA Nov. 1992   *James D. Julia, Inc.*
TABLE LAMP, Phonix glass, rev. painted shade, bronzed base, 23″ T .. $1200.00*

A-MA Nov. 1992   *James D. Julia, Inc.*
BOUDOIR LAMP, rev. and exterior painted shade signed Handel 6155 HH, bronzed base labeled, 15″ T $1900.00*

A-MA Nov. 1992   *James D. Julia, Inc.*
NIGHT LIGHT, rev. and exterior painted crackle glass shade signed Handel 8013C, metal base, rim chips, 7½″ T ... $700.00*
NIGHT LIGHT, exterior painted crackle glass shade signed Handel 7057, interior has yellow wash, gilt painted base, 7½″ T $1050.00*

A-MA Nov. 1992   *James D. Julia, Inc.*
Row 1, Left to Right
LAMPS, 3 pcs., blue glass fonts, 3″ – 3¾″ T $120.00*
Row 2, Left to Right
FINGER LAMPS, 2 pcs., lt. green glass, 3½″, blue-green glass, 4″ T $70.00*
FINGER LAMPS, 2 pcs., cobalt blue glass, 3¼″, 3½″ T $80.00*
Row 3, Left to Right
FINGER LAMPS, 2 pcs., ruby ...... NS
FINGER LAMPS, 2 pcs., blue glass fonts, 3⅝″, 4″ T $70.00*

A-MA Nov. 1992   *James D. Julia, Inc.*
Row 1, Left to Right
STEM LAMP, blue glass font, WMG base, 9¼″ T $150.00*
STEM LAMP, green panel font, clear base, 8¾″ T $75.00*
STEM LAMP, amber glass font, WMG base, 7¾″ T $95.00*
FINGER LAMP, green, 7″ T $60.00*
Row 2, Left to Right
STEM LAMP, green glass font, clear base, 9¾″ T $50.00*
STEM LAMP, embossed cobalt font, amethyst glass base, 10″ T $135.00*
STEM LAMP, blue glass, 8¼″ T ..... NS
STEM LAMP, green panel font, clear base, 9¼″ T $70.00*

A-MA Nov. 1992   *James D. Julia, Inc.*
OVERLAY LAMP, electric blue cut to clear font, WMG base, cut frosted shade, 23″ T $1800.00*
TABLE LAMP, pink alabaster font and stem, marble foot, 13¼″ T $500.00*
STEM LAMP, blue opaline font and stem, marble base, frosted shade, 15¾″ T $750.00*

A-MA Nov. 1992   *James D. Julia, Inc.*
TABLE LAMP, signed Alladin, #1763, rev. painted shade, bronzed base, 16″ T $1000.00*

A-MA Nov. 1992   *James D. Julia, Inc.*
TABLE LAMP, rev. painted shade signed Classique 1918 LK, bronzed vase marked. 22″ T $4500.00*

A-MA Mar. 1993   *Skinner, Inc.*
MIRRORED CANDLE SCONCES, pr., early 19th c., painted candle cups, imperfections, 9⅛″ D $1320.00

A-MA Jun. 1993   *Skinner, Inc.*
WALL SCONCES, pr., tin, Deer Isle, Maine, 19th c., 14⅞" H $1760.00

A-MA Nov. 1992   *James D. Julia, Inc.*
HANGING LAMP, red satin glass, yellow brass frame, crack, 35½" T $70.00*
HANGING LAMP, opalescent cranberry shade, brass holder, electified, 16½" T $200.00*

A-MA Nov. 1992   *James D. Julia, Inc.*
DESK LAMP, green painted opal glass shade signed Handel 7001 Mossering, bronzed base labeled, 12" T $700.00*

A-MA Nov. 1992   *James D. Julia, Inc.*
POND LILLY LAMP, green white 3-layered leaded shades impressed Handel, bronze base impressed Handel $1700.00*

A-MA Nov. 1992   *James D. Julia, Inc.*
TABLE LAMP, each lithophane shade panel signed and numbered, gold base signed Handel, 14" T $900.00*
SHADE, each lithophane panel signed and numbered, tin frame, 6½" T $400.00*

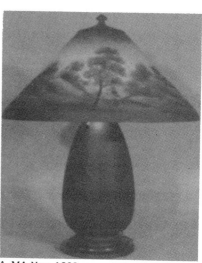

A-MA Nov. 1992   *James D. Julia, Inc.*
TABLE LAMP, rev. painted shade signed, 1802-156, bronzed base, 22" T $1200.00*

A-MA Nov. 1992   *James D. Julia, Inc.*
TABLE LAMP, rev. painted shade signed Moe Bridges Co. 192, bronzed base unsigned, 23" T $2250.00*

A-MA Nov. 1992   *James D. Julia, Inc.*
TABLE LAMP, rev. painted shade signed Handel 6930, bronzed metal base unsigned, 23" T $3500.00*

A-MA Nov. 1992   *James D. Julia, Inc.*
TABLE LAMP, Handel, pink, white, green rev. painted shade, bronzed base w/acid finished patina, 22" T $12000.00*

A-MA Nov. 1992   *James D. Julia, Inc.*
TABLE LAMP, painted WMG, green, pink, yellow, blue, 20½" T $250.00*

A-MA Nov. 1992   *James D. Julia, Inc.*
HANDEL TABLE LAMP, multi-color on shaded blue reverse painted shade signed "Handel 6688," bronzed base w/cloth label, 23" T $8500.00

A-MA Nov. 1992   *James D. Julia, Inc.*
PAIRPOINT TABLE LAMP, Ravena shade interior painted w/Pilgrim's Landing, stamped "Pairpoint Corporaton," silver-plated base mkd., 25" T $8000.00

A-MA Nov. 1992   *James D. Julia, Inc.*
PAIRPOINT TABLE LAMP, interior painted multi-color flowered shade, stamped "Pairpoint Corporation," brass base unsigned, 26" T $5750.00

A-MA Nov. 1992   *James D. Julia, Inc.*
HANDEL TABLE LAMP, multi-color pansys on mottled green leaded glass shade, bronzed base, 21" T $3700.00
HANDEL TABLE LAMP, yellow, green apple blossoms on caramel leaded glass shade signed "Handel," bronzed base w/molded signature, 26" T $3000.00

A-MA Nov. 1992   *James D. Julia, Inc.*
PAIRPOINT TABLE LAMP, Carlisle shade reverse painted in blue, green, yellow, red, stamped and labeled Pairpoint, brass base stamped, 21" T $2250.00
PAIRPOINT TABLE LAMP, Carlisle shade reverse painted in green, blue, orange, brown, stamped "Pairpoint Corporation," artist signed "Palme," bronzed base impressed "Pairpoint," 23" T $750.00
PAIRPOINT TABLE LAMP, Copley shade reverse painted in green, blue, brown, yellow, stamped "Pairpoint Corporation," artist signed "F. Motley," base unsigned, 22" T . . $500.00

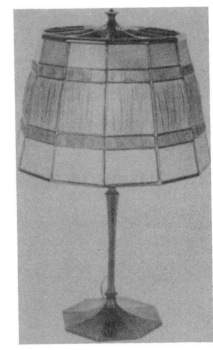

A-MA Nov. 1992   *James D. Julia, Inc.*
TABLE LAMP, Tiffany, linenfold amber glass leaded shade, bronze base, 23" T $6250.00*

A-OH Apr. 1993   *Early Auction Co.*
ASTRAL LAMP, frosted shade cut to clear, cut crystal stem, prisms, 29″ T $550.00*
ASTRAL LAMP, frosted shade cut to clear, metal stem, marble base, prisms, 20″ T $400.00*

A-MA Nov. 1992   *James D. Julia, Inc.*
Row 1, Left to Right
STEM LAMP, white striped font, brass stem, marble foot, wear, 9¾″ T $375.00*
STEM LAMP, crystal font, blue alabaster base, 13″ T $280.00*
STEM LAMP, white striped font, brass stem, marble foot, wear, 9″ T $475.00*
Row 2, Left to Right
TABLE LAMP, lt. blue cathedral font, clear stem and foot, 12¾″ T $160.00*
STEM LAMP, WMG font, green alabaster base, bruise on base, 14¼″ T $125.00*
LAMP, blue, burgundy, green WMG font, blue cut to clear stem, 13¾″ T $125.00*

A-OH Nov. 1992   *Garth's Auctions, Inc.*
Row 1, Left to Right
LAMPS, pr., clear, blown frosted fonts, pressed octagonal bases, chips, no collars, 9¼″ & 9½″ H $55.00
PITTSBURGH FLINT CANDLESTICK, clear, hexagonal, 9¾″ H $55.00
DOLPHIN CANDLESTICK, electric, blue, second period, heat check in socket, 6½″ H $225.50
FLINT LAMP, clear, brass collar, horn of plenty font, chips, 10¼″ H $220.00
Row 2, Left to Right
LAMP, clear, blown font, pressed base, pewter collar, chips, 9⅜″ H $99.00
FLINT LAMP, clear, ellipse and bull's eye font, brass collar, chips, 8⅜″ H . . . $71.50
PITTSBURGH FLINT VASE, clear, pillar mold, 9⅝″ H $115.50
LAMP, clear, blown font, pressed base, brass collar, chips, 7⅝″ H $49.50
LAMP, sanded clambroth base, clear pressed font, brass connector and collar, 9″ H $60.50

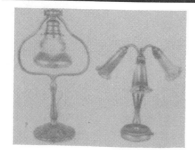

A-MA Nov. 1992   *James D. Julia, Inc.*
DESK LAMP, Tiffany Favrile, green glass shade w/iridescent purple, gold surface, silver dec., inscribed, bronzed base marked. 17″ T $1500.00
LILLY LAMP, Tiffany, signed Quezal shades, 12¾″ T . . . . NS

A-MA Nov. 1992   *James D. Julia, Inc.*
DESK LAMP, rev. painted shade signed Handel #6253, bronzed base unsigned, 10″ L, 12″ T $1600.00*

A-MA Nov. 1992   *James D. Julia, Inc.*

Row 1, Left to Right

STEM LAMP, clear glass, 6⅝″ T $975.00*
FINGER LAMPS, 2 pcs., clear glass $80.00*
FINGER LAMP, clear glass, 3¾″ T $90.00*
FINGER LAMP, clear glass, 3¾″ T $250.00*
FINGER LAMP, pressed glass, 4″ T $150.00*

Row 2, Left to Right

STEM LAMPS, 2 pcs., (1 illus.), clear glass, pewter collars, 6″ T $110.00*
STEM LAMP, clear class, 6¾″ T $400.00*
FINGER LAMPS, pr., clear glass, pewter collars, 4¾″ T $140.00*
LAMPS, 3 pcs., (1 illus.), clear glass, pewter collars, 2″ to 3½″ T $130.00*

A-MA Nov. 1992   *James D. Julia, Inc.*
TABLE LAMP, pink, yellow, white, blue, green leaded shade impressed Handel, bronze base unsigned, 28″ T .. $3500.00*

A-MA Nov. 1992   *James D. Julia, Inc.*
HANGING LAMP, cranberry glass, red brass frame, crystal prisms, losses, 40″ T $950.00*

A-MA Nov. 1992   *James D. Julia, Inc.*
HANGING BALL LIGHT, painted iridescent glass shade signed Handel 6885, Artist signed "Bedigie," bronzed stem, 31″ L, 10″ D $3200.00*

A-MA Nov. 1992   *James D. Julia, Inc.*
HANGING BALL LIGHT, painted iridescent glass shade signed Handel 6996, bronzed stem, 25″ L, 10″ D $1900.00*

A-MA Nov. 1992   *James D. Julia, Inc.*
Row 1, Left to Right
OVERLAY LAMP, white cut to clear font, mercury glass stem, slate foot, 8½" T $425.00*
LAMP FONT, Hobbs Coin Dot, blue glass $290.00*
STEM LAMP, optic swirled rib amethyst glass font, cracked brass stem, chipped marble foot, 7¼" T $55.00*
Row 2, Left to Right
STEM LAMP, green alabaster font, fluted brass stem, marble base, wear, 12" T $200.00*
STEM LAMP, blue clambroth Sandwich glass font, veined gold stem, black foot, crack, 9¾" T $250.00*
OVERLAY LAMP, white cut to clear font, brass stem, marble foot, 9" T . . . $250.00*

A-MA Nov. 1992   *James D. Julia, Inc.*
Row 1, Left to Right
STEM LAMP, Greek Key clear glass w/matching chimney, 18½" T $205.00*
STEM LAMP, clear Princess Feather glass, flakes, 9¼" T $35.00*
STEM LAMP, crystal w/lion, tiger, buffalo heads on stem, flakes, 11¾" T $125.00*
Row 2, Left to Right
STEM LAMP, clear glass, Peanut pat., 9½" T $25.00*
HOLLOW STEM LAMP, by Ripley, clear glass, 11" T $140.00*
STEM LAMP, clear Moon glass, font painted, frost w/blue daisys, 10" T $50.00*
STEM LAMP, Crown pat. clear glass, frosted/painted panels, wear, 9" T $35.00*
Row 3, Left to Right
STEM LAMP, Comen/Pinwheel crystal font, brass stem, marble foot, 9¼" T $45.00*
STEM LAMP, Shield & Star crystal font, brass stem is split, marble foot, 6¾" T . . $45.00*
STEM LAMP, Blackberry crystal font, brass stem, WMG foot, 8¼" T $175.00*

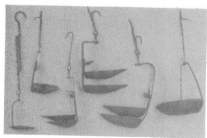

A-MA Dec. 1992   *Skinner, Inc.*
PAN LAMP, iron, 18¾" L $150.00*
DOUBLE CRUSIE, iron, "JB," 10½" L $150.00*
DOUBLE CRUSIE, iron, 12½" L $150.00*
DOUBLE CRUSIE, iron, 12" L $300.00*
CRUSIE, iron, repair, 14" L $75.00*
PAN LAMP, iron, "JB," 14½" L . . . $80.00*

A-MA Nov. 1992   *James D. Julia, Inc.*

Row 1, Left to Right

STEM LAMP, amber glass Diamond Dot font, blue glass base, 12¼" T . . . . NS
STEM LAMP, Cathedral blue glass font, clear glass stem, blue Daisy & Button shade, 18½" T $375.00*
STEM LAMP, Moon & Star blue glass base, amber font, 11½" T $50.00*

Row 2, Left to Right

STEM LAMP, opaque green Princess Feather glass, 9¾" T $200.00*
STEM LAMP, amber glass New York font, amber Chicago stem, 10½" T $55.00*
STEM LAMP, amber glass Diamond Dot font, amber Thousand Eye base, 12¼" T . . . NS
STEM LAMP, Bullseye pat., crystal font, opaque blue base, 11¼" T $350.00*

A-MA Nov. 1992   *James D. Julia, Inc.*

Row 1, Left to Right

STEM LAMP, blue, clear font embossed "Patented March 4 & June 3 1862," brass stem, marble foot, wear, 9¼" T . . $750.00*
STEM LAMP, blue alabaster font, WMG base, crack, 11⅜" T $100.00*
STEM LAMP, cranberry glass font, fluted stem, marble base, wear, dents, 9¾" T $400.00*

Row 2, Left to Right

LAMP, yellow cased glass font, cast metal stem, 7¼" T $120.00*
LAMP, embossed clear glass font, amber base, crack, clouded, 9" T $350.00*
STEM LAMP, WMG font, blue milk glass base, flake, 7⅜" T $275.00*

A-MA Nov. 1992   *James D. Julia, Inc.*

STEM LAMP, Webster vaseline font, cast iron base, dated Feb. 29, 1876, wear, 11¾" T $25.00*
LAMP, green and white milk glass font and stem, 13½" T $25.00*
LAMP, lt. green font and stem, painted metal foot, 11½" T $70.00*
FINGER LAMPS, 2 pcs., (1 illus.), green glass, 5¼", 3" T $50.00*

Row 2, Left to Right

STEM LAMPS, 2 pcs., (1 illus.), green fonts, brass stems, marble feet, 10½" T $100.00*
BANQUET LAMP BASE, nickel plated, 9¼" T $90.00*
LAMP, amber glass font, WMG base, 10½" T $70.00*
STEM LAMP, WMG font and base, 10¾" T $70.00*

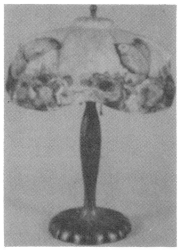

A-MA Nov. 1992   *James D. Julia, Inc.*

PAIRPOINT TABLE LAMP, multi-color des. on white ground painted shade stamped "Pairpoint Corporation," base stamped, 20" T $5500.00

A-MA Nov. 1992   *James D. Julia, Inc.*

Row 1, Left to Right
SHADES, 2 pcs., 1 signed Steuben, iridescent gold, other iridescent lily, 6" T $450.00
STEUBEN SHADES, pr., gold aurene on calcite, signed, 5" T $175.00

Row 2, Left to Right
SHADES, 3 pcs., blue hooked feather signed Luster Art; Steuben opalescent; Verre De Soire 2-color pulled feather, unsigned $600.00

Row 3, Left to Right
QUEZAL SHADE, iridescent gold, hooked feather, signed, 6" T $300.00
QUEZAL SHADES, 3 pcs, signed, opal w/green, gold pulled feathers ... $675.00

A-MA Nov. 1992   *James D. Julia, Inc.*
HANGING SHADE, leaded glass, heart and leaf border, 24" D $800.00

A-MA Nov. 1992   *James D. Julia, Inc.*

Row 1, Left to Right
STEM LAMP, opalscent in vaseline glass, chimney not original, 16¾" T $175.00*
STEM LAMP, vaseline glass, match holder base, 8" T $00.00*
STEM LAMP, vaseline glass, Sheldon Swirl pat., 8" T $225.00*
STEM LAMP, stem lamp, blue opalescent Hobbs Snowflake pat., 8¾" T $300.00*

Row 2, Left to Right
FAIRY LAMP, Prunus flower decorated Burmese shade, pottery base signed Clarke and Taylor-Tunnecliff, crack, 6¼" T $1300.00*
FINGER LAMP, clear opalescent polka dot, 5" T........................... $450.00*
STEM LAMP, amber glass, 8" T $75.00*
FAIRY LAMP, Prunus flower decorated Burmese shade, pottery base signed Clarke and Taylor-Tunnecliff, 6¼" T $1300.00*

Row 3, Left to Right
STEM LAMP, clear opalescent font, amber base, chips, 7¼" T $125.00*
STEM LAMP, clear opalescent coinspot font, crystal base, 7½" T $100.00*
STEM LAMP, blue Sheldon Swirl, flake, 8½" T $325.00*
STEM LAMP, amber glass Peacock Feather, 8" T $60.00*

A-MA Nov. 1992   *James D. Julia, Inc.*
CHANDELIER, cast iron, Lomax frosted star fonts, WMG shades, 46" L .. $425.00*

A-MA Nov. 1992   *James D. Julia, Inc.*
TABLE LAMP, rev. painted shade signed Moe Bridges co 182, bronzed base unsigned, 23″ T $3250.00*

A-MA Nov. 1992   *James D. Julia, Inc.*
TABLE LAMP, Wilkinson, red, green leaded shade, bronzed base, 24″ T . . . $1550.00*

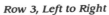

A-MA Nov. 1992   *James D. Julia, Inc.*

Row 1, Left to Right

LAMP, red stain glass, nutmeg burner, flakes, 8¾″ T $115.00*
LAMP, Nellie Bly pattern, white milk glass w/pink, multicolors, chip, 8⅝″ T $40.00*
LAMP, Nellie Bly pattern, white milk glass w/pink, multicolors, 8⅝″ T $35.00*
LAMP, milk glass, painted gray, black, orange, acorn burner, 7½″ T $600.00*
LAMP, white milk glass, painted gray, black, orange, nutmeg burner, 9″ T $175.00*

Row 2, Left to Right

LAMP, camphored glass, painted blue, red, green, nutmeg burner, 6¼″ T $105.00*
LAMP, bisque skeleton, off white, professional restoration, 5¼″ T $1400.00*
LAMP, blue milk glass, filigreed copper/gold overlay, 7½″ T $500.00*
LAMP, white milk glass, painted orange, brown, satin finish, acorn burner, 7¼″ T . . . . NS
LAMP, camphored glass, embossed, painted, nutmeg burner, wear, 8¼″ T $100.00*

Row 3, Left to Right

LAMP, milk glass painted yellow, gold trim, embossed, acorn burner, 8¼″ T . . . $200.00*
SKATER'S LANTERN, brass, globe embossed "BABY," 4½″ T $125.00*
TWO ITEMS, brass skaters lantern, 7″ T, milk glass shade, blue delft, 5″ D $125.00*
BANQUET BASE, silverplated, Hinks burner, wear, tarnish, dent, 7½″ T $85.00*

A-MA Nov. 1992   *James D. Julia, Inc.*
GWTW LAMP, painted WMG, electrified, 26″ T $500.00*

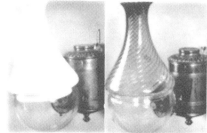

A-MA Nov. 1992   *James D. Julia, Inc.*
ANGLE LAMP, polished brass, WMG shade, all original $100.00*
ANGLE LAMP, brass plated tin, ruby shade, repro. elbow $800.00*

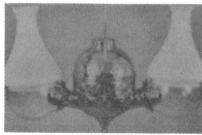

A-MA Nov. 1992   *James D. Julia, Inc.*
DOUBLE ANGLE LAMP, polished fleur-de-lis brass, repro. WMG shades $350.00*

A-MA Nov. 1992   *James D. Julia, Inc.*
MANHATTAN LAMP, nickel-plated brass, repro. WMG shade, 20¾" T $300.00*
DOUBLE STUDENT LAMP, repro., brass, onyx standard, brass fonts, floral glass shades mkd. "MGM Studio Property Culver City, CA," 25" T $250.00*

A-MA Nov. 1992   *James D. Julia, Inc.*
DOUBLE STUDENT LAMP, brass, green cased shades, electrified, 27" W, 22½" T $400.00*

A-MA Nov. 1992   *James D. Julia, Inc.*

Row 1, Left to Right
STEM LAMP, melon ribbed crystal font, cobalt base, by Central Glass, 7⅝" T . . $175.00*
STEM LAMP, opaque green glass, discolored bubble, 9¾" T $175.00*
STEM LAMP, cobalt glass, brass collar split, 8¼" T $95.00*
STEM LAMP, broad rib opaque blue font, transluscent cobalt base, 9¼" T $250.00*

Row 2, Left to Right
STEM LAMP, crystal Bullseye font, emerald glass base, 9¼" T $150.00*
STEM LAMP, amber Peacock Feather glass, 9½" T $225.00*
MAKE-DO LAMP, blue opalescent coindot font, WMG base, rough, 10¼" T . . . $160.00*
STEM LAMP, green Bullseye glass, 10" T $70.00*

Row 3, Left to Right
STEM LAMP, cranberry opalescent Snowflake font, clear base, loss, 7½" T $150.00*
STEM LAMP, cobalt Princess Feather glass, 8¼" T $300.00*
MAKE-DO LAMP, cranberry opalescent Snowflake font, WMG base, 7⅜" T $200.00*
STEM LAMP, cranberry opalescent Snowflake font, clear glass base, 9" T $400.00*

A-MA Nov. 1992   *James D. Julia, Inc.*
LIBRARY LAMP, brass frame, cranberry thumbprint shade, cranberry diamond quilted font, 3" prisims, 14" D $8000.00*
IRON HORSE HANGING LAMP, black cast iron frame, WMG shade, clear frosted glass font $275.00*

A-MA Nov. 1992   *James D. Julia, Inc.*
GONE W/THE WIND LAMP, Victoria pat., red satin glass, electrified, 27" T $475.00*
GONE W/THE WIND LAMP, Artichoke pat., milk glass painted lavender, green, electrified, 24" T $250.00*

A-MA Nov. 1992   *James D. Julia, Inc.*
HANDEL TABLE LAMP, pink, yellow, blue, green on crystal reverse painted shade signed Handel 7062BD," bronzed base unsigned, 25" T $6500.00

A-MA Nov. 1992   *James D. Julia, Inc.*
FINGER LAMP, blue glass, Janice pat., chip, 5½" T $120.00*
FINGER LAMP, sapphire glass, 3¼" T $180.00*
FINGER LAMP, sapphire glass, molded in collar, 4½" T $95.00*
FINGER LAMP, amber glass, ruffled Bullseye pat., molded in collar, 4" T $85.00*

Row 2, Left to Right
FINGER LAMP, amber glass, lock-on burner, Daisy & Button pat., bruise 3¼" T ... $95.00*
FINGER LAMP, amber glass, Diamond & Fan pat., 3⅜" T $55.00*
FINGER LAMP, optic rib cranberry glass, clear handle, 4¼" T $85.00*
FINGER LAMP, clear glass cup & saucer, 3¼" T $100.00*

Row 3, Left to Right
FINGER LAMP, cranberry optic rib glass, crystal handle, 4¼" T $125.00*
FINGER LAMP, marigold carnival glass, Zipper loop pat., chip, 5¼" T $300.00*
FINGER LAMP, blue glass, Peacock Feather pat., 6" T $150.00*
FINGER LAMP, green glass, Bullseye pat., 5¾" T $95.00*

A-MA Nov. 1992   *James D. Julia, Inc.*

Row 1, Left to Right

SOLAR LAMP, brass font, marble base, cut frosted shade, damage, 20" T $200.00*

LAMP, cranberry opalescent swirled shade, font bruised, 14¼" T $600.00*

LAMP, cobalt cut to clear font w/gilt dec., lavendar glass base, age lines, 14½" T .... NS

LAMP, white cut to clear font w/gilt dec., marble base, pressed frosted globe, 20⅜" T $500.00*

LAMP, blue cut to clear font, WMG stem and foot, cut frosted shade, wear, 23" T $1800.00*

LAMP, pink alabaster glass font and stem, marble foot, 13¼" T.............. $500.00*

LAMP, white cut to clear font and shade, WMG base, P & A Victor burner, wear, 17¼" T $550.00*

LAMP, blue opaline font and stem, marble foot, frosted shade, wear, 15¾" T ... $750.00*

Row 2, Left to Right

LAMP, green glass font, Clambroth blue base, 8½" T $400.00*

LAMPS, pr., Barlow, cobalt blue glass, pewter collars, flakes, 8¾" T $3000.00*

LAMPS, pr., Barlow, dark green glass, pewter collars, 8¼" T $200.00*

LAMP, Clambroth blue font, WMG base, 11¼" T $250.00*

LAMP, white cut to cranberry font, white alabaster base, wear, 12¼" T $700.00*

LAMP, white blown globe, WMG base, brass collar, whale oil burner, chips, 7⅛" T $300.00*

LAMP, clear opalescent Eason font, black glass stem, flake, 7¾" T $125.00*

LAMPS, pr.,Barlow, pressed amethyst glass, brass collars, chips, 9½" T $6500.00*

A-MA Nov. 1992   *James D. Julia, Inc.*

STEM LAMP, pressed, roughness, 12¾" T............................. $95.00*

STEM LIGHT, blown and cut font, pewter collar, chips, 11¼" T $105.00*

STEM LAMP, pewter collar .... NS

STEM LAMP, Sandwich, 10" T........................ $200.00*

Row 2, Left to Right

STEM LAMP, Sandwich, roughness, 10¼" T...................... $80.00*

STEM LAMP, cut font, pressed base, 9⅞" T........................ $80.00*

STEM LAMP, pressed, pewter collar, 9¼" T........................ $50.00*

STEM LAMP, pressed, roughness, 11½" T........................... $85.00*

A-MA Nov. 1992   *James D. Julia, Inc.*

DESK LAMP, rev. painted shade signed Handel 6675, bronzed base w/adjustable arm labeled, 13" T $700.00*

DESK LAMP, painted opal glass shade signed Handel Brown 7000-½, bronzed base labeled, 12" T $700.00*

A-MA Nov. 1992   *James D. Julia, Inc.*

STEM LAMPS, pr., molded WMG, pewter collars, fluid burners, 7½" T ... $1950.00*

LAMP, WMG, brass collar, whale oil burner, chips, 7⅛" T................. $300.00*

STEM LAMP, opalescent WMG, pewter collar, 7⅜" T $1050.00*

STEM LAMP, opalescent WMG, pewter collar, 6⅛" T $1100.00*

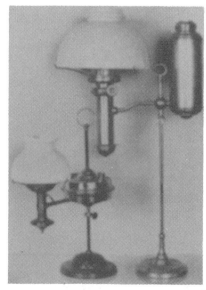

A-MA Nov. 1992   *James D. Julia, Inc.*

STUDENT LAMP, WMG shade, brass, electrified, 16" T $175.00*

STUDENT LAMP, WMG shade, nickel plated brass, electrified, 22" T .. $250.00*

A-MA Nov. 1992   *James D. Julia, Inc.*
APPLE SAUCE LAMP, crystal, fruit bowl cup w/original cork seal, paper label, roughness, crack, 21″ T. $300.00*
STEM LAMP, crystal font, amber glass base, nickle-plated brass fittings, 16″ T. . . . . . NS
STEM LAMP, green Diamond Dot font, amber Moon & Star base, 12¼″ T $70.00*
STEM LAMP, amber glass, Aquarius pat., 10″ T $125.00*
STEM LAMP, amber glass, Daisy & Button pat., flakes, bruise, 10¼″ T $55.00*

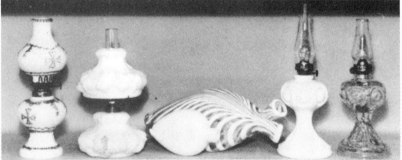

A-OH July 1993   *Garth's Auctions, Inc.*
Row 1, Left to Right
LAMP, green, brown end of day, 8½″ T $247.50
BLOWN BOTTLE, clear w/white looping, 7½″ T $22.00
NAILSEA FLASK, blown opaque white w/cranberry looping, 7″ T $121.00
LAMP, milk glass elephant base, mismatched milk glass globe w/green, 7½″ T . . $22.00
CANDY CONTAINERS, 2 pcs., lantern shaped, red, green glass, tin fittings, "Bond Pla-Mate," 4½″ T $44.00
LAMP, cranberry w/white enamel flowers on font, mismatched shade, 8¾″ T . . . $159.50
Row 2, Left to Right
LAMP, milk glass, gold painted dec., shade has chips, 9¼″ T $88.00
LAMP, molded milk glass, chips, 7″ T $104.50
PITTSBURGH LADIES FLASK, clear over opaque white, 5″ L $49.50
DOUBLE GEMEL BOTTLE, blown clear w/white looping, wear, 10¼″ L $104.50
LAMP, milk glass, 5½″ T $71.50
LAMP, clear, 5½″ T $27.50

A-MA Nov. 1992   *James D. Julia, Inc.*
LAMP, French, deep purple grape vine/leaf cameo on frosted shaded ground, signed LeGras, 19″ T $1500.00
DAUM-NANCY LAMP, golden yellow cameo glass, signed, 22″ T . . . . NS

A-MA Nov. 1992   *James D. Julia, Inc.*
TEROCA TABLE LAMP, signed caramel slag glass shade w/green, red leaded overlay dec., bronzed base, crack, 23″ T $2250.00*

A-MA Nov. 1992   *James D. Julia, Inc.*
TABLE LAMP, white cut to cranberry font, brass stem, marble foot, 9¼″ T . . $300.00
LAMP, white cut to cranberry, WMG base, flakes, wear, 14″ T $700.00
STEM LAMP, white cut to cranberry font, brass stem, marble foot, 12″ T . . . $500.00

A-MA Nov. 1992   *James D. Julia, Inc.*
HANDEL HANGING LAMP, green, brown, black on shaded yellow reverse painted iridescent shade, brass stem, artist's signature "Bedigie," 18" D $5000.00

A-MA Nov. 1992   *James D. Julia, Inc.*
MINI LAMP, blue glass, embossed daisy, nutmeg burner, 4¾" T $65.00*
MINIATURE LAMP SHADE, rainbow diamond quilted MOP in satin finish . . . $550.00*
SKELETON LAMP, white bisque w/blue, orchid, green glass eyes, 6½" T $5000.00*
MINI LAMP, green, embossed Daisy pat., acorn burner, 4¾" T $95.00*
MINI LAMP, amber, embossed Daisy pat., acorn buirner, 4¾" T $135.00*
Row 2, Left to Right
WATCH POCKET LAMP, nickel plated brass, "Watch Pocket Lamp- Folmer & Schwing Mfg.-NY-Pat. June 23-July 21, 91," includes labeled wood box w/extra lights . . . $450.00*
MATCH HOLDER LAMP, WMG, roughness, cracks, 8" T $50.00*
MATCH HOLDER LAMP, WMG, cracks, 7¾" T $100.00*
SKATERS LAMPS, pr., (1 illus.), brass w/clear globe, tin w/blue globe, 7" T $50.00*

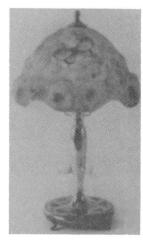

A-MA Nov. 1992   *James D. Julia, Inc.*
PAIRPOINT BOUDOIR LAMP, pastel shade stamped "Pairpoint Corporation," silver-plated base mkd., 16" T . . $3500.00

A-MA Nov. 1992   *James D. Julia, Inc.*
HANGING STORE LAMP, painted tin shade, brass font signed "The Rochester, 27" L $100.00*

A-MA Nov. 1992   *James D. Julia, Inc.*
HANGING CHANDELIER, signed Quezal, white, green on iridescent gold shades, extra shade $1600.00*

A-MA Nov. 1992   *James D. Julia, Inc.*
LAMP, cut glass, 30" T $550.00*

A-MA Nov. 1992   *James D. Julia, Inc.*
OVERLAY LAMP, blue cut to white cut to clear font, brass stem, marble base, 12" T $500.00*
STEM LAMP, green cut to clear font, figural stem, slate foot, 14¾" T . . $400.00*
STEM LAMP, green cut to clear font, brass stem, marble foot, bruise, wear, 12⅞" T $500.00*

A-MA Nov. 1992   *James D. Julia, Inc.*
OVERLAY LAMPS
Row 1, Left to Right
LAMP, white cut to green font, brass stem, marble foot, wear, 9¾" T $500.00*
LAMP, white cut to cranberry font, brass stem, marble foot, wear $300.00*
LAMP, white cut to clear font, mercury glass stem, black marble foot, 8½" T . . NS
LAMP, white cut to cobalt font, brass stem, marble foot, 9" T $400.00*
Row 2, Left to Right
LAMP, white cut to cranberry font, WMB base, 9¾" T $450.00*
LAMP, white cut to cranberry font, opalescent base, flakes, wear, 9¾" T . . $400.00*
LAMP, white cut to clear, brass stem, marble foot, 9" T . . . . NS
LAMP, white cut to clear font, brass stem, marble base, bruise, 9½" T $250.00*

A-MA Nov. 1992   *James D. Julia, Inc.*
Row 1, Left to Right
STEM LAMP, green glass font, clambroth blue base, 8½" T $400.00*
STEM LAMP, blue spatter glass font, multi-color slag glass base, flake, 9¼" T . . $200.00*
FINGER LAMP, opalescent aqua, King Melon pattern, 5¼" T $1050.00*
STEM LAMP, Eason clear opalescent font, black glass base, flake 7¾" T $125.00*
Row 2, Left to Right
STEM LAMP, clear opalescent font, amber base, 9" T $250.00*
STEM LAMP, blue-white font, brass stem, marble foot, brass cracks, 9¼" T . . . $600.00*
STEM LAMP, coindot in cranberry opalescent, manufacturing flaw, 8¼" T $175.00*
STEM LAMP, marigold Zipper Loop pattern, 9¼" T $225.00*

A-MA Jun. 1993   *Skinner, Inc.*
OVERLAY LAMP, Sandwich Glass Co., ca. 1870, 12½" T $7150.00
PRESSED TULIP LAMPS, Sandwich Glass Co., cobalt font, clambroth base, frosted globes, 19½" T $1650.00

A-MA Nov. 1992   *James D. Julia, Inc.*
OVERLAY LAMPS
Row 1, Left to Right
LAMP, cranberry cut to clear font, embossed WMG base, 13½" T $900.00*
PEG LAMPS, pr., red cut to white cut to clear, flake, 5¼" T $1150.00*
LAMP, cranberry cut to clear font, WMG base, flake, 12½" T $450.00*
Row 2, Left to Right
PEG LAMP, cranberry cut to clear font, brass stem, marble base, chip, 9¼" T $650.00*
LAMP, pink cut to white cut to clear font, opalescent base, 10¾" T $600.00*
PEG LAMP, cranberry cut to clear font, brass stem., marble foot, 9" T .. $600.00*

A-MA Nov. 1992   *James D. Julia, Inc.*
Row 1, Left to Right
PEG LAMPS, pr., (each end of row), cut crystal fonts, ceramic candlesticks, pink cased ball shades, P&A Victor burners, no chimneys, wear, 18½" T $800.00*
STEM LAMP, McKee Glass Jewel pattern, sapphire blue, 8¼" T $85.00*
GLOW LAMPS, 2 pcs., (1 illus.), embossed amethyst glass, chip, 5" T $60.00*
TWINKLE LAMP, sapphire blue glass, acorn burner, 7¼" T $175.00*
Row 2, Left to Right
FINGER LAMP, opalescent coinspot in cranberry glass, 4½" T $400.00*
LAMPS, 2 pcs., (1 illus.), white milk glass, 5½" T, clear Fire Fly font w/milk glass shade, 3½" T, both have Olmsted-type burners, flakes $75.00*
PEDESTRIAN TRAVEL LAMP, brass w/tin insert, 3¼" x 4" **$70.00***
GLOW LAMP, embossed ruby glass, glass burner, flake, 5" T $50.00*
GLOW LAMP, ruby glass, glass burner, roughness, 5" T .... NS
Row 3, Left to Right
STEM LAMP, vaseline font on white alabaster stem, flake, 7¾" T $250.00*
CHIMNEYS, 3 pcs., (1 illus.), red glass, 2 signed Macbeth #356, 1 Vulcan $200.00*
FINGER LAMP, opalescent blue glass, 2¾" T $535.00*
GLOW LAMP, embossed sapphire blue glass, glass burner, 5" T $50.00*
GLOW LAMPS, 2 pcs., (1 illus.), 1 white milk glass, 1 opalescent, 5" T $30.00*

A-MA Nov. 1992   *James D. Julia, Inc.*
STEM LAMP, blown font, scratches, 11" T $120.00*
STEM LAMP, blown frosted font, pewter collar, whale oil burner, 10¼" T $500.00*
STEM LAMP, pewter collar, 9¾" T $300.00*
STEM LAMP, blown font, pewter collar, 9¼" T $65.00*
SPARKING LAMPS, pr., (1 illus.), blown, cracks, 7½" T $145.00*

A-OH July 1993   *Garth's Auctions, Inc.*
PEWTER
Row 1, Left to Right
WATER PITCHER, "R. Gleason" touch, 8½" T $302.50
CREAMER, attributed to Hall & Cotton, Middlefield, Conn., battered, repair, 6¼" T $126.50
BEAKERS, 3 pcs., "John Warne" touch, battered, 3¾" to 4" T $148.50
PLATE, "Love" touch, wear, corroded, 7⅞" D $297.50
Row 2, Left to Right
PITCHER, attributed to D. Curtis, Albany, N.Y., wear, repair, 7⅞" T $148.50
BASIN, eagle touch by Thomas Danforth, wear, battered, 10" D $357.50
PITCHER, engraved "G," 6½" T . . $220.00

A-OH Jan. 1993   *Garth's Auctions, Inc.*
SHEAF FOOD MOLD, tin, copper, 4½ x 6" $93.50
CORN FOOD MOLD, tin, copper, holes, 4" x 6" $140.50
PEAR FOOD MOLD, tin, rust, 3½" x 5¼" $71.50
SWIRL FOOD MOLD, copper, holes, 6⅝" D $82.50
FRUIT FOOD MOLDS, 2 pcs., tin, rust $55.00
SMALL FOOD MOLDS, 5 pcs., (1 illus.), copper, similar designs, 4¼" D . . . $165.00
LARGE FOOD MOLDS, 3 pcs., (1 illus.), copper, similar designs, 9½" to 10" D $313.50
SPATULA, FORK, wrought iron, 12", 13" L $198.00
TRAMMEL, wrought iron, 19½" L $148.50
DIPPERS, 2 pcs., wrought iron, brass $88.00

A-OH May 1993   *Garth's Auctions, Inc.*
ENGLISH PEWTER
Row 1, Left to Right
CUP, wear, 4¾" H $11.00
TUMBLER, "Half Pint," 4" H $49.50
HAYSTACK MEASURE, "Gill," 3¾" H $192.50
SHAKERS, 2 pcs., 4¾" H $33.00
PITCHER, engraved monogram, resoldered, 5⅜" H $66.00
MUSTARD, crowned X mark, repair, 4¼" H $49.50
GOBLET, engraved monogram, 4⅞" H $33.00
Row 2, Left to Right
BELLIED MEASURES, set of six, ¼ gill to quart $825.00
Row 3, Left to Right
TANKARD MEASURE, 8¼"H . . $742.50
PLATE, "Townsend & Compton" touch, wear, stratches, 7¾" H $49.50
TEAPOT, Queen Anne style, rose mark, repairs, 7½" H $55.00
PLATE, "Compton" touch, wear, 8" D $115.50
TANKARD MEASURE, "Pint," 4½" H $93.50
PLATE, "Townsend & Compton" touch, wear, scratches, 7¾" D $110.00
TANKARD MEASURE, "James Birch" touch, "Quart," wear, 6¼" H $165.00

A-MA Dec. 1992   *Skinner, Inc.*
GEORG JENSEN COFFEE POT, sterling, model #80A, 14 troy oz. $770.00
GEORG JENSEN SALTS AND SPOONS, set of 6, sterling, acorn pattern, cobalt liners, 5 troy oz. $880.00

A-OH May 1993   *Garth's Auctions, Inc.*
PEWTER
Row 1, Left to Right
SYRUP PITCHER, 8⅛" H $99.00
PLATE, split, 8" D $33.00
COMMUNION CHALICES, pr., 6¼" H $275.00
PLATES, 2 pcs., dents, 10¼" D . . $231.00
TALL COFFEE POT, "Sellew & Co, Cincinnati" touch, 10" H $412.50
TEAPOT, 5⅞" H $247.50
Row 2, Left to Right
WATER PITCHER, "Sellew & Co., Cincinnati" touch, 9¼" H $742.50
PLATE, "Sheldon & Feltman, Albany" touch, 10¼" D $181.50
LAMP, matching whale oil burner, battered, 5¾" H $181.50
PLATE, scratches, 10¼" H $115.50
PITCHER, 8" H $110.00
LAMP, brass spouts, 6" H $137.50
PLATE, "Roswell Gleason" touch, 10⅞" D $247.50
WATER PITCHER, "Flagg & Homan" touch, 9" H $247.50

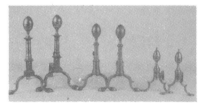

A-MA Oct. 1992   *Skinner, Inc.*
LEMON-TOP ANDIRONS, pair, brass, signed "John Molineux founder Boston," ca. 1800, 20" H $1980.00
LEMON-TOP ANDIRONS, pair, brass, 19th c., 18" H $440.00
ANDIRONS, pair, brass, ca. 1800, 11½" H $440.00

A-MA Dec. 1992   *Skinner, Inc.*
KETTLE, cast iron, 5" D $70.00*
3-LEGGED DOWN-HEARTH SKILLET, cast iron, 5½" handle, 6¼" D $60.00*
PAN, iron, 4¼" handle, 5¼" D . . $60.00*

A-MA Dec. 1992   *Skinner, Inc.*
3-LEGGED PAN, wrought iron, 11″ handle, 6½″ D $20.00
PAN, cast iron, pitted, 9″ handle, 8½″ D $75.00
3-LEGGED SKILLET, 19″ handle, 12″ D $250.00
TOASTER, wrought iron, 16″ L $250.00

A-MA Jan. 1993 *Richard A. Bourne Co., Inc.*
IRON JUG, ca. 1800, molded-in "OSIPIS," rust, 7″ T $80.00*
CALDRON, cast iron, mark, repair .. NS
MORTAR AND PESTLE, maple, age crack $50.00*
MORTAR AND PESTLE, maple, age crack in mortar $55.00*
WAFFLE IRON, heart-shaped, ca. 1800, 29½″ L $325.00*

A-MA Nov. 1992   *James D. Julia, Inc.*
TUMBLER LAMP, crystal drinking glass in tin holder w/drop in tin lamp font and burner, lid marked "STAR Patented JAN 13 1874 TUMBLER" $50.00*
CHAMBER LAMPS, pr., (1 illus.), brass, whale oil, 6″ T $50.00*
RUSH HOLDER, wrought iron, wood base, 10½″ T $50.00*
UFFORD LAMPS, pr., (1 illus.), tin shades and fonts, cast iron bases, 14½″ T $50.00*
Row 2, Left to Right
LAMPS, 2 pcs., (1 illus.), tin $35.00*
LAMPS, 5 pcs., (1 illus.), early tin $35.00*
LUCERNO LAMP, nickel plated brass, all tools, unknown hallmark, 25½″ T $50.00*
TIME LAMP, pewter, crystal font, 13½″ T $200.00*
CANDLE LANTERN, copper, tin, 19th c., 11¾″ T $25.00*

A-OH May 1993   *Garth's Auctions, Inc.*
PEWTER
Row 1, Left to Right
COMMUNION FLAGGON, "Roswell Gleason" touch, 10″ H $495.00
TEA SET, 4 pcs., copper bottomed, "D.B. Woodworth, Cinit. Britannia Co," dents, 10″ H $247.50
LIGHTHOUSE TALL POT, "R. Gleason" touch, dents, 10⅝″ H $687.50
Row 2, Left to Right
TALL POT, Boardman & Hart, N. York" touch, 11⅜″ H $330.00
CONTINENTAL CHARGER, angel touch, engraving, vintage, initials, repair, wear, 15¾″ D $247.50
COMMUNION FLAGON, dents, 14″ H $110.00
CHARGER, eagle touch, wear, scratches, 13″ D $357.50
COMMUNION FLAGON, "Smith & Feltman, Albany" touch, 10½″ H $275.00
CHARGER, English, "S. Duncomb" touch, "London," wear pitted, 14⅞″ D . . . $220.00
LIGHTHOUSE TALL POT, "I. Trask" touch, wear, resolder, 12″ H $412.50

A-OH May 1993   *Garth's Auctions, Inc.*
PEWTER
Row 1, Left to Right
TUMBLER, eagle touch, 2¾″ H .. $77.00
SPARKING LAMP, 4″ H $46.75
SPARKING LAMP, "M. Hyde," 4¼″ H $280.50
TANKARD, "T.D.B." touch, battered, repairs, 4″ H $495.00
SPARKING LAMP, loss, battered, 4¼″ H $60.50
SPARKING LAMP, "5," loss, repair, 3⅞″ H $11.00
BEAKERS, 2 pcs. (one illus.), pitted, 3⅜″ H $55.00
Row 2, Left to Right
TEAPOT, "Boardman & Hart, N. York" touch, split, 7½″ H $330.00
BASIN, eagle touch, dents, wear, scratches, 1⅞″ H, 7¾″ D $275.00
TEAPOT, "Sellew & Co. Cincinnati" touch, split, 7½″ H $220.00
Row 3, Left to Right
TEAPOT, "R. Dunham" touch, 8¼″ H $467.50
LAMP, brass burner, "Graves" touch, 7½″ H $302.50
LAMP, 5¼″ H $165.00
CANDLESTICK, "R. Gleason" touch, 7″ H $330.00
TEAPOT, "Calder, Providence" touch, old resolder, 9¼″ H $275.00

A-MA Dec. 1992   *Skinner, Inc.*
PRESENTATION CUP, silver, dated 1844, by Thomas T. Wilmot, Charleston, SC, dents, 3½" T $990.00
PRESENTATION CUP, silver, dated 1842, by Oscar T.H. Dibble, Savannah, GA, dent, 3½" T $660.00
PRESENTATION CUP, silver, dated 1845, by Nicholas J. Bogert, NY, 4" T .. $1045.00

A-MA Aug. 1993   *Skinner, Inc.*
PEWTER

Back, Left to Right
CHARGERS, 4 pcs., (1 illus.), continental, 19th c., imperfections, 8¼" to 9½" D $770.00
Center, Left to Right
MEASURES, 4 pcs, Continental, 18th c., 2 w/covers, repairs, 5" to 6¾" T $770.00
TIME LAMP, Continental, 19th c., unmarked, imperfections, 15½" T $330.00
FIVE ITEMS, (2 illus.), American and English, coffee pot, 2 plates, 2 teapots (illus.), imperfections $770.00
CANDLESTICKS, pr., Henry Hopper, New York, ca. 1840, 10" T $880.00
PORRINGER, 19 c., marked "SG," 5¼" D $275.00
Front, Left to Right
PORRINGERS, 5 pcs., New England, 19th c., 3½" to 5¼" D $660.00

A-MA Dec. 1992   *Skinner, Inc.*
CAUDLE CUP, silver, ca. 1700, by Jeremiah Dummer, Boston, repairs $2090.00

A-MA Dec. 1992   *Skinner, Inc.*
QUART MUG, pewter, ca. 1790, by Samuel Hamlin, Hartford, CT, dent, 5⅞" T $605.00

A-MA Mar. 1993   *Skinner, Inc.*
PEWTER
CHAMBER LAMPS, pr., "S. Rusts Patent New York," 8⅝" H $522.50
PLATE, PORRINGER, BASIN, marks and touches, imperfections $715.00
COFFEEPOT, Rufus Dunham, dents, 12" H $275.00
QUART MUG, "Samuel Hamlin" touch, "#330," "#331," 6" H $1540.00

A-OH Nov. 1992   *Garth's Auctions, Inc.*
ALL TOLE UNLESS NOTED
Row 1, Left to Right
TEA CADDY, dk. brown japanning, red, yellow, white, green, 4¼" H $110.00
DEED BOX, dk. brown japanning, white, green, red, 4¼" L $38.50
CREAMER, dk, brown japanning, red, yellow, green, black, white, 4" H $165.00
SYRUPER, dk. blue japanning, red, gold stenciled "Molasses," worn, 5½" H $38.50
SPICE BOX, 7 original interior canisters, brown japanning, yellow, red, stenciled labels on cannisters, 8" D $137.50
Row 2, Left to Right
COFFEE POT, rust, holes, dents, 8½" H $93.50
TEAPOT, punched tin, repairs, 5¾" H $220.00
BREAD TRAY, green, yellow, stenciled bronze design, wear, 8" x 14" $55.00
POLICE LAMP, tin, bullseye lense, damping shutter, burner, rust, holes, 7¾" H . . . $38.50
CANDLE BOX, worn red, black striping and floral design, battered, 9" L $71.50

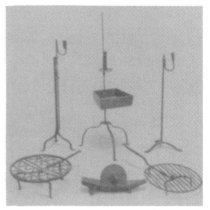

A-MA Dec. 1992   *Skinner, Inc.*
Row 1, Left to Right
RUSHLIGHT HOLDER, iron, 36⅛" H $500.00*
ADJUSTABLE CANDLEHOLDER, iron, wood box, 41½" H $1800.00*
RUSHLIGHT HOLDER, iron, rust, pitting, loss, 29½" H $250.00*
Row 2, Left to Right
TWIRLING BROILER, iron, 15" D $300.00*
HERB GRINDER, cast iron, 16" L $450.00*
TWIRLING BROILER, iron, 14" D $200.00*

A-OH July 1993   *Garth's Auctions, Inc.*
NOTE: First six items are a set of six pewter porringers with cast crown handles marked "G.S." New England, 5½" D.
Row 1, Left to Right
PORRINGER, ... $330.00
PORRINGER, ... $330.00
PORRINGER, ... $357.50
PORRINGER, ... $330.00
Row 2, Left to Right
PORRINGER, ... $330.00
PORRINGER, ... $330.00
PORRINGER, attributed to Gersham Jones, Providence, splits, 6" D $935.00
Row 3, Left to Right
PORRINGER, 5" D $275.00
ICE CREAM MOLD, pewter, duck, 4" H $71.50
PORRINGER, 5½" D $715.00
PORRINGER, 5½" D $357.50

A-MA Dec. 1992   *Skinner, Inc.*
Row 1, Left to Right
CANDLEHOLDER, iron, wood base, 7¾" H $75.00*
CANDLEHOLDER, iron, wood base, 7½" H $150.00*
CANDLEHOLDER, iron, wood base, 7½" H . . . . NS
CANDLEHOLDER, iron, wood base, crack, 9½" H $200.00*
Row 2, Left to Right
LAMP FILLER, tin, 5¾" H $75.00*
MORTAR AND PESTLE, turned maple $125.00*
DIPPER, copper, dents, handle 7", 3¾" D $60.00*
Row 3, Left to Right
MUG, copper, wrought iron handle, battered, 7½" H $50.00*
SAUCEPAN, copper, 6½" wrought iron handle, tinned interior, dovetailed, dents, 5" D $50.00*

A-NH Mar. 1993   *Northeast Auctions*
ROOSTER WEATHERVANE, molded copper, 22" H..................... NS
HORSE WEATHERVANE, copper, W.A. Snow & Co., Boston, 26" L $1000.00*
HORSE & JOCKEY WEATHERVANE, copper, cast iron, 29" L $3250.00*
MALLARDS, carved wood, tin wings, 13" L $550.00*
COW WEATHERVANE, cast iron, copper, 27" L..................... $3000.00*
BIRD WEATHERVANE, copper, 38" H......................... $5250.00*
ROOSTER WEATHERVANE, molded copper, 19" H $1700.00*

A-MA Jun. 1993   *Skinner, Inc.*
HORSE, cast iron, ca. 1900, 30" H, 23½" L $2640.00

A-MA Jun. 1993   *Skinner, Inc.*
ROOSTER WEATHER VANE, cast and sheet iron, regilt, 37" H $1540.00

A-MA Jun. 1993   *Skinner, Inc.*
SHORE BIRD WEATHER VANE, gilt metal, Long Island, NY, 20th c., 18½" H, 24" L...................... $1210.00
BUTTERFLY WEATHER VANE, sheet metal, 19th c., 16½" H, 23" L ... $1540.00

A-MA Jan. 1993   *Skinner, Inc.*
HORSE WEATHER VANE, molded copper and zink, 19th c., "Ethan Allen," 41" L $1540.00

A-MA Oct. 1992   *Skinner, Inc.*
HORSE WEATHER VANE, molded copper, 19th c., verdigris surface, imperfections, 31" L.............. $1430.00

A-MA Oct. 1992   *Skinner, Inc.*
HORSE WEATHER VANE, molded copper, verdigris surface, 19th c., 32" L........................ $1650.00

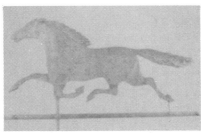

A-MA Oct. 1992   *Skinner, Inc.*
HORSE WEATHER VANE, molded copper and zinc, verdigris surface, 19th c., hole, 29" L................ $1320.00

A-MA Oct. 1992   *Skinner, Inc.*
GRASS HOPPER WEATHER VANE, copper, verdigris surface, 20th c., 35" L....................... $770.00

A-MA Oct. 1992   *Skinner, Inc.*
SHEEP WEATHER VANE, molded copper, early 20th c., verdigris surface, repairs, 28½" L............. $4125.00

A-MA Oct. 1992   *Skinner, Inc.*
OX WEATHER VANE, zinc/copper, re-gilded, loss, 19½" H, 34½" L .. $3850.00

A–PA May 1993 *Alderfer Auction Co.*
QUILT, yellow, red, green on white, 82"
sq. $725.00

A–IL Apr. 1993 *Leslie Hindman Auction*
CRAZY QUILT, 19th c., velvet, silk, embroidered, 74" x 51". $1500.00*

A–MA Jun. 1993 *Skinner, Inc.*
QUILT, 19th c., red, olive appleque on
white, feather quilting, discolored, 82" x
84" $440.00

A–MA Aug. 1993 *Skinner, Inc.*
QUILT, applique, 20th c., wear, 80" x
80" $467.50

A–MA Aug. 1993 *Skinner, Inc.*
TABLE COVER, pieced/embroidered
wool, dated 1831, losses, discolored, 64" W,
90" L. $2750.00

A–MA Jun. 1993 *Skinner, Inc.*
QUILT, 19th c., pink, red, yellow, ivory print
and solid patches, shell and conforming
quilting, soiled, 71" x 69' $412.50

A–OH Nov. 1992 *Garth's Auctions, Inc.*
QUILT, multi color calico, pink, white grid,
72" x 83" $302.50

A–MA Aug. 1993 *Skinner, Inc.*
QUILT, applique, embroidered, dated
"SCM 1860," discolored, 80" W, 93"
L. $330.00

A–MA Jan. 1993 *Skinner, Inc.*
APPLIQUED QUILT, solid cotton
patches, red, blue, plume and star pattern,
diamond and parallel line quilting, 19th c.,
82" x 84" $660.00

A-PA May 1993   *Alderfer Auction Co.*
SHOW TOWEL, by Leah Keller, 1831, 66"
L, 19" W $150.00
SHOW TOWEL, by Elisabeth Leib, 1866,
red, blue, 59½" L, 16½" W $350.00

A-MA Oct. 1992   *Skinner, Inc.*
PIECED WORSTED SPREAD, pink and
olive patches on butternut ground, feather
quilting, damage, 86" x 98" $935.00

A-PA May 1993   *Alderfer Auction Co.*
QUILT, 19th c., Lancaster Co., yellow, red,
blue, green, wear, repair, 98" x
78" $925.00

A-PA May 1993   *Alderfer Auction Co.*
HOOKED RUG, March 1925, 45" x
30" $700.00

A-PA May 1993   *Alderfer Auction Co.*
CRIB QUILT, ca. 1930, Lancaster
Co. $450.00

A-IL Apr. 1993   *Leslie Hindman Auction*
QUILT, 19th c., patchwork, house pattern
in red, green, blue calico on yellow ground,
76" x 72" $500.00*

A-MA Mar. 1993   *Skinner, Inc.*
SAMPLER, "Sally Whitney's Sampler
Worked in the eleventh year of her age AD
1797," silk on linen, shades of blue, green,
yellow, beige, 15¼" x 12" $1760.00

A-MA Oct. 1992   *Skinner, Inc.*
TABLE RUG, wool, appliqued and pieced,
red, blue, yellow, cream, brown, "E.B.
1858," discoloration, fiber loss, 66"
sq. $880.00

A-OH Apr. 1993   *Garth's Auctions, Inc.*
JACQUARD COVERLETS
Row 1, Left to Right
DOUBLE WEAVE, navy, red, wear dam-
age, 81" x 92" $440.00
SINGLE WEAVE, blue, white, corners
inscribed and dated 1849, wear, damage,
73" x 90" $440.00
SINGLE WEAVE, red, navy, white, teal,
corners inscribed and dated 1845, wear,
stains, 64" x 80" $247.50
Row 2, Left to Right
DOUBLE WEAVE, navy, red, white,
corners inscribed and dated 1839, wear,
damage, stains, 70" x 84" $319.00
SINGLE WEAVE, navy, red, white, corners
inscribed and dated 1839, wear, damage,
72" x 92" $550.00
SINGLE WEAVE, blue, red, olive, white,
corners inscribed and dated 1854, wear,
74" x 82" $440.00
Row 3, Left to Right
SINGLE WEAVE, navy, red, gold, white,
corners inscribed and dated 1855, wear,
74" x 74" $550.00
OVERSHOT WEAVE, navy, red, gold,
olive, white, wear, 74" x 90" $165.00
DOUBLE WEAVE, navy, white, holes,
stains, 74" x 88" $247.50

A-MA Oct. 1992   *Skinner, Inc.*
NEEDLEWORK PICTURE, "Shepherd-
ess," 19th c., silk threads in shades of
yellow, green, blue, bittersweet, paint and
velvet on silk inscribed, reverse painted
mat, 13¾" x 15¾" $4950.00
NEEDLEWORK PICTURE, "Shepherd-
ess," 19th c., silk threads in shades of
yellow, green, blue, bittersweet, paint and
velvet on silk inscribed, eglomise mat,
damage, 13" x 15" $770.00

A-IL Apr. 1993   *Leslie Hindman Auction*
JACQUARD COVERLET, George Washington depicted in corners, inscribed Washington, Sarah Babcock, dated 1848, 88" x 68" $2500.00*

A-PA May 1993   *Alderfer Auction Co.*
COVERLET, red, white, "Made by W. Kuder N. W. Hall Lehigh County Pa. For Feietta Miller 1862." 97" x 77" . . . $375.00

A-MA Oct. 1992   *Skinner, Inc.*
CREWEL EMBROIDERED LINEN POCKET, shades of yellow, green, blue, umber, backed w/homespun, late 18th c., fiber loss, 16¼" L $990.00
PIN CUSHION, embroidered black silk, shades of green, yellow, peach, puce, late 18th c., wear, fading, 2½" D . . . $770.00
QUILTED CHINTZ POCKET, block printed "plum tree and pheasant" pattern, ca. 1825, wear, 14" L $880.00

A-MA Aug. 1993   *Skinner, Inc.*
SAMPLER, "Hannah Currier Born January 2 1799 aged 11," 7½" W, 8½" L $1980.00
SAMPLER, "Elizabeth Buntin age 12," 8" W, 10½" L $1430.00

A-NH May. 1993   *Northeast Auctions*
NEEDLEWORK MEMORIAL, Joshua Howe and wife Hannah, dates of death 1801 and 1796, 16½" x 14" . . . $4000.00*
NEEDLEWORK MEMORIAL, George Washington, by Relief Pratt, Shrewsbury, Mass., 1804, 17½" x 15" $2000.00*

A-OH Nov. 1992   *Garth's Auctions, Inc.*
JACQUARD COVERLET, 2-pc., single weave, floral medallions, vintage borders, corners dated 1856, Navy, natural, wear, damage, stains, 82" x 92" $330.00
JACQUARD COVERLET, 2-pc., single weave, rose medallions, bird borders, corners labeled "Sarah Ann Reads, Fancy Coverlet, wove by H. Schrader, Winchester, Ohio 1844," red, sage, navy, natural, damage, 64" x 84" $165.00
JACQUARD COVERLET, 2-pc., single weave, floral and star medallions, star borders, corners labeled, "Samuel Meily, Mansfield, Richland, Ohio 1852," blue, red, natural, wear, faded, damage, 82" x 74" $137.50

A-OH Sep. 1993   *Garth's Auctions, Inc.*
APPLIQUE QUILT, 16 squares each w/different design in red, green, and yellow calico, some w/embroidery, stains, 76" x 76" $1210.00

A-MA Dec. 1992   *Skinner, Inc.*

DOLLS

ALT, BECK & GOTSCHALK BISQUE HEAD BABY, ca. 1920, sleeping brown glass eyes, impressed 1322 mark, mohair wig, bent limb composition body, 15½" H $385.00

KAMMER & REINHARDT BISQUE HEAD BABY, blue glass eyes, mohair wig, impressed K ★ R Simon & Halbig 126 mark, jointed bent limb composition body, damage, 17" H $247.50

KAMMER & REINHARDT BISQUE HEAD BABY, ca. 1913, sleeping blue glass eyes, impressed K ★ R Simon & Halbig 122 mark, mohair wig, bent limb composition body, mama voice, 18" H $412.50

BAHR & PROSCHILD BISQUE HEAD BABY, ca. 1920, sleeping blue glass eyes, 585 mark, mohair wig, bent limb composition body, scuffing, 15" H $247.50

BORGFELDT BISQUE HEAD BOY, sleeping brown glass eyes, impressed 620-3 mark, bent limb composition body, wear, 12" H $330.00

A-MA Dec. 1992   *Skinner, Inc.*
MADAME ALEXANDER DIONNE QUINTUPLETS, composition jointed bodies, cream painted crib, some clothing missing, 7" H $522.50

A-MA Jun. 1993   *Skinner, Inc.*
BYE-LO BABY W/STORK, sleeping glass eyes, impressed mard, cloth body celluloid hands, wire-legged cotton batting stork, glass eyes, each 9" T $495.00

A-MA Dec. 1992   *Skinner, Inc.*

DOLLS

CLOTH DOLL, painted hair and hands, 16½" H $275.00

TWO CLOTH DOLLS, Lenci type girl, (illus.), mohair wig, 18" H; French Poupees Greb's girl, mohair wig, 21" H $82.50

DOOR OF HOPE MISSION BRIDEGROOM, wooden head and hands, hat missing, 11½" H $165.00

MARTHA CHASE CLOTH DOLL, sateen body, stamped mark, paint loss, 23" H $357.50

SCHOENHUT GIRL, mohair wig, paint chips, 14" H $412.50

DORA PTZOLD HANDCRAFTED ART DOLL, Berlin, 1920s, molded composition head, painted features, mohair wig, stockinette and muslin body and limbs, stamped trademark, 19" H $605.00

KATHY KRUSE GIRL, c. 1914, damage, 17" H $1210.00

JOHN WRIGHT FELT "KARL," 1981, tag and card information, 18" H $385.00

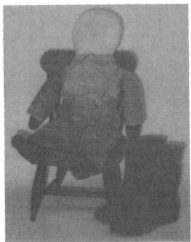

A-PA May 1993   *Alderfer Auction Co.*
DOLL, Amish boy, denim jeans, lt. blue shirt, black stockings, Lancaster Co. 350.00

DOLL CHAIR, red painted, 19th c., PA $300.00

BOOTS, leather w/stars $140.00

A-MA Dec. 1992　　　　　*Skinner, Inc.*
DOLLS

Row 1, Left to Right

KESTNER BISQUE HEAD, blue glass eyes, mohair wig, impressed "GII, 143," jointed composition body, crack, repair, 19" H $605.00
JUMEAU BISQUE HEAD, blue eyes, marked "x 11," composition body 25" H . . . . . . NS
BRU BISQUE HEAD, blue paperweight eyes, impressed "BRU JNE 10," mohair wig, jointed composition body, restored, repainted, 22" T $1760.00

BISQUE HEAD, brown glass eyes, marked "224 12," human hair wig, jointed composition body, damage, repairs, 22" T $412.50

Row 2, Left to Right

JUMEAU BISQUE HEAD, sleeping eyes, mohair wig, cork pate, stamped "Tete Jumeau," jointed composition body, repaint, 15" T . . . . NS
BISQUE SHOULDER HEAD, sleeping glass eyes, human hair wig, kid body, bisque hands, chip, 15" T $247.50
KESTER BISQUE HEAD, brown glass eyes, impressed 128 mark, mohair wig, jointed composition body, straight wrists, damage, 15" H $220.00
JUMEAU BISQUE HEAD, 19th c., impressed O mark, lamb's wool wig, jointed composition body, straight wrists, partial original costume, 15½" H $4675.00
KESTER "HILDA" BISQUE HEAD BABY, sleeping blue glass eyes, mohair wig, impressed JDK Hilda mark, bent limb composition body, scuffing, 15" T $660.00

A-MA Dec. 1992　　　　　*Skinner, Inc.*
DOLLS

Row 1, Left to Right

HERTEL, SCHWAB & CO. BABY, sleeping blue glass eyes, impressed "1524," mohair wig, bent limb composition body, scrubbed, 12" H $192.50
HEUBACH BISQUE HEAD BABY, sleeping blue glass eyes, impressed 300.2 mark, mohair wig, bent limb composition body, worn, 16" H $192.50
BISQUE HEAD BABY, "K ★ R 100," intaglio eyes, painted hair, bent limb composition body, scrubbed, 15" H . . $220.00
GRACE STORY PUTNAM BISQUE HEAD BYE-LO BABY, sleeping brown glass eyes, impressed mark, cloth body, celluloid hands, 13" H $357.50

Row 2, Left to Right

BARR & POTSCHILD BISQUE HEAD BABY, sleeping blue glass eyes, impressed 604 mark, mohair wig, jointed bent limb body, 11" H $330.00
KESTNER BISQUE HEAD BABY, blue sleeping glass eyes, impressed 152 mark, mohair wig, bent limb composition body, 11" H $220.00

HEUBACH BISQUE HEAD BABY, sleeping blue glass eyes, mohair wig, impressed 320.6/0. mark, bent limb composition body, scuffing, 11½" H $192.50
KESTNER BISQUE SHOULDER HEAD BOY, sleeping blue glass eyes, mohair wig, impressed JDK 235 mark, jointed kid body, composition arms/legs, 13" H $385.00
ALL BISQUE BABY, painted eyes, impressed "13," jointed shoulders & hips, body and arms impressed "816.13," damage, 11" H $247.50
KESTNER BISQUE HEAD BABY, sleeping blue glass eyes, mohair wig, impressed 3Dk 211 mark, bent limb composition body, 12" H $412.50

A-MA Aug. 1993   *James D. Julia, Inc.*
MICKEY MOUSE WHIRLIGIG, orig.,
box, celluloid, windup, ©Walt E. Disney, dist.
by George Borgfeldt of NY, 9″
T $5000.00*

A-MA Aug. 1993   *James D. Julia, Inc.*
MICKEY MOUSE BUBBLE BUSTER, ©Walt Disney Ent., by Kilgore Mfg. Co. of Wester-
ville, OH, cast metal, paper label around barrel, transfer on front sight, 8″ L $175.00*
MICKEY MOUSE SQUEEZE TOY, celluloid, Italy, ca. 1930, 5″ T . . . . NS
MICKEY MOUSE PIN BACK BUTTON, brass, glass top, 1″ x 1″ $45.00*
Row 2, Left to Right
MICKEY MOUSE, PLUTO ALARM CLOCK, not working, 4½″ W, 5″ T $55.00*
MICKEY AND MINNIE MOUSE TOOTHBRUSH HOLDER, bisque, ©Walt E. Disney,
Japan, 4½″ T $175.00*
SNOW WHITE TOOTHBRUSH HOLDER, porcelain, Great Britain, 6″ T $200.00*

A-MA Aug. 1993   *James D. Julia, Inc.*
MICKEY/FELIX SPARKLER, by R.S.,
Isla, Spain, ca. 1930, replacements, 5″ W,
6″ T $10000.00*

A-MA Aug. 1993   *James D. Julia, Inc.*
MICKEY MOUSE COWBOY DOLL, by Knickerbocker, complete except tail, 12″
T $5500.00*
DISNEYLAND FERRIS WHEEL, orig. box, mechanical, by Chein, ©Walt Disney Prod.,
16″ T $400.00*
RUNNING MICKEY ON PLUTO, occupied Japan, ©Walt Disney Prod., celluloid, 5″ T, 6″ L,
3½″ W $7000.00*
POPEYE & BAGGAGE WITHOUT PARROT, orig. box, by Louis Marx, ©King Features
Syn., 8″ L, 8″ T $2250.00*

A-MA Aug. 1993   *James D. Julia, Inc.*
MICKEY MOUSE RACING CAR, tin
litho, 1½″ H, 4″ L $450.00*
**FOB FOR INGERSOL MICKEY MOUSE
WATCH,** orig. strap, 1½″ D $80.00*
MICKEY MOUSE PENCIL HOLDER,
composition, by Dixon, 5″ T $275.00*

A–MA Aug. 1993   *James D. Julia, Inc.*
TOONERVILLE TROLLEY, orig. box, cast iron, by Dent, 5½" H, 4½" L $700.00*
MICKEY MOUSE SHOOFLY, by Mengel, ©Walt Disney Ent., 17" H, 13" W, 35" L $750.00*

A–MA Aug. 1993   *James D. Julia, Inc.*
FERDINAND AND THE MATADOR, tin windup, by Louis Marx Co., orig. box, works, 4½" H, 7" L $450.00*
CHAUFFER DRIVEN AUTO, possibly Fischer, tin windup, 4½" H, 7½" L .... NS
Row 2, Left to Right
MOTORCYCLE W/SIDECAR, tin windup, by Louis Marx, 4" H, 7" L .... NS
SANTA CLAUS SLEIGH, tin litho, windup, by Ferdinand Strauss Co. of NY, works, 6¼" H, 12" L $700.00*
Row 3, Left to Right
SANTA CLAUS SLEIGH, tin litho, windup, by Ferdinand Strauss, works, damaged orig. box w/no lid, 5½" H, 11½" L $1500.00*
DOUBLE DECKER BUS, tin litho, by Strauss Co., windup mec. missing, "Inter-State Bus," 6" H, 10¾" L $350.00*

A–MA Aug. 1993   *James D. Julia, Inc.*
MICKEY MOUSE HURDY GURDY, Germany, tin litho, 8" H, 3" W, 6" L $17000.00*

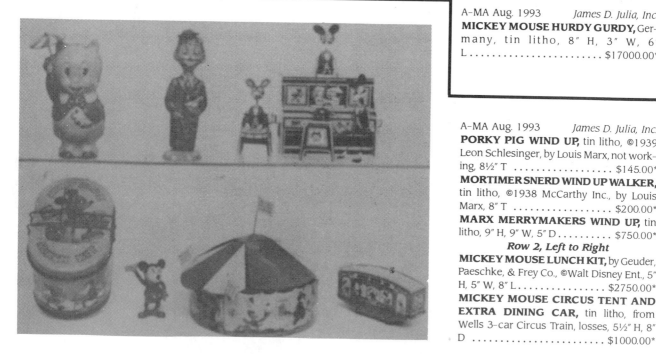

A–MA Aug. 1993   *James D. Julia, Inc.*
PORKY PIG WIND UP, tin litho, ©1939 Leon Schlesinger, by Louis Marx, not working, 8½" T $145.00*
MORTIMER SNERD WIND UP WALKER, tin litho, ©1938 McCarthy Inc., by Louis Marx, 8" T $200.00*
MARX MERRYMAKERS WIND UP, tin litho, 9" H, 9" W, 5" D $750.00*
Row 2, Left to Right
MICKEY MOUSE LUNCH KIT, by Geuder, Paeschke, & Frey Co., ©Walt Disney Ent., 5" H, 5" W, 8" L.................. $2750.00*
MICKEY MOUSE CIRCUS TENT AND EXTRA DINING CAR, tin litho, from Wells 3-car Circus Train, losses, 5½" H, 8" D $1000.00*

A-MA Aug. 1993   *James D. Julia, Inc.*

A-MA Aug. 1993   *James D. Julia, Inc.*

Row 1, Left to Right
MICKEY MOUSE STANDING ON CORK, cast figure, 1931, Germany, 5" T . . $800.00*
MICKEY MOUSE POURING SPOUTS, pr., porcelain, Germany, 3" & 4" T $300.00*
MICKEY MOUSE CONDIMENT SET, 3 pcs., Mickey mustard pot, nephew salt & peppers, repair, 4" & 2" T $500.00*

Row 2, Left to Right
MICKEY MOUSE CONDIMENT PIECE, 2" H, 3" L $425.00*
MICKEY MOUSE KNIFE REST, Germany, 3½" L $100.00*
MICKEY MOUSE CAKE DECORATIONS, pr., Germany, ca. 1931, 1½" & 1¾" T $200.00*

MICKEY MOUSE SLATE DANCER, Germany, ca. 1931, by either Saalheimer and Strauss or Wilhelm Krause, 6½" T $26500.00*

A-MA Aug. 1993   *James D. Julia, Inc.*
MICKEY MOUSE SAXOPHONE PLAYER, tin litho, squeeze toy, Japan, replacements, 6" T $3000.00*

A-MA Aug. 1993   *James D. Julia, Inc.*
TOONERVILLE TROLLEY, tin litho, contemporary, 20" H, 16" L $350.00*
DONALD DUCK WHIRLIGIG, celluloid, incomplete, 10½" T $1850.00*

Row 2, Left to Right
MICKEY MOUSE RADIO & PIN BACK BUTTON, by Emerson, radio 7½" x 7½" x 5½" $1050.00*
MICKEY MOUSE DOLL, by Character Novelty Corp., ©Walt Disney Prod., ca. 1950, 18" T $200.00*
DONALD DUCK DUET, by Louis Marx, losses, 10" T $300.00*
DONALD DUCK DOLL, by Knickerbocker, 3' T $250.00*

A-MA Aug. 1993   *James D. Julia, Inc.*
FELIX PULLED BY MULE, Spain, ca. 1928, windup, 4" H, 7" L $13500.00*

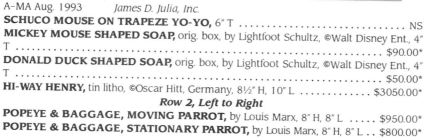

A-MA Aug. 1993   *James D. Julia, Inc.*
SCHUCO MOUSE ON TRAPEZE YO-YO, 6″ T .... NS
MICKEY MOUSE SHAPED SOAP, orig. box, by Lightfoot Schultz, ©Walt Disney Ent., 4″
T $90.00*
DONALD DUCK SHAPED SOAP, orig. box, by Lightfoot Schultz, ©Walt Disney Ent., 4″
T $50.00*
HI-WAY HENRY, tin litho, ©Oscar Hitt, Germany, 8½″ H, 10″ L $3050.00*
Row 2, Left to Right
POPEYE & BAGGAGE, MOVING PARROT, by Louis Marx, 8″ H, 8″ L $950.00*
POPEYE & BAGGAGE, STATIONARY PARROT, by Louis Marx, 8″ H, 8″ L .. $800.00*

A-MA Aug. 1993   *James D. Julia, Inc.*
POPEYE MOTORCYCLE, cast iron, by
Hubley, 5″ H, 8½″ L $4000.00*
**BARNEY GOOGLE RIDING SPARK
PLUG,** tin litho, windup, by Nifty, Germany,
7″ H, 7″ L $2450.00*
**BARNEY GOOGLE AND SPARK
PLUG RACING,** tin litho, pull toy, ©1924
King Features Syn. 6″ H, 7″ L ... $5700.00*

A-MA Aug. 1993   *James D. Julia, Inc.*
POPEYE THE ACROBAT, orig. box, mechanical, by Linemar, 9″ L, 13″ T $4000.00*
BUBBLE BLOWING POPEYE, battery operated, orig. box, by Linemar, Japan, ©King
Features Syn., 12″ T $1500.00*
SMOKING POPEYE, battery operated, orig. box, by Linemar, 6″ W, 8½″ T ... $1750.00*
POPEYE WIND UP, orig. box, celluloid, ©1929 King Features Syn., 8″ T $1500.00*

A-MA Aug. 1993   *James D. Julia, Inc.*
HAROLD LLOYD BUMPER CAR, Ger-
many, 5½″ H, 3½″ D $16000.00*
JIGGS BUMPER CAR, ca 1920, 5½″ H,
3½″ D $10000.00*

A-MA Aug. 1993   *James D. Julia, Inc.*
MICKEY MOUSE JAZZ DRUMMER SQUEEZE TOY, tin litho, ©Walt Disney, 6½" T $1750.00*
MICKEY MOUSE LAMP W/EARLY SHADE, plaster, by Soreng Manegold Co., ©Walt Disney Ent., shade not orig., 14" T $1600.00*
THREE LITTLE PIGS PITCHER, by Wade Heath of Great Britain, 10½" T $750.00*
Row 2, Left to Right
MICKEY MOUSE STERLING SILVER PINS ON ORIG. DISPLAY, © by exclusive arrangement w/Ideal Films Ltd., 12 pins, 4" W, 7" T $3250.00*
DONALD DUCK RAIL CAR, orig. box, by Lionel, ©Walt Disney Ent., 7" H, 10" L $1100.00*
DONALD DUCK BAND MASTER DOLL, by Knickerbocker, complete, all orig., ©Walt Disney Ent., 16" T $1100.00*

A-MA Aug. 1993   *James D. Julia, Inc.*
Row 1, Left to Right
MICKEY MOUSE RIDING PLUTO, tin, wind up, by Linemar, ©Walt Disney Prod., 5" H, 7" L $750.00
MICKEY MOUSE POCKET WATCH W/FOB, orig. box, by Ingersoll, ©Walt Disney, working $850.00
Row 2, Left to Right
THREE LITTLE PIGS SAND SET, orig. box, by Ohio Art $350.00

A-MA Aug. 1993   *James D. Julia, Inc.*
JEEP DOLL, no tail, cracks, 8½" T $400.00*
POPEYE BIF BAT, ©1935 by King Features Syn., ca. 1930, 11" L $70.00*
POPEYE DOLL, by EFF and Bee, ©1935 by Fleischaker & Baum, orig. tag, 17" T $200.00*
BUBBLE BLOWING POPEYE, battery operated, by Linemar, damaged orig. box, 12" T $500.00*
Row 2, Left to Right
SMITTY SCOOTER, by Louis Marx, Licensed by Famous Artists Syn., 8" H, 6" L $1450.00*
MICKEY MOUSE HANDCAR, by Lionel, orig. box, red car, 6" H, 8" L $850.00*
PETER RABBIT CHICK-MOBILE, orig. box, by Lionel, 6" H, 9" L $700.00*

A-MA Aug. 1993   *James D. Julia, Inc.*
Row 1, Left to Right
POPEYE HEAVY HITTER, tin litho, mechanical, by J. Chein, ©King Features Syn., 7" L, 12" T $4750.00*
POPEYE OVERHEAD PUNCHER, by J. Chein, ©1932 King Features Syn., 4¼" W, 4¼" D, 9½" T $4000.00*
Row 2, Left to Right
POPEYE & OLIVE OYL STRETCHY HAND CAR, orig. box, by Linemar, Japan, pull toy, 6" H, 6½" L $3000.00*
JUGGLING POPEYE & OLIVE OYL, original box, mechanical, by Linemar, 9¼" T $4000.00*

A-MA Aug. 1993   *James D. Julia, Inc.*
Row 1, Left to Right
MICKEY MOUSE CIRCUS TRAIN, orig. box, by Wells of London $1150.00*
POPEYE THE CHAMP, orig. box, by Louis Marx, tin litho, celluloid, 7"x 7" . . $3450.00*
POPEYE CYCLIST, orig. box, by Linemar, 4" W, 7" T $3500.00*
Row 2, Left to Right
POPEYE MECHANICAL TRICYCLE, orig. box, by Linemar, tin, celluloid, 3" W, 4" T $2250.00*
POPEYE MECHANICAL UNICYCLIST, orig. box, by Linemar, tin litho, no pipe, 6" T $2000.00*
EUGENE THE "JEEP" DOLL, composition, ©1935 King Features Syn., 12" T $600.00*
POPEYE BASKETBALL PLAYER, orig. box, mechanical, by Linemar, ©King Features Syn., 9" T $3800.00*

A-MA Aug. 1993   *James D. Julia, Inc.*
THREE LITTLE PIGS TOOTHBRUSH HOLDER, ©Walt Disney, Japan, 4″ T $25.00
FIDDLER PIG TOOTHBRUSH HOLDER, "Genuine Walt Disney Copyright," 4″ T $45.00
MICKEY MOUSE PENCIL CASE & POSTCARDS, by Dixon, ©Walt Disney $170.00
Row 2, Left to Right
TOONERVILLE TROLLEY, tin litho, by Nifty, 7″ H, 5½″ T $500.00
BARNEY GOOGLE RIDING SPARK PLUG, by Nifty, damage, 7″ H, 7″ L $100.00
RACING SPARK PLUG, pull toy, tin litho, wear, rust, 6″ H, 6″ L $200.00

A-MA Aug. 1993   *James D. Julia, Inc.*
HAPPY TIMES, by Kuramochi of Japan, celluloid girl in chair under umbrella that spins, works, 5″ W, 6½″ L $95.00*
ARTICULATED BLACK FIGURE, dances when crank turned, tin, 8″ T $200.00*
POLICEMAN ON MOTORCYCLE, "Champion," blue, 3″ H, 4¾″ L . . $200.00*
3 CARS, (1 illus.), 2 Tricky Taxis by Marx, Penny Toy closed truck from Germany $175.00*
POSTAL DELIVERY MOTORCYCLE, cast iron, Harley Davidson, 9″ L . . . . . . NS

A-MA Aug. 1993   *James D. Julia, Inc.*
HAPPY HOLLIGAN PULLED BY DONKEY, by Ingap of Italy, 4″ H, 7″ L $900.00
HAPPY HOLLIGAN, tin litho, windup, by J. Chein, 6″ T $550.00
FUNNY FACE, tin litho, windup, Harold Lloyd knock off, 10½″ T $350.00
RODEO JOE IN YIPEE-I-AAAY JOUNCING JEEP, orig. box, by Unique Art, 9″ H, 8″ L $350.00
Row 2, Left to Right
DISNEYLAND BISCUIT TIN, Holland, 1938, 12″ L, 8″ W, 3″ D $300.00
RACING SPARK PLUG, pull toy, tin litho, 6″ H, 9″ L $600.00

A–OH Jan. 1993   *Garth's Auctions, Inc.*
CAST IRON BANKS
Row 1, Left to Right
ELEPHANT, w/3 clowns, worn polychrome, 5¾" H $1870.00
ELEPHANT, worn gold, red, 4½" L $302.50
ORGAN BANK, w/cat, dog, worn polychrome, 7¼" H $660.00
BEAR, w/tree stump, worn black, red, 5" H.........................$550.00
EAGLE, w/eaglets, old repaint, 6" H..........................$605.00
Row 2, Left to Right
INDIAN & BEAR, worn polychrome, 10¼" L.....................$2090.00
DARKTOWN BATTERY, worn polychrome, 9¾" L...............$2145.00
ALWAYS DID 'SPISE A MULE, worn polychrome, pat. date, 10" L....$1430.00
SPEAKING DOG, worn polychrome, 7¼" L......................$935.00

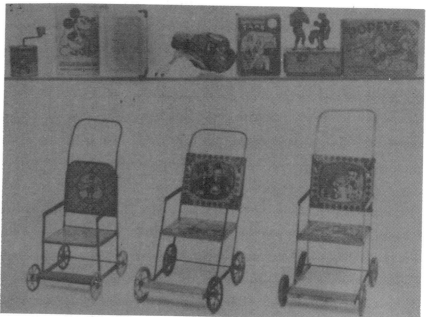

A–MA Dec. 1992   *Skinner, Inc.*
BEATRIX POTTER MINIATURE ANIMALS, 4 pcs., Austrian bronze, Benjamin Bunny, Jemima Puddleduck, Hunca Munca, Timmy and Goody Tiptoes under umbrella, ⅞" to 1½" H $495.00
BESWICK BEATRIX POTTER FIGURES AND BOOKS, Tailor of Glouchester, Hunca Munca, Flopsie Bunnies, Peter Rabbit in Jacket, Poorly Peter Rabbit, Benjamin Bunny, Mrs. Tittlemouse, Lady Mouse from Tailor of Glouchester, Little Pig Robinson, ceramic base for 6 figures, average 4" H; 21 books, pink painted case $412.00

A–MA Aug. 1993   *James D. Julia, Inc.*
Row 1, Left to Right
MICKEY, MINNIE AND FELIX MUSICAL TOY, tin litho, probably Spanish or German, 1931–1932, 2" H, 2" D $550.00*
MICKEY MOUSE BANK, orig. box, ©Walt Disney, mfg., by Zell Products, 4" H, 3" W..$500.00*
POPEYE TURNOVER TANK, orig. box, by Linemar of Japan, 2½" W, 4" L ...$1800.00*
POPEYE KNOCKOUT BANK, orig. box, by Straits Mfg. Co. of Detroit, ©King Features Syn. 1935, 5" H, 2" D, 3½" W $2050.00*
Row 2, Left to Right
MICKEY STROLLER, by Richo of Spain, 8" W, 6" D, 11" T $450.00*
LAUREL AND HARDY STROLLER, by Pico Y Cia of Spain, Felix heads in corners, 5" W, 6" D, 11" T $1400.00*
MICKEY, MINNIE, BETTY BOOP AND FELIX STROLLER, by Pico Y Cia of Spain, 5" W, 6" D, 11" T $1200.00*

A-MA Dec. 1992   *Skinner, Inc.*
NOVELTY BANK, Stevens, "patented October 28, 1873," gray, red, blue paint, wear, base 4¼" $440.00
"SPEAKING DOG" BANK, Shepherd, "patented October 20, 1885," painted, 7⅛" L $715.00
RABBIT MECHANICAL BANK, Lockwood, bronze paint, gold base, 6" H $440.00

A-OH Nov. 1992   *Garth's Auctions, Inc.*
CAST IRON BANKS
Row 1, Left to Right
TABBY BANK, paint traces, 4½" H $275.00
RABBIT IN CABBAGE, worn polychrome, loss, 4⅜" L $330.00
CHINAMAN, worn polychrome, 8¾" L $1347.50
ORGAN BANK, w/monkey, worn polychrome, replacement, repair, 5⅜" H $275.00
PIG IN HIGH CHAIR, nickel plated, 5⅞" H $907.50
Row 2, Left to Right
NOVELTY BANK, worn polychrome, 6¾" H $550.00
DINAH, worn polychrome, 6½" H $440.00
TRICK DOG, worn polychrome, loss, 8¾" L $605.00
TAMMANY BANK, worn polychrome, 5⅞" L $440.00
SANTA CLAUS, worn polychrome, 5⅞" H $1182.50
Row 3, Left to Right
STUMP SPEAKER, key trap, worn polychrome, 9⅞" H $1155.00
ORGAN BANK, w/monkey, cat, dog, worn polychrome, loss, 7⅜" H $742.50
ACROBAT, worn polychrome, 9¼" H $880.00
OWL, worn polychrome, replacement, loss, 7½" H $55.00
WILLIAM TELL, loss, 10½" H $990.00

A-OH Apr. 1993   *Garth's Auctions, Inc.*
CAST IRON BANKS
Row 1, Left to Right
HALL'S EXCELSIOR BANK, mechanical, losses, 5¼" T $82.50
RABBIT, mechanical, japanning traces, 5¾" T $467.50
RABBIT IN CABBAGE, mechanical, worn polychrome, 4¼" L $357.50
CABIN, mechanical, worn polychrome, 4¼" L $632.50
BOY AND DOG, mechanical, japanning traces, 5¼" L $247.50
SANTA CLAUS, mechanical, polychrome, 6" T $522.50
Row 2, Left to Right
KITTY, polychrome, 4⅞" T $55.00
BANK BUILDING, gold, silver, 4¾" T $60.50
SHARECROPPER, worn polychrome, 5½" T $77.00
TAMMANY BANK, mechanical, polychrome, 5⅝" T $214.50
TWO BANKS, "Beauty" and rabbit, worn, rust $143.00
Row 3, Left to Right
ARTILLERY BANK, mechanical, worn bronze paint, replacement, 8" L .. $148.50
BEAR, worn black paint, 6½" T .. $60.50
JOLLY, mechanical, worn polychrome, loss, replacement, 6¼" T $38.50
CHEIF BIG MOON, mechanical, worn polychrome, 10⅛" L $1925.00

A-MA Dec. 1992   *Skinner, Inc.*
CAST IRON BANKS
BANKS, 10 pcs., lg. two-faced black boy, (illus.), sm. two-faced black boy, Indian chief, kitty, Puppo, Fido, Fido on pillow, Billiken, shell, Elizabeth II coronation crown, Hubley orange cop cycle, chips on lot $522.50
A.C. WILLIAMS BANKS, 4 pcs., (3 illus.), Mutt & Jeff, Three Wise Monkeys, lg. camel, sm. camel, all gold painted $605.00
HUBLEY PUPPO ON PILLOW, 1920s, chips, 5¾" H $330.00
A.C. WILLIAMS MAIN STREET TROLLEY, 1920s, gold paint, 6⅝" H $550.00
DOGS, 6 pcs., lrg. St. Bernard, sm. St. Bernard, "I Hear a Call" water spaniel, boxer (bulldog), Boston bull terrier, bulldog $385.00
ANIMALS, 7 pcs., Red Goose, donkey, horse, raindeer, pig, buffalo, rooster .. $467.50

A-OH Jan. 1993   *Garth's Auctions, Inc.*
CAST IRON BANKS

Row 1, Left to Right
BATTLESHIP MAINE, gold japanning, 5¾" H $302.50
RABBIT, "1884," white, green, red, gold, wear, 2¼" H $990.00
RABBIT, brown and gold traces, 5¼" L $522.50
HEN ON NEST, worn gold, replacement, 3" H $825.00
CAT & BALL, worn gold, 5⅝" L $269.00
TEDDY BEAR, worn gold, 3⅞" L $165.00

BATTLESHIP OREGON, brown japanning w/gold, replacement, 5" L . . . $330.00

Row 2, Left to Right
SQUIRREL, gold traces, 4" H . . . $522.50
OWL, "Be Wise, Save Money," worn gold, red, 5" H $93.50
TEDDY ROOSEVELT, worn gold, red, silver, 5⅛" H $192.50
ELEPHANT, gold, 4¾" H $110.00
GIRL WITH LAMB, worn white, red, 4½" H $577.50
YOUNG BLACK MAN, worn polychrome, rust, replacement, 4⅝" H $225.50
BULL DOG, worn gold, 4" H $93.50
ROOF BANK, brown japanning w/gold, worn, 5½" H $159.50

Row 3, Left to Right
STATE BANK, brown japanning w/ bronze, 8½" H $770.00
STATE BANK, brown japanning w/ bronze, gold, 6" H $247.50
STATE BANK, brown japanning w/ bronze, gold, 4¼" H $165.00
STATE BANK, brown japanning w/ bronze, 3¼" H $137.50
CAMEL, gold, red, 7¼" H $412.50
OLD SOUTH CHURCH, white, partial label, crack in bottom, 9¼" H . . . $5005.00
DO YOU KNOW ME, gold, red, wear, 6" H $275.00
TOWER BANK, dark japanning, replacement, 9" H $275.00

A-OH Jan. 1993   *Garth's Auctions, Inc.*
CAST IRON BANKS

Row 1, Left to Right
HOUSE, gold, red, 3" H $110.00
DOMED BANK, worn silver, 3" H $60.50
RABBIT, paint traces, 3⅝" H . . . $137.50
MOSQUE BANK, no paint, 3¼" H $82.50
BASKET, nickel finish, 3" H $93.50
MOSQUE, worn gold, 3" H $27.50
PIG, gold traces, 3" H $38.50
DOMED BANK, gold traces, 3" H $66.00
SPORT SAFE, black, gold, 3" H . . $60.50

Row 2, Left to Right
DOMED BANK, gold, 4¾" H $71.50
ROOSTER, black, red, silver, 4⅝" H $159.50
BANK BUILDING, brown japanning w/ gold, replacement 3½" H $71.50
HORSE, worn gold, 4¼" H $33.00
DOG, worn gold, 4⅛" H $104.50
BANK BUILDING, brown japanning w/ gold, 3½" H $104.50
TURKEY, worn black, red, rust, 3½" H $137.50

LION, gold repaint, 4" H $38.50

Row 3, Left to Right
STATE BANK, brown japanning w/gold, bronze, 5⅞" H $192.50
STATE BANK, brown japanning w/gold, bronze, 4⅛" H $137.50
ELEPHANT, worn gold repaint, 5⅛" H $148.50
ARABIAN SAFE, worn gold, 9½" H $115.50
BEAR, worn gold, 5½" H $159.50
BUSTER BROWN, w/Tige, worn gold, red, replacement, 5⅛" H $192.50
DOMED BANK, worn silver, dk. red, 4¾" H $115.50
COIN DEPOSIT BANK, nickel finish, rust. 5¾" H $38.50

A-OH July 1993   *Garth's Auctions, Inc.*
CAST IRON BANKS unless otherwise noted.

Row 1, Left to Right

DOWER CHEST & MODEL A, 3½", 4" L $275.00
BOTTLE OPENERS, pelican, 3½" L, alligator, 6¼" L $110.00

GARAGE, traces of paint, rust, 2½"
L $71.50
BUILDINGS, 2 pcs., Mosque, black, gold,
2⅞" T, "Bank" silver, gold, rust, 3"
L $99.00

Row 2, Left to Right

LOCOMOTIVE, cast iron, tin, wind up,
"A.F. 10," red, working, 10½" L $82.50
LOCOMOTIVE, cast iron, tin, wind up,
"A.F. 16," black, red, yellow, dents, wear, not
working, 7¾" L $82.50

Row 3, Left to Right

GIVE BILLY A PENNY, silver, flesh, red,
black, wear, 4¾" T $159.50
BIRD, black patina, tail missing, 4⅞"
T $22.00
KITTY, white, blue, pink, black paint, wear,
5" T $11.00
BUILDING, "1892," red, green, yellow paint,
wear, chips, 5½" T $121.00
TWO-FACED BLACK BOY, black, gold,
wear, 4⅛" T $104.50
RABBIT, no paint, rust, 4⅝" T ... $82.50
DEPOSIT BANK, dk. bronze japanning,
silver, 4⅜" T $110.00

A-OH Nov. 1992   *Garth's Auctions, Inc.*
CAST IRON BANKS

Row 1, Left to Right

LION, blue over gold, 5½" L $33.00
BEAR, traces of paint, 4" L $49.50
SEATED CAT, modern, polychrome has wear, 4¼" H $60.50
HOUSE, traces of gold, 3¼" H $60.50
DONKEY, worn blue, 4½" H $71.50

ELEPHANT, grey, gold and silver, minor
wear, 3½" H $71.50
LION, gold has some wear, 3⅝" H .. NS

Row 2, Left to Right

SHARECROPPER, Polychrome, minor
wear 5½" H $137.50
BLACK MAMMY, polychrome, minor
wear, 6" H $104.50
STAG, gold, wear, 6¼" H $22.00
"BANK" BUILDING, silver, some wear,
3¾" H $38.50
RABBIT, gold, wear, 5¼" H $60.50
BEAR, gold, wear, 5⅜" H $49.50
ELEPHANT, mechanical, old repaint,
alligatored, 5½" H $187.00
JOLLY BLACK MAN, mechanical, worn
polychrome, rust, 6" H $220.00

Row 3, Left to Right

"TRICK PONY," mechanical, polychrome
repaint, trap missing, 7⅞" H ... $203.50
SPEAKING DOG," mechanical, worn
polychrome, no trap, 7" H $412.50
EAGLE AND EAGLETTS, mechanical,
worn polychrome, pin holding eagle and
trap replaced, glass eyes missing, 5¾"
H $302.50
**"FIDELITY TRUST VAULT, COUNT-
ING HOUSE,"** black with brown graining
over white undercoat, 6⅝" H .. $330.00
"I ALWAYS DID 'SPISE A MULE,"
mechanical, worn polychrome, reins and
trap replaced, 10¼" L $225.50

A-MA Dec. 1992   *Skinner, Inc.*
DAILY DIME BANKS, ten pcs., lithographed metal, 1920–1960, 2½" sq. ... $467.50

A-MA Dec. 1992   *Skinner, Inc.*
PENNY FIRE PUMPER, lithographed
tin, 5½" L $330.00
PENNY TOY HANSOM CAB, Germany,
lithographed tin, 4½" L $385.00
PENNY TOY TOURING CAR, Germany,
lithographed tin, 3¼" L $302.50
THREE TOYS, 2 tin rowboats, each
w/standing flat figure, 2⅝" L; Nuremberg
lady, wood, 2¾" H $110.00

A-OH Nov. 1992   *Garth's Auctions, Inc.*
CAST IRON UNLESS NOTED

Row 1, Left to Right

LOCOMOTIVE ENGINE, black, gold, wear, 7" L $88.00
BUILDING BANK, "Moore 1183," worn silver/gold, 4¾" H $71.50
SQUIRREL NUT CRACKER and TOY FOOD GRINDER, (1 illus.), late, rust ... $22.00
CATERPILLER, tin, wind-up, polychrome, white rubber treads, working, 7½" L .. $49.50

Row 2, Left to Right

GOAT AND FROG BANK, mechanical, "Initiating Bank 2nd degree," "Norman 3010,"
worn polychrome, base 7½" L $412.50
U.S. and SPAIN BANK, mechanical, "Norman 5800-a," loss, wear, 8¼" L $935.00
REPRODUCTION BANKS, 2 pcs., mechanical, cast metal and chrome shooting gallery,
cast iron and tin "Race Course Bank" $13.75

Row 3, Left to Right

ROYAL SAFE DEPOSIT BANK, worn black paint, lock incomplete, 6" H $38.50
JOLLY BLACK BANK, cast aluminum, mechanical, "Norman 3270," 6⅛" H $231.00
FLATIRON SKYSCRAPER BANK, "M1161," silver/gold, 5½" H $121.00
HORSE PULL TOY, wood, papier mache, hair cloth, damage, wear, 8" H $192.50
WORLD'S FAIR COLUMBUS BANK, mechanical bank, worn white paint, "Norman
6040-A" $165.00

A-OH Apr. 1993   *Garth's Auctions, Inc.*
CAST IRON MECHANICAL BANKS

Row 1, Left to Right

BULL DOG, worn paint, glass eyes, chip
replacement, 7¾" T $880.00
INDIAN AND BEAR, old polychrome,
10½" L $1320.00
TEDDY AND THE BEAR, worn polychrome, 9¼" T $1210.00
STUMP SPEAKER, worn polychrome,
crack, 10" T $1980.00

Row 2, Left to Right

UNCLE SAM, worn polychrome, crack,
11½" T $1760.00
SPEAKING DOG, worn polychrome, 7"
T $1980.00
WILLIAM TELL, worn polychrome,
10½" L $935.00
OWL, glass eyes, loss, 7¼" T $495.00
CAT AND MOUSE, worn polychrome,
repair, lost leg, 11½" T **$1450.00**

A-IL Apr. 1993   *Leslie Hindman Auction*
STAFFORDSHIRE COTTAGE BANKS,
3 pcs., pottery, 19th c., to 4" T .. $750.00*
STAFFORDSHIRE COTTAGE BANKS,
3 pcs., pottery, 19th c., to 5" T .. $600.00*

A-MA Aug. 1993   *James D. Julia, Inc.*
PEDAL CAR, pressed steel, red, gold stripes, repainted, 19" H, 36" L . . . $200.00

A-MA Dec. 1992   *Skinner, Inc.*
DONALD DUCK JALOPY, Linemar, Lithographed Metal, 5½" L $385.00
MECHANICAL MICKEY & DRIVER, Linemar, box, 6⅝" H $825.00
MECHANICAL KNITTING MINNEY, Linemar, box, 6¾" H $770.00
VELVETEEN MICKEY, wire armature, felt ears, fading, loss, 9¼" H $550.00
DISNEY ITEMS, 3 pcs., Noma Mickey Mouse Christmas Lights, (illus.), box; Japanese bisque Donald Duck, 3¼" H; Mattel "Mousekantooner" panograph, damage, 14¾" H, 8¾" W $192.50
SPORTS CAR W/HOUSE TRAILER, car cream w/red, trailer white w/blue, friction powered, box, total 11⅞" L $247.50
MECHANICAL PINOCCHIO THE ACROBAT, Marx, lithographed metal, 1939, wear, 16½" H $165.00

A-MA Dec. 1992   *Skinner, Inc.*
CLOCKWORK BICYCLE RACE GAME, French, painted metal and pewter cyclists, box, damage, 19" H, 18⅛" sq. . . $1760.00

A-MA Aug. 1993   *James D. Julia, Inc.*
PEDAL CAR, sheet metal, ca. 1950, cream, red stripe, 19" H, 44" L . . . $475.00

A-MA Aug. 1993   *James D. Julia, Inc.*
CAST IRON TOYS
Row 1, Left to Right
5 TRAIN CARS, clockwork Ives train engine; Ives baggage car; Ives baggage and mail car; 2 American Flyer cars $100.00*
2 ITEMS, red gas pump, 4¼" T; Avery tractor, 3" H, 4¾" L $150.00*
REFRIGERATOR, by Hubley, 1920 GE, wear, 3⅝" W, 7" T $20.00*
Row 2, Left to Right
FIRE LADDER TRUCK, by Hubley, nickel driver, repainted, repair, replacements, 6½" H, 16" L $135.00*
SEDAN, molded-in wheels, lt. green, paint loss, 2¼" H, 6½" L $110.00*

A-MA Dec. 1992   *Skinner, Inc.*
"LIBERTY" HOSE REEL, Hull & Stafford, painted tin, ca. 1870, 15⅜" L $22000.00

A-MA Aug. 1993   *James D. Julia, Inc.*
FIRE ENGINE PEDAL CAR, by American National, restored w/new parts, 30" H, 24" W, 64" L $3500.00*

A-MA Aug. 1993   *James D. Julia, Inc.*
SKIPPY DESOTO PEDAL CAR, by Pioneer(?), ca. 1935, cream w/red, wear, rust, 27" H, 38" L $900.00*

A-MA Aug. 1993   *James D. Julia, Inc.*
MOTORCYCLE DAREDEVIL, by Arnold, tin, orig. box, 11" H, 8¾" L $550.00*
CLOWN, tin windup, plays trombone, 9" T $170.00*
AUTO SPEEDWAY, tin race track, 2 garages, 3 windup race cars, orig. box, 10" W, 17" L $275.00*

Row 2, Left to Right
COWBOY, tin litho, windup, works, 9" T $90.00*
LIMPING LIZZY, by Louis Marx, Co., tin, wind up, orig. box, works, 4" H, 6¾" L $375.00*

A-MA Aug. 1993   *James D. Julia, Inc.*
PEDAL CAR, ca. 1935, blue, rubber tires, dents, rust, 21" H, 40" L $300.00*

A-MA Aug. 1993   *James D. Julia, Inc.*
PEDAL CAR, 50s style, Gran Turismo, cream, silver paint, 18½" H, 44" L $250.00*

A-MA Aug. 1993   *James D. Julia, Inc.*
Row 1, Left to Right
MAMMY W/BROOM, by Lindstrom, tin litho, windup, 8" T $150.00*
BLACK MAMMY, by Lindstrom, tin litho, 8" T $175.00*
Row 2, Left to Right
COO COO CAR, by Marx, windup, tin litho, 5½" H, 8" L $300.00*
VAQUERO MARADO, Spanish copy of Rodeo Joe, 6" H, 5" L . . . . NS
PECKING GOOSE, by Louis Marx, tin litho, windup, 5" H, 9" L $60.00*
Row 3, Left to Right
BALKING MULE, by Lehmann, tin windup, works, 5½" H, 7¾" L $200.00*
MOTORCYCLE W/SIDECAR, by Ingap, tin windup, works, 3¾" H, 5¼" L $650.00*
WHOOPEE CAR, tin windup, works, 5½" H, 8" L $225.00*

A-MA Aug. 1993   *James D. Julia, Inc.*
PEDAL CAR, ca. 1914, red, black stripe, wood steering wheel, 30" H, 42" L $300.00*

A-MA Aug. 1993   *James D. Julia, Inc.*
Row 1, Left to Right
MILK MAN W/WAGON, mechanical, by Welsotoys of England, orig. box, 5¾″ L.... NS
CLOCKWORK TRAIN, cast iron, by Bing of Germany, works, 3¼″ H, 7″ L...... $75.00*
Row 2, Left to Right
THIMBLEDRONE CHAMPION RACER, no driver, black w/red, silver, wear, 9½″
L $150.00*
U.S. ARMY TANK, by Gama of West Germany, orig. box, windup, orig. key, works, 4″ H,
7½″ L.. $275.00*
TOURING CAR, by Dayton, red body, gold fenders, 3″ H, 10½″ L $45.00*
Row 3, Left to Right
MOTORCYCLE DELIVERY WAGON, by KO of Japan, orig. box, friction powered, self-
changing direction, 5″ H, 6½″ L $150.00*
DELIVERY TRUCK, by Dayton, "Williams, The Little Shop with Big Values, Main Street,
Hannibal," friction powered, red w/green fenders, works, 6″ H, 11½″ L........ $350.00*

A-MA Aug. 1993   *James D. Julia, Inc.*
PRESSED STEEL TOY VEHICLES
Row 1, Left to Right
LINCOLN SEDAN, by Turner, green-grey paint, black strips & Roof, rubber tires w/logo,
yellow interior, 10½″ H, 27″ L $4250.00*
COAL TRUCK, by Sturdy Toy, separate coal chute, repaint, 10¾″ H, 27½″ L .. $2700.00*
Row 2, Left to Right
AMERICAN NATIONAL PACKARD ROADSTER, "Firechief" model, by Buddy "L," ca.
1928, 13½″ H, 29″ L $3750.00*
DELIVERY TRUCK, by Kingsbury of Keene, NH, motor driven, blue cab, orange rack,
"Motor Driven Truck, Kingsbury Mnfct. Co.," rubber tires w/logo, 10″ H, 25″ L .. $4250.00*

A-MA Aug. 1993   *James D. Julia, Inc.*
PEDAL CAR, ca. 1930, silver plated grill,
dents, 17″ H, 38″ L $400.00*

A-MA Aug. 1993   *James D. Julia, Inc.*
PEDAL CAR, ca. 1960, red, w/white
stripe, repainted, 18″ W, 47″ L .. $150.00*

A-MA Aug. 1993   *James D. Julia, Inc.*
PEDAL CAR, sheet metal, ca. 1938, maroon, repainted, 19″ H, 42″ L.... $300.00*

A-MA Aug. 1993   *James D. Julia, Inc.*
PEDAL CAR, ca. 1933, "Renault," repainted, 19″ H, 42″ L $700.00*

A-MA Aug. 1993   *James D. Julia, Inc.*
PEDAL CAR, ca. 1950, green, repainted,
dents, 17″ H, 37″ L $325.00*

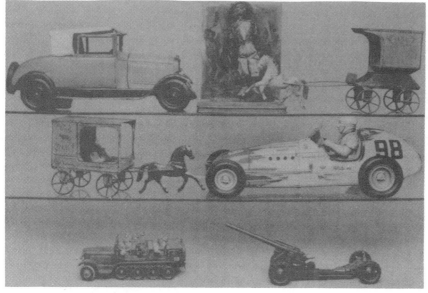

A-MA Aug. 1993   *James D. Julia, Inc.*
PUMPER PEDAL CAR, by Toledo Co., tin boiler, fuel compartment, maroon and red, black fenders, tin radiator, hand brake, replaced dashboard, pedal assembly removed, repaint, 34″ H, 60″ L . . . $2000.00*

A-MA Aug. 1993   *James D. Julia, Inc.*

Row 1, Left to Right
CONVERTIBLE, by Citroen of France, tin, green body, black fenders, Michelin rubber tires, working wind up, replacements, 6¾″ H, 15″ L $900.00*
DANCING JIGGER TOY, ca. 1890, wind up, 9″ T . . . . NS
GROCERY DELIVERY WAGON, tin, stenciled "Fine Groceries," green w/orange, gold, horse is yellow w/red, 7″ H, 14″ L $1700.00*

Row 2, Left to Right
MILK DELIVERY WAGON, tin, ca. 1880, stenciled "Pure Milk," red, orange, horse is brown w/red, 6¼″ H, 13″ L $1400.00*
RACE CAR, tin, by E.T. of Japan, "98 Champion Racer," cream body, red flames, driver has yellow shirt w/blue, white helmet, 7″ H, 19″ L $3100.00*

Row 3, Left to Right
GERMAN TRANSPORT CARRIER W/2 TRAILERS, 9 SOLDIERS, by Tipp & Company, windup, chain driven, 1 trailer has mounted cannon, papier mache soldiers in Nazi uniforms, 22″ L $800.00*

A-MA Aug. 1993   *James D. Julia, Inc.*
PEDAL CAR, by American National, black fenders, orange hood, yellow stripes, has tool box, headlights, license plate, handbrake, windshield, bulb horn, steering wheel has imitation spark advance, 26″ H, 21½″ W, 44″ L $5500.00*

A-MA Aug. 1993   *James D. Julia, Inc.*
TOURING CAR, hand made model of Stanley Steamer, ca. 1917, working levers, hand brake, clutch, chain driven, many details, padded seats, rear door, needs repairs, 7½″ H, 18″ L $2700.00*
RACE CAR INK WELL, silver plated, 1910–1912, inkwell under hood, pen storage under spare tire, 5″ H, 12½″ L $2500.00*

Row 2, Left to Right
FORD TIRE CARRIER TRUCK, replacement International decals, paint loss, 3¾″ H, 11¼″ L $500.00*
COCA-COLA TRUCK, by Metalcraft, red truck, yellow back end, electric lights, 6″ H, 11½″ L $875.00*

Row 3, Left to Right
CAR AND TRAILER, by Wyandotte, 1936 Cord car w/wood wheels, red w/yellow top, 4½″ H, 24″ L $600.00*
BELL TOY, cast iron, black boy riding alligator on wheels, 5″ H, 5½″ L . . . . NS

A-MA Aug. 1993   *James D. Julia, Inc.*
CAST IRON TOY VEHICLES
Row 1, Left to Right
FIVE TON TRUCK, by Hubley, green, red hood and tool boxes, 5¾" H, 17" L $400.00*
ARMY MOTOR TRUCK #807, by Kenton, orange, wear, 6½" H, 15" L . . . . . . NS
Row 2, Left to Right
CHEVY COUPE, by arcade, black, grey, paint loss, 4" H, 8" L $475.00*
ICE TRUCK, by Arcade, blue, nickel driver, replacements, 4" H, 8" L . . . . NS
Row 3, Left to Right
ROAD ROLLER, by Hubley, "Huber," green body, red wheels, restored, 4" H, 14" L $750.00*
OIL TRUCK, by Dent Mfg., "American Oil Co.," repainted, 6" H, 15¼" L $700.00*

A-MA Aug. 1993   *James D. Julia, Inc.*
PEDAL CAR, pressed steel, blue, white strips, repainted, 16" H, 42" L $300.00

A-MA Aug. 1993   *James D. Julia, Inc.*
PEDAL CAR, ca. 1928, red, metal wheels, repainted, 20" H, 36" L $400.00

A-MA Aug. 1993   *James D. Julia, Inc.*
PEDAL CAR, wood, ca. 1930, 23" H, 53" L $300.00

A-MA Aug. 1993   *James D. Julia, Inc.*
CAST IRON TOY VEHICLES
Row 1, Left to Right
TWO-DOOR COUPE, red, 3¼" H, 6½" L $375.00*
JAEGER CEMENT MIXER, by Kenton, orange, aluminum dump chute and container, 6¼" H, 6½" L $200.00*
FIRE CHIEF CAR, by Kenton, molded-in driver, red paint, 2½" H, 5½" L . . $775.00*
Row 2, Left to Right
HORSE DRAWN MILK WAGON, ca. 1920, white wagon, black horse, red hitch, 5¾" H, 12½" L $225.00*
HORSE DRAWN BAKERY WAGON, ca. 1920, white wagon, black horse, red harness, 5¾" H, 12½" L $200.00*
Row 3, Left to Right
HORSE DRAWN SAND & GRAVEL WAGON, green wagon, red wheels, black and white horses, sand dumps from bottom, 4½" H, 14½" L $150.00*
DUMP TRUCK, by Arcade, green cab, yellow sheet metal dump, 11¼" L . . $160.00*

A-MA Aug. 1993   *James D. Julia, Inc.*
THE WRIGHT PLANE #20, tin, America, blue body, yellow wings, red tail, 7½" H, 26½" W, 29" L $400.00*
THE EMPIRE EXPRESS MONOPLANE, tin, "Made in U.S.A.," silver body, red wing, scratches, 18" W, 20" L $90.00*
LOCKHEED SIRUS AIRPLANE, by Steel craft, pressed steel, white enamel body, red wings, electric wing lights, 21¾" W, 21½" L $1100.00*

A-MA Aug. 1993   *James D. Julia, Inc.*
PRESSED STEEL TOY VEHICLES

LA FRANCE WATER TOWER, by Sturdy Toy of MA, hand crank water pump, paint loss, wear, 12" H, 32" L $400.00*
ARMY SCOUT PLANE, by Steel craft, green body, wing and tail yellow, US insignia on wing tips $800.00*
INTERCITY BUS, by Steelcraft, electric lights, green, 6" H, 24" L $400.00*

A-MA Aug. 1993   *James D. Julia, Inc.*
FLYING ZEPPELIN, by Ferdinand Strauss, aluminum, never painted, orig. box, working mec., 16" L $375.00*
U.S. MAIL TRANSPORT PLANE, by Steelcraft, pressed steel, tri-motor, w/ canvas mailbag, repainted, 26½" W, 23½" L $550.00*

A-MA Aug. 1993   *James D. Julia, Inc.*
AIRPLANE PEDAL CAR, by Steelcraft, black body, red wing & tail w/white stripes, stenciled "Red Wing," paint loss, rust, 23" H, 50" L $900.00*

A-MA Aug. 1993   *James D. Julia, Inc.*
CAST IRON TOY VEHICLES

Row 1, Left to Right
ICE TRUCK, by Arcade, blue, nickel plated grill, rubber tires, 3¼" H, 6⅝" L $350.00*
AMPHIBIOUS AIRPLANE, "Sea Gull," repainted, 3¼" H, 8" W, 8" L $200.00*
Row 2, Left to Right
YELLOW CAB, by Arcade, paint loss, 3⅝" H, 8" L $775.00*
ONE-DOOR COUPE, by Freidag(?), yellow, 3" H, 5" L $400.00*
TWO-DOOR COUPE, by Hubley, green, gold, molded-in driver, 3¼" H, 6½" L . . $675.00*
Row 3, Left to Right
GREYHOUND BUS, by Arcade, later model, repainted, 2¾" H, 8¾" L $200.00*
FIRE TRUCK, by arcade, ca. 1937, molded-in driver and firemen, nickel plated grill and bumper, ladders missing, no brakes, 3¼" H, 9½" L $275.00*

A-MA Aug. 1993   *James D. Julia, Inc.*
AIRPLANE PEDAL CAR, by Toledo Mfg. Co., pressed steel, yellow body, red wing, wood prop., "Falcon" stencil, w/oil can, 26" H, 28" W, 60" L $2950.00*

A-MA Aug. 1993   *James D. Julia, Inc.*
CAST IRON TOYS
Row 1, Left to Right
HORSE DRAWN FIRE PATROL WAGON,
one black horse, 2 nickle plated, axle
replaced, 8" H, 19½" L $500.00*
HORSE DRAWN FIRE HOSE REEL,
breaks, losses, 6½" H, 18" L $400.00*
Row 2, Left to Right
FIRE LADDER TRUCK, 2 firemen, 3
ladders, 6" H, 16½" L $600.00*
FIRE LADDER TRUCK, ca. 1920, nickle-
plated ladders, racks, 5½" H, 13"
L $900.00*
Row 3, Left to Right
HORSE DRAWN FIRE PATROL WAGON,
black, white horses, replaced driver, no
firemen, 7" H, 20½" L $800.00*
FIRE PUMPER, ca. 1919, by Hubley, re-
pair, 7" H, 11¾" L $275.00*

A-MA Aug. 1993   *James D. Julia, Inc.*
METALCRAFT TOY TRUCKS
Row 1, Left to Right
RACK TRUCK, "Drink Smile," red, electric
lights, rust, repair, 4" H, 12" L . . . $100.00*
2 TRUCKS, Shell Motor Oil truck, red cab,
yellow rack, electric lights, 4" H, 12¼" L;
Sunshine Biscuits truck, red cab, blue rack,
4" H, 12" L $250.00*
Row 2, Left to Right
HEINZ TRUCK, electric lights, 5" H, 12"
L $200.00*
BUNTE CANDIES DUMP TRUCK, elec-
tric lights, Goodrich tires, red cab, white
body, 4¼" H, 12¼" L $450.00*
Row 3, Left to Right
PURE OIL COMPANY TRUCK, pressed
steel, blue, nickel plated radiator and
bumpers, 4½" H, 15" L $1050.00*
HEINZ TRUCK, restored, 5¼" H, 12"
L $175.00*

A-MA Aug. 1993   *James D. Julia, Inc.*
TWO TOYS, US Air Force Helicopter, by
TN of Japan, orig. box, 5" H, 10" L; firechief
car, by TN of Japan, 3¼" H, 8" L . . $65.00*
HILLCLIMBER TRUCK, sheet metal,
flywheel mec., blue w/yellow, wear, 7" H,
11" L $200.00*
Row 2, Left to Right
HARDY'S SALT TRUCK, by Metalcraft,
sheet metal, wear, 5" H, 11" L . . . $225.00*
SAND TRUCK, by Louis Marx, sheet
metal, red, black, 4" H, 10½" L . . . $75.00*
Row 3, Left to Right
CANNON, cast iron, patented 1907, turn
crank to shoot pellets, 7" H, 16"
L $135.00*
ARMY TRANSPORT TRUCK, by Louis
Marx, sheet metal, orig. box, canvas top, 4"
H, 13½" L $250.00*

A-IL Apr. 1993   *Leslie Hindman Auction*
POTTERY BANK, pearlware, 19th c., blue, ochre, brown, 8½" H $500.00*
POTTERY FIGURINE, pearlware, 19th c., ochre, green, blue, 8" H $500.00*

A-OH Nov. 1992   *Garth's Auctions, Inc.*

Row 1, Left to Right

TOURING CAR, cast iron, green, orange, white, rubber wheels, 5" L $181.50
MICKEY MOUSE RACING CAR, tin, wind-up, rubber wheels, wear, 4" L . . $148.50
AIRPLANE, "Hubley," cast white metal, red folding wings, 6¼" L $27.50
"TEXACO" TRUCK, "Hubley," cast white metal, mint with red trim, worn white rubber wheels, 4¾" L $71.50
SEDAN, "Hubley," cast white metal, mint w/red trim, rubber wheels, 5¼" L . . .$71.50
AIRPLANE, "Hubley," cast white metal, "Flying Circus," yellow, orange, 7½". . .$27.50
SEDAN, "Hubley," cast white metal, mint w/red trim, rubber wheels, 5¼" L . . .$60.50

Row 2, Left to Right

HORSE AND CART, tin pull toy, worn green, yellow, orange, black, 9½" L . . $286.00
TRAIN, tin pull toy, worn green, red and black, 9½" L $275.00
CLIMBING MONKEY, tin, polychrome paint, flaking, 7½" L $27.50
HOUSE BANK, tin, red, yellow and black, chimney bent, 3¼" H $104.50

Row 3, Left to Right

"COO—COO CAR," tin, wind-up, working, wear, 9" L $93.50
POLICE CAR, tin, wind-up, "Dunlap, made in France," working, 7" L $192.50
"ROYAL" RANGE, cast iron, worn silver, 4½" H $5.50
BOOK-SHAPED BLOCKS, set of 16, wood with colored printed paper, A.B.C.s plus numbers and ampersand, wear, 3" L $379.50

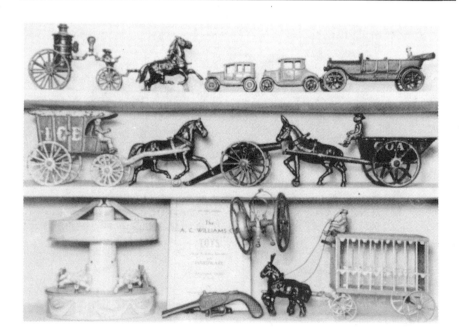

A-OH Nov. 1992   *Garth's Auctions, Inc.*

CAST IRON UNLESS NOTED

Row 1, Left to Right

FIRE PUMPER, 2 horses w/no wheels, black, red, gold paint, 14½" L $93.50
SEDAN, orange, black, wear, 4½" L $85.00
COUPE, olive and silver, wear, "Kilcare," 5⅛" L $115.50
TOURING CAR, green red, silver, black, wear, driver missing, 9½" L . . . $165.00

Row 2, Left to Right

"ICE" WAGON, black, red, yellow, gold, silver, wear, 16" L $275.00
CANNON, red, black, wear, 8½" L $115.50
"COAL" CART, worn yellow, black, red and blue, cart dumps cargo . . . $412.50
BELL TOY, some tin, worn polychrome, 5" D $27.50

Row 3, Left to Right

"MERRY-GO-ROUND," tin, lever action, by Wolverine, worn polychrome, non-working, 10" D, 10¼" H $27.50
CATALOGUE, paper bound, "The A.C. Williams Co., Ravenna, Ohio, Toys and Hardware 51st ed.," wear 7⅜" x 10½" $88.00
AMERICAN BULLDOG BOOT JACK, in shape of revolver, 8¼" L $66.00
CIRCUS WAGON, cast iron, wood, sheet metal, paper label "Arcade," polychrome, 14½ L $352.00

A-MA Aug. 1993   *James D. Julia, Inc.*
CAST IRON TOY VEHICLES
Row 1, Left to Right
JAEGER CEMENT MIXER, by Kenton, cast aluminum chute and bowl, 7½" H, 9½" L $125.00*
TRUCK, by Arcade, red, decal, 3¼" H, 7¼" L $450.00*
TRUCK, by Arcade Toys, black cab, stake body stripped, 3⅞" H, 9" L $400.00*
COUPE, by Arcade, scratches, chips, 4" H, 6¼" L $185.00*
Row 2, Left to Right
2 ITEMS, (1 illus.), dump truck by Kilgore, blue body, red dump, 3½" H, 8½" L; tractor w/cattle trailer, 30's style, 4¼" H, 13½" L................................. $125.00*
McCORMACK-DEERING WAGON W/HORSES, by Arcade, black horses, green wagon, 4¼" H, 12" L $200.00*
LOW ROOF COUPE, by Arcade, black, no driver, 3½" H, 6¾" L $250.00*
Row 3, Left to Right
GREYHOUND BUS, by Arcade, blue, white, nickel plated radiator, windshield and rear piece, 2¼" H, 8¾" L $200.00*
TEN TON TRUCK, by Hubley, ca. 1930, cab orange, nickel plated grill and body, 2⅝" H, 8¼" L.. $350.00*
INTERNATIONAL DUMP TRUCK, by Arcade, ca. 1940, red cab, silver dump, 3½" H, 11" L $550.00*

A-MA Aug. 1993   *James D. Julia, Inc.*
POLICE PATROL, by Buddy "L," pressed steel, black cab, grated enclosure for criminals, rust, paint loss, 27" L $650.00*

A-MA Aug. 1993   *James D. Julia, Inc.*
EXPRESS LINE, by Buddy "L," green, working rear doors, 25" L..... $1150.00*

A-MA Aug. 1993   *James D. Julia, Inc.*
WATER TOWER FIRE TRUCK, by Keystone, pressed steel, working pump, 32" L......................... $500.00*

A-MA Aug. 1993   *James D. Julia, Inc.*
BUS, by Keystone, pressed steel, "Keystone Bus, Built by Keystone Mnfct. Co., Boston, MA," decals listing cities traveled to, rust, 32" L...................... $850.00*

A-MA Aug. 1993   *James D. Julia, Inc.*
CAST IRON BELL TELEPHONE TRUCKS BY HUBLEY
Row 1, Left to Right
CABLE LAYER TRUCK, complete w/tools, tires, ditch digger, pully holder, 5" H, 9" L $450.00*
TRUCK, molded-in driver, no tools, replaced tires, crack, 4¼" H, 8" L.. $150.00*
Row 2, Left to Right
TRUCK, molded-in driver, no tools, rust, 3½" H, 6¾" L $200.00*
TRUCK, green paint, wear, 2" H, 3¾" L $125.00*
TRUCK, wear, chips, 1½" H, 3" L $125.00*
TRUCK, molded-in driver, green paint, 3" H, 5" L $200.00*

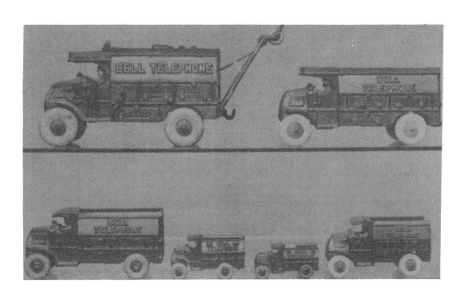

A-MA Aug. 1993   *James D. Julia, Inc.*
**CAST IRON TOY TRUCKS BY
ARCADE TOYS**
Row 1, Left to Right
INTERNATIONAL TRUCK, nickel grill,
paint wear, rust, 2 tires replaced, 3¼" H,
11½" L $900.00*
PICK UP, "Anchor Truck Company," re-
painted, 3¾" H, 8¾" L . . . . NS
Row 2, Left to Right
INTERNATIONAL TRUCK, 2 replaced
tires, overall paint loss, 3" H, 11½"
L $925.00*
PICK UP, by Freidag(?), molded-in driver,
green paint, 3½" H, 7½" L $1100.00*
Row 3, Left to Right
FORD TRUCK, nickel driver, 4" H, 8½"
L $900.00*
ONE-TON PICK UP, nickel driver, 4" H,
8¼" L $800.00*

A-MA Aug. 1993   *James D. Julia, Inc.*
1903 MODEL "A" FORD, 1978 Ford
Motor Company Diamond Jubilee Com-
memorative Model, fully working scale
model, sterling silver, gold, 2 diamonds, 1
ruby, 7½" H, 14" L $4500.00*

A-MA Aug. 1993   *James D. Julia, Inc.*
CAST IRON TOY VEHICLES
Row 1, Left to Right
INTERNATIONAL HARVESTER DUMP TRUCK, by Arcade, red chipped paint, 4⅜" H,
10½" L $400.00*
COUPE, by Arcade, black body, orange tires, orange wheels, nickel plated driver, repainted,
4¼" H, 8½" L $900.00*
Row 2, Left to Right
CHEVY SUPERIOR TOURING SEDAN, black, nickel driver, repainted, 3¾" H, 6¾"
L $1000.00*
BORDEN'S MILK TRUCK, by Hubley, repainted, 3⅜" H, 5¾" L $450.00*
Row 3, Left to Right
CHEVY SUPERIOR COUPE, by Arcade, no driver, wear, 3½" H, 6¾" L $900.00*
MACK TRUCK W/BACKHOE, by Hubley, green truck, embossed driver, red derrick,
nickel clamshell, impressed "General," 3¼" H, 8" L $600.00*
MODEL T TOURING CAR, by Arcade, black, nickel wheels, 4" H, 6¼" L $150.00*

A-MA Aug. 1993   *James D. Julia, Inc.*
TOURING CAR, salesman's display to
demonstrate electric mec. for canvas top,
ca. 1925, electric lights, glass windshield,
wood steering wheel, spark advance, plush
seats, 21" H, 37" L $3500.00*

A-MA Aug. 1993   *James D. Julia, Inc.*
Row 1, Left to Right
TOY TOWN RAILROAD GAME, orig. box, penny toy train, coal car, caboose all tin, many other pieces, buildings, cardboard figures $2000.00*
CHEVROLET UTILITY TRUCK, by Arcade, black body, grey rack, driver, 4" H, 8¾" L $400.00*
Row 2, Left to Right
HARDY'S SALT DELIVERY TRUCK, by Metalcraft, black cab, green body, 5¼" H, 11¼" L $900.00*
SUNSHINE BISCUITS VAN TRUCK, by Metalcraft, yellow w/blue, electric lights, 5¼" H, 12¼" L $450.00*
Row 3, Left to Right
2 METALCRAFT TOYS, machinery hauler truck, "Forbes Quality Coffee Machinery Hauling," red cab, green bed w/wench, 4" H, 12" L; steam shovel on platform, 8" H, 5" L $850.00*
WHITE KING DELIVERY TRUCK, by Metalcraft, red cab, yellow box, 4" H, 12" L $400.00*

A-MA Aug. 1993   *James D. Julia, Inc.*
Row 1, Left to Right
FLIVVER W/DUMP BODY, Buddy "L," repainted, 4½" H, 11" L $900.00*
DREDGE, Buddy "L," pressed steel, 22½" H, 15" L $350.00*
Row 2, Left to Right
TANK TRUCK, Buddy "L," pressed steel, 12½" H, 25" L $1450.00*

A-MA Aug. 1993   *James D. Julia, Inc.*
CAST IRON TOY VEHICLES
DITCH DIGGER, by Kenton, crack in side, 6½" H, 12" L $1050.00*
SIGHT SEEING BUS, by Kenton, "Seeing New York 1899," yellow-orange paint, 3 replaced figures, 6¾" H, 10" L $2700.00*
Row 2, Left to Right
CAR CARRIER, by Kenton, trailer w/molded-in blue cars, 10" L $1900.00*
BUS, by Arcade, black, yellow, grey, "Yellow Coach," nickel driver, 3½" H, 13" L . . . . . . NS
Row 3, Left to Right
3 PIECES, by Arcade, green tractor, green dump w/red body, red cradle w/green side dump, 3" H, 21" L $3500.00*
DELIVERY TRUCK, by Freidag, molded-in driver, white paint, 3½" H, 7⅜" L . . $850.00*

A-MA Aug. 1993   *James D. Julia, Inc.*

STEAM SHOVEL, by Buddy "L," pressed steel, 14" H, 20" L $100.00*
DUMP TRUCK, by Buddy "L," ride-on, ca. 1930 International truck, grey, blue, wear, rust, 11" H, 25" L $350.00*

A-MA Aug. 1993   *James D. Julia, Inc.*

CAST IRON TOY VEHICLES MADE BY ARCADE TOYS
Row 1, Left to Right
MACK DUMP TRUCK, red paint, losses, 5" H, 12" L $200.00*
INTERNATIONAL TRUCK, "Red Baby," nickel driver, wear, rust, 4¼" H, 10" L . . . . . . NS
Row 2, Left to Right
INTERNATIONAL DUMP TRUCK, well worn, tires gone, 3½" H, 10½" L $950.00*
MODEL T HIGH HIP ROOF COUPE, no driver, old repaint, 3¾" H, 6" L $200.00*
Row 3, Left to Right
YELLOW CAB, yellow, black top & hood, nickel plated driver, 4½" H, 9" L $350.00*
DUMP TRUCK, cast iron, by Freidag, molded-in driver, red cab, orange dump, chips, wear, 3⅝" H, 8" L $700.00*
CHEVY SUPERIOR COUPE, cast iron, black, nickel plated driver, 3½" H, 6¾" L . . . . NS

A-MA Aug. 1993   *James D. Julia, Inc.*

PRESSED STEEL BUDDY "L" TRUCKS

WRECKER TRUCK, seat for child, pull handle, ca. 1931-1932, 14" H, 26" L $600.00*
EXPRESS LINE TRUCK, wear, chips, 10¾" H, 24" L $425.00*
FLIVVER SERIES TRUCK, dump body, repainted, 4½" H, 12½" L $1000.00*

A-MA Aug. 1993   *James D. Julia, Inc.*

PRESSED STEEL BUDDY "L" TOY VEHICLES

COUPE, touring car w/working steering wheel, paint loss, rust, 11" L $550.00*
DUMP TRUCK, black w/red fender, paint loss, rust, 25" L $450.00*
TRUCK, black cab, flip down gate, chips, 28" L $650.00*

A-MA Aug. 1993   *James D. Julia, Inc.*

TANK TRUCK, by Buddy "L," pressed steel, black cab, green tank, 27" L $1000.00*
TANK TRUCK, by Buddy "L," pressed steel, black cab, green tank, rust, 27" L $700.00*

A-OH Jan. 1993　　　*Garth's Auctions, Inc.*
Row 1, Left to Right
TRAIN, cast iron, 5 pc., nickel finish, marked "M.C.R.R.,"losses, 31" L ... $82.50
Row 2, Left to Right
BLACK MAN PUSHING CART, tin, mechanical, "Tip-Top" by "Straus," wear, 6¼" L $115.50
TRAIN ENGINE, cast iron, mechanical, black, red, gold, 6½" L $99.00
TRAIN ENGINE, cast iron, worn black, red, 7¼" L $93.50
COCKATOO BOTTLE OPENER, worn polychrome, 5½" L $71.50
PIP SQUEEK, bisque head, silent, 5½" H $38.50
WOOD BOOT, sliding lid and pop up snake, black, yellow, red, 3½" H ... $81.50
Row 3, Left to Right
EASTER RABBIT, nodder, papier mache, worn polychrome, 9¾" H $55.00
BOTTLE OPENER, cork screw, cast iron, label "Bishop & Babcock," nickel finish, worn, 6⅝" H $93.50
CLOWN ON UNICYCLE, tin, mechanical, "Marx," rust wear, 9" H $385.00
BIRD, tin, mechanical, yellow, velvet, felt, 9⅝" H $98.50
COCKATOO DOORSTOP, cast iron, polychrome, 8" H............. $187.00
DUCK DOORSTOP, polychrome, 7¾" H.......................... $550.00
PENGUIN DOORSTOP, cast iron, worn polychrome, 10" H $302.50

A-MA Aug. 1993　　　*James D. Julia, Inc.*
CAST IRON TOYS
Row 1, Left to Right
HIGH ROOF COUPE, by Arcade, re-painted, 4" H, 6½" L.......... $225.00*
CEMENT MIXER, motorized, wear, losses, 6" H, 6½" L............ $125.00*
MOTORIZED PUMPER, by Arcade, re-painted, replacements, 4¾" H, 7" L.......................... $95.00*
Row 2, Left to Right
MACK ICE TRUCK, by Arcade, wear, 3¼" H, 6¾" L $125.00*
MACK DUMP TRUCK, by Champion, red cab, blue dump, losses, 6¾" L ... $50.00*
Row 3, Left to Right
3 BUSSES, Greyhound by Arcade; red bus w/nickel plated wheels; blue bus w/molded-in passengers and driver $175.00*

A-MA Aug. 1993　　　*James D. Julia, Inc.*
Row 1, Left to Right
HORSE DRAWN LADDER WAGON, cast iron, by Hubley, all original, 7" H, 20" L $250.00*
Row 2, Left to Right
U.S. MAIL DELIVERY TRUCK, by Lindstrom Toy Co., windup, blue, loss, rust, 5½" H, 8" L $150.00*
C.W. BRAND COFFEE TRUCK, by Metalcraft, green, red, 5¼" H, 10¾" L..... $300.00*
TRUCK, by Metalcraft, sheet metal, red cab, yellow body, Shell decal, repainted, 4½" H, 12" L $105.00*
Row 3, Left to Right
BELL TELEPHONE TRUCK, ca. 1940, green paint on white metal .... NS
HARDY'S SALT TRUCK, by Metalcraft, 5¼" H, 11" L $65.00*
COCA COLA TRUCK, by metalcraft, red cab, yellow body, 5¾" H, 11" L $250.00*

A-MA Aug. 1993   *James D. Julia, Inc.*

TOY VEHICLES BY BUDDY "L"

Row 1, Left to Right

CATAPULT AIRPLANE W/HANGER, when lever on hangar is pulled, doors open and plane shoots out, orange wings, black body, 10" W, 6¾" L, hanger is grey w/orange, 6" H, 8" W, 12" L $900.00*
LADDER TRUCK, sheet metal, battery operated headlights, red paint, 9½" H, 21½" L $275.00*
CEMENT MIXER, pressed steel, rust, 13½" H, 16" L $400.00*

Row 2, Left to Right

AERIAL LADDER FIRETRUCK, 2 ladders missing, rust, 9" H, 33" L $350.00*
FLIVVER SERIES MODEL T, 7" H, 11" L $850.00*
JUNIOR SERIES TRUCK, ca 1930, repainted, 22" L $650.00*

A-MA Aug. 1993   *James D. Julia, Inc.*

SHEET METAL TOY TRUCKS

Row 1, Left to Right

BABY RUTH TRACTOR & 2 TRAILERS, by Buddy "L," ca. 1930, yellow, red, green, wear, 9½" H, 36" L $600.00*

Row 2, Left to Right

DELIVERY TRUCK, by Metalcraft, black, green box, rust, 5¼" H, 10¾" L $275.00*
WRECKER TRUCK, by Metalcraft, "Hardy's Salts, St. Louis," black, red, 4" H, 10¼" L $400.00*
RAILWAY EXPRESS TRUCK, Wrigley's Spearmint Chewing Gum trailer, wear, repainting, repair, 9" H, 23" L $500.00*

Row 3, Left to Right

TRUCK, by Cor-Cor Toys, black, red, losses, 7¼" H, 24" L $100.00*
FIRE PUMPER, by Dayton, cast iron driver and fireman, tin boiler, 7¼" H, 14½" L $300.00*

A-MA Aug. 1993   *James D. Julia, Inc.*

PRESSED STEEL BUDDY "L" TOY VEHICLES

SAND SCREENER, complete, wear, 21½" H, 24" W $500.00*
COAL TRUCK, no coal chute, wear, 12" H, 25½" L $650.00*
ROAD ROLLER, gears for turning and powering wheels, no driver, 9¼" H, 19" L $1700.00*

A-MA Aug. 1993   *James D. Julia, Inc.*

BUDDY "L" TRUCKS

Row 1, Left to Right

WRECKER, pressed steel, black cab, red chassis & crane, rust, 12" H, 26½" L $1700.00*

Row 2, Left to Right

ONE TON EXPRESS TRUCK, touchups to paint, 6½" H, 14" L $2100.00*
BUDDY L HUXTER TRUCK, for peddling fruit, black paint, replaced tailgate, 6" H, 14" L $2800.00*

A-MA Aug. 1993   *James D. Julia, Inc.*

PRESSED STEEL TOY VEHICLES

Row 1, Left to Right

STEAM SHOVEL, "Riding Toy," red, grey, wear, 12" H, 20" L $65.00*
TWO TOYS, fire truck by Structo, electric lights, no ladders, wear, 5½" H, 22½" L; red tractor w/green cattle trailer, (not illus.), by Wyandotte, ca. 1930, 5¾" H, 20½" L $175.00*

Row 2, Left to Right

CORD AUTO, ca. 1930, by Wyandotte Toys, yellow, red top, 4" H, 13" L $175.00*
DUMP TRUCK, by Republic Toys, 8" H, 19½" L $225.00*

Row 3, Left to Right

DUMP TRUCK, by Turner, yellow cab, green dump, wear, 8" H, 26" L $150.00*
TWO AUTOS, LaSalle, ca. 1930, red, white top, "Made in U.S.A.," 3½" H, 11" L; LaSalle convertible, (not illus.), ca. 1930, red, blue windshield, tin plated radiator, bumper and lights, 3¼" H, 10¾" L $250.00*

A-MA Aug. 1993   *James D. Julia, Inc.*

PRESSED STEEL TOY TRUCKS

Row 1, Left to Right

DUMP TRUCK, by Turner, seat style cab, losses, replacements, 11¾" H, 31" L ... $375.00*
HYDRAULIC DUMP TRUCK, by Keystone, worn paint, 10" H, 27½" L $800.00*

Row 2, Left to Right

DUMP TRUCK, by Steelcraft, blue cab, grey body, rubber tires, 7½" H, 27" L ... $250.00*
DUMP TRUCK, by Sturdy Toy, repainted, 10½" H, 27" L $625.00*

A-MA Aug. 1993   *James D. Julia, Inc.*

PRESSED STEEL TRUCKS BY KEYSTONE

Row 1, Left to Right

WRECKER TRUCK, repainted, 11" H, 27" L $500.00*
DUMP TRUCK, wear, paint loss, rust, 10½" H, 27" L $275.00*
DUMP TRUCK, wear, 7¼" H, 26" L $150.00*

A-MA Aug. 1993   *James D. Julia, Inc.*

BUDDY "L" TOY TRUCKS

DUMP TRUCK, pressed steel, chain dump, black, red, wear, 24" L ... $400.00*
DELIVERY TRUCK, ride-on, grey w/red, gold, blue, 8¼" H, 22" L $500.00*
DUMP TRUCK, chain dump, black, red, repainted, 9½" H, 24" L $400.00*

A-MA Aug. 1993   *James D. Julia, Inc.*

MOVING VAN, cast iron, by Arcade of the White Motor Company, blue w/gold stripe and lettering, red wheels, white tires, 4½" H, 13" L $15000.00*

A–MA Aug. 1993   *James D. Julia, Inc.*
OUTDOOR RAILROAD SET, 8 pcs., (4 illus.), by Buddy "L," pressed steel, steam engine, coal car, closed box car, oil tanker, flat bed, livestock carrier, open carrier, track $4000.00*

A–MA Oct. 1992   *Skinner, Inc.*
MINIATURE BUREAU, grain painted, ca. 1830, wear, 9½" H, 9" L, 6" D $660.00
SHOE-SHAPED MATCHBOX, carved, polychromed yellow, black, red, ochre, paint loss, 2¼" H, 5¼" L $605.00
NOAH'S ARK W/ANIMALS, carved, painted, late 19th c., imperfections 5¾" H, 10" L $990.00
JIG TOY, carved and painted wood head and body, celluloid hands, early 20th c., wear, losses, 11" H $330.00
MINIATURE WALL BOX, grain painted, carved, 19th c., crack, 2½" H . . $247.50
CARVED SONGBIRDS, 2, painted, robin and Baltimore oriole, chips, repair, 8" to 6½" L $247.50

A–MA Dec. 1992   *Skinner, Inc.*
BLACK DANCERS, American Clockwork, ca. 1870, man plays bell as lady dances, wood base, 9" H, 8⅝" L $1320.00

A–MA Aug. 1993   *James D. Julia, Inc.*
Row 1, Left to Right
TRAIN SET, by Lionel, 9 standard gauge pcs., (3 illus.), engine, 4 different coal cars, cattle car, searchlight car, caboose, crane car $600.00*
Row 2, Left to Right
PASSENGER TRAIN SET, by Lionel, 4 standard gauge pcs., (3 illus.), engine, mail and baggage car, pullman car, observation car, mostly grey and maroon $400.00*
IVES RAILWAY TRAIN SET, 4 standard gauge pcs., (2 illus.), engine, observation car, parlor car, buffet car, rust $300.00*

A–MA Aug. 1993   *James D. Julia, Inc.*
FIRE TRUCK, Buddy "L," pressed steel, nickel ladders, 9" H, 29½" L $400.00*
WATER TOWER FIRE TRUCK, by Keystone, pressed steel, "With Real Pump," has crank that pumps water to hose, 13" H, 32" L $700.00*

A–MA Aug. 1993   *James D. Julia, Inc.*
CAST IRON TOY VEHICLES
Row 1, Left to Right
AIRPLANE, Lindy-type, nickel plated engine, stars on wing, 2½" H, 6" L $275.00*
SEDAN, by Freidag(?), wear, paint loss, rust, 3" H, 5" L $250.00*
Row 2, Left to Right
CITY AMBULANCE, by Arcade, blue, 2½" H, 5¾" L $375.00*
SEDAN, by Arcade, paint loss, crack, wear, 3¾" H, 6½" L $200.00*
TOURING SEDAN, molded-in driver, green w/white, yellow, 3" H, 6" L $600.00*
Row 3, Left to Right
JAEGER CEMENT MIXER, by Kenton, loss, wear, paint loss, 6" H, 6½" L $200.00*
MODEL "T" TRUCK, by Arcade Mfg., restored, 3" H, 9" L $225.00*

A-MA Dec. 1992   *Skinner, Inc.*
STUFFED BEARS UNLESS OTHERWISE NOTED
Row 1, Left to Right
THREE TOYS, cinnamon mohair teddy, (illus.), glass eyes, jointed, driving goggles, fiber loss, 15" H; Marx Snow White and the Seven Dwarfs, boxed, plastic, ⅞" H; cast iron locomotive and passenger car, poor $137.50
YELLOW MOHAIR, shoebutton eyes, extensive fur loss, damage, 16½" H .... NS
YELLOW MOHAIR, fully jointed, glass eyes, embroidered features, felt pads, excelsior stuffing, fur and fiber loss, 17" H $247.50
YELLOW MOHAIR, Germany, ca. 1906, fully jointed, shoebutton eyes, embroidered features, excelsior stuffing, fur/fiber loss, replacements, 16½" H $550.00
GOLDEN MOHAIR, Germany, 1906, fully jointed, shoebutton eyes, embroidered features, felt pads, excelsior stuffing, losses, 16" H $880.00
TAN MOHAIR, fully jointed, shoebutton eyes, embroidered features, felt pads, fur/fiber loss, 15" H $825.00
Row 2, Left to Right
BLONDE MOHAIR W/BEAR STORY BOOK, English, ca. 1907, fully jointed, shoebutton eyes, felt pads, excelsior stuffing, fiber loss, 19¾" H $330.00
YELLOW MOHAIR, fully jointed, replacements, fur/fiber loss $220.00
STEIFF YELLOW MOHAIR, ca. 1910, ear button, fully jointed, glass eyes, embroidered snout, excelsior stuffing, fiber loss, repair, 18" H $990.00
GOLDEN MOHAIR, Germany, ca. 1906, fully jointed shoebutton eyes, embroidered features, felt pads, excelsior stuffing, losses, 21" H $2090.00
YELLOW MOHAIR, ca. 1910, fully jointed, shoebutton eyes, embroidered features, woven pads, excelsior stuffing, extensive fur/fiber loss, 18" H $220.00
STEIFF BRONZE MOHAIR, Germany, ca. 1906, fully jointed, shoebutton eyes, embroidered features, excelsior stuffing, ear button, fur/fiber loss, 18" H ... $1870.00
DRESSED GOLDEN MOHAIR W/CHAIR, Germany, fully jointed, shoebutton eyes, embroidered features, felt pads, wicker chair, extensive fur/fiber loss, 16" H... $550.00
Front Row, Left to Right
GRAY FROSTED MOHAIR, on all fours, jointed head, glass eyes, embroidered features, losses, 7½" H, 12" L $165.00
STUFFED MOHAIR TOYS, 4 pcs, Teddy bear, (illus.), shoe button eyes, 11¾" H, Steiff blonde kitty, fully jointed, glass eyes, ear button, 10¾" L; Steiff tiger puppet, 8" H; cocker spaniel puppet, 8" H $220.00
MOHAIR, jointed, long snout, wool stuffing, damage, 13" H................... NS
STEIFF BLONDE MOHAIR, ca. 1906, fully jointed, black steel eyes, embroidered snout, overalls, knitted slippers, fiber loss, 8½" H $522.50
TAN MOHAIR AND CLOTH, jointed, wool and cotton body, losses, 10" H ...... NS

A-MA Jan. 1993   *Skinner, Inc.*
SIGNAL CANNON, painted wood, ca. 1870, 60" L $605.00

A-MA Mar. 1993   *Skinner, Inc.*
REINDEER TOYS, 2 pcs., velveteen, imperfections, 7½" H, 3½" H $440.00

A-MA Dec. 1992   *Skinner, Inc.*
DANCING RABBIT, Schuco, mohair, fabric, wood, metal, glass eyes, 8" H........................ $275.00
MOTOR CAR, Lehmann, 1903, #420, box, 5" L $1430.00
MECHANICAL POPEYE THE PILOT, Mark, lithographed tin, ca. 1930, losses, 8½" L $154.00

A-MA Dec. 1992   *Skinner, Inc.*
HORSE PULL TOY, black mohair, steel eyes, leatherette tack, wood platform, metal wheels, fiber loss, 7¾" H, 5¾" L......................... $137.50
DOUBLE HORSE TEAM, flannel cover, metal eyes, leatherette tack, mohair mane and tail, wood platforms, metal wheels, damage, 12½" H, 12⅜" L...... $770.00
HORSE ON WHEELS, felt, shoebutton eyes, red saddle blanket, leather saddle, stamped "Steiff", metal wheels, ca. 1913, losses, 9" L, 9½" H $385.00

A-MA Jan. 1993   *Skinner, Inc.*
PLANE, whalebone, 19th c., mustard pigment, 8½" L, 2" w $660.00
GLOBE, wood, painted and inscribed, 19th c., 5½" $825.00
CRIBBAGE BOARD, ivory inlaid mahogany, 19th c., 10¾" H, ⅞" H . $440.00

A-FL Jan. 1993   *Gary Kirsner Auctions*
POTTERY, .5L, mkd. 446, Hauber & Reuther, pewter lid $275.00
POTTERY, .5L, mkd. 1221, J.W. Remy, inlaid lid $264.00
POTTERY, .5L, mkd. 1171, Merkelbach & Wick, pewter lid, tear $242.00

A-FL Jan. 1993   *Gary Kirsner Auctions*
Row 1, Left to Right
METTLACH, .4L, 2106, inlaid lid $4290.00
METTLACH, .5L, 3167, inlaid lid, Hohlwein $1815.00
METTLACH, .5L, 3281, inlaid lid, Hohlwein, loose lid $2035.00
METTLACH, .5L, 3090, inlaid lid $935.00
METTLACH, .5L, 2024, inlaid lid $1045.00
METTLACH, .5L, 2093, inlaid lid $770.00
Row 2, Left to Right
METTLACH, 1L, 5023, faience, pewter lid, repair $2640.00
METTLACH, 1L, 5394, faience, pewter lid, repair $1245.00
METTLACH, 1L, 5394, faience, pewter lid, replacements, flakes $632.50
METTLACH, 1L, 2530, cameo, inlaid lid $1265.00
METTLACH, 1L, 2778, inlaid lid $1815.00
METTLACH, 1L, 2027, inlaid lid, repair $1100.00

A-FL Jan. 1993   *Gary Kirsner Auctions*
METTLACH, .5L, 983 (1909), P.U.G., pewter lid $297.00
METTLACH, .5L, 993 (1909), pewter lid $357.50
METTLACH, .5L, 833 (2140), pewter lid, flakes $495.00
METTLACH, .5L, 678 (280), pewter lid, wear $231.00

A-FL Jan. 1993   *Gary Kirsner Auctions*
Row 1, Left to Right
WILHELM III, .5L, porcelain, Musterschutz $1705.00
MUNICH CHILD ON BARREL, .5L, porcelain, Musterschutz $797.50
JUDGE, .5L, porcelain, Musterschutz, hairline $1210.00
GENTLEMAN RABBIT, .5L, porcelain, Musterschutz $2640.00
POTATO HEAD, .5L, porcelain, Musterschutz, wear $1650.00
LADY WITH BUSTLE, .5L, stoneware, mkd. HR, Hauber & Reuther $1155.00
Row 2, Left to Right
METTLACH, .5L, 2723, inlaid lid $2200.00
METTLACH, .5L, 2134, inlaid lid $2970.00
METTLACH, .5L, 2277, inlaid lid $1925.00
METTLACH, .5L, 2829, inlaid lid $1870.00
METTLACH, .5L, 2765, inlaid lid $2090.00
METTLACH, .5L, 1733, inlaid lid, hairline $880.00

A-FL Jan. 1993   *Gary Kirsner Auctions*
Row 1, Left to Right
METTLACH, .5L, 2001F, Architecture, inlaid lid $852.50
METTLACH, .5L, 2001D, Mathematics, inlaid lid $907.50
METTLACH, .5L, 2001B, Medicine, inlaid lid $605.00
METTLACH, .5L, 2001A, Law, inlaid lid $632.50
Row 2, Left to Right
METTLACH, .5L, 2001K, Banking, inlaid lid $550.00
METTLACH, .5L, 2002, inlaid lid $467.50
METTLACH, .3L, 2035, inlaid lid $209.00
METTLACH, .3L, 2833D, inlaid lid $440.00

A-FL Jan. 1993   *Gary Kirsner Auctions*
REGIMENTAL, .5L, pottery, 1898, 9½"
H.., ... $605.00
REGIMENTAL, .5L, porcelain, 1896,
faded, 8⅝" H $385.50
REGIMENTAL, .5L, porcelain, 1895,
repair, 8⅝" H $357.50
REGIMENTAL, .5L, porcelain, 1896, chip,
bent lid, 9⅝" H $242.00

A-FL Jan. 1993   *Gary Kirsner Auctions*
HANS BUTTNER, 1L, porcelain, photograph lithophane, pewter tear . . . $253.00
HANS BUTTNER, .5L, porcelain, photograph lithophane, pewter lid $242.00
LITHOPHANE, .5L, porcelain, transfer,
pewter lid and base $286.00

A-FL Jan. 1993   *Gary Kirsner Auctions*
Row 1, Left to Right
PIG W/PIPE, .5L, porcelain, mkd. Musterschuytz $577.50
BERLIN BEAR, .5L, porcelain, mkd. Musterschutz $1155.00
SEATED RAM, .5L, porcelain, mkd. Musterschutz $687.50
CAT W/HANGOVER, .5L, porcelain, mkd. Musterschutz 770.00
CAT W/LETTER, .5L, pottery, mkd. 767 . . . . 385.00
MAN W/FLOWER, .5L, porcelain, mkd. 765 . . . . 495.00
MUNICH CHILD, .25L, porcelain, lithophane, mkd. Martin Pauson $412.50
MUNICH CHILD, .5L, porcelain, Gruss aus Muchen $495.00
Row 2, Left to Right
REGIMENTAL, .5L, porcelain, 2 scenes, 1900-03 . . . . $577.50
REGIMENTAL, .5L, porcelain, 2 scenes, 1905-07 . . . . $632.50
REGIMENTAL, .5L, porcelain, 2 scenes, 1902-05 . . . . $852.50
REGIMENTAL, .5L, porcelain, 4 scenes, 1905-08 . . . . $660.00
REGIMENTAL, .5L, porcelain, 4 scenes, 1907-09 . . . . $522.50
REGIMENTAL, .5L, porcelain, 2 scenes, 1902-05 . . . . $440.00
REGIMENTAL, .5L, porcelain, 4 scenes, 1912-14 . . . . $522.50
Row 3, Left to Right
REGIMENTAL, 1L, porcelain, 2 scenes, 1909-12, repair $825.00
REGIMENTAL, 1L, porcelain, 2 scenes, 1907-10, loss $825.00
REGIMENTAL, 1L, porcelain, 2 scenes, 1907-10, repair, replacement $605.00
REGIMENTAL, .5L, porcelain, 4 scenes, 1910-12, loss $467.50
REGIMENTAL, .5L, porcelain, 2 scenes, 1907-09, flakes $297.00
REGIMENTAL, .5L, porcelain, 2 scenes, 1908-10, repairs $330.00
REGIMENTAL, 1L, porcelain, 2 scenes, loss $962.50

A-FL Jan. 1993   *Gary Kirsner Auctions*
SOLDIER, 1L, porcelain, photograph lithophane, pewter lid scratches $467.50
BREWER, .5L, porcelain, lithophane, transfer, pewter lid . . . . NS
BLACKSMITH, .5L, porcelain, lithophane,
transfer, 1930 . . . . $357.50

A-FL Jan. 1993   *Gary Kirsner Auctions*
LITHOPHANE, .5L, porcelain, hand
painted, pewter lid $385.00
LITHOPHANE, .5L, porcelain, transfer,
"Aus Grosser Zeit, Weltkrieg, 1914-1916,"
pewter lid $286.00
LITHOPHANE, .5L, porcelain, transfer,
Hindenburg, pewter lid $297.00
LITHOPHANE, .5L, porcelain, transfer,
pewter lid, repair $198.00

A-FL Jan. 1993   *Gary Kirsner Auctions*

Row 1, Left to Right
WOOD STEIN, 1L, Norwegian, carved, dated 1872 ....$990.00
STONEWARE, 1L, Westerwald, ca. 1780, pewter lid, repair $495.00
STONEWARE, .5L, Westerwald, ca. 1780, pewter lid, chips $308.00
STONEWARE, .6L, Frankonian, ca. 1700, pewter lid, replacement, repair $308.00
STONEWARE, 1L, Creussen, Christ & Apostles, ca. 1700, pewter lid $4510.00

Row 2, Left to Right
FAIENCE, .75L, Zerbst, ca. 1700, pewter lid, loss $880.00
FAIENCE, 1L, Bayreuth, ca. 1780, pewter lid, loss, replacement $1485.00
FAIENCE, .75L, Thuringen, pewter lid dated 1754, loss dents $1375.00
FAIENCE, .5L, Bayreuth, ca. 1780, pewter lid, chips, loss, hairline $907.50
FAIENCE, .5L, Schrezheim, ca. 1800, pewter lid, flakes $797.50
FAIENCE, .75L, ca. 1800, pewter lid, chip $577.50

A-FL Jan. 1993   *Gary Kirsner Auctions*

Row 1, Left to Right
METTLACH, .25L, 1803, mosaic, inlaid lid $412.50
METTLACH, .25L, 1828, mosaic, inlaid lid $385.00
METTLACH, .5L, 1570, mosaic, inlaid lid $440.00
METTLACH, .5L, 3282/536, Bavaria, inlaid lid $440.00

Row 2, Left to Right
METTLACH, .5L, 3282/535, Bavaria, inlaid lid, hairline $154.00
METTLACH, .3L, 2099, mosaic, inlaid lid $209.00
METTLACH, .5L, Pretzel, inlaid lid $412.50
METTLACH, .25L, 2800, inlaid lid, repair $220.00

A-FL Jan. 1993   *Gary Kirsner Auctions*

Row 1, Left to Right
GLASS, .25L, blue opaline, ca. 1870, enameled, inlaid lid $2695.00
GLASS, .5L, blown pink opaline, ca. 1870, enameled, inlaid lid $3410.00
GLASS, .5L, blown overlay, blue, clear, ca. 1880, silver lid, repair, chip $412.50
GLASS, .75L, blown, red flashed, silver dec., pewter lid $412.50
GLASS, .5L, blown overlay, red, clear, ca. 1880, silver plated lid, repair, scratches .... NS
GLASS, .5L, blown, red, enameled, etched, inlaid glass lid $319.00
GLASS, .5L, blown, pink opaline, ca. 1870, pewter lid $797.50

Row 2, Left to Right
PORCELAIN, .5L, Beehive mark, royal Vienna, porcelain inlaid lid $2310.00
PORCELAIN, .5L, Beehive mark, royal Vienna, porcelain inlaid lid $2420.00
PORCELAIN, 1L, Beehive mark, signed Sihl, royal Vienna, gold plated lid $2035.00
PORCELAIN, .5L, Beehive mark, royal Vienna, porcelain inlaid lid, repair $1760.00
PORCELAIN, .5L, Beehive mark, royal Vienna, loss, flakes $1100.00
PORCELAIN, .5L, Capo di Monte, inlaid lid $330.00

A-FL Jan. 1993   *Gary Kirsner Auctions*
STONEWARE, .5L, mkd. 2351, pewter lid $297.00
STONEWARE, .5L, mkd. 2131, pewter lid $143.00
STONEWARE, .5L, pewter lid ..$132.00

A-FL Jan. 1993   *Gary Kirsner Auctions*
MILITARY, .5L, porcelain, 1928, 12" H.........................$852.50
REGIMENTAL, .5L, porcelain, 1911, 11⅜" H.........................$550.00
REGIMENTAL, .5L, pottery, 1903, 11⅝" H.........................$687.50
REGIMENTAL, .5L, porcelain, 1904, 11¼" H.........................$467.50

A-FL Jan. 1993   *Gary Kirsner Auctions*

Row 1, Left to Right
VIKING, pottery, .5L, mkd. 570, Merkelbach, relief pewter lid $308.00
CHILDREN, pottery, .5L, mkd. 1463, pewter lid $88.00
BABIES, pottery, .5L, mkd. 1276, pewter lid, dents $154.00
SOLDIERS, pottery, .5L, mkd. 1194, Merkelbach, 1870/1871 commerative $176.00
SOLDIERS, pottery, .5L, mkd. 125/18, inlaid bronze lid, chip $187.00
SOLDIERS, pottery, .5L, mkd. 1173, Merkelbach, pewter lid $187.00
GENERALS, stoneware, .5L, mkd. 207, saltglazed, pewter lid $176.00
STONEWARE, .5L, mkd. music box base, pewter lid $88.00

Row 2, Left to Right
STONEWARE, .5L, mkd. 1770/16, Marzi & Remi, designed by Gorig, pewter . . . $198.00
CLOVERS, stoneware, .5L, mkd. 1169A, Merkelbach & Wick, pewter lid $198.00
STONEWARE, .4L, pewter lid, loss, hairline $154.00
STONEWARE, , .5L, mkd. 6117, blue, white, 8 sides, pewter lid $143.00
MONKEY, pottery, .5L, mkd. 1257, inlaid lid $264.00
POTTERY, , .5L, mkd. 0130, inlaid lid, hairline $220.00
CARDS, pottery, .5L, mkd. 1255, pewter lid $220.00
JOHN KRESS, pottery, .5L, mkd. 944, Merkelbach, pewter lid $467.50

A-FL Jan. 1993   *Gary Kirsner Auctions*
METTLACH, 3.2L, 171, pewter lid $242.00
METTLACH, 3.2L, 953 (2183), P.U.G., inlaid lid $715.00
METTLACH, 2.2L, 2784/6129, Rookwood type, pewter lid, scratches $605.00

A-FL Jan. 1993   *Gary Kirsner Auctions*
METTLACH, .5L, 171 . . . . $242.00
METTLACH, .5L, 171 . . . . $198.00
METTLACH, .5L, 2182 . . . . $275.00
METTLACH, .5L, 2182 . . . . $242.00

A-FL Jan. 1993   *Gary Kirsner Auctions*

Row 1, Left to Right
PORCELAIN, .5L, pewter lid $242.00
PORCELAIN, .5L, hunting, cherubs, inlaid lid, repairs $264.00
PORCELAIN, .5L, mkd. C.A.C. Lenox, copper & silver lid $467.50
PORCELAIN, .5L, mkd. C.A.C., silver lid $412.50
POTTERY, .5L, mkd. Thos. Maddock Sons Co., Trenton N.J., Princeton University tavern scenes, inlaid lid $357.50
PORCELAIN, .5L, lithophane, pewter lid $209.00
PORCELAIN, .5L, lithophane, pewter lid $143.00

Row 2, Left to Right
SAD RADISH, .5L, porcelain, mkd. Musterschutz $440.00
HAPPY RADISH, .5L, porcelain, mkd. Musterschutz $522.50
HOPS LADY, .5L, porcelain, mkd. Musterschutz $742.50
CAROLINE, .5L, porcelain, mkd. Musterschutz $522.50
SKULL, .5L, porcelain, bisque glaze $605.00
SKULL ON BOOK, .3L, porcelain, E. Bohne Sohne, bisque glaze $660.00
DEVIL, .5L, porcelain, mkd. E. Bohne Sohne, bisque glaze $440.00

A-FL Jan. 1993   *Gary Kirsner Auctions*
STONEWARE, 1L, transfer, pewter lid $143.00
ARTILLERY SHELL, .5L, porcelain, lithophane, wear $357.50
MUNICH CHILD, 1L, pottery, mkd. Reinimann $385.00

A-FL Jan. 1993   *Gary Kirsner Auctions*
PEWTER PITCHER, 1L, uneven patina $110.00
PEWTER PITCHER, .5L, dent . . $110.00
BEARDED KNIGHT, 1.5L, stoneware, saltglazed, repair $154.00

A-FL Jan. 1993 *Gary Kirsner Auctions*

BLOWN GLASS, .5L, red, pewter lid, handle, base and overlay $660.00
PITCHER, blown amber glass, pewter overlay, handle, base and stopper $412.50
BLOWN GLASS, 1L, clear, helmet-shaped pewter lid $1017.50
BLOWN GLASS, .5L, swirl, cranberry to clear, engraved name, pewter lid $187.00
BLOWN GLASS, .5L, enameled amber, pewter lid and foot ring $308.00
BARREL, blown green glass, enameled, metal straps, loss $154.00

A-FL Jan. 1993 *Gary Kirsner Auctions*
ART NOUVEAU, 1L, stoneware, mkd.
1569, pewter lid $209.00
ART NOUVEAU, 1L, stoneware, mkd.
2238, pewter lid $357.50
STEIN, .5L, etched pottery, mkd. 1220, by
J.W. Remy, inlaid lid $220.00

A-FL Jan. 1993 *Gary Kirsner Auctions*

METTLACH, 1L, 2880, etched, inlaid lid $632.50
METTLACH, 1L, 1154, etched, silver plated lid $467.50
METTLACH, 1L, 2090, etched, inlaid lid $715.00
METTLACH, 1L, 2002, etched, inlaid lid $660.00
METTLACH, 1L, 2028, etched, inlaid lid $660.00
METTLACH, 1L, 1932, etched, inlaid lid $632.00
METTLACH, 1L, 2520, etched, inlaid lid, chips $412.50

A-FL Jan. 1993 *Gary Kirsner Auctions*
MONK, .5L, stoneware, blue saltglaze,
copper lid, flakes $165.00
MONK, .5L, stoneware, blue, purple saltglazes, mkd. M.W.G. $253.00
BOWLING PIN, .5L, porcelain,
relief $231.00

A-FL Jan. 1993 *Gary Kirsner Auctions*

Row 1, Left to Right

METTLACH, .5L, 2833F, etched, inlaid lid $440.00
METTLACH, .5L, 2833C, etched, inlaid lid $495.00
METTLACH, .5L, 2090, etched, inlaid lid, flake $467.50
METTLACH, .5L, 2092, etched, inlaid lid $962.50
METTLACH, .5L, 2091, etched, inlaid lid $1045.00
METTLACH, .5L, 1478, etched, inlaid lid $770.00
METTLACH, .5L, 2025, etched, inlaid lid $495.00
METTLACH, .5L, 2714, cameo, inlaid lid $962.50

Row 2, Left to Right

POTTERY, .5L, hand painted, 1913, pewter lid $187.00
POTTERY, .5L, transfer, Heidelberg & 4F, relief pewter lid Father John $385.00
STONEWARE, .5L, transfer, relief pewter lid man shooting rifle $440.00
STONEWARE, .5L, transfer, "Ostdeutsche Austellung, Posen 1911," pewter lid . . $330.00
STONEWARE, .5L, transfer and enameled, pewter lid $143.00
STONEWARE, .5L, transfer, mkd. Sarregumines, pewter lid $77.00
POTTERY, .5L, transfer, "Pschorr-Brau, Muchen," incised pewter lid, flakes $176.00
STONEWARE, .5L, transfer and enameled, "1821-1911," relief pewter lid $357.50

A-FL Jan. 1993 *Gary Kirsner Auctions*
FRAUENKIRCHE TOWER, .5L, stone-
ware, blue, purple saltglazes, mkd.
T.W. $385.00
LISL (BARMAID), .5L, stoneware, blue,
purple saltgrazes, mkd. J.
Reinemann $495.00
RICH MAN, .5L, stoneware, blue, purple
saltglazes, mkd. M.W.G. $275.00

A-FL Jan. 1993 *Gary Kirsner Auctions*
CAVALIER, .5L, porcelain, transfer, lithophane, pewter lid $220.00
DUELING SOCIETY, .5L, porcelain, hand
painted, lithophane, pewter lid . . . $440.00
BRICKLAYER, .5L, porcelain, transfer,
lithophane, pewter lid repaired . . $319.00
LOGGER, .5L, porcelain, transfer, lithophane, pewter lid $605.00

A-FL Jan. 1993   *Gary Kirsner Auctions*

Row 1, Left to Right

MASONIC, , pottery, .5L, mkd. 247, pewter lid, repair $357.50
POTTERY, , .5L, mkd. 579, pewter lid, repair $187.00
SHIP, pottery, .5L, mkd. 1411, German, pewter lid $308.00
SOLDIERS, pottery, .5L, mkd. 2395, pewter lid, repair $132.00
OPERA, pottery, .5L, mkd. 390, KB, pewter lid $209.00
PUB, stoneware, .5L, mkd. 1802, Marzi & Remi, pewter lid $209.00
CARDS, pottery, .5L, mkd. 215, pewter lid $209.00
BAND, pottery, .5L, mkd. 457, Hauber & Reuther, pewter lid $198.00

Row 2, Left to Right

HUNTER, pottery, 1L, mkd. 1147, pottery lid $242.00
CASTLE, pottery, .5L, pottery lid $242.00
BOATMAN, pottery, 1L, mkd. 1283, KB, pottery lid $319.00
CONICAL, pottery, .5L, mkd. inlaid pottery lid, pewter tear $308.00
FISH, pottery, .5L, mkd. 1245, KB, pottery lid $605.00
KNIGHT, pottery, .5L, pottery lid $264.00
POTTERY, .5L, mkd. 1044, inlaid lid, chip $143.00

A-FL Jan. 1993   *Gary Kirsner Auctions*
METTLACH, 5.5L, 2126, pewter
lid $6875.00
METTLACH, 5.7L, 2102, pewter
lid $6600.00
METTLACH, 6.8L, 2455, pewter lid, repair,
replacement $3850.00

A-FL Jan. 1993   *Gary Kirsner Auctions*
STONEWARE, 2L, mkd. 843, saltglazed,
inlaid lid $297.00
POTTERY, 1.5L, mkd. 1611, inlaid lid,
flakes $253.00
POTTERY, 1L, mkd. 851, inlaid
lid $220.00
POTTERY, 1L, mkd. 743, D.R.G.M., Diesin-
ger, loss $242.00
POTTERY, 1L, mkd. 692, boar
lid $412.50
POTTERY, 1.5L, mkd. 1250, threading,
pewter lid $242.00
POTTERY, 1.5L, mkd. 163, pottery
lid $357.50
CHINESE MAN, 1L, faience, chips,
flakes $605.00

A-FL Jan. 1993   *Gary Kirsner Auctions*
EWER, stoneware, mkd. 108, saltglaze, loss, 19" H $330.00
STONEWARE, 4L, mkd. O, Whites Utica, blue, brown, green glaze, pewter lid . . $1430.00
PORCELAIN, 3L, mkd. Ceramic Art Company, A. Heidrich 1896, silver lid $742.50
POTTERY, 3L, mkd. 1390, J.W. Remy, inlaid lid, chip $385.00
POTTERY, 2L, mkd. 155, G.K., pottery lid, flake $308.00
POTTERY, 2L, mkd. 272, pewter lid $357.50

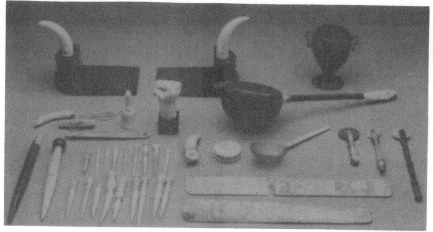

A-MA Oct. 1992   *Skinner, Inc.*

SEVEN PIECE LOT, 2 bone and wood fids, ivory pickwick, ivory twister, ivory box engraved "W. Speer," bone cased razor, ivory handle w/eagle, all 19th c..... $412.50
WHALE'S TOOTH BOOKENDS, pair, mahogany mounted, cracks, 5¾" ... $330.00
CARVED COCONUT CUP, tin mounted, 19th c., imperfections, 4½" H..... $165.00
FIST CANE HANDLE, carved ivory, 19th c., imperfections, 3¼" H $880.00
PENDANT, carved ivory joined to whale's tooth, 19th c., 3½" L........... $440.00
DIPPER AND SPOON, coconut shell dipper w/rosewood and ivory handle, carved bone and ivory spoon, 14¼", 7½" $440.00
JAGGING WHEELS, 3 pcs., whalebone and wood, 19th c., 4½" to 8" L..... $247.50
WHALEBONE AND IVORY IMPLEMENTS, 18 pcs., 2½" to 5" L $440.00
BUSK, engraved whalebone, eagle, women, bird, designs, break, losses, 13½"L... NS
BUSK, engraved whalebone, eagle, woman, flowers, 19th c., 12" L $302.50

A-MA Mar. 1993   *Skinner, Inc.*
SCRIMSHAW BUSK, engraved, sun, mourning scene, bird, primrose, 13¼" L $467.50
SCRIMSHAW BUSK, engraved, eye, compass, ship, bird, loss, 12⅞" L ..... NS
SCRIMSHAW BUSK, engraved, columbia, flowers, lighthouse, lady slipper, initialed "FS," 12½" L.............. $440.00
WALKING STICK, carved whalebone, tooth handle, crack, 30½" L $330.00
WALKING STICK, carved whalebone, ivory handle, baleen spacer, 33" L $440.00
WALKING STICK, carved whalebone, ivory handle, initials "AG," 32¾" L $550.00

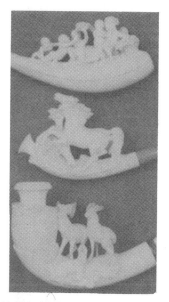

A-MA Oct. 1992 *Skinner, Inc.*
JAGGING WHEEL, carved ivory, 19th c., 6½" L.............. $1980.00

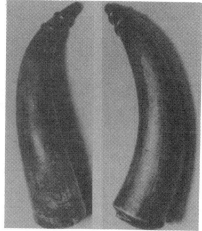

A-MA Nov. 1991   *Skinner, Inc.*
IVORY TUSK, Meiji period, carved and pierced w/dragons, wood base, 14" L......................... $1210.00

A-MA Mar. 1993   *Skinner, Inc.*
MEERSCHAUM FIGURAL PIPE, bacchanalian scene, amber stem, fitted case, 8⅝" L $660.00
MEERSCHAUM FIGURAL CHEROOT HOLDER, 2 galloping horses, amber stem, damage, fitted case, 7⅛" L $357.50
MEERSCHAUM FIGURAL PIPE, deer buck, doe and fawn beside bellflower bowl, amber and meerschaum stem, amber mouth piece, damage, fitted case, 11⅝" L $467.50

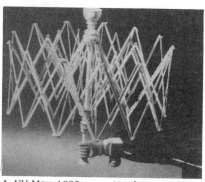

A-NH May. 1993   *Northeast Auctions*
SCRIMSHAW SWIFT W/CLINCHED FIST, handle w/MOP ruffle, 15" H $4500.00*

A-OH Nov. 1992   *Garth's Auctions, Inc.*
POWDER HORN, engraved with ship, flowers and "William Mott's horn made August ye 29th AD 1758, Made at Fort Cosby at Schonectady (sic)," damage and hole at tip, 14" L........... $2420.00

A-MA Jan. 1993   *Skinner, Inc.*
"HARVARD" MODEL, painted basswood & mahogany, cased, 71" H, 70" L, 27" W $4400.00

A-NH Aug. 1993   *Northeast Auctions*
EAGLE WALL PLAQUE, stamped brass, 23" L $350.00*
SOVEREIGN OF THE SEAS, sailor-made model of famous clipper, 36" L . . . $2000.00*
TERRESTRIAL GLOBE, 17" T $2400.00*
UMBRELLA STAND, cast iron, sailor form, 27" T $1500.00*
SHADOW BOX, top sail schooner, 27" H, 46" L $2500.00*
PARLOR GAMES TABLE, inlaid, made at Thomaston, MN prison, 28" L $2700.00*
TUG BOAT, "E.M. Card," carved, painted, 32" L $3500.00*
WEATHERVANE, copper, single masted ship, 21" L $750.00*

A-MA Mar. 1993   *Skinner, Inc.*
NANTUCKET BASKET, swing handle, incised base, varnished exterior, 5" H, 11" D $605.00
NANTUCKET BASKET, swing handle incised base, 4¾" H, 9" D $550.00
NANTUCKET BASKET, swing handle, incised base, 4½" H, 10" D $550.00

A-MA Jun. 1993   *Skinner, Inc.*
SHAKER BASKETS, 4 pcs., imperfections, 11" to 22" W $2860.00

A-ME Feb. 1993   *James D, Julia, Inc.*
Row 1, Left to Right
BASKET, kicked up bottom, 6" H, 10½" D $275.00*
BURLED CHOPPING BOWL, 4" H, 8¼" W, 15" L $475.00*
BASKET, 4¾" H, 7½" D $125.00*
Center
BURL BOWL, 5½" H, 14" D . . . $800.00*
Row 2, Left to Right
INDIAN BASKET, decorated, 10" H, 13½" D $125.00*
WOOD BOWL, turned, mustard paint, old wax crack repairs, 6" H, 16" D . . $400.00*
BASKET . . . . NS

A-MA Jan. 1993   *Skinner, Inc.*
LIGHTSHIP BASKET, early 20th c., swing handle, 8" H, 6½" D $1100.00
NANTUCKET BASKETS, two, oval, swing handles, 20th c., 5¼" H x 11" L, 4½" H x 8" L $467.50

A-PA May 1993   *Alderfer Auction Co.*
POTATO STAMP BASKET, blue dec., Pennacook, 19th c. $2250.00

A-IL Apr. 1993   *Leslie Hindman Auction*
GEORGE III TEA CADDY, mahogany, 18th c., 6" H, 12" W, 6" D $350.00*
REGENCY TEA CADDY, rosewood w/ line inlay, 19th c., 8" H, 8½" W, 5½" D $550.00*

A-IL Apr. 1993   *Leslie Hindman Auction*
GEORGE III TEA CADDY, mahogany, 18th c., brass bail handle opening to 3 brass tea canisters, 5" H, 10" W, 5½" D $700.00*
GEORGE III TEA CADDY, mahogany, 18th c., 5" H, 5½" W, 5" D $450.00*

A-MA Aug. 1993   *Skinner, Inc.*
HAT BOX, Baltimore and Ohio Railroad, blue, yellow, red wallpaper covered, coach "B & O Carrol of Carroll," newspaper lining dated Newbury port June 7, 1833, water stains, stitch repairs, 13½" H, 16" W $11000.00

A-MA Jun. 1993   *Skinner, Inc.*
HAT BOX, wallpaper "Drapery swag with Three Roses and Vase," ca. 1830, 10½" H $495.00
HAT BOX, wallpaper covered wood, attributed to Hannah Davis, Jaffrey, NH, ca. 1850, 14" H $330.00
HAT BOX, brick house and farm, ca. 1830, 11" H $880.00

A-NH Mar. 1993   *Northeast Auctions*
NESTED HATBOXES, 2pcs., (1 illus.), 19" L $1500.00*
HATBOX, "A Peep at the Moon" wallpaper, blue, labeled "Hannah Davis," $1900.00*
HATBOXES, 2 pcs., (1 illus.), yellow, 19" L $750.00*
HATBOXES, 2 pcs., (1 illus.), yellow, 16" L $650.00*

A-OH Nov. 1992   *Garth's Auctions, Inc.*
HIGH CHEST, cherry, poplar, refinished, replacements, damage, age cracks, 51" H, 43" W, 19½" D $797.50
BAND BOX, bentwood, white, green, brown wallpaper, label "Hannah Davis, Jeffrey N.H.," 12" H, 16" L $220.00
BAND BOX, cardboard, blue, green, yellow, damage, faded, 20" L $440.00
BAND BOX, cardboard, pink, white, green, yellow, damage, 17" L $357.50
BAND BOX, cardboard, shades of blue on white, damage, 14" L $165.00

A-MA Jan. 1993   *Skinner, Inc.*
WALLPAPER COVERED BOXES
Top Row, Left to Right
BAND BOX, 19th c., hand blocked blue, tan, white, 12" H, 15" L $330.00
HAT BOX, ca. 1830, "Patriot Marine Journal," 13½" H, 19½" L $605.00
BOX, ca. 1835, Clayton's Ascent pattern, pink, yellow, white, 11" H $495.00
Bottom Row, Right to Left
BOX, ca. 1830, Quadriga Filled with Flowers pattern, 12" H, 19" W .. $550.00
BAND BOX, 19th c., blue, white ... NS
HAT BOX, ca. 1830, "Les Trois Jours" pattern .... NS
HAT BOX, ca. 1830, "Heraea Games" pattern, 13½" H, 19½" L $357.50

A-MA Dec. 1992   *Skinner, Inc.*
GEORGE III CUTLERY BOXES, pr., mahogany, 14½" H $1980.00

A-NH May. 1993   *Northeast Auctions*
HEPPLEWHITE KNIFE BOXES, 2 pcs., inlaid mahogany, fitted interior, 15" H $5750.00*

A-IL Apr. 1993   *Leslie Hindman Auction*
GEORGE III KNIFE BOXES, pr., inlaid mahogany, fitted inter., 15" H . . $2000.00*

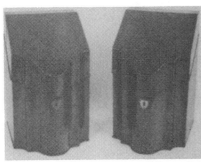

A-MA Jun. 1993   *Skinner, Inc.*
KNIFE BOXES, 2 pcs., inlaid mahogany, ca 1790, 14½" H, 9" W, 11" D . . . $1980.00

A-OH March. 1993   *Garth's Auctions, Inc.*
Row 1, Left to Right
HOGSCRAPER CANDLESTICK, tin, pushup marked "Patented 1853," 5⅛" H $165.00
HOG SCRAPER CANDLESTICK, tin, 6¼" H $110.00
BETTY LAMP, wrought iron, bird cut-out finial, loss, 3½" H $357.50
BETTY LAMP, sheet iron, worn black paint, 3¾" H $220.00
BETTY LAMP, sheet iron, losses, repair, 3½" H $33.00
BANK, brass, traces of gilt, 3" H . . $60.50
DOUBLE CRUSIE LAMP, tin, bird crests, 8½" H $165.00
DOUBLE CRUSIE LAMP, tin, thistle crests, 7¼" H $165.00
Row 2, Left to Right
RUSH LAMP, wrought iron, candle socket counter weight, twisted stem, pitted, wood base, 11" H $170.50
REDWARE JAR, dk. brown glaze, wear, hairline, 9¼" H $82.50
LIGHTING DEVICE, wrought iron, twisted stem, candle and spring socket, 7¾" H $412.50
REDWARE APPLE BUTTER JAR, dk. brown glaze, wear, 6¾" H $82.50
CANDLE MOLD, 8 tube, tin, w/tin scissor wick trimmer, 9¾" H $165.00

A-IL Apr. 1993   *Leslie Hindman Auction*
FEDERAL KNIFE BOXES, pr., inlaid mahogany, urn-form, 26" T $3200.00*

A-OH July 1993   *Garth's Auctions, Inc.*
Row 1, Left to Right
PULL TOY, tin, horse & cart, worn red, green, white, yellow paint, 5" L . . . $165.00
LION PAPERWEIGHT, red clay, brown, black glaze, flakes, 3¾" L $165.00
LADY BUG TOY, tin, wind-up, marked "D.R.P.," working, 5¼" L $165.00
TREEN BUCKET, blue w/polychrome, 2¾" H, 3" D $33.00
Row 2, Left to Right
APPLE SHAPED BOX, painted wood, hinged lid, crack, hole, 4¾" T . . . $1100.00
BUCKET, alternating pine, walnut staves, metal bands, tin bale, old varnish, 3⅜" H, 4½" D $49.50
CAPSTAN CANDLESTICK, brass, 4¾" T $412.50
APPLE SHAPED BOX, painted wood, 3½" T $55.00
APPLE SHAPED BOX, hardwood, natural finish, scarred ribs, hinged lid, ring handle, lock w/key, 4½" T $1760.00
Row 3, Left to Right
CANDLESTICK, steel, hogscraper, old black paint, partial label, brass ring, 6⅛" T $165.00
CANDLESTICK, brass, 5¾" T . . $159.50
CANDLESTICK, steel, hogscraper, old black paint, pushup marked "Birmh," 5" T $170.50
CANDLESTICK, tin, hogscraper, 4¼" T $104.50
CANDLESTICK, tin, hogscraper, old lt. blue paint, 5" T $126.50
CANDLESTICK, steel, hogscraper, pushup marked "Shaw's Birhm," old black paint, battered, 7⅛" T $159.50

A-MA July 1993   *Skinner, Inc.*
NOAH'S ARK, painted wood, 27 animals, Noah and wife, Germany, 7½" H, 17⅛" L $660.00

A-PA May 1993   *Glass Works Auctions*
GERMAN KUGELS

GRAPES KUGEL, ca. 1880–1910, German, silver, 7¼" L $425.00*

A-OH March. 1993   *Garth's Auctions, Inc.*
CHRISTMAS ORNAMENTS
Row 1, Left to Right
BASKET OF FRUIT, glass, polychrome $5.50
SHOES, pr., purple velvet, pearl buttons, satin pin cushion top, replacements $38.50
SANTA, painted bisque face, red flannel coat, composition trim, loss, 5" H $22.00
SANTAS, 5 pcs., 4 w/pipe cleaner construction, 1 w/composition body $27.50
Row 2, Left to Right
BIRDS, 2 pcs., glass, angel hair tails, tin clips, polychrome, 1 incomplete $16.50
BIRDS, 4 pcs., glass, angel hair tails, polychrome, 3 w/tin clips, 1 in basket $33.00
Row 3, Left to Right
FOUR PCS., santa, star, fish, horn, glass, polychrome $26.40
FIVE PCS., 2 circles, 2 indents, almond, tinsel, silvered, 1 worn $60.50

A-PA May 1993   *Glass Works Auctions*
GRAPES KUGEL, ca. 1880–1910, German, gold, 4½" L $160.00*

A-MA Dec. 1992   *Skinner, Inc.*
CHRISTMAS ORNAMENTS, 4 pcs., (2 illus.), cotton batting Santa and girl w/Dresden trim, cardboard manger w/scrap baby Jesus, flat angel hair and scrap ornament, 3¼", 4½", 5" H $275.00
SANTA CANDY CONTAINER, papier-mache, cloth, loss, 12½" H $1430.00
EASTER VEHICLES, 3 pcs., Chein, lithographed metal, 6⅜", 6⅞", 8½" L $104.50
JACK-O-LANTERNS, 6 pcs., (3 illus.), 1 tin, 6½" D; 4 papier-mache 3¼", 4¾", 6½" D; 1 painted glass, 4" D, some lot damage $357.50

A-PA May 1993   *Glass Works Auctions*
GERMAN KUGELS

GRAPES, ca. 1880–1910, red, 2⅞" L $500.00*
GRAPES, ca. 1880–1910, purple, 2⅞" L $575.00*

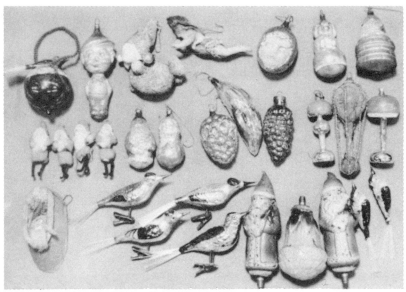

A-OH Nov. 1992   *Garth's Auctions, Inc.*
NOTE: *All Christmas tree ornaments are glass unless otherwise noted.*

Row 1, Left to Right
BALL, red with frosting and tinsel, glass bird with angel hair tail, 3¼" H $8.80
BOY WITH CAP, pastel colors 5" H $49.50
FLYING DWARF, papier maché, paint and glitter, 4¾" H $9.90
ANGEL, bisque, pink paint and lace, repair, incomplete, 4½" L $16.50
HEAD OF CHILD, shades of pink, probably had glass eyes, 2¾" H $7.70
DOG ON BALL & SANTA IN CHIMNEY, two pcs., worn polychrome, 3½" H . . . . NS

Row 2, Left to Right
FIBER SANTAS, four pcs., painted bisque faces, "Made in Japan," 3" H $33.00
SANTA and GIRL IN BAG, two ornaments, worn polychrome, 3" H $55.00
FRUIT, three ornaments, silver banana, silvered grapes w/gold wash, clear grapes
w/bronze wash, 3" to 4½" $29.70
ORNAMENTS, three, two mushrooms, unsilvered double sphere w/tinsel and scrap, 5"
H $16.50

Row 3, Left to Right
SHOE CANDY CONTAINER, paper w/net, painted bisque Santa face, "Made in Japan,"
4¼" L $16.50
BIRDS, four pcs., tin clips, angel hair tails, polychrome $55.00
ELECTRIC BULBS, three pcs., 2 Santas, flower, worn polychrome, 5¾" H $5.50
BIRDS, eight pcs., (two illus.), feather or angel hair tails $26.40

A-PA May 1993   *Glass Works Auctions*
GRAPES KUGEL, ca. 1880-1910, German, silver, 4¼" L $80.00*

A-PA May 1993   *Glass Works Auctions*
GRAPES KUGEL, ca. 1880-1910, German, cobalt, 4" L $350.00*

A-OH Nov. 1992   *Garth's Auctions, Inc.*
Row 1, Left to Right
JACK-O-LANTERN, cardboard, polychrome, tinsel, "Germany," 5" H . . . $66.00
EASTER EGG BOXES, 3 pcs., (2 illus.), decoupaged, 3¼" to 4½" L $33.00
EASTER EGG BOXES, 2 pcs., decoupage, lithographed, 5½" and 7" L . . . $33.00
HALLOWEEN TOYS, 2 pcs., papier maché jack-o-lantern, 2¾" H; pipe lithographed $49.50
JACK-O-LANTERNS, 2 pcs., tin, "Trick or Treat," 4" and 5¼" H $66.00

Row 2, Left to Right
SANTA, red flannel coat, bisque face, pack, ball, "Made in Japan," 6" H $49.50
SLEIGHS, 2 pcs., Santa, reindeer, damaged, "Made in Japan," 7¼", 8" L $5.50
BUILDINGS, 13 pcs. from Christmas village, (2 illus.), cardboard w/snow, glitter, etc., some marked "Japan," wear, damage $82.50

Row 3, Left to Right
BUILDINGS, 7 pcs. from christmas village, (2 illus.), ... $82.50
SANTAS, 5 pcs., plastic w/red flannel costume, 11" H; 4 cardboard cut-out Santas, (not illus.), 14½" H $16.50

SULPHIDE, sheep, chips, 2"
D $137.50
SULPHIDE, sheep, wear, 1⅞"
D $104.50
SULPHIDE, bird, chips, 1⅞" D ... $82.50
SULPHIDE, porcupine, chips, 1½"
D $104.50

Row 2, Left to Right

SULPHIDE, rabbit, chips, 1½" D .... NS
SWIRLS, 2 pcs., wear, chips, 1¾"
D $99.00
SULPHIDE, rabbit, chips, 1½"
D $49.50

Row 3, Left to Right

SCENT BOTTLE, cobalt, pewter cap,
2½" D $93.50
SWIRLS, 2 pcs., chips, 1⅜", 1⅞"
D $132.00
SULPHIDE, dog, damage, 1½"
D $104.50
SCENT BOTTLE, fiery opalescent, pewter
cap damaged, 2⅜" T $49.50

Row 4, Left to Right

PILL BOX, reddish agate, gilded metal fit-
tings, 2" L $22.00
SWIRLS, 4 pcs., chips, wear, 1½" to 2"
D $154.00
MALACHITE, 1¼" D $55.00

A–OH July 1993   *Garth's Auctions, Inc.*
MARBLES, unless otherwise noted.

Row 1, Left to Right

SULPHIDE, dog on cushion, wear, chips, 2¼" D $60.50

A–OH Nov. 1992   *Garth's Auctions, Inc.*
MARBLES

Row 1, Left to Right

POTTERY, blue, white, 2" D $115.50
SULFIDE, with dog, wear, ground spot,
1⅞" D $82.50
SULFIDE, with sheep, wear, flakes, 1¾"
D $66.00
SULFIDE, with squirrel, wear, 1⅝"
D $132.00
SULFIDE, with dog, wear, 1⅛"
D $82.50
SULFIDE, with bird, ground spot, 2½"
D $203.50

Row 2, Left to Right

SWIRLS, 3 pcs., multi color, wear, flakes, 2"
D, 1⅞" D, 1¾" D $231.00
MULTI COLOR, 4 pcs., 2 swirl, 2 end of
day, wear, 1½ to 1¾" D $286.00

Row 3, Left to Right

POTTERY, 7 pcs., 5 small Bennington
type, 2 brown-white carpet balls, 2"
D $19.25

Row 4, Left to Right

BENNINGTON TYPE, approx. 65 pcs., blue, orig. box $110.00
BENNINGTON TYPE, approx. 60 pcs., brown $110.00
POTTERY, approx. 77 pcs., multi color $82.50

A-OH March. 1993   *Garth's Auctions, Inc.*

Row 1, Left to Right

INK WELL, treen, brown graining w/gold stenciled decoration, labeled "S. Silliman & Co.," glass insert, wear, 3⅛" D $99.00

BENTWOOD BOX, pine, oval, chip carving, laced seams, 5⅝" L $192.50

WOVEN SPLINT BASKET, round, 8" D, 3" H $55.00

CUP, coin silver, marked "W.B. Heyer," engraved "Eckford," dents, 2⅝" H $192.50

Row 2, Left to Right

PITTSBURGH TUMBLER, cobalt blue, panels and arches, 3⅜" H $88.00

PUFFIN, carved wood, original polychrome, damage, wear, 4" H $115.50

SUGAR BOWL, pottery, green glaze, medallion, eagle, wear, chips, 5⅜" H $82.50

TREEN, 3 pcs., 2 jars, goblet, mahogany, rosewood $16.50

CHRISTMAS LIGHT, cobalt blue, diamond quilted, 4⅞" H $11.00

Row 3, Left to Right

REDWARE BANK, incised "Save all you can is a very good plan. John Albert Willars, March 14th 1883. Economy is the true source of wealth." repairs, 7½" H $137.50

CHALK DOG, worn polychrome, 6¾" H $38.50

DECORATED BOX, old red, black, yellow, gilt, not original, damage, 9" L...... $214.50

CHALK DOG, worn polychrome, 5" H $38.50

BOOK BOTTLE, pottery, blue glaze, "Coming Thro the Rye," repair, 5" H $38.50

A-OH Nov. 1992   *Garth's Auctions, Inc.*

QUEEN ANNE SWING-LEG TABLE, maple and other hardwood, stained refinish, repairs, 12¾" x 39", 29" H . . $907.50

PLATES, pair, English pewter, "London" touch, 9½"................... $143.00

TEAPOT, pewter, "Putnam" touch, battered, split base, repairs, 7¾" . . $110.00

BLANKET CHEST, miniature, cherry, worn finish, dovetailed case, brass escutcheon, edge repairs, 12⅜" L ... $715.00

LAMP, pewter, "Sellew & Co. Cincinnati," burning fluid burner, dents, crack, 8¾".......................... $412.50

CANDLESTICK, pewter, 7¼" . $137.50

PORRINGER, pewter, cast flowered handle, dents, repairs, 5½" $203.50

ANDIRONS, pair, cast iron, 14" H.......................... $181.50

A-OH Nov. 1992   *Garth's Auctions, Inc.*

Row 1, Left to Right

FROG, cast iron, green paint, "I Croak for the Jackson Wagon," 5¼" $275.00

SEWERPIPE FROG, black glass, marble eyes, repair, chips, 5¼" $165.00

SEWERPIPE FROG, 4¼" $220.00

FROG, cast iron, old green, 4¾" . . $55.00

Row 2, Left to Right

TABLESPOONS, 4 pcs., pewter . . $55.00

CLAY MARBLES, approx. 58, blue glazed Bennington type, original cardboard box, marked "Made in Germany" $192.50

FORKS, nine, steel, wood handles trimed in pewter $19.80

CLAY MARBLES, approx. 80, various sizes, some worn $93.50

TEASPOONS, 4 pcs., pewter $44.00

CLAY MARBLES, approx. 95, Bennington type, marked "Made in Germany" $148.50

TABLESPOONS, two similar, pewter, one marked "L.B.," 7½" & 8¼" $88.00

Row 3, Left to Right

COOKIE CUTTERS, three, tin, 2 hearts and crimped diamond w/tulips ... $33.00

BURL DOOR KNOBS, matched set, brass trim, steel shank $38.50

INVALID FEEDER, pewter, marked "M.A.W. Aldersgate St.," 5" L...... $38.50

INVALID FEEDER, pewter, marked "1800, X, Kent," 5" L $27.50

A-OH Nov. 1992　　*Garth's Auctions, Inc.*
NOTE: *These paintings are by the North Dakota folk artist Emily Lunde.*
PAINT ON CANVAS, farmers eating at kitchen table on thrashing day, signed "Lunde," framed, 27¾" x 30¼" . $385.00
PAINT ON CANVAS, Country Auction, unsigned, framed, 24" x 24" ... $165.00
PAINT ON MASONITE, Country Fair, signed "Lunde," framed, 26" x 38" $412.50

A-ME Mar. 1993　　*James D, Julia, Inc.*
DAGUERREOTYPE, of Den Tillotson, stagecoach driver for the Bradford & Montpelier, Vermont stage line, case split, spots $1250.00*

A-MA Oct. 1992　　*Skinner, Inc.*
MEMORIAL PICTURE, watercolor and ink on paper, "Sacred to the Memory of Mrs. Rebecca Barber who Departed this Life, September the 4th, 1828, Aged 48 Years," damage, 18½" x 15" .. $2200.00

A-ME Mar. 1993　　*James D, Julia, Inc.*
TIN TYPES, 4 pcs., (2 illus.), civil war soldiers $400.00*
TIN TYPE, civil war sailors ... $600.00*

A-PA May 1993　　*Alderfer Auction Co.*
BOOKPLATE, Hanna Hunsberger, 1804, wear, 6¾" x 4" $700.00
BOOKMARK, Catherine Shaddinge, 6" x 3½" $900.00
BOOKPLATE, Johannes Biebighaus, dated November 18, 1812, red, yellow, black, damage, 5¾" x 3¾" $4000.00

A-ME Mar. 1993　　*James D, Julia, Inc.*
DAGUERREOTYPE, Mary Coburn, case marked "J.G. Holcumb of Augusta, Main $200.00*
DAGUERREOTYPES, pr., framed, Mr. & Mrs. Samuel Pickard of Auburn, Maine $450.00*
AMBROTYPE, Maungwudaus, Chief of the Ojibway tribe of PA $2900.00*

A-ME Feb. 1993　　*James D. Julia, Inc.*
CURRIER & IVES PRINT, "Mr. August Belmon's Potomac (Hamilton Up) and Masher (Bergen Up)," 20" x 27¾"........................ $700.00

A-MA Mar. 1993　　*Skinner, Inc.*
PAINTING, watercolor on paper, unsigned, stains, tear, 7½" x 9¾" $2090.00

A-MA Mar. 1993　　*Skinner, Inc.*
PAINTING, "A Primrose," signed "Painted by Sally Stearns 1857," watercolor, ink on paper, stains, tears, 8¼" x 6¾" ... $835.00

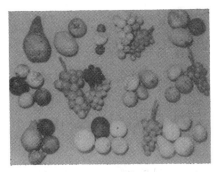

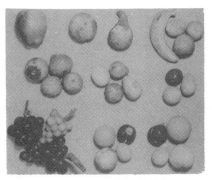

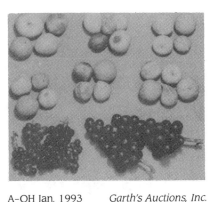

A-OH March. 1993   *Garth's Auctions, Inc.*
STONE FRUIT
Row 1, Left to Right
PEAR, 7½" L $71.50
LEMON, TOMATO, late $11.00
PEACH, 2 STRAWBERRYS, ... $16.50
GRAPES, 2 bunches, white $44.00
LEMON, APPLE, PLUM, wear .. $16.50
Row 2, Left to Right
2 APPLES, 3 PLUMS, losses.... $68.75
GRAPES, 3 bunches, 1 black, 2
white $253.00
PEAR, LEMON, APPLE, PLUM,
wear $132.00
APPLE, PLUM, PEACH, GRAPES,
wear $132.00
Row 3, Left to Right
FIGS, 4 pcs., chips, wear $22.00
2 PEACHES, 2 LEMONS, LIME,
wear $55.00
GRAPES, 2 PEARS, APPLE, PEACH,
FIG, some late, 2 alabaster $49.50

A-OH Nov. 1992   *Garth's Auctions, Inc.*
STONE FRUIT
Row 1, Left to Right

APPLE, lg., 4" $247.50
PEACH, lg., 3¼" $247.50
GOURD, 4½" $170.50
BANANA, LEMON, PEACH, ORANGE,
4 pcs. $330.00
Row 2, Left to Right
POMEGRANATE, PEAR, PEACH,
APPLE, 4 pcs. $242.00
LEMON, PEAR, PEACH, POTATO, 4
pcs. $154.00
FIG, PEACH, POTATO, 3
pcs. $115.50
Row 3, Left to Right
GRAPES, 3 bunches, red, white,
black $445.50
ORANGE, PEACH, FIG, PLUM, 4
pcs. $286.00
FIG, ORANGE, PEACH, GREEN FIG, 4
pcs. $418.00

A-OH Jan. 1993   *Garth's Auctions, Inc.*
STONE FRUIT
Row 1, Left to Right
APPLE, ORANGE, PEACH,
LEMON $154.00
TOMATO, PEACH, PLUM, ORANGE,
FIG $181.50
PEACH, APPLE, PLUM,
ORANGE $66.00
Row 2, Left to Right
PEAR, APPLE, FIG,
ORANGE $154.00
PEAR, APPLE, PEACH,
ORANGE $149.60
FIG, 2 APPLES, PEACH,
ORANGE $192.50
Row 3, Left to Right
PURPLE GRAPES, 5 small bunches
.... $192.50
PURPLE GRAPES, 2 large bunches
.... $143.00

A-ME May 1993   *James D. Julia, Inc.*
WEIGHT SCALE, Planters Peanut, chips, 20" x 45" x 22" $16250.00*
GUM VENDOR, 1 cent, black baker boy, 8" x 16" x 6" $5250.00*
SLOT MACHINE, Caille Superior Jackpot, 25 cent, new door, 14"x 24"x 14" .. $1000.00*

A-OH July 1993   *Garth's Auctions, Inc.*
STONE FRUIT
Row 1, Left to Right
APPLE, PEAR, PEACH, crack .. $49.50
ORANGE, PLUM, LEMON $57.75
TWO APPLES, PLUM $90.75
POMEGRANATE, PEACH,
FIG $49.50
Row 2, Left to Right
PLUM, TWO PEACHES $74.25
PLUM, PEACH, GRAPES $123.75
WHITE GRAPES, 2 bunches ... $148.50
Row 3, Left to Right
GRAPES, 2 bunches, white,
black $192.50
TWO BANANAS, EGG, traces of
paint...................... $189.75

A-OH Nov. 1992   *Garth's Auctions, Inc.*
NOTE: *Pieces on top row are English match boxes also known as "going to bed" lamps.*

Row 1, Left to Right
MATCH BOX, bear, gilded brass, glass eyes, 3" H $104.50
MATCH BOX, box w/miniature chamber stick attached, silver, English, 3⅛" H $93.50
MATCH BOX, grill work cylinder, gilded brass, 2⅞" H $49.50
MATCH BOX, ornate chest, gilded brass, 3" L $50.50
MATCH BOX, embossed brass, agate in lid, 2" x 2", 1¾" H $49.50
MATCH BOXES, 2 pcs., red plaid decoupage, ivory finials, 2¾", 2⅞" H . . . $132.00

Row 2, Left to Right
CHRISTMAS ORNAMENT, cobalt, unsilvered grapes, brass hanger, 6" L $165.00
CHALISES, 2 pcs., green $27.50
CHOCOLATE MOLDS, 2 pcs., tin multiple molds, 3 rabbits, 3 sheep, "Germany," rust, 10½" L $110.00
WOODEN TIGER, polychrome, holes at mouth, 3⅜" L $60.50
CHOCOLATE MOLDS, 2 pcs., tin, rabbit w/pack, 4½" H, running rabbit, "U.S.A.," 5¼" L $99.00

Row 3, Left to Right
FRUIT BASKET BOOK END, cast iron, polychrome, 5½" T $33.00
CHOCOLATE MOLDS, 3 tin rabbits, 1 mkd. "U.S.A.," 4" to 6" T $99.00
SNOWBIRD EAGLES, 6 pcs., (1 illus.), cast iron, dk. patina. 6¼" T $264.00

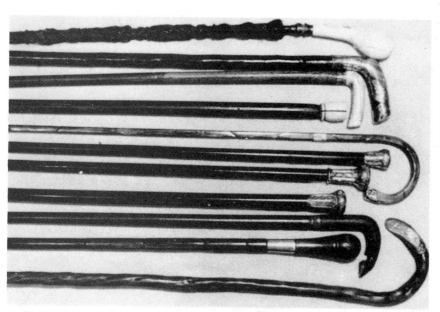

A-OH Jan. 1993   *Garth's Auctions, Inc.*
WALKING STICKS OR CANES
Top to Bottom
EBONY, w/macreme string painted black, carved ivory handle, brass collar, damage, hairlines, 33" L $247.50
SAPLING SHAFT, tooled silver overlay handle, "P.C. '94," damage, 35" L $165.00
MAHOGANY, worn orange lacquer, ivory handle, cracks, 33" L $55.00
PINE, w/bone knob, ebonized finish, crack, 32¾" L $38.50
SQUARE FAUX BAMBOO, battered silver trim, 33" L $38.50
EBONIZED, silver plated knob, 32" L $71.50
EBONIZED, gold knob, marked "T.D. & V.," engraved monogram, dent, 36" L . . . $104.50
EBONIZED, gold knob, floral tooling, engraved inscription, "1881," 35½" L $165.00
HORN HOOF HANDLE, mahogany, damage, 34½" L $93.50
GAMBLER'S STICK, foux bamboo, screw off end holds ivory dice, 35" L $220.00
KNOBBY VINE, sterling overlay handle, fooling and engraved "K," 31" L $82.50

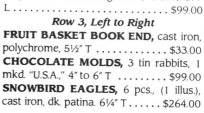

A-PA May 1993   *Conestoga Auction Co.*
STANGL, MARKED
Row 1, Left to Right
COCKATOO, 9" T $75.00*
DOUBLE PARAKEET, 7" T . . . $120.00*
DOUBLE BLUEBIRD, *" T $90.00*
Row 2, Left to Right
SPECKLED HEN, 7" T $130.00*
PAINTED BUNTING, 5" T $95.00*
MALE PHEASANT, 5¾" T $130.00*

A-MA Oct. 1992   Skinner, Inc.
WALKING STICKS, two, (first and last pictured), carved ivory and whalebone, 19th c., 33½" and 32½" $825.00
WALKING STICK, carved walrus ivory w/whalebone, cracks, 34½" . . . $990.00
WALKING STICK, carved ivory w/ ebony, 19th c, cracks, 34½" . . $1210.00
WALKING STICK, carved whalebone, tortoise shell w/ivory knop, 19th c., 37¼" $1210.00

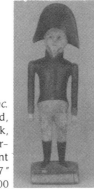

A-MA Oct. 1992
Skinner, Inc.
SOLDIER, carved, painted blue, black, white, mustard, red, articulated arms, paint wear, chips, 17" H $8250.00

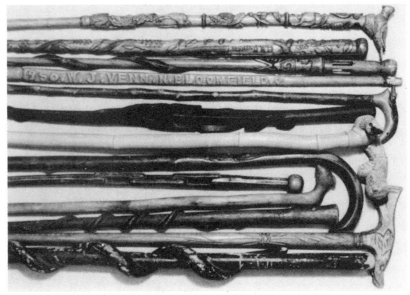

A-OH Jan. 1993   Garth's Auctions, Inc.
FOLK ART WALKING STICKS OR CANES
Top to Bottom
BIRD HANDLE, hardwood, carved animals, flowers, monogram, chip, 35" L . . . $385.00
CARVED ASH, vine, leaves, Masonic emblems, inscription, "1920," 5½" L $330.00
CARVED SNAKE, rinestone eyes, old polychrome, 37" L $220.00
ROOTHEAD, "1950, W.J. Wenn, N., Bloomfield, O.," 34" L $71.50
ALLIGATOR HANDLE, knobby shaft, worn paint, 35½" L $104.50
WILLOW, stylized diamond shapes, dk. finish, 35" L $55.00
BAMBOO ROOT HEAD, convoluted natural growth handle, natural, 31" L $38.50
KNOBBY SAPLING, carved alligator shaft, two-tone, 34" L $49.50
CHAIN LINK CARVED, worn red, 34¾" L $82.50
ROOTHEAD, carved mouse head handle, cracks, 37¾" L $71.50
CARVED SNAKE, worn finish, 33" L $93.50
TOMAHAWK HANDLE, decal "Souvenir of Wisconsin Dells," 37¼" L $48.50
CARVED SNAKE, worn black paint over white, 35" L $49.50

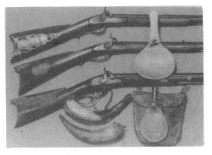

A-OH Apr. 1993   Garth's Auctions, Inc.
KENTUCKY RIFLE, curly maple stock, percussian lock conversion from flint lock, engraved silver dec., 56" L $1320.00
KENTUCKY RIFLE, curly maple stock, percussion lock, cracks 56" L $522.50
KENTUCKY RIFLE, walnut stock, percussion lock marked "Henry Parker Warrented," octagonal barrel initialed "R.B.," brass inlays, 48½" L $935.00
BUTTER PADDLE, maple, 10½" L $71.50
POWDER HORN, carved w/animal and inscription, cracks, 10½" L $55.00
SHOT FLASK AND BAG, leather, wear $38.50

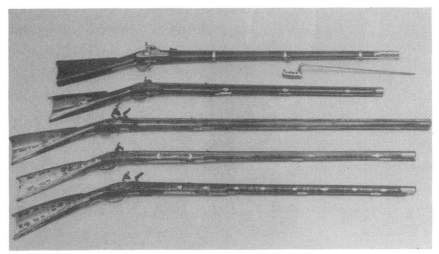

A-NH May. 1993   Northeast Auctions
MUSKET, Colt M1861 Special, Flayderman 5B-255, dated 1864, unissued . . . $2750.00*
NEW ENGLAND KENTUCKY RIFLE, by H. Pratt, militia rifle w/patch box, orig. percussion $2000.00*
MILITARY KENTUCKY RIFLE, by J. Dickert, ca. 1790, stamped "P" and "PR," orig. flint $7500.00*
KENTUCKY RIFLE, carved, orig. percussion, silver inlays, silver patchbox and thimbles $2000.00*
KENTUCKY RIFLE, curly maple, silver inlays, ca. 1820-1830, reconversion . . $1750.00*

A-OH Nov. 1992   *Garth's Auctions, Inc.*
RATTLE, turned wood, carved "A.T. Junior," 14" L $60.50
TURTLE, wood, tin, old paint, rust, 8" L $192.50
CLOTHES HANGER, 15" L $5.50
CARVED BONE KNIFE, engraved designs, chip, 9⅝" L $16.50
"EZY RAISIN SEEDER," cast iron, "Pat. May 21, 1895," "Scald the Raisins," 6" L $104.50
COOKIE CUTTERS, 6 pcs., (2 illus.) tin, man, woman, teddy bear, horse, rooster, lion $72.60
BIRD ROASTING SPIT, brass, wrought iron, 12" L $38.50
PIPE, pottery, wood, metal, bowl has troubadour and "1761," 13¾" L $11.00
TRIVET, wrought iron, 10½" L . . $178.75
IRON CHOPPER, ROCKINGHAM CUSPIDOR, (not illus.), ... $27.50
FORKS, 6 pcs., steel, bone handles, 7" L $13.20
CHILD'S KNIFE and FORK, steel, bone handles, 7" L $17.60
TRIVET, wrought iron, rusted, 9½" L $33.00

A-OH Nov. 1992   *Garth's Auctions, Inc.*
DECORATED MIRROR, two part, worn original brown sponging, gilt, reverse glass painting has flaking, 22¼" x 11¾" $159.50
FRAME, red flame graining, gold liner, 1¾" molding, 12¾ x 16¾" $82.50
CHARCOAL DRAWING, on paper, black, white, Rhineland scene, 16½" x 21¼" . . . . NS
SPINDLE BACK CHAIR, youth size, black paint w/gold trim, 11" seat, 26½" H $38.50
SERVER, poplar, cherry, worn brown finish, 35" W, 18" D, 28¾" H $495.00
ASSEMBLED TEA SET, pewter, 3 pcs., copper bottom pot, pot and creamer marked "Homan & Co. Cincinnati," sugar marked "Flagg & Homan," repairs 10" H $93.50
ASSEMBLED TEA SET, pewter, 3 pcs., copper bottom pots marked "Cin'ti Britannia Co.," battered, repairs, 10¼" H $82.50
SHIP DOORSTOP, cast iron, old polychrome, wear, 10½" H $82.50
SHIP DOORSTOP, cast iron, old polychrome, wear, 11½" H $60.50
SHIP DOORSTOP, cast iron, white, green and red paint, 10½" H $49.50

A-OH Feb. 1993   *Garth's Auctions, Inc.*
CHEESE BASKET, damage, 21" D, 7" H $275.00
HOBBY HORSE, black wool, brown fur mane, button eyes, wear, repair, 46½" L $126.50
QUEEN ANNE TAVERN TABLE, birch base, replaced pine top, damage, repairs, 24" x 31½", 25½" H $770.00
BOWBACK WINDSOR ARMCHAIR, added rockers, worn varnish, damage, 36" H $220.00
CANDLESTICK, iron, push up, lip hanger, worn black paint, 7¼" H $220.00
COOKIE BOARD, wood, cat on one side, equestrian on other, cracks, repairs, 6½" x 10" $77.00
CANDLESTICK, tin, push up, 7" H $93.50
REDWARE JUG, ovoid, amber glaze, wear, flakes, 11½" H $115.50
MAPLE CANDY MOLD, wood, varnish, 3" x 18" $126.50

A-OH Apr. 1993   *Garth's Auctions, Inc.*
QUILT, red, green applique on white, stains, 83" x 88½" $880.00
CANNONBALL ROPE BED, birch, pine, old refinish, replaced rails, 48" H, 53" W, 74" L $247.50
BASKET, weathered, damage, 7" H, 17½" W, 13" D $126.50
BASKET, weathered, damage, 8½" H, 17" D $44.00

A-PA May 1993   *Alderfer Auction Co.*
BOX, slide lid, salmon, brown . . . $190.00
PANTRY BOX, wood, blue, 11¾" T $225.00
BOX, bas relief hearts, drawer, ca. 1900 . . . . $375.00

A-OH Nov. 1992   *Garth's Auctions, Inc.*
CHIPPENDALE BLANKET CHEST, poplar, old alligatored green repaint, loss, 54½" W, 24" D, 29¼" H $275.00
STONEWARE JAR, blue stencil "Hamilton & Jones, Greensboro, Pa 1½," chips, 9¼" H $110.00
BIBLE BOX, softwood, old green, red, orange repaint, deteriorated, worm eaten, 10" x 17" x 22" $137.50
SUGAR BUCKET, all wood, stave constructed, worn, 8¾" H $99.00
CANADA GOOSE SWIMMER, glass eyes, old paint, repair, 24" L $55.00

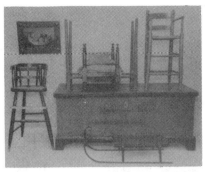

A-OH Nov. 1992   *Garth's Auctions, Inc.*
OIL ON BOARD, still life, green painted frame, 14¼" x 18½" $99.00
HIGH CHAIR, stenciled "Sterling," replacements, 32" H $165.00
BLANKET CHEST, pine, red, black repaint, German label, "Klara Lower, Nach Bremen, nach Americka," replacements, 52½" W, 23½" D, 22¼" H $412.50
PENCIL POST DOLL BED, chestnut, old red, 13" x 26¾", 27" H $55.00
DOLL BED, old finish, mattress, bolster, quilt, 13½" x 19", 18" H $302.50
HIGH CHAIR, natural finish, woven splint seat, 30¾" H $126.50
CHILD'S SLED, steel frame, wood top, 29" L $93.50

A-OH Nov. 1992   *Garth's Auctions, Inc.*
CHEESE DRAINER, tin, punched circles with compass stars, old black patina, short ball feet, 13½" x 14", 2½" H . . . $770.00
OIL ON CANVAS, primative portrait, minor surface damage, rosewood frame damage, 34" x 26¼" $605.00
LADDERBACK ARMCHAIR ROCKER, worn yellow repaint, worn splint seat, 41½" H $302.50
BLANKET CHEST, pine, brown paint, staple hinges, till with secret compartment, replacements, 29¼" x 12¼", 15¾" H $330.00
SEWING BOX, pine, old brownish graining, chip carved edges, lift lid compartment, replacements, 9¾" x 10", 11¼" H $302.50

A-OH Jan. 1993   *Garth's Auctions, Inc.*
Row 1, Left to Right
BOTTLE, redware, green glaze, brown flecks, label, "Made by I.S. Stahl, 11-1-1939," 5¾" H $55.00
JAR, stoneware, grey salt glaze, cobalt dec., 8¾" H $159.50
BASKET, burl, one piece, 7" H . . $330.00
JUG, redware, Galena pottery, green-amber glaze, orange spots, wear, flakes, 9½" H $192.50
FLOWER POT, pottery, brown Albany slip, unglazed tan clay, mustard paint, wear, chips, 4⅞" H $192.50
Row 2, Left to Right
HANGING BOX, glass sides, pine, green paint, cracks, holes, 10½" H $275.00
FOLK ART MAN, carved pine, wear, cracks, 10" H $192.50
SGRAFFITO BOWL, redware, eagle, "1827," flakes, 2½" H, 12½" D . . . $412.50
HOUR GLASS, all wood, gold, green repaint, 8¼" H $55.00
BARN LANTERN, wood frame, tin socket, wavy glass, red paint, crack, 11" H $522.50

A-OH Nov. 1992   *Garth's Auctions, Inc.*
SHERATON CHEST, cherry, curly maple, walnut, poplar, chestnut, refinished, replacements, 37" W, 17½" D, 40" H $522.50
SAMPLER, wool on linen, "Mary Margret Callishaw '76," 16¾" x 15¾" $275.00
SAMPLER, silk on homespun linen, wear, damage, faded, 18⅝" x 8½" $330.00
JACQUARD COVERLET, deep salmon, dk. teal, white ground, "W. Minster Allen Co, 1856," frayed, 70" x 88" $467.50
ROCKINGHAM SHOE BOTTLE, 9" L $60.50
HEPPLEWHITE CANDLESTAND, cherry, refinished, repair, age cracks, 15¼" x 16¾", 28½" H $467.50

A-MA Dec. 1992   *Skinner, Inc.*
STERNBOARD EAGLE, carved, red, white, blue, black, gold, 83" L . . . $850.00*
MARKET BASKET, losses, 14" W, 16" L $60.00*
SPLINT BASKET, decorated, faded, 8¾" W, 9¾" L $45.00*
GATHERING BASKET, 15½" W, 18¼" L $100.00*
WALL POCKET BASKET, painted yellow, white, red, 9" L $100.00*
QUEEN ANNE TAVERN TABLE, restored, 27½" H $325.00*
SHERATON TAVERN TABLE, pine, birch, refinished, 29½" H, 35" W, 24" D $900.00*

A-OH Jan. 1993   *Garth's Auctions, Inc.*
TRAMMEL, wrought iron, 12¾" L $93.50
BOX LOCK, cast iron, 4¼" x 7" . . $38.50
BED WARMER, copper, turned handle, 6¾" W, 7¾" L $60.50
LADLE, pewter, 6" L $165.00
CHOPPER, steel, burl handle, 6¾" W, 7¾" L $60.50
SHOOTING GALLERY BIRD, cast iron, 4¼" L $38.50
SHOOTING GALLERY DUCK, cast iron, 5½" L $60.50
4 PCS., horn handled fork, child's fork, cork screw, leather marking tool marked "C.S. Osborne & Co" $38.50
CAMPAIGN HORNS, 2 pcs., tin, "Patriotism, Prosperity, Protection" $71.50
SHOOTING GALLERY BIRDS, 2 pcs., cast iron $93.50
SHOOTING GALLERY DUCK, cast iron, 7" L $93.50

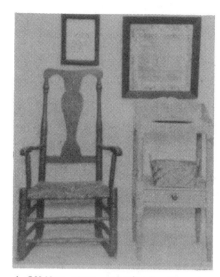

A-OH Nov. 1992   *Garth's Auctions, Inc.*
APPLIQUE PANEL, wool and other fabrics, brown and black ground, worn and faded, repairs, 34½ x 34 ½" . . $5.50
WINDSOR STOOL, bamboo turnings, worn green paint, cracks, 23¾", 34½" H $715.00
HEPPLEWHITE TABLE, poplar, green paint, octagonal top, 24½" x 25", 29¼" H $1320.00
DECORATED BOX, pine, worn original graining and paint, 12" L $71.50
WINDSOR STOOL, original red paint, alligatored, 10½", 12½" H $192.50

A-OH Nov. 1992   *Garth's Auctions, Inc.*
WATERCOLOR THEOREM, on paper, bird in tree, frame with half turnings, corner blocks, dark paint, 12¾" x 9½" $990.00
NEEDLEWORK SAMPLER, homespun linen, white satin border, silk needlework, "Family Register, " "Wrought by Rhoda Stearns, Cambridge 1814," wear, damage, 20½" x 18¾" $880.00
QUEEN ANNE ARMCHAIR ROCKER, old dark red repaint, old repair, worn paper rush seat, 40¾" H $330.00
SHERATON WASHSTAND, pine, original deep yellow graining, paint decorated, 16" W x 13½" D, 28¾" H $357.50
WOVEN SPLINT BASKET, watercolor polka dots in yellow and black, Woodlands Indian origin, 10½" D, 4½" H . . $269.50

A-OH Nov. 1992   *Garth's Auctions, Inc.*
CHIPPENDALE CHEST, walnut and pine, refinished, dovetailed drawers, replacements, repairs, 37" x 20", 35½" H $2866.00
PEARLWARE PITCHER, Leeds five color decoration, "William Wane, Nottingham 1803," wear and scratches, 9⅜" H $2172.50
STAFFORDSHIRE PLATTER, medium blue stansfer of ship and seashell border, 18" L $797.50
PEARLWARE PITCHER, Leeds blue and white gaudy floral design, leaf handle, edge flakes, 8½" H $715.00
STAFFORDSHIRE PLATTER, dark blue transfer, "Cornwall Terrace, Regents Park London," 10⅜" L $715.00

A-MA Oct. 1992   *Skinner, Inc.*
FISH DECOYS, 4, wood and tin, carved, painted, 20th c., 5" to 6¾" L . . . $357.50

A-OH Nov. 1992   *Garth's Auctions, Inc.*
SILHOUETTES, set of 3, traces of gold brushed details, mahogany veneer frames, damage, 15" x 10" $742.50
IMMIGRANT'S CHEST, red pine, blue, red, yellow and black paint, initials and "1815," 36" L $715.00
WINDSOR SIDE CHAIR, bamboo, old refinish, replacements, 34" H $71.50
SPATTER PITCHER, blue/white spongeing, 8¼" H $220.00
SPATTER BOWL, 2-tone blue spongeing, 8¾" D, 3" H $27.50
SPATTER TEAPOT, olive and white spongeing, chips, 7¼" H $291.50

A-MA Oct. 1992   *Skinner, Inc.*
U.S. MAIL DELIVERY CART, painted, 19th c., 37" L $3520.00

A-OH March. 1993   *Garth's Auctions, Inc.*
QUILT, stars and scalloped border in blue/white print, feather quilted circles, wear, stains, 86" x 100" $1045.00
CANNONBALL ROPE BED, cherry, poplar, refinished, head/foot not matching, replacement, 54" x 72½", 48" H . . $385.00
VELOCIPEDE, steel, black paint, wear, loss $165.00

A-OH Nov. 1992   *Garth's Auctions, Inc.*
FRAME, pine, original red and black graining, yellow stenciled decoration, 2" molding, 17¼" x 14¼" $137.50
WINDSOR STOOL, refinished, traces of old green, 15" D, 24¼" H $104.50
SHAKER ARMCHAIR ROCKER, Mt. Lebanon, worn dark finish, new red and black taped seat and back, unmarked, 37" H $715.00
SHAKER BOX, oval bentwood, worn original blue paint, wrought iron tacks, 9¼" L $770.00
PIN CUSHIONS, pr., shaker type, woven ivory, pink velvet inserts, Oval 4¼" L, rectangular 4¼" L $22.00

A-OH Feb. 1993   *Garth's Auctions, Inc.*
NOTE: *All decoys contemporary.*
LADDERBACK CHAIR, black repaint, old splint seat, 46" H $357.50
CHIPPENDALE CHEST, curly maple, honey colored refinish, replacements, damage, repairs, 38½" W, 18" D $1265.00
BLUEBILL HEN, glass eyes, distressed paint, initialed "AC," 8½" L $126.50
BLACK DUCK, glass eyes, cracks, 16½" L $82.50
CANVASBACK DRAKE, hollow, glass eyes, initialed "P.A.," 16½" L $77.00
SNOW GOOSE, glass eyes, initialed "TM," crack, 20½" L $60.50

A-OH Nov. 1992   *Garth's Auctions, Inc.*
QUILT, pink, green, yellow calico on white, wear, fading, 75" x 86" $82.50
QUILT, appliqued, green calico, red on white, feather wreath quilting, wear, stains, frayed, 96" x 96" $495.00
DRY SINK, pine, old refinish, repairs, replacement, 60¾" W, 18" D, 30¼" H. $715.00
BIRD CAGE, tin, blue paint, 13½" D, 20½" H. $192.50
BED WARMER, copper, brass, 42" L. $187.00
STONEWARE JUG, 16¾" H $82.50
TRIANGULAR LANTERN, tin, old red repaint, glass bottom, 28" H $192.50

A-OH Jan. 1993   *Garth's Auctions, Inc.*
SHERATON CARD TABLE, cherry, curly maple and mahogany veneer, repairs, 36¼" W, 18¾" D $990.00
CANDLESTICKS, pr., pewter, w/pushups, 8" H $220.00
PLATTER, creamware, blue, white, chips, 16⅜" L $825.00
SPOOL CHEST, maple inlaid walnut, replacements, 17½" H, 23½" W, 14¼" D $495.00

A-OH Feb. 1993   *Garth's Auctions, Inc.*
KRAUT CUTTER, walnut, old finish, 7¼" x 22½" $170.50
POPLAR PEEL, old refinish, 33½" L $93.50
SPOON, hardwood, chip carved, 26" L $38.50
HOOKED RUG, 23" x 38" $275.00
DRYING RACK, pine, old green repaint, damage, 20" W, 33" H $148.50
HEPPLEWHITE DESK, pine, 32" W, 25½" D, 36½" H $440.00
WOVEN SPLINT BASKET, damage, 9½" D, 4¾" H $104.50
FOOTSTOOL, old drk. paint, 8" x 11½", 6" H $71.50
STONEWARE JAR, cobalt design, label "Cowden & Wilcox 2," 10" H . . $440.00
BENTWOOD BOX, old worn patina, 19" D, 8" H. $71.50

A-OH Jan. 1993   *Garth's Auctions, Inc.*
QUEEN ANNE MULE CHEST, maple, pine, refinished, damage, losses, 46½" H, 37¾" W, 18¾" D $825.00
SEWERPIPE DOG, dark glaze, firing cracks, 7¾" H $110.00
SPICE BOX, poplar, old red, 12½" W $770.00
SEWERPIPE LION, incised "L.E. Sr., #16, 9 - 16 - 52, Wadsworth, Ohio," 1954 pencil inscription, 8½" L $275.00
OVOID CHURN, stoneware, impressed "3," cobalt dec., chips, wooden lid, 15¼" H. $330.00

A-OH Apr. 1993   *Garth's Auctions, Inc.*
HERB DRYING BASKET, damage, 6¾"
H, 16" D $236.50
TRADE SIGN, pocket watch, handmade
wood, rope, gold, white, black paint, 2-
sided, 28" H $192.50
CHEESE BASKET, 15" D $126.50
HEPPLEWHITE WORK TABLE, walnut,
pine, top replaced, 29" H, 59" W, 33¼"
D $660.00
PLATE, pewter, "Compton, London"
touch, pitted, 8" D $82.50
PLATE, pewter, Edgar Curtis touch, wear,
crack, 8" D $93.50
WRITING BOX, poplar, old red, black
repaint, 18" L, 13½" D $209.00
SYRUP, pewter, "Homan & Co. Cincinnati,"
flower finial, splits, 6" H $55.00
PLATE, pewter, Edgar Curtis touch, wear,
scratches, 7⅞" D $82.50
PLATE, Thomas Danforth Boardman
eagle touch, wear, 7¾" D $357.50

A-OH Nov. 1992   *Garth's Auctions, Inc.*
STEPBACK WALL CUPBOARD, poplar,
weathered surface, greyish paint, 33" H,
18½" D, 70¾" H $1100.00
REDWARE CHARGER, coggeled edge,
yellow slip decor., chips, wear, hairlines,
14½" D $286.00
BENTWOOD BOXES, nesting set of 5, old
green paint, 1 labeled in pencil "Joseph W.
Smith 2/5/23," 10" D $577.50

A-OH Nov. 1992   *Garth's Auctions, Inc.*
DRYING RACK, folding, 2-part, walnut,
loss, each section 30" x 61½" $11.00
JACQUARD COVERLET, navy, teal,
salmon, on natural, "Lima, Ohio," wear,
holes, 65" x 69" $49.50
QUILT, yellow, green, red on white, wear,
stains, damage, machined binding, 69" x
74" $71.50
REEL, walnut, cast iron, incomplete, 54"
L $5.50
CRADLE, pine, old refinish, repairs, re-
placements, 38" L $104.50
STONEWARE, 2 pcs., Albany slip, jug 8¼"
H, pitcher 8¼" H $22.00

A-OH Nov. 1992   *Garth's Auctions, Inc.*
QUILT, pieced and applique, red and
green calico, stains, 63" x 63" . . $302.50
BLANKET CHEST, pine and walnut,
worn red and green repaint, 41" x 19¼",
23¾" H $385.00
LANTERN, punched tin, oversized, electrified, open bottom, old patina, rust, not
period, 20" H $385.00
WOVEN SPLINT BASKET, worn patina,
minor damage, 10" D, 5½" H . . $104.50
HORSE SCULPTURE, sheet iron, arc
welded, rusted, modern stand, 26"
H $302.50
ROTARY BROILER, wrought iron,
twisted and scrolled detail, brass inlay
handle, "1763," 12" x 26" $440.00
FOOT WARMER, punched tin, wooden
top and bottom, refinished, repaired, 7½"
x 8½", 5½" H $165.00

A-OH Nov. 1992   *Garth's Auctions, Inc.*
SHERATON WORK TABLE, mahogany,
dark reddish varnish, dovetailed drawer,
opalescent pulls, 16½" x 18", 28½"
H. $4125.00
CANDLESTICK, brass, repair, small
crack, 7⅜" H $165.00

A-MA Jun. 1993   *Skinner, Inc.*
SHAKER TOOL BOX, walnut, bird's eye
maple, ca. 1850, fitted tray, paint spatter,
13" H, 24⅝" W, 13¾" D $1210.00
SHAKER TABLE, cherry, Canterbury,
19th c., drawer inscribed "Shaker," 28½" H,
36" W, 24" D $1650.00
SHAKER LADDER, painted, labeled "L.A.
Shepard Canterbury, N.H.," 109" H, 12"
W $1650.00
DRYING RACK, grain painted, also 3
work boards, 19th c. $192.50

A-OH Nov. 1992   *Garth's Auctions, Inc.*
MULE CHEST, maple, refinished, 37¾" W, 17" D, 40" H $440.00
CHAIR, old worn black repaint, gold striping, 39¾" H $115.50
PITCHER, tin, punched and tooled design, 11" H $137.50
PAINTED BOX, pine, old green, 18" L $137.50
COFFEE POT, tin, stamped "J. Brinkhouse," 10½" H $440.00
BLANKET CHEST, miniature, oak, green repaint, polychrome angels, flowers, 12¼" L $137.50
BENTWOOD BOX, brown, 11½" D, 6¼" H $137.50
SUGAR BUCKET, all wood, stave constructed, refinished, 9" H $49.50
COCK WEATHERVANE, sheet metal, weathered polychrome, 18½" H . . $396.00

A-OH Nov. 1992   *Garth's Auctions, Inc.*
PENSYLVANIA WATER BENCH, pine and poplar, old brown finish, 45¼" W, 15¼" D, 45½" H $2750.00
GROTESQUE JUG, pottery, green ash glaze, "Lanier Meaders," 8¾" . . $880.00
OVOID JAR, stoneware, "1/2," cobalt slip, stains, 6¾" H $104.50
GROTESQUE JUG, pottery, green ash glaze, "Lanier Meaders," 9" . . . $1045.00
OVOID JAR, stoneware, cobalt blue brushed floral design around shoulders, chips and hairlines, 12" H $302.50
GROTESQUE JUG, contemporary, redware, white and grey spiral glaze, impressed initials "C.L.," 12½" H $385.50
BOTTLE OR VASE, southern pottery, green ash glaze, "Lanier Meaders," 11" H $605.00
JAR, stoneware, tulip and "2" in cobalt blue slip, impressed label "Burger & Co. Rochester, N.Y.," lip chips, 11" H $247.50
OVOID JAR, stoneware, cobalt blue brushed foliage designs on shoulder, out of round, hairlines and chips, 15¾" H $302.50

A-OH May 1993   *Garth's Auctions, Inc.*
Row 1, Left to Right
TAPER JACK, silver plated, "Exeter," worn, 5½" H $275.00
BETTY LAMP, brass, 5" H $115.50
CANDLESTICK, iron, hog scraper, "Shaw," 6⅝" H $165.00
LARD LAMP, tole, old black, gold repaint, battered, 6¾" H $77.00
LAMPS, pr., blue japanning, brass, tin whale oil burners, 3¾" H $242.00
LAMP FILLER, polished brass, 4⅞" H $71.50
Row 2, Left to Right
BETTY LAMP, wrought iron, 4" H $220.00
LIGHTING STAND, pine, poplar, crack, 8" H $297.00
TREEN BOX, walnut, cracks, repairs, 12" H $170.50
SPOUT LAMP, brass, battered, polished, 11" H $71.50
LIGHTING STAND, poplar, 8¼" H $165.00
CANDLESTICK, wrought iron, 8½" H $192.50
LANTERN, tin, blown globe, worn, stained, 10" H $440.00
BETTY LAMP, copper, home made, 4½" H $55.00
LIGHTING STAND, cherry, poplar, refinished, 7" H $38.50

A-OH Nov. 1992   *Garth's Auctions, Inc.*
DECORATED CHEST, pine, brown vinegar graining, rebuilt from mule chest, 41½" W, 19¼" D, 34" H $935.00
CANDLESTICK, early square base, 6½" H $220.00
BOX, pine, poplar, brown alligatored finish, gold stenciled floral, cracks, repairs, 10" L $412.50
CANDLESTICK, brass, early square base, crack, 8" H $209.00
REDWARE PLATE, incised distlefink w/flowers, German inscription, name, dk. amber glaze, 10½" D $192.50

A-OH March. 1993   *Garth's Auctions, Inc.*
HOOKED RAG RUGS, pr., bright colors, modern, 18" x 34" $121.00
COUCH, walnut, old finish, old blue/white reupholstery, 77" L $522.50
BOX, pine, paint grained, bluish sponging, iron lock/hasp, crack, 30" L $330.00

A-OH March. 1993   *Garth's Auctions, Inc.*
POTTY CHAIR, old brown, yellow, floral paint, loss, ironstone chamber pot, 39" H $49.50
EMPIRE CHEST, cherry, worn finish, 42¼" W, 20" D, 47" H $522.50
STONEWARE PITCHER, blue, white, chip, 8⅞" H $302.50
CHECKERBOARD, olive, red, grey paint, 12" x 14" $330.00
STONEWARE PITCHER, blue, white, hairline, 9" H $275.00

A-OH Jan. 1993   *Garth's Auctions, Inc.*
BUTTER PRINT, tulip, scrubbed, cracks, 5½" H, 3¼" W $104.50
STAG COOKIE CUTTER, tin, 8¼" H $341.00
STAG COOKIE CUTTER, tin, 6½" L $93.50
COOKIE BOARD, drk. patina, 6¾" H, 5¼" W $247.50
COOKIE BOARD, animals, fish, fruit, birds, man, mermaid, drk. patina, 20" H, 5" W $357.50
SPOON, curly maple, cracks, 17" L $93.50
ROUND COOKIE BOARD, poplar, cracks, 25½" D $203.50
CARVER'S WHIMSEY, incomplete, 16" L $126.50
COOKIE BOARD, hardwood, grapes, damage, 19¼" H, 3½" W $214.50
HORSE COOKIE CUTTER, tin, 6½" L $170.50
BIRD COOKIE CUTTER, tin, 5" H $38.50
HORSE COOKIE CUTTER, tin, 7¾" L $104.50
BIRD COOKIE CUTTER, tin, 6" L $71.50
BIRD COOKIE CUTTERS, 2 pcs., tin, rust $44.00

A-OH Jan. 1993   *Garth's Auctions, Inc.*
POWDER HORN, engraved, "Britannia," "Sea Horse," "Sea Unicorn," ships, verse, mottos, "Nathaniel Munden, April 2nd 1829," 15" L $275.00
RUM HORN, engraved animals, birds, man with tail, etc., damage 8¾" L $88.00
HORN, engraved floral, fish, stars, heart, "F.B. Ano. d. 1833," loss, holes, 6½" L $137.50
POWDER HORN, carved eagle, shield, "V.D. Courtenay to S.B. Blackwell," crack, 8" L $137.50
NEEDLEWORK PANEL, soft faded colors on black ground, damage, 12" x 12" $192.50
FISH DECOY, wood, tin, painted, 6½" L $77.00
BIRD DECOY, tin, folding, 9½" L $192.50
BIRD DECOY, tin folding, 11¼" L $197.50
WICK TRIMMER, brass, on tray, 9¾" L $137.50
COOKIE BOARD, carved, mahogany, "E. Pluribus Unum," 11¾" x 12" $2640.00

A-OH Feb. 1993   *Garth's Auctions, Inc.*
BLANKET CHEST, pine, poplar, old refinish, losses, 40½" W, 18½" D, 23½" H $357.50
LADDERBACK ROCKER, natural refinish, 44" H $38.50
REDWARE PITCHER, brown glaze, wear, chips, 10¼" H $71.50
MINIATURE BLANKET CHEST, poplar, old drk. refinish, till w/lid, 19" L $495.00
REDWARE PITCHER, tooled lines, red glaze, 10¼" H $55.00
WOVEN SPLINT BASKET, damage, 14" x 15", 6½" H $104.50
REDWARE PAN, yellow slip decoration, chips, repair, 17½" L $99.00
SUGAR BUCKET, all wooden, old worn brownish red, finger construction bands, 8" H $115.50

A-NH Mar. 1993   *Northeast Auctions*
APOTHECARY CHEST, 30" W $1600.00*
CHILD'S BLANKET BOX, 27" L $950.00*
BLANKET BOX, grain painted, 42" L $1200.00*
SHERATON WORK TABLE, blue paint 36" L $350.00*
ROCKING HORSE, carved, leather saddle, horsehair tail, mane, 37" L . . $400.00*

A-OH Nov. 1992   *Garth's Auctions, Inc.*
OHIO BLANKET CHEST, miniature, poplar, original brown graining, dovetailed case, 13" L $2915.00
SEWERPIPE DOG, molded and tooled detail w/feet, chips, 13" L $1100.00
BURL BOWL, covered, ash, scrubbed finish, 7¼" D, 5¾" H $3520.00
OHIO WHITE CLAY DOG, blue and white, label insc. "Ned", chips on base, 6¾" H $302.50
CANDLE MOLD, miniature, 4 tube, handle resoldered, 6⅛" H $385.00

A-OH May 1993   *Garth's Auctions, Inc.*
EMPIRE MIRROR, two part, mahogany, flaking, loss, 32¾" H, 18" W $247.50
WALL CLOCK, resewood veneer, brass works, label "Seth Thomas," replacement, 25¼" H $165.00
EMPIRE MIRROR, two part, mahogany, losses, 30" H, 19" W $275.00
CHAIRS, 6 pcs., (2 illus.), old black, gold repaint, "Chas. B. Lourence decorator, Nov. 1924," recaned w/plastic, 1 damaged, 33¼" H $247.50
EMPIRE WASH STAND, pine, old dk. refinish, gold striping, 39¾" H, 22½" W, 15" D $275.00

A-OH Nov. 1992   *Garth's Auctions, Inc.*
JACQUARD COVERLET, red, navy, white, "J.C. Adams 1859," 72" x 84" $495.00
JELLY CUPBOARD, poplar, pine, old brown paint over blue, worn, 31¾" W, 15¾" D, 36¾" H $440.00
CORNER CHAIR, birch, refinished, 31" H........................ $275.00
NOGGIN PITCHER, made from 1 pc. of wood, age cracks $220.00
BENTWOOD BOX, old dk. green paint, 9½" D...................... $192.50
BENTWOOD BOX, old white repaint, 6" D $148.50
BENTWOOD BOX, green lid, 3⅛" D $82.50
STONEWARE JUG, brushed cobalt design, chips, 13½" H $126.50

A-ME May 1993   *James D. Julia, Inc.*
MUTOSCOPE, cast iron, Charlie Chaplin reel, 1 cent, old repaint, chips, replacements, 18" x 76" x 18" $2250.00*
MUTOSCOPE, cast iron, Hoot Gibson reel, replacements, 18" x 75" x 18" $900.00*
POSTAGE STAMP VENDOR, Mills, cast pot metal front, oak case, 5 cent, beveled mirror, 11" x 22" x 8" $1750.00*
GUM MACHINE, Pulver, 1 cent, red, white paint, ca. 1950, composition clown, 8½" x 20" x 4½" $450.00*

A-OH Apr. 1993   *Garth's Auctions, Inc.*
CORNER CUPBOARD, pine, old wavy glass, replacements, 74½" H, 44½" W $2090.00
ROAD RUNNER, carved wood, glass eyes, 30" L...................... $550.00
STONEWARE JAR, label "I.M. Mead," chips, hairline, 15½" T......... $275.00

A-OH Feb. 1993   *Garth's Auctions, Inc.*
SAMPLER, silk on homespun linen, damage, 17½" x 17¾" $165.00
EMPIRE STAND, cherry, refinished, replacements, 19¼" sq., 29¼" H .. $220.00
HEPPLEWHITE CHEST, cherry, refinished, replacements, damage, repairs, 46¾" W, 20" D $467.50
ROCKINGHAM FOOD MOLD, tulip design, wear, hairlines, 9" D $27.50
ROCKINGHAM BOWL, 11½" D, 3¼" H........................ $126.50
ROCKINGHAM BOWL, 9½" D, 4¼" H........................ $132.00
ROCKINGHAM BOWL, 9¼" D, 2¼" H........................ $55.00
ROCKINGHAM BOWL, wear, hairlines, flakes, 12½" D, 3½" H $82.50

A-OH Nov. 1992   *Garth's Auctions, Inc.*
HOOKED RAG RUG, rich red, blue, yellow, green, white, beige, grey, 41" W, 29" L........................... $66.00
ARMCHAIR, old red, yellow, green paint, damage, 38½" H $192.50
SHERATON STAND, pine, poplar, old yellow grained repaint, some mahogany flame veneer, stamped drawer, 32½" H, 19½" W, 17" D $770.00
BUTTER CROCK, w/lid, stoneware, cobalt dec., chips, 7½" H, 12" D .. $484.00
OVOID JAR, stoneware, impressed label "Norton & Fenton, Bennington, Vt.," cobalt dec., 12¾" H $385.00

A-OH Nov. 1992   *Garth's Auctions, Inc.*

Row 1, Left to Right
COW AND CALF, crocheted, starch stiffened, painted, 8" L $11.00
BERRY BASKET, 5" D $11.00
BENTWOOD BOX, worn green paint, 6½" D $203.50
FOLK ART BIRDS, 3 pcs., carved wood, cardinal, bluejay, song bird, 4" H $66.00

Row 2, Left to Right
BENTWOOD BOX, spring latch lid, burned decoration, 10¼" L $192.50
WOVEN SPLINT BASKET, red, black star flower, damage, 8" D, 4½" H $66.00
SCRODDLEWARE MATCH HOLDER, red, yellow clay, chips, worn, 5½" H $16.50
THREAD CADDY, hardwood, wire pins, pin cushion top, replacement, 6" H $27.50

Row 3, Left to Right
PIPSQUEEK, papier mache rooster and hen in wood cage, loss, silent, 7⅝" H ... $99.00
HORSE WHIRLIGIG, animated, wood, polychrome, 15" L $220.00
CHALK CAT, white, grey, beige paint, chips, damage, 7½" H $38.50
STONEWARE FIGURE, hen and rooster, damage, repair, 9" H $104.50

A-OH March. 1993   *Garth's Auctions, Inc.*
BLANKET CHEST, pine, dk. finish, replacements, age crack, worn, 45½" W, 21" D, 26" H $110.00
FIRESIDE BROILER, wrought iron, adjustable, 28" H $1100.00
PRESERVING JAR, stoneware, cobalt brushed, stenciled, flake, 8" H $170.50
LIGHTING STAND, wrought iron, adjustable octagagon pan, replacement, 20½" H $385.00
PERSERVING JAR, stoneware, cobalt stencil "Hartford City Salt Co, Dealers in Salt & General Merchandise, Hartford City, W. Va," chips, hairlines, 6¾" H $275.00
LIGHTING STAND, wrought iron, candle and spring sockets, 17½" H $302.50
OWL CONFIDENCE DECOY, papier mache, "Souler Swicher, Decatur, Illinois, Pat. Pend," glass eyes, original paint, wear, 14¼" H $104.50
FOOTSTOOL, poplar, worn red repaint, losses, crack, 14" L $82.50

A-OH Nov. 1992   *Garth's Auctions, Inc.*
EMPIRE SERVER, cherry, old worn refinish, repairs, replacements, 42½" W, 20" D, 33" H plus crest $385.00
ROCKINGHAM PIE PLATES, set of 4, 1 chip, 8" D $198.00
ROCKINGHAM PIE PLATE, 9⅜" D $71.50
ROCKINGHAM BOWL, 11½" D, 3¼" H $93.50
ROCKINGHAM PIE PLATES, 2 pcs., wear, 1 chipped, 10¼ D $99.00
ROCKINGHAM PLATTER, chip, 15" L $170.50

A-OH Jan. 1993   *Garth's Auctions, Inc.*
LITHOGRAPH, "Currier & Ives," "The Celebrated Trotting Team Edward and Swiveller . . .," C#940 (pub. 1882), stains, tears, 27¼" H, 39½" W $440.00
CHIPPENDALE BLANKET CHEST, walnut, old refinish, pine, poplar, repairs, 31½" H, 52¾" W, 23¾" D $3575.00
WOOD BOWL, old blue paint, 4¾" H, 13¾" W, 23½" L $577.50
DOME TOP BOX, pine, red graining, cracks, loss, 15" L $110.00

A-OH March. 1993   *Garth's Auctions, Inc.*
WALL CUPBOARD, yellow pine, poplar, 25" W, 9¼" D, 41¾" H $302.50
PENNY RUG, wool, olive, grey, maroon, red, wear, repairs, 28" x 46" $187.00
CRADLE, cherry, worn red paint, repairs, cracks, 42" L $302.50
ROPE BED, poplar, old grey repaint, 42" x 57", 32½" H $154.00
BEE KEEP, rye straw, was used as hive, wear, 17" D, 17" H $231.00

A-OH Feb. 1993   *Garth's Auctions, Inc.*
Row 1, Left to Right
REDWARE BOWLS, 2 pcs., (opposite ends), cream slip, brown spots, flakes, hairline, 7" D, 6½" H $143.00
REDWARE POT, dark glaze w/brown splotches, lid replaced, chips, 5" H $71.50
MORTAR AND PESTLE, brass, 4¼" H $33.00
REDWARE BOWL, worn yellow slip, 5½" D $71.50
Row 2, Left to Right
REDWARE FLOWER POT, amber glaze, brown sponging, hairline, 5" H $27.50
REDWARE JAR, lid, drk. glaze, brown splotches, chips, hairlines, 6¾" H $220.00
SKATER'S LAMP, tin, clear globe, 6¾" H $77.00
MORTAR AND PESTLE, ash, refinished, worn, hairlines, 5½" H $93.50
REDWARE JAR, ovoid, brown metallic glaze, 5¾" H $55.00
Row 3, Left to Right
SEWERPIPE BIRD HOUSE, 8½" H $522.50
EAGLE CARVING, repairs, damage 8" H $38.50
SALT BOX, poplar, old red, lid marked in pencil: "L.G. Adam, September 13, 1883," 8" x 8" x 8" $220.00
REDWARE JAR, lid, ovoid, drk. orange glaze, brown splotches, chips, 6" H $49.50

A-ME May 1993   *James D. Julia, Inc.*
NATIONAL CASH REGISTER #311, bronze, brass, restored, 10½" x 21" x 16½" $500.00*
NATIONAL CASH REGISTER #5, bronze, restored, loss, 9½" x 21" x 16" $450.00*
NATIONAL CASH REGISTER #33, 1903, restored, losses, 16" x 22" x 15" . . . $200.00*

A-OH March. 1993   *Garth's Auctions, Inc.*
BED WARMER, brass, floral engraved lid, 44" L $302.50
CHURN, stoneware, cobalt slip decoration, incised lines, "2," loss, 14" H $319.00
CUPBOARD, pine, original yellow graining, originally built-in, additions, 38½" W, 13¼" D, 80" H $440.00
FOOTSTOOL, pine, old brown repaint, 9½" x 19", 7¾" H $93.50

A-OH Nov. 1992   *Garth's Auctions, Inc.*
SIGN BRACKET, cast iron, 20½" D, 15" H $247.50
HUTCH TABLE, pine and poplar, brown paint over pinkish grey, repairs, replacements, 29½ x 38½, 27" H $247.50
BURL JAR, turned from one piece of wood, soft finish, age crack, 8" D, 9½" H $2750.00
BURL BOWL, worn patina, 14¼" x 15½", 6½" H $4400.00
SEWERPIPE DOG, molded and tooled, firing crack, chips, 11½" H $770.00

A-MA Jun. 1993   *Skinner, Inc.*
CELESTIAL TABLE GLOBE, Merriam
Moore & Co., Troy, NY, 19th c., 12"
H $1210.00
CELESTIAL TABLE GLOBE, Gilman
Joslin, Boston, 19th c., 14½" H . . $2420.00

A-OH Nov. 1992   *Garth's Auctions, Inc.*
Row 1, Left to Right
YELLOWWARE FOOD MOLD, ear of corn design, 3½" x 3¾", 2⅛" H $82.50
YELLOWWARE CHAMBER POT, miniature, white, brown, 2⅝" D, 1⅞" H $44.00
ADVERTISING POTTERY, 8 pcs., (2 illus.), most ash trays, desk pieces . . . $148.50
POTTERY MARBLE, blue and white, wear and chips, 1¾" D $181.50
CARPET BALL, green and white, 2⅛" $208.50
CARPET BALL, purple and white, 2⅛" $214.50
Row 2, Left to Right
SEWERPIPE SCOTTIE, chip, 3" H $49.50
SEWERPIPE PIG, molded flowers on back, 6⅝" L $357.50
SEWERPIPE CAT, tooling, broken tail, 7⅜" L $192.50
SEWERPIPE MAN IN SHOE, hand formed and tooled, 3" H $192.50
Row 3, Left to Right
SEWERTILE CAMEL, incised initials, "E.J.E.," 5½" H $330.00
REDWARE GROTESQUE JUG, stamped "Brown's Pottery, Arden, N.C.," brown glaze,
white teeth, 4¾" H $225.50
SEWERPIPE SHOE, tooled, 4¼" H $27.50
SEWERPIPE BOOT, finely molded, 4" H $38.50
SEWERPIPE SHOE, finely molded and tooled, 5" H $137.50

A-OH July 1993   *Garth's Auctions, Inc.*
MULE CHEST, butternut, red stain, attrib-
uted to Shakers, replacements, repairs, dam-
age, 43" H, 43½" W, 20½" D $2035.00
PRESERVING JAR, stoneware, cobalt
stencil, "Wilkinson & Fleming, Shinnston,
W.Va.," 10" T $275.00
PRESERVING JAR, stoneware, cobalt
stencil, "A. Conrad, New Geneva, Pa," 8½"
T $220.00
PRESERVING JAR, stoneware, cobalt
stencil, "New Geneva Pottery," flake, 9½"
T $269.50
STONEWARE JUG, cobalt quill work, label
"Bergan & Foy 3," 15" T $1072.50

A-ME May 1993   *James D. Julia, Inc.*
STRAW HOLDERS, brass, glass, 12" H,
4" D $275.00*

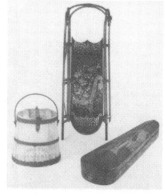

A-MA Mar. 1993   *Skinner, Inc.*
COVERED BUCKET, "Boston Oyster
Company," iron hoop, bail and hasp, losses,
12¼" H $302.50
SLED, painted, 42" L $880.00

VIOLIN CASE, red paint w/American
eagle, shield, inscribed "BG," "Musician,"
paint loss, 30½" L $467.50

A-OH Jan. 1993   *Garth's Auctions, Inc.*
AMISH QUILT, bright solid colors, 3 quilt-
ing patterns, 85" x 87" $1292.50
OIL PAINTING, flaking, 28" H, 23"
W $495.00
ROPE BED, curly maple, old refinish, 54"
H, 46" x 53" $550.00
SPLINT BASKET, damage, wear, 12½" H,
14½" sq. $71.50
SPLINT BASKET, 10" H, 17½" W, 9"
D $126.50

A-OH Nov. 1992   *Garth's Auctions, Inc.*

Row 1, Left to Right

TOP HAT, black beaver, miniature, "Knox, New York," orig. box worn $137.50
FEDORA, miniature, olive felt, silk band, "Stetson," orig. box $121.00
STRAW "BOATER," miniature, "Austin Co., New York," 5½" L $132.00
DERBY, miniature, brown felt, box has "Brown Derby" restaurant ad photos $104.50

Row 2, Left to Right

OXEN PULL TOY, wood, brown, blue paint, damage, losses, 11" L $660.00
PIPSQUEAK, rooster in wood cage, felt/feather bird, damage, silent, 4⅜" H $77.00
GRASSHOPPER PULL TOY, wood, animated, damage, 10" L.............. $148.50
BUTTER MOLD, pomegranate, crack, 4¾" D $38.50

Row 3, Left to Right

MEAT TENDERIZER, stoneware, "Pat'd Dec 25, 1877," wood handle, 9½" H $71.50
BUTTER MOLD, stave constructed w/pewter bands, wear, damage, 4½" H..... $93.50
PAPIER MACHE CAT, glass eyes, worn, damage repairs, 8" H $19.25
CUPBOARD, miniature, pine, cardboard back, damage, 9½" W, 10½" H $77.00
MINIATURE MUGS, 2 pcs., buff clay, blue glaze, 1⅜" H $5.50
CANDLESTICK, wood, blue paint, "Juan Jimez" scratched on bottom, 8½" H $27.50
REDWARE PITCHER, hound handle, molded floral, cherub design, dk. brown glaze, impressed label "Nathaniel Sellers, Upper Hanover, Pa.," chips, 8" H $192.50

A-OH Jan. 1993   *Garth's Auctions, Inc.*
OHIO WALL CUPBOARD, walnut, 2-pc., 85½" H, 52¼" W, 20½" D $7920.00
PEA PICKING BASKET, old red, 10" L.......................... $220.00
PEA PICKING BASKET, old white, 6" L.......................... $82.50
SPLINT BASKET, red, damage, 12" L.......................... $49.50
MELON RIB BASKET, damage, 15" D $60.50

A-OH Jan. 1993   *Garth's Auctions, Inc.*
CHIPPENDALE DESK, maple, refinished, repairs, replacements, 43½" H, 40" W, 19½" D $1430.00
THEOREMS, pr., on velvet, fruit, 9½" x 11½"...................... $880.00
PITCHER, flint enamel glaze, chips, 8⅝" H........................... $192.50
ROCKINGHAM CUSPIDOR, 3½" H........................... $181.50
ROCKINGHAM BOWL, wear, 3¼" H, 11½" D...................... $82.50
ROCKINGHAM SOAP DISH, 4⅞" L........................... $49.50
ROCKINGHAM PIE PLATES, 2 pcs., 9⅝", 10" D $143.00

A-ME May 1993   *James D. Julia, Inc.*
SIGN, Granite Iron Ware, paper, wrinkled, 12" x 28" $1450.00*
SIGN, Roessle Brewery, paper, 28" x 20" $650.00*
SCHOOLHOUSE CLOCK, Kramer Service Co., oak case, reversed numbers to be viewed in barbershop mirror, 14" x 22" x 4½" $400.00*

A-OH Jan. 1993   *Garth's Auctions, Inc.*
Row 1, Left to Right
DUCK PULL TOY, papier mache, 4"
L $115.50
CHICKS IN A BASKET BANK, redware,
flaking, 3¼" H $192.50
BIRD, carved wood, natural patina, label
"Canton, Ohio 1880" $49.50
CHILD IN HIGHCHAIR, tin, poly-
chrome $247.50
GRASSHOPPER, papier mache, worn
polychrome, glass eyes, loss, 7"
L $258.50
Row 2, Left to Right
BURL JAR, pin cushion lid, chip, 4¼" H,
4" D $93.50
WOOD BOOK, chip carved, 4⅝"
L $137.50
DESK SET, carved red stone, stump
shaped, worn red, green paint, chips, 6¾"
L $16.50
PEAFOWL NODDER, carved wood, 5"
H $77.00
Row 3, Left to Right
MINIATURE JUG, redware, yellow glaze,
4½" H $48.50
PIP SQUEAK, papier mache, felt, crepe
paper, "Germany," repair, 5" H $71.50
TURKEY CANDY CONTAINER, papier
mache, worn polychrome, 5½" H . . $38.50
WOOD CARVINGS, 3 pcs., 2 roosters, 1
squirrel, 3⅝" to 5¾" H $478.50

A-OH Jan. 1993   *Garth's Auctions, Inc.*
MINIATURE CHEST, pine, 4⅜" H, 5½"
W $49.50
BENTWOOD BOX, red, 5¼" H, 7½"
D $357.50
SPICE BOX, refinished cherry, 9"
L $110.00
BULL DOG, Ohio white clay, brown glaze,
8½" L $275.00
SHOREBIRD, painted wood, 11"
H $115.50
TREEN PLATE, 6" D $313.50
BENTWOOD BOX, jewel colored dec.,
3¼" D $93.50
SHAKER BOX, black repaint, stenciled
dec., copper tacks, 9" L $258.50
BENTWOOD HARVARD BOX, green
wash, loss, 6¼" L $187.00
BULL DOG, Ohio white clay, "Fred,"
broken, 5⅝" L $11.00
Row 1, Left to Right
OVOID JAR, redware, broken, 8⅜"
H $38.50
DECORATED BOX, beech, polychrome,
damage, 8⅝" L $561.00
BENTWOOD BOX, blue, red, green, rose,
crack, 4½" D $71.50
OVOID JUG, stoneware, grey salt glaze,
brown dec., incised fish, chips, hairlines,
10" H $302.50
OVOID JAR, stoneware, grey, brown, im-
pressed "Boston 1804," firing chips, 9½"
H $1210.00

A-OH Nov. 1992   *Garth's Auctions, Inc.*
HEPPLEWHITE BLANKET CHEST, pine,
red graining, repairs, replacements, 50" W,
22¾" D, 25¼" H $660.00
WOVEN SPLINT BASKET, 10" x 14",
8¾" H $192.50
BLANKET CHEST, miniature, pine, pop-
lar, black graining on red, repairs, replace-
ments, 18½" L $385.00
CARVED QUAIL, painted, "Will Birch
Chincoteague Island, Va.," 13" L . . . $82.50
WOVEN SPLINT BASKET, 10" x 14", 6"
H $93.50
HOGSCRAPER CANDLESTICK, iron,
push up, lip hanger, dent, 9" H . . . $275.00
HOGSCRAPER CANDLESTICK, iron,
push up marked "Fisher," lip hanger, re-
placements, 7¼" H $137.50
HOGSCRAPER CANDLESTICK, iron,
push up, loss, 7¾" H $66.00
CANDLE BOX, pine, orange paint, sliding
lid, 13¾" L $93.50

A-OH Apr. 1993   *Garth's Auctions, Inc.*
HANGING SHELVES, pine, old green
paint, cracks, 22" H, 20½" W, 7¼"
D $247.50
Row 1, Left to Right
SAFFRON BOX, Lehnware, poplar, paint

and decoupage dec., repair, wear, 5"
T $467.50
SUGAR BOWL, tole, brown, yellow on
red, battered, 3½" T $165.00
SNUFF BOX, birch bark, German inscrip-
tions, wear, 4" L $93.50
BENTWOOD BOX, poplar, white, blue on
red paint, 4½" L $302.50
SHORE BIRD, carved wood, black, grey
paint, 5" T $27.50
Row 2, Left to Right
TREEN BOX, beech, polychrome floral
dec., crack, 4" D $275.00
DOME TOP BOX, pine, polychrome floral
dec. on blue-green, replacements, chip, 7"
L $2.50
TREEN BOX, poplar, polychrome floral
dec. on brown, 4" D $247.50
Row 3, Left to Right
BOX, poplar, black, blue on red, repair,
10¼" L $522.50

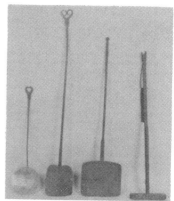

A-MA Dec. 1992   *Skinner, Inc.*
SKIMMER, brass, copper rivets, wrought
iron handle, 26¼" L $125.00*
PEEL, iron, bent, 44" L $150.00*
PEEL, iron, 37½" L $75.00*
DOUBLE CANDLEHOLDER, wood,
ratchet type, split, replacement, 34" to
44" L $175.00*

A-MA Jan. 1993   *Skinner, Inc.*
"DEWEY BOY" WHIRLIGIG, carved, painted, ca. 1900' 12" H $935.00
ROMAN SOLDIER WHIRLIGIG, carved, ca. 1900, 12" H $220.00

A-MA Oct. 1992   *Skinner, Inc.*
CHALKWARE STAG, polychrome, 19th c., paint loss, 16" H, 16" L $935.00

A-NY Nov. 1992   *David Rago Gallery*
ANDIRONS, pr., w/fireplace fender, marked Bradley & Hubbard, cast iron, wear $500.00*

A-OH Apr. 1993   *Garth's Auctions, Inc.*
SUGAR BUCKET, all wood, orange stain, damage, 7¼" T $192.50
BRONZE MOLD, for casting pewter spoons, 9" L $330.00
BOX, curly maple, walnut trim, old refinish, 10⅝" L $286.00
BENTWOOD BOX, Harvard Shaker, old varnish, damage, 5½" L $49.50
CUSTARD CUP, blue, white sponge spatter, chip, 2⅜" T $49.50
BETTY LAMP, wrought iron, swivel lid, no pick, 3½" T $137.50
MINER'S LAMP, cast iron, indistinct label, hammers, 3½" T $170.50
CHAMBER POT, yellowware, white, dk. brown, red, wear, hairlines, 4" H, 6" D $192.50
Row 2, Left to Right
PLATE, purple, white stick spatter, impressed "George Jones, Stoke on Trent," stains, hairlines $27.50
FLOWER POT, pottery, green, brown speckled glaze, 5" T $33.00
BASKET, green paint, polychrome fruit, 9¼" L $104.50
CHARGER, redware, coggeled rim, wear, flakes, hairline $82.50
THREAD CADDY, bentwood, pincushion top, old varnish, repair, losses, 3¾" T $8.25
SKATER'S LAMP, brass, "Orion, Made in Germany," 6½" T $126.50
CUP & SAUCER, oversize, blue, white sponge spatter, chip $60.50

A-ME Feb. 1993   *James D, Julia, Inc.*
SCONCES, pr., tin, mirrored, 12" W, 20" T $300.00*
DOUBLE CANDLE HOLDER, carved wood, 35" L $1100.00*
EGG CRATE, Pennsylvania Dutch, 11" H, 10" W, 5¼" D $125.00*

A-ME Feb. 1993   *James D, Julia, Inc.*
BLANKET CHEST, red, black swirl paint, 22" H, 42" W, 16" D $450.00*
HAT BOX, labeled "Fancy boxes, hat cases and band boxes, William Warren, Baltimore," form of Admiral's hat, no cover, 11" H, 21" L $250.00*
WELCOME MAT, hooked, 22" x 34" $500.00*
BAND BOX, labeled "Henry Barnes No. 33, Jones Alley, Philadelphia," wallpaper w/columns, swags, roses, 12" H, 17" W, 13" D $600.00*

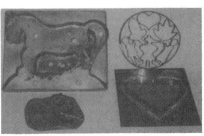

A-PA May 1993   *Alderfer Auction Co.*
TIN COOKIE CUTTERS
Row 1, Left to Right
HORSE, 9½" L $150.00
ROUND, w/men and Mickey Mouse $35.00
Row 2, Left to Right
EAGLE AND HEART $55.00

A-MA Aug. 1993   *Skinner, Inc.*
SHELLWORK VALENTINE, 19th c., imperfections, 10" D $3575.00

A-MA July 1993   *Skinner, Inc.*
VICTOR TALKING MACHINE, oak
horn $2090.00

A-NY Nov. 1992   *David Rago Gallery*
BOOKENDS, 5 pcs., hammered copper, each w/Roycroft orb and cross mark, 8¾" H,
5¾" W $275.00*
TABLE LAMP, unmarked Heintz Art Metal Shop, sterling on bronze helmet shade, 15"
T $700.00*
BUD VASES, pr., by Wilcox Silver Plate Co. .... NS
CHAMBER STICK, Roycroft orb and cross mark, hammered copper, 5¾" L .. $100.00*
OVAL TRAY, hammered copper, unmarked Gustav Stickley, 11¼" W, 23" L ... $300.00*
VASE, by Heintz Art Metal Shop, sterling-on-bronze, 6" T $150.00*
HUMIDOR TROPHY, sterling on bronze, by Heintz Art Metal Shop, 10" T $150.00*
BOOKENDS, pr., hammered copper, Roycroft orb & cross mark, 5" H, 4" W ... $225.00*

A-OH Nov. 1992   *Garth's Auctions, Inc.*
NOTE: *All Pewter unless noted.*
MULE CHEST, walnut, soft finish, hinged
lid with till, minor edge damage, age
cracks, replacements, 41" W, 18½" D, 39"
H....................... $1100.00
TALL POT, "Calder" touch, Jacobs #68,
wear, pitting, holes, 11¼" H ... $104.50
PLATE, "Love" touch, Jacobs #207, minor
scratches, 7⅞" $242.00
COMMUNION GOBLET, pitting, 5¼"
H...........................$11.00
PLATE, wear, pitting, 8⅜" $88.00
CANDLESTICK, 10¾" H.......$82.50
TUMBLER, 3⅛" H $60.50
TUMBLER, "A.G." touch, Jacobs #155,
wear, pitting, 3⅛" H $27.50
PLATE, Eagle touch marks, "G. Lightner,
Baltimore, Jacobs #205, wear, pitting,
7⅞"........................$77.00
TALLPOT, "H. Homan" touch, wear, poor
repairs, 11¼" H...............$55.00

A-PA May 1993   *Alderfer Auction Co.*
CORNER CUPBOARD, figured woods $2700.00
HAT BOX, decorated wood $200.00
BASKET, decorated Algonkian $85.00
QUILT, Lone Star $1950.00
CHAIRS, 6 pcs., (2 illus.), decorated $1650.00
STAND, salmon decorated... $2700.00
FLOWERPOT, yellow, green brown $1050.00
RUNNER, Shahsivan.. $500.00

A-OH Apr. 1993　　*Garth's Auctions, Inc.*
Row 1, Left to Right
COOKIE BOARD, carved beech, metal edging, age cracks, 6¼" x 18" $357.50
BUTTER PRINT, poplar, 3½" x 5" $165.00
ORNAMENT, carved wood, "E.R.," 1¾" x 5½" $198.00
FRINEDSHIP FAN, all poplar, inscriptions and autographs, 1876, damage .. $110.00
LEATHER WORKING TOOL, all wood, maple, burl, 8" L $44.00
Row 2, Left to Right
BUTTER PRINT, acorn, oak leaf, 3¾" D $220.00
DOUGH SCRAPER, wrought iron, damage, 4" L $110.00
Row 3, Left to Right
BUTTER PRINT, tulip, star, cracks, 3¼" x 4⅞" $181.50
BUTTER WORKER, initials "M.A.A.," 7¾" L $33.00
FROG, cast iron, old green, 5½" L $60.50
BUTTER PRINT, carved sheaf, 8½" T $27.50

A-PA May 1993　　*Alderfer Auction Co.*
DUTCH CUPBOARD, grained $15000.00
BASKET, Algonkian, square base $300.00
QUILT, Sixteen Stars $525.00
WINDSOR CHAIR, ca. 1790 .... $450.00
TALL CLOCK, Michael Strieby $5400.00
RUNNER, Anatolian $850.00

A-OH Apr. 1993　　*Garth's Auctions, Inc.*
CUPBOARD, pine, refinished, replacements, 90" H, 58" W, 17¾" D $495.00
STONEWARE CROCK, by Red Wing, cobalt quill work, "20," 22½" T .. $165.00

A-OH Nov. 1992　　*Garth's Auctions, Inc.*
BANQUET TABLES, pr., refinished mahogany, veneered aprons, damage, repairs, replacements, additions, 21½" x 46½", 30" H $495.00
CANDLESTICKS, set of 4, brass, victorian, 10" H $242.00
HOT WATER PLATE, English pewter, Henry & Richard Joseph touchmarks, battered, 8" D $165.00
COMMUNION FLAGON, pewter, repair, 14½" H $49.50
HOT WATER PLATE, English pewter, "Cocks, London," losses, 7¾" D $5.50
KETTLE SHELF, wrought iron, reticulated brass top, 11¾" H $313.50
GLASS GLOBE, silver mercury, 8" H $93.50

A-OH Nov. 1992　　*Garth's Auctions, Inc.*
CORNER CUPBOARD, walnut, old glass, old refinish, replacements, repairs, 84" H, 59" W $1540.00
JACQUARD COVERLET, navy, natural, wear, damage, 80" x 86" $660.00
HORSE WEATHERVANE, wood, white paint, repairs, damage, 24" H $77.00
STONEWARE JUG, cobalt slip dec., chips, 16" H $220.00

A-OH Nov. 1992   *Garth's Auctions, Inc.*
NOTE: Top row carved wooden whirlygig ornaments w/worn polychrome.
Row 1, Left to Right
HOBO, cracks, chip, 10" H $66.00
SAIL BOAT, loss, 11" H $27.50
MAN, w/cigar, 7¾" H $93.50
MAN, w/staff, 11½" H $27.50
PUPPET HEAD, Punch, red leather collar, cap, 9" H $71.50
Row 2, Left to Right
CARVED BIRD, blue, red paint, on driftwood, 5" H $11.00
HEART BOX, mahogany, damage, 2⅝" L $137.50
BIRD TOY, pewter, 1⅞" H $11.00
RATTLE, tin, gold, red japanning, porcelain mouth piece, 6¼" L $27.50
Row 3, Left to Right
CARPET BALL, black, white spatter, 3⅝" D $170.50
CARPET BALL, black, white spatter, 3½" D $220.00
CARPET BALL, brown, white plaid, 3¼" D $126.50
CARPET BALL, black, white plaid, damage, 3¼" D $55.00
PIPSQUEAK, chicken, papier mache, yellow, red, black damage, 8¾" H ... $49.50

A-OH Feb. 1993   *Garth's Auctions, Inc.*
CHIPPENDALE HIGH CHEST, maple, pine, poplar, secret drawer, refinished, repairs, replacements, 39¾" W, 20¾" D, 56½" H $5610.00
STONEWARE JUG, labeled "Nichols and Boynton, Burlington Vt. 4," cobalt decoration, hairline, 17¼" H $126.50

A-MA Jun. 1993   *Skinner, Inc.*
CAROUSEL HORSE, carved wood, old repaint, 19th c., 37" H, 48" W, 13" D $1650.00

A-ME Feb. 1993   *James D, Julia, Inc.*
CAROUSEL HORSE, carved, 58" H, 52" L $1700.00*

A-OH Nov. 1992   *Garth's Auctions, Inc.*
WINDSOR HIGH CHAIR, bamboo, adult size, old black repaint over green and earlier colors, damage, repairs, 30¼" seat, 47¼" H $605.00
DESK, walnut with poplar, dovetailed feet and drawers, lid has scratch carved compass design, edge damage, age cracks, replacements, 30" W, 19" D, 44¼" H $1265.00
CANDLESTICKS, pewter, pair, pushups, 8¾" H $253.00
TEAPOT, pewter, "Morey & Ober, Boston" touch, 6⅝" H $214.50
CREAMER, pewter, "Sellew & Co., Cincinnati," 6" H $148.50

A-OH Nov. 1992   *Garth's Auctions, Inc.*
PIE SAFE, butternut, refinished, punched tin panels, loss, 37¾" W, 17¾" D, 51" H plus crest $825.00
BATTER PITCHER, stoneware, dk. brown Albany slip, Impressed "4," loss, 9¼" H $82.50
DOME TOP BOX, old black paint, wear, 12¾" L $165.00
REDWARE PITCHER, green-amber glaze, chips, wear, 8¼" H $209.00
BEDWARMER, brass, tooled lid, refinished handle, 43" L $357.50

A-PA May 1993   *Alderfer Auction Co.*
COFFEE GRINDER, Enterprise, Philadelphia, worn paint, rrepair, 27" T ... $500.00

A-OH March. 1993   *Garth's Auctions, Inc.*
QUILT, Carolina lily, red, blue on white ground, wear, stains, 71" x 71" ... $187.00
ARROWBACK SETTLE BENCH, repairs, replacements, refinished, 76" L .. $385.00

A-OH Nov. 1992   *Garth's Auctions, Inc.*
Row 1, Left to Right
BUTTER MOLD, rose design, old varnish, 5" x 8" $71.50
PAUL REVERE LANTERN, miniature, punched tin, rust, 5¾" H $93.50
PRESSING IRON, brass, engraved designs, small iron ingot, 5¾" L $170.50
TEA KETTLE, miniature, copper, 2" H $104.50
BUTTER MOLD, 4-part "TC" design, scrubbed, cracks, losses, 5½" x 6¼" $11.00
EAGLE SNOWBIRDS, pr., cast iron, black tar over pitted iron, 5¼" H $33.00
Row 2, Left to Right
STONEWARE PITCHER, blue, white, molded bark, King Gambrinus, 7½" H . . . $165.00
CAT DOORSTOP, cast iron, black, 8" H $71.50
GREYHOUND DOORSTOP, cast iron, red, 12½" L $148.50
PITCHER, red clay, shiny black glaze, chip, 7" H $22.00
CARVED BEAR, old finish, age cracks, 8" H $71.50
Row 3, Left to Right
BOSTON BULL DOORSTOP, cast iron, old brown, white repaint, 9¼" H $60.50
COFFEE GRINDER, cherry, pewter hopper, "E. Nagle, Maker," 10" H $165.00
CAMPBELL KIDS DOORSTOP, cast iron, worn polychrome, 8½" H $159.50
BOSTON BULL DOORSTOP, cast iron, worn black, white paint, 9¼" H $60.50

A-OH Jan. 1993   *Garth's Auctions, Inc.*
BEDWARMER, brass, engraved rooster, cherry handle, 44½" L $440.00
KRAUT CUTTER, pine, red finish, scratch carved "1801," 19¼" L $93.50
CUTTING BOARD, *butternut, 17½" H, 10" W* *$71.50*
GRATER, punched tin, pine back, 13½" L $137.50
COOKIE BOARD, poplar, 19" x 23" $159.50
BENTWOOD CARRIER, worn red paint, repair, damage, 12¼" L $379.50
BOX, pine, grey, black repaint, damage, 14" H, 15½" W, 13¾" D $82.50
COUNTRY BIN, pine, hardwood, wear, damage, repairs, 41" H, 38" W, 18" D $715.00
NOGGIN PITCHERS, 3 pcs., old patina, 5½" H to 8¾" H $643.50

A-OH Feb. 1993   *Garth's Auctions, Inc.*
CHIPPENDALE CHEST, cherry, pine, old refinish, replacements, repair, 41¾" W, 20½" D, 35¼" H $2640.00
PEWTER LAMP, marked "Sellew & Co, Cincinnati," battered, repairs, 8½" H $2640.00
CANTON VEGETABLE DISH, lid, blue, white, "China," flakes, 10½" L $93.50
BRASS LAMP, replaced burner, 8½" H $55.00
CANTON TALL PITCHER, blue, white, 15¾" H $1155.00

A-MA Mar. 1993   *Skinner, Inc.*
FIRE BUCKET, painted, decorated w/ burning building, "Charles W. Eliot," cracks, paint loss, 8½" H $880.00

A-ME May 1993   *James D. Julia, Inc.*
LUNCH BOX, Bagley's Burley Boy, tin, chips, rust, scratches, 6½" x 4" x 5" $2200.00*

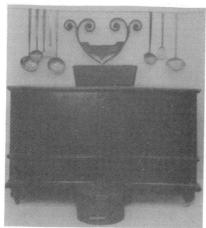

A-OH Nov. 1992   *Garth's Auctions, Inc.*
UTENSILS, set of 5, iron and brass, all marked, "F.B.S. Canton, O. Pat. Jan. 26 '86," pitting, 19" L $398.75
BOOT SCRAPER, wrought iron, 23½" W., 20½" H $770.00
UTENSILS, set of 3, iron and brass, 2 marked, "F.B.S. Canton, O. Pat. Jan. 26 '86." $398.75
DECORATED BOX, Pine with worn original red paint with black and yellow striping, damage, age crack on bottom, 11¼" x 17¼", 5¾" H $132.00
BENTWOOD BOX, round, lid, wire bail, copper tacks, edge damage, 12" D, 6¾" H $247.50
OHIO BLANKET CHEST, poplar, worn brown and green repaint, dovetailed case, replacements, faded initials and date "D.N. 1859," 49¾" W, 20¾" D., 31" H $330.00

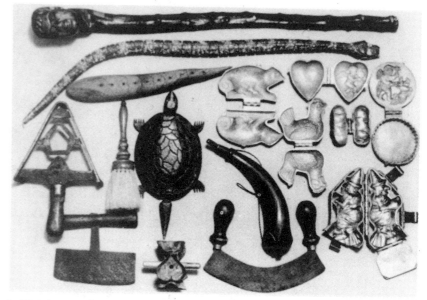

A-OH Feb. 1993   *Garth's Auctions, Inc.*
WALKING STICK, age cracks, damage, 27½" L $181.50
WOODEN SNAKE, jointed, original yellow, black, brown paint, 29" L $159.50
WOODEN FISH, jointed, natural patina, 12½" L $27.50
ICE CREAM MOLD, pewter, possom, 5" L $115.50
ICE CREAM MOLDS, 3 pcs, heart, cherubs, potato $148.50
TRIVET, wrought iron, wood handle, 9¾" L $27.50
HORSE HAIR BRUSH, ash handle, 8¼" L $11.00
TURTLE PULL-TOY, homemade, articulated leather feet, wood head and tail, old polychrome, 11" L $137.50
FOOD CHOPPERS, 2 pcs., straight blade w/handle, crescent blade w/double handles, both have label, cracks $88.00
MULTIPLE ROLLING COOKIE CUTTER, tin, aluminum, also wooden funnel and square tin sander not illus. $104.50
POWDER HORN, 10" L $71.50
CHOCOLATE MOLD, folding tin, 6" H $93.50

A-OH March. 1993   *Garth's Auctions, Inc.*
HOOKED RAG RUG, grey stripe, oak leaf borders, shades of rose, green, purple, ivory, 28" x 92" $467.50
MULE CHEST, pine, chestnut, red-brown flame graining, damage, replacements, 40½" W, 17" D, 37½" H $1430.00
SALT BOX, mahogany, old refinish, 8½" W, 13¾" H $577.50
TREEN COMPOTE, red, black, green paint, worn, 12" D, 5¾" H $550.00

A-OH Nov. 1992   *Garth's Auctions, Inc.*
CUPBOARD, poplar, cleaned to old blue, 3 shelves, hole in door has tin repair, 49¼" W, 15¾" D, 72" H $1540.00
JACQUARD COVERLET, two piece, single weave, labeled corners, "W. in Mt. Vernon, Knox County, Ohio by Jacob and Michael Ardner 1855," navy and natural white, wear, 74" x 84" $99.00
KETTLE SHELF, iron and brass, reticulated top $286.00
SHAKER SPINNING WHEEL, hardwood, natural finish, branded label "Thompson," distaff incomplete, replacement, 33" H $192.50

A-OH Nov. 1992   *Garth's Auctions, Inc.*
PEWTER UNLESS NOTED
PEWTER CUPBOARD, walnut, 1-piece, old refinish, repairs, replacements, 40½" W, 18½" D, 76½" H $1100.00

Row 1, Left to Right
FRENCH MEASURES, 7 pcs., various makers $423.50
CONTINENTAL PLATES, pr., crowned rose touch, scratches, 9" D $121.00
INKWELL, hinged lid, loss, 2¼" H $82.50
QUART MEASURE, brass rim, English, "John Warne," battered, 5¾" H $93.50

Row 2, Left to Right
SIDE SPOUT MEASURE, English, battered, repair $93.50
PLATES, 2 pcs., 1 w/angel touch, wear, scratches, 9½" D $121.00
PINT MEASURE, English, monogramed, dents, 6¼" H $49.50
CONTINENTAL FLAGON, 3 satyr heads, damage, 7¾" H $11.00
BELLIED TANKARD, hinged lid, crack, repair, 7" H $115.50
SIDE SPOUT POT, English, wood handle, "Sheffield," 8" H $115.50

Row 3, Left to Right
CONTINENTAL PITCHER, swirl design, hinged lid, angel touch 6½" H $71.50
CONTINENTAL PITCHER, hinged lid, wear, battered, repair, 4¾" H $11.00
CONTINENTAL PLATES, 3 pcs., angel touch, wear, scratches, 9" D $165.00
CONTINENTAL PORRINGER, double handled, out of round, 5¾" D $49.50
INKWELL, wide flat base, hinged lid, ceramic insert, 7" D $137.50
BELLIED TANKARDS, 2 pcs., engraved "Elsia May" and "Mary Jane," battered, 3¼" H, 3" H $77.00
TEA CADDY, American, almond shaped, cut designs, "B.G.S. & Co." touch, wear, pitted, 3¾" H $330.00

Row 4, Left to Right
CONTINENTAL FLAGON, lid engraved "G.O.P. 1842," German eagle touch, 10" H $192.50
CONTINENTAL CHARGER, angel touch, "Georg Kling," wear, 12½" D $110.00
CONTINENTAL FLAGON, lid engraved "A.R.G. 1811," fleur de lies touch, battered, repair, 12½" H $192.50
CONTINENTAL GREASE LAMP, tin wick support, 10¼" H $71.50
CONTINENTAL FLAGON, twist ring lid, spout flap and shield, "B.W.," battered, 11¾" H $143.00
CONTINENTAL PLATE, faint touch, wear, scratches, 11½" D $82.50
CONTINENTAL FLAGON, floral engraving w/couple on bench, German inscription, "F.C.S. 1809," repair, 9½" H . . $165.00

Bottom
CONTINENTAL PLATE, engraved designs, "B.S. 1790," 12½" D $143.00

A-OH Nov. 1992   *Garth's Auctions, Inc.*
Row 1, Left to Right
TRIVET, adjustable, iron, hoof-like feet $99.00
TRIVET, wrought iron, shoe feet $27.50
FRUIT SHAPED BANKS, seven pieces, Mexican pottery, painted bright colors $60.50
JUG, white clay, black sponging, 5½" H $22.00

Row 2, Left to Right
LOOM LIGHT, wrought iron, sawtooth ratchet w/rushlight holder, oval pan, two candle sockets w/pushups . . . $880.00
WOOD CARVING, woodpecker on tree, age cracks 12" H $27.50
FIGURAL CLOCK, cast iron, worn polychrome, marked "Bradley & Hubbard, Patented July 14, 1857," working, replacements, damage, 16¼" H $715.00
WOOD CARVING, bearded man, worn polychrome, wear, edge damage, 10½" H $55.00
SEWERPIPE OWL, incised "Ross Clay Plant," chipped and damaged, not free standing, 12¼" H $77.00
LOOM LIGHT, wrought iron, adjustable candle socket, heart shaped hanger, pitted, 23" H $275.00

A-OH Jan. 1993   *Garth's Auctions, Inc.*
EMPIRE STAND, cherry, curly maple, burl veneer, refinished, stained, repairs, 29½" H, 22" W, 19" D $715.00
WINDSOR ARMCHAIR, added rockers, new paint, 43¾" H $605.00
HORSE PULL TOY, wood, cast iron wheels, replacements, losses, 19½" L $192.50
CANDLE BOX, poplar, worn brown, red, white, black, tan, damage, 14¼" L $550.00
CHALK CAT, brown, white, blue, wear, chips, 12" L $110.00

A-OH Apr. 1993   *Garth's Auctions, Inc.*
SAMPLER, silk on homespun linen, black, olive, lt. blue, stains, holes, 13½" x 11" $476.50
SPICE BOX, walnut, refinished, repairs $110.00
SAMPLER, silk on homespun linen, black, rust, olive, yellow, green, white, inscribed and dated 1811, 16½" x 11" $275.00
MULE CHEST, poplar, refinished, repairs, mismatched pulls, 43" H, 41" W, 18½" D $330.00
BEDWARMER, engraved copper, refinished handle, split, replacement, 45½" L $165.00
STONEWARE JUG, cobalt brush work, labeled, "C. Crolius Manufacturer, New York," professionally restored $110.00

A-OH July 1993   *Garth's Auctions, Inc.*
GERMAN VORSCHRIFT FRAKTUR, pen, ink, watercolor on paper, signed "P.W.J. Brown 1792," Penn., damage, stains, repair, 15¾" H, 18" W $550.00
FRAKTUR BIRTH RECORD, pen, ink, watercolor on paper, 1840 birth of Mahlon B. Spang, damage, 11⅝" H, 9⅝" W $1210.00*
GERMAN CALLIGRAPHY, black ink on paper, stains, tape, 15½" H, 19" W $33.00
BLANKET CHEST, pine, brown, yellow vinegar graining, wear, damage, repair, 29¾" H, 48½" W, 20½" D $715.00
COOT, by Bill Goenne, wear, glass eyes, 11½" L $82.50
CANADA GOOSE, by Phil Soukup, Ohio, cork body, wood head, glass eyes, 21" L $181.50
CANADA GOOSE, by Phil Soukup, Ohio, cork body, wood head, glass eyes, 19" L $181.50

A-OH Jan. 1993   *Garth's Auctions, Inc.*
BLANKET CHEST, poplar, worn red graining, 9½" H, 12½" W, 8" D $550.00
DOUBLE SALT, treen, maple, floral engraved, "F.J. 1890," crack, 7¾" H $1952.50
WATERCOLOR, ink, on paper, inscription "Canada," stains, 9½" x 7¾" $38.50
STONEWARE DOG, white clay, clear glaze, green spots, 6¼" H $770.00

A-OH July 1993   *Garth's Auctions, Inc.*
WATER BENCH, pine, poplar, refinished, 54" H, 42" W, 18" D $1760.00
STONEWARE JUG, labeled "J. & E. Norton, Bennington," cobalt slip dec., wear, chips, 10½" T $357.50
SEWERPIPE BANK, molded and tooled pig, green-brown salt glaze, no bottom, 9¼" T $423.50
BASKET, black paint, wear, damage, 15" x 17", 9" T $137.50
STONEWARE PITCHER, cobalt brushed dec., 14½" T $1760.00

A-OH March. 1993   *Garth's Auctions, Inc.*
CUTTING BOARDS, 3 pcs., (1 illus.), wear, cracks, 8½" x 16½" $57.75
FIREPLACE TRAMMEL, 3 part, 40½" W $385.00
FOOD MOLD, tin, fish, 12" L $27.50
CUTTING BOARD, wear, 11" x 22½" $27.50
HIGH CHAIR, natural finish, splint seat, 31" H $247.50
SAUSAGE GRINDER, cherry and others, metal teeth, refinished, 17" L $38.50
ARMCHAIR ROCKER, maple, old refinish, added rockers, 40½" H $110.00
CARVED CHICKEN, 20th c. folk art, 15" L $60.50
ANDIRONS, pr., losses, 11½" H .. $49.50

A-OH Feb. 1993   *Garth's Auctions, Inc.*
HOOKED RUG, floral design, sculptural detail, soft colors, wear, damage, 18" x 28" $159.50
DRYING RACK, pine, dark patina, mortised and pinned bars, 47" W, 64" H $192.50
SPLAY LEG STAND, walnut, cherry, refinished, replacements, 20¾" sq., 27¾" H $220.00
CRADLE, poplar, worn drk. finish, dovetailed, 42" L $275.00
FRUIT COMPOTE, wood, worn brown w/blue stripes, 8½" sq., 7½" H ...$38.50
WOVEN SPLINT BASKET, weathered grey, damage, 14" x 18", 8" H $93.50
WOVEN SPLINT BASKET, oval, weathered grey, 11" x 16", 8½" H $60.50
WOVEN SPLINT BASKET, oval, old varnish, 15" x 16", 6½" H $203.50
WOVEN SPLINT BASKET, traces of red, damage 10½" x 13½", 5" H...$82.50
STONEWARE JAR, ovoid, labeled "Hamilton, Greensboro, Pa. 8," brushed cobalt decoration, crack, 18½" H $853.50

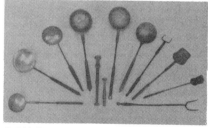

A-MA Dec. 1992   *Skinner, Inc.*
LADLE, copper, wrought iron handle, 17¾" L $120.00*
LADLE, brass, wrought iron handle, 19½" L $140.00*
SKIMMER, copper, wrought iron handle, repair, 18½" L $90.00*
DIPPER, copper, wrought iron handle, dents, 20¾" L $40.00*
MUDDLER, wood, 12½" L $35.00*
MUDDLER, maple, 7" L $30.00*
DIPPER, copper, wrought iron handle, repairs, dents, 23½" L $40.00*
LADLE, wrought iron, 19⅜" L .. $50.00*
FORK, wrought iron, 19½" L.... $25.00*
SPATULA, wrought iron, 19" L $100.00*
SPATULA, wrought iron, 15¾" L $22.00*
FORK, wrought iron, 19⅝" L.... $30.00*

A-OH Nov. 1992   *Garth's Auctions, Inc.*
CRIB QUILT, pieced twenty-five patch, lavender, white, gold, 32" x 46½" $88.00
CHIPPENDALE TILT-TOP TEA TABLE, maple, worn reddish brown finish, repair, replacement, 26½" D, 26" H . . $1100.00
KNIFE BOX, cleaned to old red and green, edge damage, 9" x 15" . . $214.50

A-OH May 1993   *Garth's Auctions, Inc.*
ROUND BUTTER PRINTS
Row 1, Left to Right
LOLLIPOP, star, worn, 7⅜" L . . . $302.50
EAGLE, repair, 4⅜" D $220.00
POMEGRANATE, 5⅛" D $247.50
COW & DOLL, 3" D $275.00
LOLLIPOP, star flower, 9" L $110.00
Row 2, Left to Right
FLOWERS, loss, 4" D $49.50
FLOWERS, 3½" D $110.00
SHEAF, yellow, 4¼" D $330.00
Row 3, Left to Right
FLOWER, damage, 3½" D $55.00
LEAF, loss, 4⅞" D $82.50
POMEGRANATE, chips, crack, 4¼" D $71.50
Row 4, Left to Right
STAR FLOWER, crack, 5½" D . . $127.50
FRUIT, stains, 4" D $330.00
PINEAPPLE, scrubbed, 4½" D . . $165.00
STAR, wear, cracks, 5½" D $60.50

A-OH Jan. 1993   *Garth's Auctions, Inc.*
TREEN ITEMS
BUTTER PADDLE, ivory inlaid maple, "Annie 1924," 10¼" L $330.00
CARVED SPOON, engraved bowl, 6¼" L $60.50
BUTTER PRINT, pine, star flower design both sides, 8¾" L.............$550.00
BUTTER SCOOP, burl, 11½"L . . $583.00
MINIATURE PADDLE, burl, 4¾" L $335.50
MINIATURE SPOON, burl, 5" L $165.00
BUTTER PRINT, heart, scrubbed, stains, 6½" L $165.00
BUTTER PADDLE, bird's head hook, wear, 10" L.................$495.00
BUTTER PRINT, walnut, tulip, scrubbed, loss, 4½" D.................$115.50
BUTTER PRINT, flower, scrubbed, stains, crack, 3⅜" D $104.50
BUTTER PADDLE, maple, worn, cracks, 11" L........................$71.50
BUTTER PADDLE, maple, refinished, 9½" L $165.00
BUTTER PADDLE, chestnut, 12¼" L $184.50
ROLLING PIN, curly maple, 21" L $148.50

A-OH July 1993   *Garth's Auctions, Inc.*
WINDSOR ARMCHAIR, dk. varnish stain, red base, signed "Burgess," old repairs, 37¼" T $330.00
ANDIRONS, wrought iron, spit rests, 13½" T $412.50
ARCHITECTURAL MIRROR, refinished pine, repairs, 21½" H, 13½" W . . . $165.00
CHALK DOG, red, green, brown paint, wear, damage, 6" H $363.00
CHIPPENDALE CANDLESTAND, cherry, black paint, replacement, 25" T. . . $660.00

A-OH March. 1993   *Garth's Auctions, Inc.*
QUILT, star pat. in blue print, white, red, pink calico, goldenrod, stains, tear, 70" x 70" $495.00
ROPE BED, poplar, refinished, 55" x 72", 43½" H $203.50
JACQUARD COVERLET, blue, gold, rose, natural, wear, stains, fading, bleeding, damage, 76" x 86" $49.50
CABIN CRUISER MODEL, motor driven prop, lights, "John Conrad, Bermuda," damage, 34" L...................$522.50

A-MA Jan. 1993   *Skinner, Inc.*
CHIME CABINET, painted poplar, ca. 1840, 48" H, 15" W, 7" D $660.00

A-OH Apr. 1993   *Garth's Auctions, Inc.*
CANDLE CHANDELIER, wire arms, tin sockets, old repro., 19" T $220.00
CHEESE PRESS, pine, hardwood, age cracks, 45¾" T $82.50
CUPBOARD, pine, worn refinish, 75" H, 30" W, 14¾" D $330.00
BASKET, blue trim, damage, 13" H, 16" D $33.00
CANDLE MOLD, tin, 52" L $357.50

A-OH Nov. 1992   *Garth's Auctions, Inc.*
CHEST, miniature, pine, brown graining over grey, red paint trim, wear, chipping, 11" W, 6½" D, 10½" H ... $687.50
HANGING BOX, pine and poplar, original red, black and white paint, hinged lid, 15½" H $2805.00
FOLK ART CARVING, comical stylized details, original polychrome paint, by Anton Zeleznick, Potter Co., N.Y., 11½" H $1375.00
PAUL REVERE LANTERN, miniature, punched brass, 3⅜" H $440.00
KETTLE LAMP, miniature, wrought iron and brass, fine details, 3⅝" H .. $880.00

A-OH Apr. 1993   *Garth's Auctions, Inc.*
SAMPLER, silk on homespun linen, shades of green, brown, blue, pink, black, white, "Catherine Carpenter, her sampler, aged 9 years, 1787," 16¾" x 18" $3210.00
CANDLE BOX, tin, black paint, 10½" L $132.00
CHIPPENDALE CANDLESTAND, cherry refinished, repairs, replacements, cracks, 20¼" H, 16½" x 16¼" $385.00
WINDSOR SIDE CHAIR, bamboo turnings, legs, crack, 37" H $275.00
TOASTING FORK, brass, adjustable, weighted bvase, dents $165.00

A-OH Apr. 1993   *Garth's Auctions, Inc.*
APOTHECARY CHEST, pine, replacements, 36" H, 33" W, 18¼" D ... $2310.00
FRAKTUR CERTIFICATE, ink, watercolor, German text w/"P. Bergman 1776," stains, damage, 18½" x 15" $220.00
WINDSOR SIDE CHAIRS, set of 6, (1 illus.), bamboo, 33¾" T $627.00
CANDLE LANTERN, tin, glass sides, black paint, 11¼" T $137.50
CANDLE SCONCE, label "J.S. Grose," 13½" T $137.50
CANDLE LANTERN, tin, black paint, 13" T $137.50
CANDLE LANTERN, tin, glass sides, damage 11½" T $115.50
FOOT WARMER, punched tin, walnut frame, 5¾" H, 7½" W, 9" D $330.00

A-OH Nov. 1992   *Garth's Auctions, Inc.*
PIECED QUILT, prints, navy blue and pink calico, stains, wear, 70" x 80" $440.00
CANNONBALL ROPE BED, maple and cherry, refinished, blanket rail moved, replacements 55" x 78", 59" H ... $357.50
STAND, cherry, refinished, dovetailed drawer, 18½" x 19", 29" H $357.50
CHEST, curly maple, old finish, cockbeaded drawers, handmade reproduction, 16⅜" x 27½", 27" H $770.00

A-OH Nov. 1992   *Garth's Auctions, Inc.*
OIL ON WOODEN KEG LID, primitive landscape by Seymore Lindsay, Lexington, OH 1848-1927, unsigned, 14" ... $66.00
FOLK ART COFFEE TABLE, mahogany, relief carved zodiac, flowers, animals, etc., 26" x 44", 17" H $385.00
CARVED BIRD, polychrome paint, button eyes, damage, repairs, 17" H ... $220.00
CARVED BALD EAGLE, painted, 30" H $275.00
TRAIN, tin, flaking original black, gold and red paint, 38" L $3080.00

A-OH Nov. 1992 *Garth's Auctions, Inc.*

Row 1, Left to Right

BURL BOWL, worn original red paint with red and black swags, rim crack, 4½" D, 2" H $357.50

DIPPER, maple with burl, minor rim crack, 2¾" D $467.50

CARVED BOWL, butternut, oblong, old varnish, 2⅝" x 4⅝" $82.50

TURNED JAR, lid, old varnish, 3⅜" D, 2¾" H $93.50

Row 2, Left to Right

PEASE TURNED JAR, lid, old worn varnish, 4½" H $181.50

PEASE TURNED JAR, lid, old varnish, 3½" H $115.50

PEASE TURNED JAR, lid, old varnish, 2¾" H $181.50

PEASE TURNED JAR, lid, old varnish, 2¾" H $170.50

PEASE TURNED JAR, lid, old varnish, 2⅜" H $192.50

PEASE TURNED JAR, lid, 1½" H $280.50

GOBLET, ash burl, shiny varnish, 3⅜" H $60.50

Row 3, Left to Right

BURL BOWL, old finish, stains, 5" D, 1⅝" H $476.50

BOWL, birch, with worn brown paint, 4" x 6", 1" H $214.50

PEASE TEAPOT, old dark finish, wire bail, drilled hole in bottom, 5" D, 2⅞" H $357.50

BURL BOWL, medium finish, 5" D, 1⅞" H $302.50

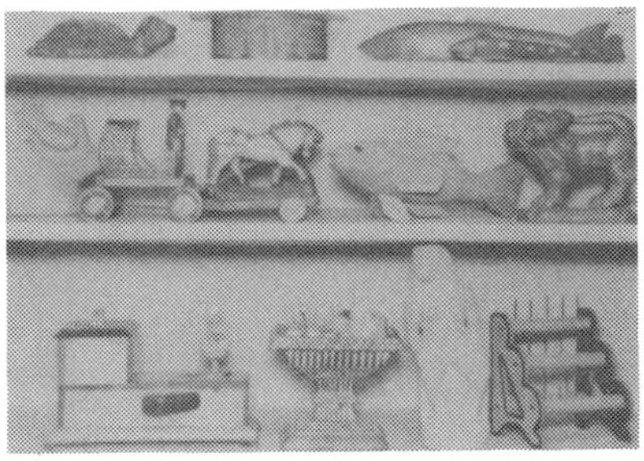

A-OH Nov. 1992 *Garth's Auctions, Inc.*

Row 1, Left to Right

SEWERPIPE TURTLE, hand molded, 7½" L $302.50

BENTWOOD BOX, oval, spring latch lid, chip carved floral design, "STOCKHOLM" in original polychrome, 8" L ... $220.00

FISH DECOY, wood and tin, glass eyes, original polychrome, 13" L $220.00

FISH DECOY, wood and tin, original polychrome, 9" L $93.50

Row 2, Left to Right

FOLK ART CARVING, eagle on nest, natural finish, signed "David Arthur Myers, 5¾" H $93.50

RUSSIAN TOY, carved wood, original polychrome, 3 horses, 12" L ... $330.00

CARVED FISH, wood, glass eyes, Signed "E. Reed," 12" L $225.50

CARVED LION, wood, grey stain, paper label "Carved by a black man near Ramseur, N.C. about 1940," 6" H $38.50

Row 3, Left to Right

TOY CIGARETTE DISPENSER, wood, varnish, polychrome, duck grabs cigarette when lever pushed, 10½" L $38.50

COMPOTE, cast iron, white and black repaint highlights, 5¾" x 7", 5¾" H $137.50

STONE FRUIT, miniature, 15 peices $577.50

SANDSTONE CARVING, naked woman, grey, signed "E. Reed," 10½" H .. $302.50

SPOOL CADDY, plywood, metal pins, orange, black and red, 7¼" H $27.50

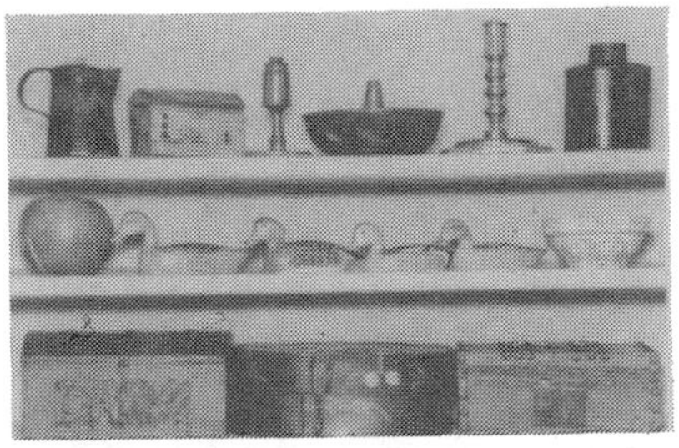

A-OH Nov. 1992 *Garth's Auctions, Inc.*

Row 1, Left to Right

CREAMER, tole, red, yellow, green on black, battered, 4⅛" H $220.00

BOX, pine, white paint, damage, wear, 4¼" L $275.00

LAMP, pewter, 3⅞" H $126.50

FOOD MOLD, redware, amber glaze, 6" D $55.00

CANDLESTICK, brass, 5⅝" H .. $245.50

TEA CADDY, tole, green, yellow, red, pink on dk. brown japanning, 4½" H .. $110.00

Row 2, Left to Right

APPLE BANK, redware, worn paint, 3¼" H $135.50

PINTAIL HEN, "Carved by J.F. Rider, Port Clinton, Ohio," 7" L $302.50

WOOD DUCK, , "Carved by J.F. Rider, Port Clinton, Ohio," 5¾" L $605.00

GREENWING TEAL DRAKE, "Carved by J.F. Rider, Port Clinton, Ohio," 5¼" L $440.00

GREENWING TEAL HEN, "Carved by J.F. Rider, Port Clinton, Ohio," 5¼" L .. $275.00

BOWL, brown, blue, cream sponge spatter, 4¼" D $71.50

Row 3, Left to Right

DOME TOP BOX, walnut, polychrome, wrought iron hinges, 8¼" L $363.00

BENTWOOD BOX, pine, polychrome, 9½" L $385.00

LEATHER BOUND BOX, brass studs, handle, label "E.A.G. Roulstone, Boston," wear, damage, 8" L $209.00

A-OH May 1993 *Garth's Auctions, Inc.*

Row 1, Left to Right

PLATE, redware, coggled rim, yellow slip dec., wear, chips, hairlines, 9" D .. $220.00

CHARCOAL IRON, black paint, wood handle, damage, 8" H $60.50

FOOD MOLD, redwear, turk's head, white, brown slip dec., chip $71.50

COW CREAMER, Rockingham, repair, 5½" H $104.50

PIE PLATE, redware, yellow slip dec., hairlines, chips, 8¼" D $302.50

Row 2, Left to Right

SEWING BOX, poplar, stenciled floral dec. on yellow paint, loss, cracks, wear, 8" H $1320.00

PIE PLATE, redware, coggled rim, yellow slip dec., chips, wear, hairlines, 10⅜" D $220.00

PITCHER, redware, brown, "Michael Feders 1835," chips, 7" H $192.50

SHAVING MIRROR, curly maple veneer, loss, 7¾" L $302.50

A-PA May 1993 *Alderfer Auction Co.*

STRING HOLDER, PA, ca. 1850 .... $350.00

BUTTER MOLD, eagle, 3¾" D .. $125.00

BUTTER PRINT, acorn $80.00

BUTTER PRINT, half moon, wheat $215.00

BUTTER PRINT, eagle $80.00

CANDLE HOLDERS, smoke grained $1780.00

A-OH Jan. 1993   *Garth's Auctions, Inc.*
LITHOGRAPH, "Amos" by "N. Currier," restored, stains, 17½" H, 13½" W $137.50
LITHOGRAPH, "The King of the Turf St. Julian..." by "Currier & Ives," C#3339, 29¾" H, 37¾" W $605.00
WINDSOR SIDE CHAIR, bamboo, old varnish, labeled "Spooner & Fitts...," damage, 33½" H $275.00
SHERATON PEMBROKE TABLE, cherry, curly maple, old refinish, damage, 28¾" H, 35½" W, 18" D $440.00
BELLIED MEASURES, 6 pcs., English pewter, qt. mark "Yates and Birch," pt. mark "James Yates," 2" to 6" H $561.00
TEAPOT, American pewter, battered, loss, 6½" H $71.50
COFFEE POT, pewter, "Sellew and Co, Cincinnati," battered, 11¼" H $71.50
CHARGER, English pewter, damage, 16½" D $330.00

A-OH March. 1993   *Garth's Auctions, Inc.*
ENGRAVINGS, 2 pcs., handcolored, from "The Botanical Magazine," signed "W. Curtis 1792," 13½" H, 10⅜" W $187.00
CHIPPENDALE MIRROR, walnut, repairs, loss, 20¼" H, 12¼" W, ... $192.50
SHERATON DESK, walnut, curly maple/birdseye veneeer, damage, cracks, replacements, 42" W, 21" D, 45" H $2310.00
PITCHER, clear flint, pillar mold, 9⅝" H $330.00

A-OH Nov. 1992   *Garth's Auctions, Inc.*
SHERATON CHEST, curly birch, pine, alligatored red-brown finish, 43" W, 20⅜" D, 38" H $3080.00
PEWTER PLATE, "Made in London," wear, 8¾" D $60.50
PEWTER CANDLESTICKS, pr., beaded trim, loss, 8" H $275.00
PEWTER PLATES, 2 pcs., rampant lion insignias, 1 has scissors w/"Schneider, I has grain vat w/"Beaver," 9" D . . . $99.00
BOX, pine, black, orange paint, stenciled "Deborah W. Holway," 12¾" L . . . $110.00
PEWTER PLATE, angel touch, engraved initials, 8⅜" D $82.50

A-OH Jan. 1993   *Garth's Auctions, Inc.*
CHIPPENDALE MIRROR, walnut, refinished, repair, 20¾" H, 12¾" W . . $330.00
LITHOGRAPH, "Partrigge Shooting," by Currier & Ives, 11¾" x 15¾" $385.00
HEPPLEWHITE CHADLESTAND, birch, old refinish, leg replaced, cracks, 29½" H $302.50
WINDSOR SIDE CHAIR, bamboo turnings, old black repaint, 17½" H . . $550.00
SEWERPIPE LION, 10" L $385.00

A-MA Dec. 1992   *Skinner, Inc.*
PAINTING, "Portrait of A Dark-haired Lady," signed William Matthew Prior, repair $3500.00*
SIDE CHAIR, old repaint $350.00*
DOWN-HEARTH SKILLET, iron, pitting, 43" L $150.00*
DOWN-HEARTH COFFEE ROASTER, sheet metal, iron rod, wood handle, damage, repair, 51" L $125.00*
SIDE CHAIR, old repaint, chip $400.00*

A-OH Nov. 1992   *Garth's Auctions, Inc.*
WINDSOR POTTY CHAIR, black paint, worn stencil, replacements, 41" H $27.50
DRAWING, ink, pencil, watercolor on paper, 9¾" x 10" $126.50
HOMESPUN, cotton, brown, white, wear, holes, 24" x 76" $49.50
BLANKET CHEST, poplar, brown-grey graining, white ground, paint decor., 37½" W, 16½" D, 20" H $577.50
STONEWARE PITCHER, cobalt brushed decor., chip, 10½" H $660.00
DOLL CRADLE, pine, brown graining, paint decor., damage, 19" L $165.00
RAG DOLL, button eyes, embroidered mouth, old worn dress $27.50
WINDSOR FOOTSTOOL, old worn black paint over red, upholstered top, 12" L $38.50

A-OH May 1993   *Garth's Auctions, Inc.*
JACQUARD COVERLET, red, blue, natural, "Loudonville, Ohio 1868 wove by Peter Grimm," 69" x 86" $1100.00
CANNONBALL ROPE BED, poplar, old dk. brown repaint, 43" H, 39" W, 69" L $440.00
WINDSOR FOOTSTOOL, poplar, old repaint, 6¾" x 13" $38.50
JUG, stoneware, grey salt glaze, brown top, molded raised "The Ohio Stonware (sic) Co. Akron, Ohio," hairline, chips, 11" H $82.50

A-OH Nov. 1992   *Garth's Auctions, Inc.*
EMPIRE STAND, cherry and poplar, old finish, 2 dovetailed drawers, top w/cut ovolo corners, floral relief carving, 21" x 21", 28¾" H $880.00
VICTORIAN CANDLESTICKS, pr., brass, pushups, marked "England," 8¾" H $187.00
VICTORIAN CANDLESTICKS, pr., brass, pushups, 7" H $104.50
CANDLESTICK, brass, pan base, side pushup, 7⅝" H $368.50

A-OH Jan. 1993   *Garth's Auctions, Inc.*
EMPIRE CHEST, cherry curly maple, refinished, losses, 56½" H, 46" W, 22¼" D $1265.00
STORE DISPLAY CASE, pine, drk. finish, 8" x 11¾" x 13" $192.50
WOOD BASKET, worn white paint, birds, flowers, etc. in gold, blue, repair, 3" H, 7¼" x 9" $137.50
CROCK, stoneware, cobalt label "6 Butter 1870," 13¾" H $385.00
BIRD CAGE, wood, wire, brown-red paint, 14" L $330.00

A-OH Nov. 1992   *Garth's Auctions, Inc.*
WINGBACK CHAIR, New Hampshire Chippendale, chestnut, dark finish, worn reupholstery, 42" H $1650.00
DRAWING, ink and crayon on paper, eagle, American flags, drum, halbreth, rifles, 19½" x 21" $110.00
EMPIRE STAND, cherry, missing drops, 18½" x 18½", 27½" H $577.50
TALL POT, American pewter, repairs, 11½" H $104.50
FOOTSTOOL, brown varnish over gold paint, twine top, 9½" x 9½", 5¾" H $22.00

A-OH Nov. 1992   *Garth's Auctions, Inc.*
PASTEL DRAWING, on paper, by Ernie Arnon, 31" x 40¾" $1567.50
PENSYLVANIA BLANKET CHEST, pine and poplar, original red flame graining, dovetailed case, wrought iron hinges, replacements, 49½" W, 22½" D, 25½" H $412.50
DECORATED BOX, poplar, original yellow, black, green and olive paint, some wear, 16" L $1650.00
RACCOON, carved and painted, by "David Alvarez," some damage, 19" L . . $357.50

A-OH Feb. 1993   *Garth's Auctions, Inc.*
LITHOGRAPHS, 2 pcs., handcolored, from "Birds of America" by Autubon, "American Ptarmigan," and "Ivory Gull," 6¾" x 10½" $143.00
CHIPPENDALE SLANT FRONT DESK, curly maple, chestnut, old honey colored refinish, repairs, cracks, 35½" W, 18" D, 42" H $4730.00
BUFFLEHEADS, pr., contemp., cedar, initialed "W.M.," 10¼" L $121.00
BIRDS, 2 pcs., contemp., 8¼", 11" H $143.00

A-OH Feb. 1993   *Garth's Auctions, Inc.*
GRANDFATHER'S CLOCK, cherry, brass works, painted face w/phase of moon dial, repairs, 93" H $2365.00
FEDERAL MIRROR, pine, 2 part, flaked, worn, 29½" H, 15¾" W $412.50
EMPIRE SHELF CLOCK, mahogany veneer, 2 part, wooden works, labeled "Eli Terry patent, manufactured & sold by Mark Lane, Elizabethtown, N.J.," wear, damage, repairs, 34¼" H $302.50
SHERATON CHEST, cherry, poplar, old refinish, replacements, 42¾" W, 19¾" D, 44½" H $825.00

A-OH Nov. 1992   *Garth's Auctions, Inc.*
CREWEL PANEL, wool on cotton, stains, holes, 17¼" x 15¼" $220.00
CREWEL PANEL, wool on cotton, stains, frame repainted, 27¼" sq. $165.00
ARMCHAIR ROCKER, worn black repaint, repairs, 41" H $192.50
HEPPLEWHITE TABLE, poplar, red paint, cracks, replacements, 25" x 27" .. $192.50
CANDLE BOX, pine, red, black, white paint, sliding lid, 14" L $220.00
STONEWARE JAR, 14" H $49.50

A-OH Nov. 1992   *Garth's Auctions, Inc.*
THREE TIER RACK, pine, original green, blue, red, white and yellow paint, holes for pipes, edge damage, age cracks, 14" H, 6½" D, 13" H $715.00
RUG, wool felt, embroidery and applique in rich colors on black ground, 23" x 34¼" $385.00
WINDSOR ARMCHAIR, worn brown finish, green beneath, replacements, 28½" H $385.00
MULE CHEST, walnut, miniature, traces of old red, square nail construction, edge damage, repairs, 19¾" W, 10½" D, 15½" H $550.00
HORSE TETHER DOORSTOP, cast iron, 13½" H $71.50

A-OH Nov. 1992   *Garth's Auctions, Inc.*
NOTE: *Miniature decoys are all by John Rider, Port Clinton, Ohio. All are marked by a paper or stamped label and have original paint and bead eyes.*
HANGING SHELF, pine, greyish green repaint over dark green, late, 19¾" W, 6¼" D, 17¾" H $275.00
PINTAIL DRAKE, 7" L $511.50
PINTAIL HEN, 7" L $385.00
WOOD DUCK DRAKE, 5¾" L $385.00
MALLARD HEN, 6½" L $192.50
CANADA GOOSE, 7¾" L $220.00
WIDGEON, 5¾" L $363.00
REDHEAD DRAKE, 6⅝" L ... $495.00
REDHEAD HEN, 6½" L $275.00
BLACK DUCK, 6¼" L $220.00

A-OH Feb. 1993   *Garth's Auctions, Inc.*
QUILT, pieced, appliqued, multi color on white and blue-green ground, stains, 76" x 90" $275.00
WEATHERVANE, galvanized sheet metal, brown, black paint, 27" L, 77" H $247.50
HUTCH-TOP DRY SINK, poplar, brown flame graining, zinc lined well, cast iron and brass thumb latches, damage, 36" W, 19" D, 74¼" H $1650.00
WOVEN SPLINT BASKET, contemp., 18" x 27", 12½" H $71.50
SNOW GOOSE, contemp., by Tom Martindale, Ontario, crack, 20½" L $60.50

A-OH Nov. 1992   *Garth's Auctions, Inc.*
QUILT, lavender, green, on white ground, 76" x 96" $165.00
HUTCH TABLE, poplar, refinished, replacements, 34" x 65", 28¼" H $1045.00
COPPER PANS, set of 5, cast steel handles, tin lining, worn, rust, 5" to 10" D $247.50
CARRY ALL, poplar, refinished, 13" x 22¼" $82.50

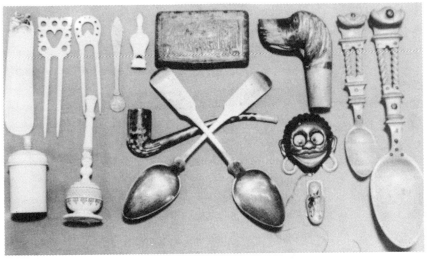

A-OH Nov. 1992   *Garth's Auctions, Inc.*
Row 1, Left to Right
SHOE HORN, ivory, oriental, carved mouse on handle, 5¼" L $11.00
HAIR COMB, ivory, 5¼" L $38.50
HAIR COMB, ivory, 4⅜" L $11.00
SALT SPOON, bone, 4¼" L $11.00
WHISTLE, bone, turned handle, 2⅜" L $33.00
SNUFF BOX, burl, tortoise shell lining, carved scene of people dancing, minor age crack, 4" L $165.00
DOG WALKING STICK HEAD, wood, black paint, glass eyes, 4¼ H $60.50
SPOONS, two, carved wood with inlay, 7" and 10" L $11.00
Row 2, Left to Right
CYLINDRICAL BOX, ivory, threaded lid, minor damage 3⅛" H $104.50
GLOVE DUSTER, ivory, carved and painted, 5¼" H $16.50
CLAY PIPE, Whieldon-type tortoise shell glaze, 6¼" L $412.50
TABLESPOONS, pair, coin silver, "W. Pitkin, L.M. & A.C. Root," 8⅜" L $27.50
HALLOWEEN CLICKER AND FACE OF BLACK PERSON, two pieces, tin, face has spring loaded eyes that spin when string is pulled, wear, ...$55.00

A-MA Nov. 1992   *James D. Julia, Inc.*
Row 1, Left to Right
DOUBLE CRUISE LAMPS, pr., wrought iron, 11½" T $75.00*
BETTY LAMPS, pr., quadruple wick, wrought iron . . . . NS
Row 2, Left to Right
LAMPS, 2 pcs., cast iron . . . . NS

A-OH Nov. 1992   *Garth's Auctions, Inc.*
Row 1, Left to Right
LIGHTING TRAMMEL, Wrought iron, brass fittings, bone finial, 16" L $4070.00
BUTTER PRINT, one-piece turned handle, primitive eagle, worn patina, 3" D . . . $192.50
BUTTER PRINT, star flower, chip carved edges, worn patina, 4⅝" D $55.00
TRIVET, wrought iron, hearts and starflower, boot feet, 11¼" L $522.50

BUTTER PRINT, one-piece turned handle, cow, dark finish 4½" $330.00
BUTTER PRINT, one-piece turned handle, fox, scrubbed finish 3½" $632.50
Row 2, Left to Right
BUTTER WHEEL, acorn and foliage, scrubbed finish, 5½" D $49.50
PORRINGER, cast iron, pierced handle, 3" $22.00
BUTTER PRINT, inserted turned handle, thistle, scrubbed finish, 2½" $82.50
BUTTER PRINT, inserted turned handle, cow, scrubbed finish, 2½" $137.50
TRIVET, wrought iron, double heart, shoe feet, black paint, rust, 4½" L $165.00
Row 3, Left to Right
TRIVET, cast iron, hearts, 5¾" L $93.50
BUTTER PRINT, one-piece whittled handle, strawberry, foliage and flower, scrubbed finish, 4¼" $165.00
TRIVET, wrought iron, heart, two legs, 5½" L $8.25
TRIVET, cast iron, hearts 8" L $93.50

A-OH Sep. 1993   *Garth's Auctions, Inc.*

DROP LEAF TABLE, curly maple, old worn refinish, mortised and pinned apron, 29" H, 41¾" W, 19¾" D $907.50

PENNSYLVANIA CHECKERBOARD, handpainted "oil cloth" on wood frame, black w/finely detailed floral design several colors, wear, holes, 21" x 23" $522.50

PAPER CUTOUT, birds, flowers, animals and men on horseback, tramp art frame, damage, 12" W, 14" H $302.50

BASKET, matural patina, damage, 10" x 10" $82.50

BASKET, finely woven, natural patina, damage, 6½" x 7" $159.50

BASKET, natural patina, damage, 11" x 12" $148.50

STONEWARE JUG, cobalt slip dec., impressed label "West Troy Pottery," chips, handle glued, 12" T $275.00

STONEWARE JUG, cobalt stenciled label "Jas Hamilton & Co, Greensboro, PA, 4," hairlines, 15" T $181.50

STONEWARE JUG, cobalt quill work dec., impressed label "Ottman Bros. Fort Edward, N.Y.," chip, hairline in handle, 11¾" T $181.50

A-OH Sep. 1993   *Garth's Auctions, Inc.*

BLANKET CHEST, poplar, old red finish. dovetailed case and bracket feet, till w/lid, 23½" H, 42½" W, 18¾" D $385.00

TABLE TOP WRITING BOX, oak, old finish, relief carving w/initials, decorative iron strap hinges, 8" H, 13" W, 10" D $165.00

FRISIAN CARVED BOX, two-tone varnish, alligatored, 14¾" H, 8½" W, 4¾" D $247.50

MINIATURE CHEST OF DRAWERS, mahogany veneer on pine, turned feet, repairs, 8" H, 9¾" W, 6" D $165.00

EUREOPEAN BOX, walnut, old finish, carved panels, brass reinforcements, wrought iron hinges, tooled brass escutcheon, till w/lid, lock missing, edge damage, 14¾" L $137.50

ANDIRONS, pr., wrought iron . . $110.00

TRIVET, wrought iron, brass, wood handle, 7" H, 11" L $220.00

TEA KETTLE, copper, dovetailed, hinged flap on goose neck spout, damage to handle, 5¾" H $82.50

A-OH Sep. 1993   *Garth's Auctions, Inc.*
TIN COOKIE CUTTERS UNLESS OTHER-WISE NOTED
Row 1, Left to Right
CUTTING BOARD, cutout crest, 9″ W, 15″ L $71.50
HEART IN HAND, traces of japanning, handle missing, repair, 4¼″ L $258.50
ROOSTER, loss, 4½″ L $148.50
SANTA & BOOT, ... $66.00
HORSE, 5¼″ L $27.50
DUTCHMAN, 7¼″ L $170.50
Row 2, Left to Right
ELEPHANT & BIRD, ... $132.00
MAN & WOMAN, 4″ L $55.00
CHICKEN & LEAF W/TULIP, . . $44.00
Row 3, Left to Right
TWO FISH, 6¾″ & 4″ L $44.00
DOG, 6″ L $82.50
TWO MEN & WOMAN, ... $49.50

A-OH Sep. 1993   *Garth's Auctions, Inc.*
OHIO HANGING SHELVES, walnut, scrubbed grey finish, square nail construction, repaired split, 23½″ W, 36½″ T $1210.00
Row 1, Left to Right
BURL BOWL, ash, 2⅛″ H, 6¼″ D $330.00
TREEN SOUVENIR BUCKET, probably by Pease, "Pan America 1090," 2¼″ H $60.50
TWO BASKETS, splint and sweet grass, 4″ H, 3″ D; cane and splint, 2½″ H, 7¾″ D $38.50
Row 2, Left to Right
DECORATED TREEN JAR, poplar w/orig. red sponged flame graining, wear, 7½″ T $533.50
BASKET, woven splint, 3¾″ H, 6¾″ D $49.50
TREEN JAR, old dk. finish, 8¼″ T $66.00
Row 3, Left to Right
BASKET, woven splint, 5″ H, 8″ D $104.50
BASKET, woven splint, 6″ x 7″, 3″ H $16.50
BASKET, woven splint, faded watercolor dec., red, blue, 9″ x 11″, 4″ H $33.00
Bottom
HANGING LOOM BASKET, natural dk. patina w/black and faded red, wear, damage, repair, losses, 11½″ W, 8½″ H $71.50

A-OH Sep. 1993   *Garth's Auctions, Inc.*
QUILT, Linsey woolsey w/nine patch design in black and redish salmon, wear, damage, 86" x 98" $605.00
SCHOOL MASTER'S DESK, refinished walnut, dovetailed drawer and gallery, 29" H, 42" W, 31¾" D $715.00
CUPBOARD TOP, refinished walnut and cherry, molded base trim, beaded edge trim, 37½" H, 34" W, 12¾" D $495.00
HANGING DRYING RACK, folding arms, poplar, old worn patina, damage, 2 arms missing, 33" H $330.00
MALLARD DRAKE, by Dave Hodgman, Niles, MI, unsigned, orig. paint, glass eyes, metal tail feathers, 16½" L $60.50
CANVASBACK HEN, by Madison Mitchell, unsigned, branded "D. Yundt," orig. paint, 16" L $280.50
MALLARD DRAKE, by Dave Hodgman, orig. paint, glass eyes, branded "Hall," age crack, edge wear, 16" L $71.50
PRIMITIVE BRANDT, hollow block, old repaint, shot scars, putty around neck is loose, 16¾" L $93.50
BASKET, bentwood rim handles, old patina, 22" D, 9" H $181.50
GATHERING BASKET, old worn varnish, 12" x 15½" $71.50

A-OH Sep. 1993   *Garth's Auctions, Inc.*
SHAKER WOOD BIN, poplar, layers of old worn paint, turned pegs added to ends, Union Village, 38¼" H, 35" W, 19" D $385.00
SHAKER WEAVER'S CHAIR, refinished, plugged holes in posts, new seat, 34" T $192.50
SHAKER TEA KETTLE, tin, Mt. Lebanon, NY, old repairs, 7" T $165.00
SHAKER BASKET, Union Village, 13" D $110.00
SHAKER COFFEE POT, tin, Mt. Lebanon, NY, old repairs, 11½" T $137.50
KRAUT CUTTER, walnut, old patina, rounded ends, 20" L $66.00
KRAUT CUTTER, cherry, old patina, lollypop crest, no blade, 18" L $49.50
WOODLANDS INDIAN BASKET, two-tone splint, 12" x 22½" $49.50
CHEROKEE INDIAN BASKET, woven cane, red, black, natural, damage, 6¾" x 14" $115.50

A-OH Sep. 1993 *Garth's Auctions, Inc.*
BLANKET CHEST, poplar, PA, old refinish, 27" H, 51½" W, 23¼" D $825.00
ROCKINGHAM
Back Row, Left to Right
PIE PLATE, 10" D $71.50
PIE PLATE, 8⅜" D $60.50
PIE PLATE, wear, 10⅛" D $22.00
PIE PLATE, 9" D $82.50
PIE PLATE, 10¼" D $71.50
Front Row, Left to Right
BOWL, chip, 4¼" H, 10" D $49.50
POT W/LID, 4⅝" H.......... $280.50
BOWL, 3½" H, 8½" D $60.50
BOTTOM
BED PANS, 2 pcs., chips, 13" to 15"
L $33.00

A-OH Sep. 1993 *Garth's Auctions, Inc.*
QUILT, orange, white, 71"x75" .. $110.00
BLANKET CHEST, pine, poplar, red stain, damage, age cracks, 25½" H, 52" W, 23¼" D $368.50

SPUN BRASS BUCKETS W/IRON BALE
Top Row, Left to Right
BUCKET, dk. patina, 8¼" D $55.00
BUCKET, "Hayden's Patent" label, dk. patina, 9½" D $49.50
BUCKET, "Hayden's Patent" label, 10¾" D $49.50
BUCKET, "Hayden's Patent" label, 11¾" D $49.50
Bottom Row, Left to Right
BUCKET, 12¾" D.............. $49.50
BUCKET, "Hayden's Patent" label, 13¾" D $49.50
BUCKET, "American Brass Kettle," 12½" D $49.50

A-MA Aug. 1993 *Skinner, Inc.*
SPOOL STAND, pin cushion top, sailor-made, exotic wood, carved ivory, 19th c., 10" T $1045.00
BOX, whale bone/exotic wood inlaid mahogany, 19th c., 7" H, 12" W $412.50

A-MA Oct. 1992 *Skinner, Inc.*
DOMED TOP BOX, poplar, early 19th c., 11½" H, 28" W, 14¼" D $1100.00

A-IL Apr. 1993 *Leslie Hindman Auction*
MINIATURE CHEST, mahogany, 19th c., 14" H, 14" W, 9" D $2800.00*
MINIATURE CUPBOARD, birds-eye maple, walnut, 19th c., 18½" H, 14" W, 6" D $1100.00*

A-ME Feb. 1993 *James D, Julia, Inc.*
DOCUMENT BOX, ca. 1820, coral, red, yellow, white on black paint, 5" H, 12" L $4500.00*

A-PA May 1993 *Alderfer Auction Co.*
BOX, blue dec., 19th c., wear, 13" H, 28" W $425.00

A-OH Nov. 1992 *Garth's Auctions, Inc.*
DECORATED BOX, poplar, original brown flame graining, gold striping and polychrome floral design, 18½" L .. $550.00
HAND MIRROR, carved wood frame, old worn gold paint, 13⅜" L ... $104.50
TOY BIRD, carved painted wood, bird pecks, 5" L................... $60.50

A-MA Jun. 1993 *Skinner, Inc.*
SHAKER CHILD'S BLANKET BOX, pine, Canterbury, New Hampshire, ca. 1800, red stain, repairs, 24¾" H, 33¼" W, 16¼" D $8250.00

A-OH July 1993   *Garth's Auctions, Inc.*
PAINTING, oil on canvas, patch, damaged
frame, 14¼" H, 22¼" W $192.50
WINDSOR SIDE CHAIR, bamboo legs,
dk. brown refinish, 37¾" T $192.50
MINIATURE CUPBOARD, curly maple,
handmade repro., 21¼" T $385.00
STAND, cherry, old refinish, 27½" H, 20" W,
17¾" D $434.50
STONEWARE JAR, cobalt quill work, im-
pressed label "New York Stoneware Co.,
Fort Edward, NY. 5," lime deposits, 14½"
T $302.50

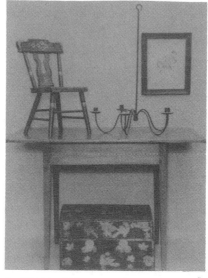

A-OH Nov. 1992   *Garth's Auctions, Inc.*
WATERCOLOR THEOREM, on paper,
rose, good color, 14¼" x 11¼" . $121.00
HEPPLWHITE TAVERN TABLE, hardwood, hickory and pine, refinished, 23½"
x 39¾", 27" H $495.00
PENNSYLVANIA CHILD'S CHAIR, original brown paint with black and red polychrome, labeled "Made by J.S Ebersol
Gordonville, Pa. 1951," wear, 20¾"
H $137.50
CHANDELIER, wrought iron, 27¼"
H $1760.00
DOME TOP BOX, beech, worn original
blue, white and red paint, iron lock and
hasp, damage, worm hole, replacements,
18¾" L $192.50

A-NH Aug. 1993   *Northeast Auctions*
GOOSE DECOY, carved, painted, 25"
L $600.00*
QUILT, red, white, blue $400.00*
WEATHER VANE, copper rooster, 19"
T $900.00*
CHIPPENDALE BLANKET CHEST, blue
paint, New England, dated 1789, 39"
W $4750.00*
WINDSOR CHAIR, black painted, New
England $1100.00*
FEDERAL TILT-TOP CANDLESTAND,
red painted, 27" H, 16" W, 15½"
D $2000.00*
DOCUMENT BOX, red, black grained, 16"
L $375.00*
HOOKED RUG, pink floral on striated
green ground, 9'3" x 6'4" $3000.00*

A-OH May 1993   *Garth's Auctions, Inc.*
FOLDING SHELF, walnut, old varnish,
masonic dec., loss, 15½" H $55.00
TEXTILE, cotton, brown roller printed
design. "William Henry Harrison," stains,
repairs, damage, 26½ x 28½ $660.00
SIDE CHAIR, dk. brown repaint, old
replaced seat, 42½" H $1100.00
CHIPPENDALE TILT-TOP TEA TABLE,
walnut, cracks, repairs, 27½" H, 32"
D $1155.00
CANDLESTICK, brass, hex base, 9⅝"
H $275.00

A-OH Sep. 1993   *Garth's Auctions, Inc.*
LITHOGRAPH, "Washington and his
Family, Published Phila. 1864," stains, dam-
age, fading, 28" H, 35" W $165.00
MAMMY'S BENCH, poplar, old patina,
burns, 57" L $1045.00
STONEWARE CROCK, impressed "4,"
cobalt dec., 10" T............. $330.00
STONEWARE CROCK, impressed label
"N.A. White & Son Utica, N.Y. 2," brushed
cobalt dec., hairline, 9" T $137.50

A-OH July 1993   *Garth's Auctions, Inc.*
CHIPPENDALE TILT-TOP TEA TABLE,
cherry, walnut, refinished, mismatched top,
replacements, 28¾" H, 27" D $495.00
QUEEN ANNE SIDE CHAIR, walnut, dk.
varnish, 41" H $275.00
MINIATURE DROP LEAF STAND, ma-
hogany, 10¼" H, 8¾" W, 7½" D .. $357.50
PAINTING, oil on canvas, "Ace 4 Weeks,"
Initials "N.B.L. '98," 13½" H, 10"
W $445.50
CHALK CAT, black paint, gold markings,
red, blue, green bow, chips, touch-ups,
11¾" L $115.50

A-OH July 1993   *Garth's Auctions, Inc.*
CHIPPENDALE HIGH CHEST, curly maple, pine, old refinish, repairs, replacements, 47" H, 37¾" W, 19¾" D $4180.00
QUEEN ANNE CANDLESTICK, brass, splits, 7⅜" T $187.00
CANDLESTICK, brass, mismatched socket, 10½" T $82.50
PEARLWARE PLATTER, Leeds blue feather edge, gaudy floral in blue, green, yellow, stains, wear, 13" L $1870.00
CANDLESTICK, brass, 6¼" T . . $247.50
CANDLESTICK, brass, dents, 10⅜" T $93.50

A-OH July 1993   *Garth's Auctions, Inc.*
CHIPPENDALE BUTLER'S DESK, cherry, poplar, old refinish, repairs, replacements, 38" H, 43¼" W, 24" D . . . $1375.00
DOME TOP BOX, pine, brown vinegar graining, painted initials "MAB 1822" in black, olive, yellow, wear, 12¾" L $357.50
BLACK BALL BOX, walnut, w/marbles, labeled "Parson & Co, Manufacturers of Regalia . . .," 9½" L $110.00
BOX, walnut, refinish, 12¼" L . . $275.50
SPLINT BASKET, some age, 10½" x 11½", 5½" H $71.50

A-OH July 1993   *Garth's Auctions, Inc.*
CRIB QUILT, red, white, machine sewn, wear, 30" x 31" $170.50
HANGING SHELVES, walnut, 3 curved shelves, bottom w/bent wood gallery, 28" H, 20" W, 18⅛" D $330.00
HEPPLEWHITE STAND, pine, hardwood legs, reddish stain from stripped paint, age crack in top, 29" H, 20" W, 17¾" D $170.50
TALL POT, pewter, eagle touch "Boardman & Co., New York," 11½" T . . $330.00
STONEWARE JAR, cobalt stenceled "L.B. Milliner, New Geneva, PA, 6," 16½" T $715.00
HANGING CUPBOARD, pine, old blue, green, red repaint, worm holes, age cracks, iron lock, pintel hinges, 25¼" H, 20¾" W, 14½" D $660.00
TAVERN TABLE, pine, hardwood, refinished, top and stretcher replaced, 26" H, 39¾" W, 26¾" D $660.00
ASTRAL LAMP, pewter, drilled, electrified, damage, repair, 24" T $27.50
CUTOUT SILHOUETTE, wood, young woman, worn white, salmon, silver, brown paint, damage, loss, 27¼" T $5.50
SHOESHINE STAND, pine, cast iron foot rest, refinished, 20" T $99.00

A-NH May. 1993   *Northeast Auctions*
SHERATON CARD TABLE, lunette inlaid mahogany, bird's eye maple, Boston, 36" L $4750.00*
BANJO CLOCK, carved mahogany, eghlomise, 31" H $1400.00*
HEPPLEWHITE BOW FRONT CHEST, inlaid mahogany, Mass. 37" W $1750.00*

A-OH July 1993   *Garth's Auctions, Inc.*
HEPPLEWHITE CHEST, inlayed cherry, replacements, 43¼" H, 38¾" W, 20½" D $2200.00
DEED BOX, tole, dk. brown japanning w/white, yellow, green, red, black, wear, 8" L $302.50
BREAD TRAY, tole, dk. brown japanning w/crystalized brown, yellow, green, black, olive, red, wear, 12¾" L $192.50
TEA CADDY, tole, dk. brown japanning w/red, green, yellow, wear, 5¾" H $165.00
TEA CADDY, tole, dk. brown jappaning w/yellow, green, red, wear, 5⅜" H $27.50

A-OH Nov. 1992   *Garth's Auctions, Inc.*
QUILT TOP, multi-colored prints, machine sewn, 69" x 95" $16.50
TAVERN TABLE, maple, refinished, restored, 29" x 47", 27¾" H $330.00
REDWARE SGRAFFITO CHARGERS, pr., slip decor., signed Lester and Barbara Breininger, dated 1979, 13" D . . . $137.50
REDWARE PLATE, slip decor., signed Lester Breininger, "Money Wanted," "1974," 12½" D $49.50
STONEWARE CROCK, cobalt brushed vintage, "6," hairlines, 13" H $49.50

A-ME May 1993

James D. Julia, Inc.

BARBER POLE, glass, porcelainized steel, restored, electrified, 96" H, 16" D $850.00*

A-OH May 1993   *Garth's Auctions, Inc.*
KRAUT CUTTER, pine, old red, chip carved, 21¼" L $330.00
KRAUT CUTTER, walnut, chip & scratch carved, loss, crack, 17¾" L $192.50
KRAUT CUTTER, walnut, old refinish, 16¾" L $176.00
KRAUT CUTTER, walnut, scrubbed, damage, loss, 18" L................ $71.50
KRAUT CUTTER, walnut, worn, 19¼" L $60.50
KRAUT CUTTER, cherry, branded "A.J. Kuhn," double blade, 25½" L $110.00
QUEEN ANNE WORK TABLE, butternut, old grey paint, damage, wear, cracks, 28½" H, 62¼" W, 28½" D $605.00
BURL BOWL, ash, scrubbed, cracks, holes, 6¾" H, 15½" D $1210.00
KNIFE BOX, pine, black paint, wear, damage, 12" x 19"................. $137.50
DOUGH BOX, poplar, old red, cracks, damage, 33½" L $302.50

A-OH Apr. 1993   *Garth's Auctions, Inc.*
Row 1, Left to Right
ABC PLATE, tin, rust, 8" D $110.00
CHEESE SIEVE, punched tin, 4" D $99.00
ABC PLATE, tin, 7¾" D $121.00
Row 2, Left to Right
TIN ITEMS, horse cookie cutter, eagle cookie cutter, skimmer $66.00
FOOD MOLD, tin, lion, 5¼" L ... $44.00
Row 3, Left to Right
FOOD MOLD, copper, tin, pears, battered, repair, 6½" L $33.00
CHOCOLATE MOLD, tin plated steel, 3 rabbits, 2-part folding, 10½" L $44.00
FOOD MOLD, melon, rust, loss, 7¼" L $4.40

A-OH Feb. 1993   *Garth's Auctions, Inc.*
WALL CUPBOARD, poplar, red repaint, damage, repairs, 40½" W, 20" D, 71" H......................... $1210.00
HAYSTACK MEASURES, 5 pcs., quart, pint, 2 half pints, gill, some marks or pub names, battered, 3¾" to 7⅜" H . $605.00
HAYSTACK MEASURE, pewter, gallon, battered, 11¾" H $577.50

A-OH July 1993   *Garth's Auctions, Inc.*
PEWTER CUPBOARD, walnut, damage, losses, 86" H, 47" W, 22" D $2530.00

ENGLISH PEWTER
Row 1, Left to Right
PINT TANKARD, "Watts & Harton, London," 5¼" T $93.50
PLATE, David Melville touch, wear, battered, split, 8⅛" D $247.50
PINT TANKARD, old repair, 4¾" T........................$115.50
PINT TANKARD, battered, 4¾" T........................$159.50
PLATE, back engraved "Olea," wear, scratches, 8⅜" D $38.50
PINT TANKARD, "R. Reym---," battered, 5" T........................$22.00
Row 2, Left to Right
COVERED TANKARD, side spout, "Pint," "Alderson," old repair, 5¾" T $159.50
BASIN "Townsend & Compton, London" touch, wear, scratches, damage, 11" D $220.00
COVERED TANKARD, dents, repair, 7½" T $357.50
HOT WATER PLATE, "John Home, London" touch, wear, scratches, damage, 9" D $27.50

COVERED TANKARD, 6" T $165.00
BASIN, "I.M." touch, 10¾" D $110.00
Row 3, Left to Right
PLATE, "Rd King" touch, wear, dents, scratches, 8½" D $38.50
PLATE, "Samuell Ellis" touch, wear, battering, 7¾" D $71.50
ALE PITCHER, engraved monogram, battered, wear, 8" T............ $330.00
PLATE, worn touch marks, scratches, 8½" D $60.50
PLATE, "George Grenfell, London" touch, wear, scratches, 8⅝" D $66.00
Row 4, Left to Right
BASIN, "Townsend and Compton" touch, wear, scratches, 13" D $220.00
BASIN, wear, dents, repairs, 13" D $275.00
CHARGER, angel touch. wear, dents, 14" D $247.50
Bottom
CHARGER, faint touch, hammered booge, wear, pitted, 15½" D $275.00
CHARGER, fleur-de-lis touch, wear scratches, 15" D $231.00

A-OH July 1993   *Garth's Auctions, Inc.*
BEDSIDE STAND, curly maple, poplar, refinished, 27½" H, 23" W, 18¼" D $935.00
STONEWARE JAR, cobalt stenciled label "McIntire & Brand, 4208 Butler St., Pitts., Pa., 2," hairlines, 10" T $165.00

A-OH Nov. 1992   *Garth's Auctions, Inc.*
PEWTER CUPBOARD, one piece, walnut cleaned to traces of old green, cornice missing, replacements, edge damage, age cracks, 71¼" H, 47" W, 22" D $797.50

REDWARE JARS, two, interior glaze, one has hairline, 7½", 7¾" H $99.00
REDWARE BEDPANS, two, clear glaze, brown sponging, chips $44.00
STONEWARE JUG, cobalt blue brushed vintage, chips, 11½" H $137.50
STONEWARE CROCK, cobalt blue brushed leaves, impressed "5," chips, hairline, 12¾" H $60.50

A-OH July 1993   *Garth's Auctions, Inc.*
CANDLE SCONCE, tin, crimped edge, punched heart, 16½" T $137.50
ORNAMENTS, 2 pcs., tin, horse with movable legs, head and tail, 9½" L, punched star, 9½" H $104.50
WINDSOR SIDE CHAIR, green repaint, branded "T.B. Ackley," damage, 38½" H. $440.00
FOOTSTOOL, walnut, engraved brass plaque, "This footstool belonged to Jennett Rowland Johnson . . . Phila. . . . from marriage date April 5th, 1805. Repaired by Geo. C. Johnson, Dec 1919 . . .," 11¾" L $137.50
HANGING SHELVES, mahogany, sun-bleached finish, dovetailed, 37½" H, 27¼" W, 9" D $742.50
OHIO BLANKET CHEST, poplar, salmon gray paint, dovetailed case, Darke Co., Ohio, 19¾" H, 37" W, 17¾" D $440.00
BONNET, anniversary tin, cloth trim, 8" T $770.00
BOUQUET, 8 anniversary tin flowers, 16" L $550.00
TOP HAT, anniversary tin, 6¼" T $275.00
MALLET, anniversary tin, filled w/noise making rattles, 14½" L $55.00

A-OH Sep. 1993   *Garth's Auctions, Inc.*
CRADLE, walnut, old refinish, age cracks, 27½" H, 40" W, 22" D $165.00
WINDSOR CANDLESTAND, hardwood, alligatored dk. green paint, replacement, 31½" T $1870.00
STONEWARE JAR, cobalt dec., stenciled "Hamilton & Jones, Greensboro, Pa., 3," 13¾" T $3300.00
STONEWARE JAR, cobalt quill work "2," chips, 11" T $93.50

A-NH Aug. 1993   *Northeast Auctions*
Row 1, Left to Right
DOME-TOP BOX, painted . . . $450.00*
SHAKER BOX, grey paint . . . $1600.00*
Row 2, Left to Right
SCONCES, pr., (ends of row), punched tin $900.00*
DECOY, shore bird $250.00*
COVERED CUP, Lehn-ware $50.00*
BASKETS, 2 pcs., (one on bottom row), Apache $1100.00*
Row 3, Left to Right
DOUBLE SILHOUTTE $600.00*
SHAKER CARRIER, salmon colored stain $1800.00*
CAMPAIGN TORCH, eagle . . $1550.00*

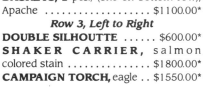

A-OH July 1993   *Garth's Auctions, Inc.*
CHIPPENDALE CHEST, maple w/curl, chestnut, refinished, repairs, replacements, 33¾" H, 38¾" W, 19¼" D $1980.00
BAND BOX, bentwood, wallpaper covered, white, brown, black, red, on blue ground, labeled "Warranted Nailed Band-Boxes Made by Hannah Davis, Jaffrey N.H.," wear, damage, 20" L $687.50
STONEWARE JUG, brushed cobalt dec., "2," stains, chips, crazing, 14" T . . . $82.50

A-OH Nov. 1992   *Garth's Auctions, Inc.*
HANGING SHELF, pine, original varnish, black painted sawtooth edge on crest and sides, screw and wire nail construction, damage, 19¼" W, 5¾" D, 30½" H.......................... $192.50
PRINTED FRAKTUR, block printed color, "Geburts and Taufschein" recording 1835 birth in Ohio, signed "Levine Runkel, creases and fold lines, 17½" x 14½" ... $121.00
STOOL, old brown finish, new blue and ecru woven seat, 13" x 13¼", 17¼" H........................... $60.50
SHAKER ARMCHAIR ROCKER, old black repaint, new blue and ecru woven seat and back, 34" H $495.00
WOVEN SPLINT BASKET, good detail, age and color, bentwood handle, minor damage, rim repair, 11" x 11½" $313.50

A-NH May. 1993   *Northeast Auctions*
CANDLESTAND, adjustable twin-arm, 40" H $1400.00*
CANDLEHOLDER, adjustable twin, ratchet, 23½" H $2250.00*
QUEEN ANNE ARMCHAIR, stained maple, New England $5000.00*
BLANKET CHEST, red painted pine, Mass, 38" W $5750.00*
TEA TABLE, grain painted, label J. Morris, 25⅝" H, 38" W, 26" D $6500.00*
QUEEN ANNE SIDE CHAIRS, pr., red painted maple, New England $6750.00*

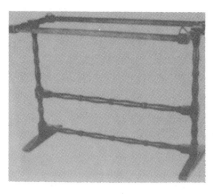

A-ME Feb. 1993   *James D, Julia, Inc.*
EMBROIDERING RACK, 18th c., red paint, 32" H, 43" L $350.00*

A-OH July 1993   *Garth's Auctions, Inc.*
SHERATON CHEST, birch, bird's eye maple, poplar, pine, old cherry-colored finish, crack, loss, 43" H, 41" W, 19½" D $935.00
FLOWER POT, Bennington, brown glaze, molded cat tails, 10¼" T $148.50

A-MA Oct. 1992   *Skinner, Inc.*
FEDERAL HALL TREE, maple, ca. 1820, 70½" H $1320.00

A-OH March. 1993   *Garth's Auctions, Inc.*
Row 1, Left to Right
SHAKER SEWING BOX, pine, ivory eyelets, pin cushion finial, refinished, repair, cracks, 6¼" H $192.50
REDWARE DISH, coggeled rim, yellow slip decoration, chips, 6½" D $104.50
CANDLE BOX, pine, soft patina, ivory inlay, repair, 7¼" L $33.00
MARQUETRY BOX, ebonized finish, dogs in veneer, 8⅜" L $55.00
Row 2, Left to Right
BENNINGTON CUSPIDOR, brown glaze, amber highlights, impressed 1849 mark, hairlines, chips, 8" D $27.50
REDWARE TURK'S HEAD MOLD, exterior amber glaze w/brown, interior pale salmon, 9" D $60.50
REDWARE SHAVING MUG, dk. brown glaze, chips, hairline, 4¼" H $77.00
ROCKINGHAM CUSPIDOR, chips, 8" D $27.50
Row 3, Left to Right
BANK, mechanical, cast iron, "Novelty Bank, Norman 2460-B," worn red, yellow, blue paint, loss $143.00
STRONG BOX, wrought iron, 9¼" L $302.50
BANK BUILDING, cast iron, "Moore 1125," replacement, 5½" H $137.50
SAFE DEPOSIT BANK, cast iron, "Henry Chart Mfg. Co. Detroit, Mich. Pat. May 12, 1885," worn red, 5⅛" H . . $71.50
PIPSQUEAK, sheep in cage, wood, printed paper, wear, silent, 5¾" H $148.50

A-OH Nov. 1992   *Garth's Auctions, Inc.*
WOODEN HORSE, carved, black and white with blue, red and white, 20th c. folk art, 8⅛" H $49.50
WOODEN BIRD, carved and painted, glass eyes, wire feet, 4¾" H $27.50
SHAVING MIRROR, tramp art, two drawers, edge damage, discolored mirrors, 9¾" W, 7" H $110.00
STONEWARE BIRD, grey, traces of tan paint, 6¼" L $33.00
COTTAGE DOORSTOP, cast iron, old paint, 5½" H $126.50
TRAMP ART BOX, hinged lid, brown alligatored finish, 8¼" L $82.50
SEWERPIPE DOG, flakes, 7¾ L $220.00
Row 2, Left to Right
PEDESTAL BOX, tramp art, hinged lid, old finish, 9" H $269.50
GEESE DOORSTOP, cast iron, worn polychrome, rust, 8¼" H $30.25
COCKATOO DOORSTOP, cast iron, worn polychrome repaint, 8" H . . . $93.50
CHANDELIER PEG LAMP, tin, miniature, six arms with crimped pans, old repairs, 10½" D $330.00
CANDLEHOLDERS, two, tin, shaker, rectangular $247.50
DOVETAILED BOX, poplar, walnut and maple inlay, old finish, 8¾" L $27.50

A-MA Jun. 1993   *Skinner, Inc.*
NANTUCKET POCKETBOOK., signed Stanley Roop, carved ivory dolphin plaque, 8" H $1100.00
SHELL-WORK VALENTINE, 19th c., 18½" W $1430.00
SPINNING JENNEY, French prisoner of war carved bone, w/bone bodkin and needlecase in wood box dated 2-23-1873 . . . . $660.00
BUSK, engraved whalebone, 19th c., 13¼" L $1320.00
JAGGING WHEEL, carved, inlaid ivory, 19th c., 7½" L . . . . NS
FOOD CHOPPER, bone and composition inlaid handle, 19th c., 7" H $357.50

A-OH Jan. 1993   *Garth's Auctions, Inc.*
Treen ware, most made by Pease.
Row 1, Left to Right
WINE, red sponging, 3¼" H $110.00
CARVED CUP, reddish, cracks, 2" H $121.00
WINE, red, green, 3½" H $55.00
LIDDED JAR, worn varnish, 2¾" H $605.00
LIDDED JAR, worn varnish, 2" H $192.50
LIDDED JAR, worn varnish, crack, 2¼" H $165.00
LIDDED JAR, worn varnish, 2½" H $192.50
LIDDED JAR, worn varnish, crack, 3⅜" H $203.50
Row 2, Left to Right
LIDDED JAR, worn varnish, 4½" H $247.50
LIDDED JAR, worn varnish, 5¾" H $275.00
LIDDED JAR, worn varnish, repair, 4¾" H $71.50
TURNED SANDER, worn varnish, 3⅜" H $82.50
BASKETRY JAR, wood base, lid, 4" H $82.50

A-ME Feb. 1993   *James D, Julia, Inc.*
EAGLE WEATHERVANE, gilded copper, 38" W, 34" H $1350.00*

A-ME Feb. 1993   *James D, Julia, Inc.*
SONG BIRD TREE, carved, painted, 6 different song birds, 21" T $2600.00*
WOOD DUCKS, carved, by John Templeton Coolidge, Milton, Mass., 9" T $1400.00*

INDEX